From Communists to Foreign Capitalists

From Communists to Foreign Capitalists

THE SOCIAL FOUNDATIONS
OF FOREIGN DIRECT INVESTMENT
IN POSTSOCIALIST EUROPE

Nina Bandelj

PRINCETON UNIVERSITY PRESS

PRINCETON AND OXFORD

Library of Congress Cataloging-in-Publication Data
Bandelj, Nina.
From Communists to foreign capitalists : the social foundations
of foreign direct investment in postsocialist Europe / Nina Bandelj.
p. cm.
Includes bibliographical referneces and index.
ISBN-13: 978-0-691-12912-9 (cloth : alk. paper)
1. Investments, Foreign—Europe, Eastern. 2. Investments, Foreign—Europe,
Central. 3. Post-communism—Social aspects. I. Title.
HG5430.7.A3B36 2008
332.67'30947—dc22   2007015167

British Library Cataloging-in-Publication Data is available

moji družini

_____

CONTENTS

TABLES

FIGURES

ACKNOWLEDGMENTS

ALMOST AS TUMULTUOUS and exciting as the postsocialist transformations, this project has taken nearly a decade from the initial ideas to the final form. I am grateful to Viviana Zelizer, Bruce Western, and Paul DiMaggio for their wonderful mentoring during my work on this project as a graduate student in the Department of Sociology at Princeton University. In my early graduate student years, Viviana recommended me as the Noah Cotsen Junior Teaching Fellow. A lucky set of circumstances that brought us together turned out to be the most precious opportunity to learn from Viviana as a teacher, scholar, and person. No words can justly describe my gratitude and appreciation for Viviana's incredible generosity, unwavering support, care, and wisdom that have sustained me over my years in graduate school and beyond.

Since my first empirical paper in graduate school, which instigated this research, Bruce Western's encouragement, support, and advice have been crucial and invaluable. His patient insistence on relevance of inquiry, conceptual clarity, and methodological rigor have greatly improved the project and significantly shaped my thinking about sociological research more generally. Learning from him has been a great privilege and an incredibly rewarding experience.

I have also been very fortunate that Paul DiMaggio, in response to my ideas, generously shared his amazing breadth of knowledge. Whether the project was my dissertation on foreign investment or an article on the creativity of actors, Paul always provided stimulating ideas and practical suggestions that helped me to think more critically and write more clearly.

At Princeton, I benefited also from discussions with Alejandro Portes, Miguel Centeno, Michèle Lamont, Frank Dobbin, Marta Tienda, Patricia Fernandez-Kelly, Wally Wallace, and Scott Lynch, as well as collegial support and stimulation from Adriana Abdenur, Sada Aksartova, Donnell Butler, Wendy Cadge, Marion Carter, Marion Fourcade-Gourinchas, Josh Guetzkow, Eszter Hargittai, Kristen Harknett, Kieran Healy, Leslie Hinkson, Alexandra Kalev, Erin Kelly, Meredith Kleykamp, Grégoire Mallard, Virág Molnár, Margarita Mooney, Ann Morning, Cesar Rosado, Gabriel Rossman, Kyoko Sato, Brian Steensland, Craig Upright, Margaret Usdansky, Olav Velthuis, and Frederick Wherry. I am especially grateful to Eszter and Sandra for being such terrific friends and for making a difference in so many ways. At Princeton I was also lucky to meet my compatriots Petra Munih, Uroš Seljak, and little Nika, who provided a family away from home.

Moving on from Princeton, I found a wonderfully supportive home in the Department of Sociology at the University of California, Irvine. I have benefited from comments and feedback on this project from Calvin Morrill, David Snow, and Wang Feng, and exchanges with David Meyer, Judy Stepan-Norris, David Smith, David Frank, Judy Treas, Belinda Robnett-Olsen, Frank Bean, Katie Faust, Lin Freeman, Jennifer Lee, and Rubén Rumbaut. My junior colleagues and friends Jen'nan Read, Matt Huffman, Joy Pixley, Carter Butts, Cynthia Feliciano, Stan Bailey, Su Yang, and Susan Brown have also been very supportive. Thanks to Russ Dalton, Rein Taagepera, Bernie Grofman, and Willie Schonfeld at UCI's Center for the Study of Democracy, and David Obstfeld, Christine Beckman, and especially Martha Feldman of UCI's Center for Organizational Research. Matthew Mahutga and Bogdan Radu provided excellent research assistance. I am most grateful to the Chair of Sociology, Calvin Morrill, for his steadfast support and to Dean Barbara Dosher for approving my leave in Europe to finish the writing. I was tremendously lucky to have received financial and intellectual support to do so from the Robert Schuman Centre for Advanced Studies of the European University Institute in Florence, and from the Max Planck Institute for the Study of Societies in Cologne. At the EUI, a group of economists at the 2005–6 European Forum extended a warm welcome to an economic sociologist. At Max Planck, Jens Beckert ensured that I had a most stimulating and enjoyable time, as did Sabine Köszegi, Patrik Aspers, and other junior colleagues. I thank Sabina Avdagić for initiating the first contact and Wolfgang Streeck for extending the invitation.

The research would have not been possible without the generosity and goodwill of many experts, informants, and respondents in the eleven countries of Central and Eastern Europe examined in this study. I thank them all for sharing their time and information. The substance of the arguments has been improved by comments from the participants and discussants at the European Political Economy Infrastructure Consortium Advance Training Workshops, Society of Comparative Research Graduate Student Retreats, RC09 International Sociological Association sessions, Duke University FDI Workshop, Cultural Politics of Globalization and Community in East Central Europe Workshop in Budapest, as well as numerous other occasions where I presented parts of this work. I am grateful for comments and suggestions from Ákos Róna-Tas, József Böröcz, Abby Innes, David Stark, Iván Szelényi, Lisa Keister, Bai Gao, Gary Gereffi, Larry King, Ulrike Schuerkens, Michael Kennedy, Mitchell Orenstein, and Gail Kligman. Thanks to the 2004 Martin Seymour Lipset Dissertation Award Committee of the Society for Comparative Research for expressing their support of this project. In the final stages of writing two Princeton University Press reviewers provided terrific comments that substantially improved the work, as did Nathan Jensen's generous methodological advice.

The book may have never happened if it weren't for Tim Sullivan, who has been the best editor a first-time book author could imagine. I thank Tim for taking a chance with me and guiding me along the way. I am also grateful for the assistance I have received from the production team at Princeton University Press and to Richard Isomaki for his excellent editing.

For financial support I thank the Graduate School, the Council on Regional Studies, the Center for International Studies, the Center for Migration and Development, all of Princeton University, as well as the National Science Foundation, the Center for the Study of Democracy and the Center for Organizational Research at the University of California, Irvine, the Max Planck Institute for the Study of Societies, and the European University Institute. I have also received great support over the years from IEDC-Bled School of Management in Slovenia, and kindly thank Danica Purg and her excellent team.

Finally, I wanted to finish this book to be able to write in it thanks to my family. *Dragi moji, iskrena hvala za vašo podporo in ljubezen.* The unconditional love and support from my parents Olga and Bojan and my sisters Ana and Eva have been more important to me than they know and have mattered more than I can say. My family-in-law, Vida and Janez, and Mojca and Marko, have always been very supportive. Marko Studen, my better half, has inspired me, supported me, and taken care of me in every possible way for the whole fourteen years of my personal postsocialist transformation. I could not have done this if it hadn't been for him. At the end of the day, it is he who gives it all sense.

PROLOGUE

AN ENGINEER in his late fifties, a member of the top management of a middle-sized firm in Central Europe, told me the following story of his working life before and after the postsocialist transformation.

• • •

Twenty-five years ago, I was an enthusiast, not only because I was younger. Everyone had work, no matter what. In our firm, we organized our activities based on a five-year plan of production issued by the central state authorities controlled by the Communist Party. We had no idea what a firm strategy is, and even less how to formulate one. We knew that if we wanted to be acknowledged as a successful enterprise, we needed to guarantee work to as many people as possible. We wanted to be big. Back then we had 33,000 people working for the holding company.

The production was not driven by demand. Nobody thought about "demand." In fact, you could sell everything that you produced. And if your costs went up because of inflation or increased expenses for material inputs, you never considered firing people or automating production or increasing productivity standards. Sometimes you could negotiate a higher price with the central authority, or you just didn't meet the yearly quota. And if the enterprise was doing well, you wanted to build another satellite firm of the holding to get even bigger and greater. If your company was big in terms of size, you could get paid more. The director of the enterprise was appointed by the Party, and promotions were influenced by people's political affiliations.

The system proclaimed that everyone was equal, but it wasn't quite like that. Still, we were much more equal then than we are today! Just imagine, then the standards were set so that the salary of the director compared to the lowest rank in the firm was about 5 to 1; today that ratio is probably 30 to 1.

Who owned the company? Everyone. It was the property of the "whole of the people," like everything else. The political ideology of the system was to abolish private property in favor of collective ownership. So there were also no private foreign investors, who chart the economic landscape for us today. Because everything was everyone's and really nobody's, it was hard to hold anyone accountable for that common ownership.

Although purchasing power was low, people got by. They got meals at the place where they worked, and their transportation to work was paid for. They put their kids in kindergartens and schools for free, went on vacation in company-owned trailers on the coast, and got free health care. Housing was widely available and rents were heavily subsidized. Credit was easy to get. And even those who didn't work for various reasons were taken care of by generous social provisions. This was socialism. And after thirty-five years of work, spent often in just one company, you could retire and receive your guaranteed pension. . . .

It wasn't like everyone in the firm could just do—or not do—anything they wanted. There were norms and standards. As a firm we had to produce a certain amount dictated by the five-year plan. But those norms were low, loose, and not related to pay. You could get to work a bit later, leave a bit early, go for coffee in-between. . . . Stress? I don't think there was even a word for it. Just like *job security*. If jobs are there for everyone, taken for granted, you don't need words to speak about it.

And today? I'm not an enthusiast anymore. Today I worry. It's great that I don't have to work for three months to buy a bicycle or a year to afford a new kitchen. But I am very worried about how our firm will survive the increased competitive pressures on global markets. We're completely on our own now. What we took for granted in socialism, the guaranteed sales for everything we produced, the subsidies . . . vanished overnight. The firms had to turn around 180 degrees. Many failed. You survived if you quickly learned the new ways of organizing, the new culture of business, the new standards of success. It's profitability and added value per capita employee that I worry about today. I worry about increasing the stock price, fighting the fierce competition from China, and satisfying demanding customers in Germany and the United States. To be competitive, that's what we have to do. If we were smaller and more flexible, maybe I wouldn't worry so much. But I'm not sure. I'm really uncomfortable with firing people. I guess it's the socialist in me. . . .

Where would we be if we had let those American investors buy us eight years ago? I try not to think about that. In the abstract, foreign capital may have seemed such a natural path to success for our firm, but in reality, it was complicated. There were emotions, and politics and misunderstandings. . . . It was anything *but* natural.

• • •

This engineer reflecting about the past and anxiously anticipating the future is my father. Seeing in his personal experience a microcosm of grand social transformations that fundamentally changed lives of more than 100 million people from Central and Eastern Europe after the collapse of Communist regimes, is the sociological imagination that inspires this book.

From Communists to Foreign Capitalists

Chapter 1

SOCIAL FOUNDATIONS OF THE ECONOMY

IN 1985, THE ECONOMIC order of the day in socialist Central and Eastern Europe[1] was full employment and absence of private property, domestic or foreign. Only fifteen years later, in 2000, the economic systems were based on private ownership and market competitiveness. Numerous postsocialist firms were in the hands of foreign investors, absorbing some of the $1.4 trillion of that year's world foreign direct investment, which itself has increased more than twentyfold since 1985. In only fifteen years, how did we get from there to here?

This book is about the confluence of two grand processes of economic transformation that define our times: the transformation from command economies of state socialism to liberal market capitalism, and the intensification of transnational flows of capital as the defining characteristic of contemporary economic globalization. The book addresses two broad concerns. On the one hand, how have the economies in Central and Eastern Europe changed over the first decade after the fall of the Berlin Wall? How has market-based activity proliferated, and how do these newly established markets operate? On the other hand, what patterns global economic exchange? What influences whether a nation is more or less integrated into global capital flows, or whether a firm is controlled by foreign or domestic owners? Examining the determinants of foreign direct investment in Central and Eastern Europe is a strategic research site that allows me to simultaneously engage both sets of issues.

Foreign direct investment (FDI) is investment made by a company in the investor country in a foreign, host country. FDI refers to business transactions and does not include contributions from foreign governments, such as foreign aid. The objective of FDI is to obtain a lasting interest and an active role in a host company. The lasting interest implies the existence of a long-term relationship between the investor and the host and a significant degree of influence by an investor on the management of a company in a host country. Hence, FDI is usually classified as investment leading to ownership of 10 percent or more of the host firm, as opposed to portfolio investment, which refers to purchase of smaller equity shares.[2] FDI can take the form of foreign acquisition, in which the investor obtains partial or full ownership in an existing company. On the other hand, foreign investors can establish new companies in the host country, referred to as *greenfield* investment, wholly foreign-owned or in partnership with domestic investors (Dunning and Rojec 1993).

From a macroeconomic perspective, FDI is a crucial medium through which national economies become interconnected on a global basis. In fact, world FDI flows in the past three decades show exponential growth in the intensity of global exchanges, and an ever more pronounced role of multinational corporations (MNCs) in creating a global economy. While in 1970, annual world FDI flows were a mere $12 million, in 1990 this figure was up to $200 billion, and by 2000 FDI had increased dramatically to $1.4 trillion (UNCTAD 2002).

FDI in postsocialist countries provides an ideal research opportunity because it allows us to examine how certain economic activity comes into existence *de novo*. These formerly socialist countries received virtually no foreign investment before 1989 because regimes were closed and private firms did not exist. Just fifteen years later, however, Central and Eastern Europe was very substantially penetrated by foreign capital. In 2004, average FDI stock as a share in gross domestic product (GDP) for these countries reached 39 percent, which is almost twice the average for the developed economies and significantly higher than the share in developing countries. To compare, FDI stock as share in GDP of China, one of today's premier investment locations, was (only) 16 percent in 2004 (UNCTAD 2006).

The goal of this book is to exploit the advantages of this unique research setting in three ways: first, to trace the origins of FDI flows to postsocialist Europe and empirically examine the determinants of cross-border investment exchanges; second, to use this empirical case to learn more about the actual process of economic transformations in postsocialism; and third, to theoretically build on the empirical findings and advance our understanding of the creation and operation of markets in conditions of uncertainty.

THE ARGUMENT

On November 9, 1989, the Berlin Wall, which separated the socialist East from the capitalist West, fell. The fall symbolized what may be the most dramatic and revolutionary transformation of political and economic institutions in the twentieth century—the collapse of Communist regimes and socialist command economies. Vindicated by the eventual dismantling of the Iron Curtain, neoliberals[3] saw the collapse of Communism as an impetus to unleash the "natural" form of economic organization: free-market capitalism. After all, in the eyes of these observers, planned socialist economies were artificially manufactured systems that created inefficiencies, which would be corrected once the intervention of the Party state in the economy was eliminated and free markets were allowed to emerge. This view reflected the notion that in a socialist system, economic organization is closely intertwined with politics and ideology. In fact, the close coupling of economic and noneconomic institutions, or *economic embeddedness* as defined by Karl Polanyi (1944, 1957), may have been the key distinguishing feature of the socialist system. At the same time, according to the neoliberal view, self-regulating markets are by nature free of political and social constraints on efficiency-seeking economic agents. From this perspective, to "transition" to market means to "disembed" the socialist economy, that is, to remove the political, social, and ideological influences that are assumed to impede the emergence of markets and constrain the natural propensity of economic agents to maximize efficiency. But does the "disembeddedness" perspective capture the character of *actual* economic changes in Central and Eastern Europe after 1989?

In this book, I use a case study of foreign direct investment in eleven postsocialist European countries, Bulgaria, Croatia, the Czech Republic, Estonia, Hungary, Latvia, Lithuania, Poland, Romania, Slovakia, and Slovenia, to empirically examine claims about spontaneous market emergence and the asocial nature of market exchanges. (See the map of the region in figure 1.1.) In fact, I am skeptical about both of these assumptions. First, as research in economic sociology contends, markets are institutions that do not emerge naturally or spontaneously but are socially created (Polanyi 1944; Swedberg and Granovetter 1992; Swedberg 1994, 2005; Lie 1997; Fligstein 2002). The socialist command economies were created by the Communist rulers. In a similar vein, markets in Central and Eastern Europe have been created by postsocialist states, international organizations, foreign investors, and domestic economic actors who had to learn new rules of economic behavior. Market "transition" has involved a transformation of one type of institutional order, socialism, into another, capitalism.[4] Importantly, this transformation is not about eradicating social influences from the economic sphere. It is not about eliminating the role of the state in economic activity, and erasing the influence of ideational structures and political arrangements on economic transactions. Rather, it is about changing *how* these social forces structure the new market-based system of economic organization. From this perspective, socialist command economies and free-market systems are *formally very similar*, in the sense that both are socially constructed instituted systems, and in both, economic exchanges are embedded in social forces. However, these two economic systems are *substantively very different*. They exhibit different varieties of economic embeddedness. That is, each system is a configuration of different kinds of social-structural, political, and cultural influences on economic life.[5]

Second, I follow a sociological perspective on economic behavior, which understands *economic* transactions as *social* relations, enabled and

Figure 1.1. Map of Central and Eastern Europe

constrained by three key social forces: social structures, power, and culture (Zukin and DiMaggio 1990).[6] Structural conditions encompass the
influence of repeated patterns of social interaction, which can take the
form of social networks or social institutions, both consequential for economic processes. The role of power is visible because of the uneven distribution of resources, which gives rise to issues of control and disposal,
and stimulates the pursuit of political interests and power struggles in
the economic sphere. Culture is consequential because shared collective
understandings and meanings shape economic strategies and goals, and
affect the interpretations of economic situations. In this view, social influences of different kinds course through *any* economic transaction,
whether it occurs in a competitive market or in a redistributive system
of a command economy. Importantly, social forces not only *constrain*

efficiency-seeking economic agents, as most analysts emphasize, but they *enable and empower* social actors to construct and then execute economic strategies of action in conditions of uncertainty.

This perspective, that social forces not merely constrain but constitute economic behavior, rests on the distinction between two different analytic understandings of the nature of economic worlds and economic action, which I call the *instrumentalist* and the *constructivist* perspectives (table 1.1). On the one hand, from the instrumentalist standpoint, economic action is perfectly possible without the interference of social structures, politics, or culture. Such may very well be the ideal conditions for economic exchange. This is because social forces are conceived as something separate from and outside of the economic sphere. Should they transgress into the economic domain, they can be accounted for as constraints that shape the structure of incentives for rational actors. They either impede economic efficiency because they raise transaction costs, or they can be strategically employed as an efficiency-enhancing mechanism. The rational actor model aligns well with the instrumentalist perspective: economic agents are independent in their decision-making, with known, stable, and transitive preferences, and guided by inherent self-interest to maximize economic utility. When they make decisions, they follow a means-ends logic: they have *a priori* determined goals (ends), usually profit maximization, and compare and evaluate possible strategies of action (means) to select the one that is estimated to yield the greatest profits. Worlds in which these economic agents conduct exchanges are conceived as inherently knowable so that any uncertainty is treated as ignorance of objectively available information. But economic agents are seen as capable of dealing with such uncertainties by reducing them into risk probabilities, which can then be integrated into utility maximization calculations.

On the other hand, the social-constructivist model sees economic actors as always interdependent (embedded in social networks), influenced by interests and politics (politically embedded), and guided by culturally specific preferences and goals (culturally embedded). The socially constructed nature of social worlds implies that economic processes are inherently uncertain and not objectively knowable. Actors can deal with uncertainty only if they rely on social forces, which make their decision-making possible by helping them to construct strategies of economic action and providing them with a framework to evaluate them. Within stable worlds, where social forces congeal into institutions, taken-for-granted rules of interaction allow actors to reach a common basis of understanding—a common evaluation metric—and treat uncertainty as risk. However, in changing environments during unsettled times,[7] economic actors may not have clear and consistent preferences, may be unable to reliably evaluate alternatives, and may have difficulty judging probabilities of future (truly uncertain) outcomes. Hence, they are incapable of

TABLE 1.1
Instrumentalist and Constructivist Perspectives on Economic Issues

Economic Issue	Instrumentalist Perspective	Constructivist Perspective
Relationship between the social and economic spheres	Separated; if acknowledged, social forces considered as context for economic action	Permeated and embedded; economic action is social action; social forces constitute economic action
Nature of economic worlds	Objectively knowable	Inherently uncertain
Treatment of uncertainty	Uncertainty can be turned into calculable risk	Uncertainty necessitates reliance on social forces
Model of economic actor	Rational	Practical
Goals of economic action	Effficiency maximization	Multiple goals, economic and noneconomic
Strategy of economic action	Means-ends instrumental rationality	Substantive and procedural varieties of action
View of economic change	Natural evolution to one best way of free-market organization	Institutional transformation from one kind of embedded, socially constituted economy to another

turning uncertainties into risk probabilities, and will at best satisfice (Simon 1957) rather than maximize. Moreover, in conditions of radical uncertainty, economic actors may be ambiguous even about their goals of action; they may be attached to certain strategies rather than set on goals, or forced by contingencies to adjust both ends and means during the action process itself. To accommodate these circumstances, actors adopt economic strategies outside of the clear means-ends framework of instrumental rationality, such as following commitments, muddling through situational contingency, or improvisation. This means that economic action has multiple substantive and procedural varieties. To account for this diversity and flexibility of strategies, the social-constructivist model aligns best with the conception of actors as *practical* (Bourdieu 1980) rather than rational. Depending on context, economic-social actors will hold both economic and noneconomic motives for action, and their attempts at instrumental calculations will be mixed with, or even replaced by, affect, value judgments, and routine, which *may or may not* lead to efficiency maximization.

Needless to say, the social-constructivist model treats economic behavior as fundamentally social. Social forces are not imagined as something separate from the economic sphere. Instead, the social and the economic worlds interpenetrate so much that economic action is impossible without social structures, politics, or culture, which come to constitute economic behavior.[8] While often these social forces support bounded rationality of actors, and help them enhance their material positions, social forces sometimes limit efficiency, as economic actors follow value commitments, get caught up in political games, or are hindered by social networks in which they are embedded. Hence, while the instrumentalist view on economic life sees economic action as a rational search for material efficiency, the social-constructivist perspective focuses on actors' practical engagement in the processes of production, consumption, distribution, and exchange, and is agnostic about the resultant efficiency. That is, the constructivist approach does not assume maximization *a priori* but relies on concrete empirical investigation to specify the conditions in which economic behavior is or is not efficiency enhancing.

The instrumentalist and constructivist perspectives have different implications for the study of foreign direct investment in postsocialist Europe. From the instrumentalist perspective, which has dominated existing research, FDI is *a product of an investor's calculation of risk and return* to determine the investment that yields the highest profit. In this view, the collapse of Communist regimes and withdrawal of the Party states from the economy liberates Western corporations to pursue investment opportunities in Central and Eastern Europe. The investors compare likely investment profit across different alternatives, calculate expected returns and costs, and then invest in those places that promise the highest returns for the lowest costs.

In contrast, this book applies the constructivist perspective to FDI. The tenets regarding the socially constructed character of economic systems and social nature of economic transactions lead me to theorize and empirically analyze FDI as a *socially constituted relational process, negotiated by practical economic actors*. Fundamentally, FDI is a relational process— an exchange between two sides to the transaction, investor and host. Not only investors' but also hosts' actions play an important role in shaping FDI. Specifically, it is not the state's withdrawal from the socialist economy upon the collapse of Communist regimes that induces FDI inflows. On the contrary, postsocialist states need to be significantly involved in constructing FDI markets by institutionalizing and legitimizing exchanges with foreigners as appropriate and desirable economic behavior. In particular, because of the increased international integration of economies induced by globalization, postsocialist states shape FDI flows by negotiating liberalization pressures from the international environment with often protectionist domestic interests grounded in nationalist discourse. Because of the relational nature of FDI, the investment flows are not shaped only by the host country's economic and political characteristics (as cues for investors' calculations of risk and return) but are channeled through the existing network of social relations between countries.

Moreover, if FDI is a *socially constituted* process, transactions at the level of firms will be heavily influenced by (*a*) business and personal networks in which investors and hosts are embedded, (*b*) political interests and vying for power between and within firms engaged in FDI transactions, and (*c*) culturally embedded understandings that investors and hosts have about appropriate economic partners, desirable economic goals, and plausible strategies to reach them. These social forces will not simply impose constraints on otherwise universally rational investors and hosts by increasing transaction costs. Rather, facing radical uncertainty that characterizes fundamental transformations in postsocialist Europe, investors and hosts will be able to accomplish FDI transactions *only if* they rely on social forces and act practically. Embeddedness in networks, institutional arrangements, power distributions, and cultural understandings will enable and empower both hosts and investors to partake in FDI transactions because it will help them manage the unpredictability of doing business in a turbulent environment. Paradoxically, being rational in conditions of unmeasurable uncertainty is an impediment. In such conditions, investors and hosts would likely be incapacitated because they could not precisely calculate the risk and returns of all possible investment alternatives. Or, should they nevertheless follow an *a priori* determined satisficing strategy, they would sacrifice precious flexibility to adjust when unexpected events came their way. Therefore, investors and hosts *act practically.* They use their social ties, draw on extant cultural conceptions, and sway with political currents. The social embeddedness of their actions gives rise to practical economic strategies, such as following commitments, muddling through situational contingency, or improvising. Some of these strategies may turn out to be suboptimal with respect to material efficiency. FDI business in unsettled times may or may not result in profit maximization. Uncertainty may help open up new strategic opportunities for entrepreneurial profits (Knight 2002) but it may also limit efficiency.

In the next section I detail the social-constructivist perspective on economic organization and action that provides the basis of the arguments advanced in this book and informs the empirical analyses of FDI flows to postsocialist Europe, which follow in subsequent chapters.

A Social-Constructivist Perspective
on Economic Organization and Action

Departing from the neoclassical conception of a market as an abstraction equilibrating supply and demand via a price-setting mechanism, sociologists have pointed to the social-network, cultural, political, and state-institutional dimensions of markets (for a recent review see Smelser and Swedberg 2005). One of the most prominent strands in this research takes off from the famous statement by Mark Granovetter that economic behavior is "constrained by ongoing social relations" (1985, 481) and examines the role of networks in economic activity.[9] The network approach has provided a powerful antidote to atomistic conceptions of economic actors prevalent in economics. Nevertheless, this research has been critiqued for its lack of attention to cultural, political, and institutional forces (Zelizer 1988, 2001, 2002a; Fligstein and Mara-Drita 1996; Emirbayer and Goodwin 1994; Barber 1995; Nee and Ingram 1998; Spillman 1999; Krippner 2001; Bandelj 2002; Fligstein 2002), which have been shown to importantly structure economic life. Hence, we now have a smaller but growing body of work in economic sociology, which has responded to Viviana Zelizer's (1988, 618) call to avoid "social structural reductionism" and pay attention also to cultural dimensions of economy (e.g., Zelizer 1979, 1987, 1994, 2005; Biggart 1989; Smith 1990; DiMaggio 1994; Dobbin 1994a; Abolafia 1996, 1998; Beckert 2004; Velthuis 2005). A third prominent line of work in economic sociology, closely aligned with political economy research, took seriously Max Weber's (1978, 67) suggestion that "it is essential to include the criterion of power of control and disposal . . . in the sociological concept of economic action" (e.g., Mills 1956; Zeitlin 1974; Mintz and Schwartz 1985; Fligstein 1990, 1996; Carruthers 1996; Roy 1997; Bourdieu 2005). A variety of this research investigates the role of states in economic development (e.g., Evans 1979, 1995; Block 1994; Ó Riain 2000; Fligstein 2001a; Block and Evans 2005) or broadly accounts for the political-legal and institutional bases of markets (e.g., Hamilton and Biggart 1988; Campbell and Lindberg 1990; Gao 1997, 2001; Biggart and Guillén 1999; Campbell and Pedersen 2001; Fligstein and Stone Sweet 2002; Guillén 2001b; Nee 2005).

As this short, in no way exhaustive, literature review shows, economic sociology is a very vital and diverse field of inquiry.[10] It harbors multiple approaches, often distinguished by the one social force that researchers privilege in their analyses.[11] For instance, research in the network tradition almost exclusively focuses on the role of social structures. Political economists stress state institutions as paramount. Cultural analyses underscore the importance of symbolic meanings. Often, then, vying for theoretical territory and armed with their one favored explanatory factor, scholars engage in debates over "structure versus culture" or "power versus institutions." Not only are such theoretical debates largely counterproductive, but various research in economic sociology shows that social structures (networks, institutions, and states), power, and culture *all* matter for economic activity. The social constructivist perspective, which I advance in this book, takes this as a basic premise. Indeed, if the economy is an integral part of society, and if economic action is socially constituted, then social structural, political, and cultural forces all course through any economic transaction, at the micro level, and their configurations constitute every economic system, at the macro level of analysis. The constructivist perspective encourages the analytical integration of these three key social mechanisms, and the empirical examination of their *concurrent* influences on economic organization and economic action. Such analyses avoid one-sided explanations, which are likely skewed because they leave important causal factors unconsidered.

At the macro level of economic systems, examining all three key social forces allows us to identify the social organization of economies. Analysis of merely the structural, political, or cultural dimensions of economy will not be sufficient for this task since it is precisely the configurations of, and interrelations between, different social forces that characterize unique varieties of economic organization. For instance, state socialism, as an ideal type, is characterized by structures of redistribution, central planning, an absence of private enterprise, autocratic power of the Communist Party, and a prevalent ideology of Marxism-Leninism, which privileges collective interest. The structures-power-culture configuration of Western capitalism is marked by private property rights and competitive market structures, a multiparty polity, and an ideology of individualization that privileges self-interest. As I will try to show, tracing the *re*configuration of the structures-power-culture nexus helps us explain the paths to economic transformation.

At the micro level of economic action, exchanges are social relations that have structural properties, but they also require attendant frameworks of understanding that enable actors to make sense of their role position. At the same time, any single position in the structure of social relations comes with different resources/power vis-à-vis actors in other positions. In addition, cultural understandings shape the articulation of interests (desired goals, preferred means) that actors pursue in exchanges. Thus, every economic exchange will be simultaneously influenced by social structures, cultural understandings, and distributions of power. While some of these forces may be causally more important than others for any specific economic transaction, we need to disentangle these relationships in rigorous empirical research that concurrently considers all three aspects.

Furthermore, the social-constructivist focus (on how economic outcomes result from mutual shaping of structures, power, and culture) underscores that social forces do not only comprise a "context" for what is otherwise an inherently asocial autonomous economic transaction (cf. Zelizer 2001, 2002a). Rather, social factors generate and constitute economic activity—by providing cultural and material resources, which help actors to make sense of economic situations, enable them to construct economic strategies of action, and empower them to engage in economic interactions. The emphasis on the constitutive rather than merely contextual properties of social forces underscores that economic exchanges are social relations, navigated by practical actors. It is also on this count that the social-constructivist view on economic life sharply departs not only from neoclassical economic tradition but also from transaction cost institutional economics and rational-choice economic sociology. While these latter two perspectives acknowledge the role of social forces, they treat them as part of the context that shapes incentives for rational actors: either as transaction costs that impede the pursuit of inherent self-interest, or as efficiency-enhancing mechanisms that rational agents strategically employ.

Substantive Varieties of Embedded Economies

A basic assumption is that not structures (states, institutions, networks) alone, not culture alone, and not power alone, but all of these social forces together, matter in constituting economic activities. However, the real and challenging task for analysts of economic processes is to articulate the different *substantive varieties*[12]—different types and kinds—of political factors, cultural understandings, institutional arrangements, and social ties that shape different systems of economic organization at the macro level, or different economic outcomes at the micro level.[13] Moreover, if any economic system is a configuration of different kinds of social structures, power distributions, and cultural understandings, then economic change needs to be conceptualized as a *re*-configuration, a movement from one kind of embedding to another, that is, a change in the substantive variety of economic embeddedness.

The fundamental transformation from command economies to market economies—which is "nothing short of revolution" (Szelényi, Beckett, and King 1994, 242)—provides a particularly fruitful area in which to examine the reconfiguration process. So far scholars have largely disagreed on how market transition is (best) accomplished because they operate with different assumptions about institutional change. On one hand, many prominent economists propose what may be called blueprint capitalism (Sachs 1989; Lipton and Sachs 1990; Sachs and Lipton 1990; Blanchard et al. 1991; Fischer and Gelb 1991; Aslund 1992, 1994, 1995; but see Murrell 1992; North 1990, 2005). This perspective is grounded in neoclassical economics and the assumption that the Western economic model of a market and the profit maximization principle is universally applicable. Thus Eastern European countries are advised (often quite literally by international financial organizations and Western experts) to quickly—as in shock therapy—implement tight monetary policy, restricted fiscal policy, and export-led growth, which will yield markets. Advocating that capitalist institutions should be replicated according to

Western experts' blueprints, this perspective assumes a clean slate, *tabula rasa*, after the fall of socialism, which allows for a rapid emergence of a new system. Underlying this blueprint capitalism (or shock therapy) perspective is the assumption that laissez-faire is the one best and most efficient way to organize contemporary capitalism. Once inefficient state intervention is eliminated, the invisible hand of the market will demonstrate its powers.

On the other hand, scholars working in the tradition of historical institutionalism emphasize that change is "path dependent" because structures inherited from before and during the state-socialist period influence the postsocialist transformation (Comisso 1991, 1995; Bruszt 1992; Stark 1992, 1996; Campbell and Pedersen 1996; Szelényi and Kostello 1996; Verdery 1996b, 2003; Róna-Tas 1997; Stark and Bruszt 1998; McDermott 2002; Ekiert and Hanson 2003). Policymakers who align with this perspective advocate a gradual transformation, not shock therapy. This historically grounded perspective privileges continuity between socialist and postsocialist periods. It suggests that multiple transformations—not a transition with a single known destination—occur *with* (not merely *on*) the ruins of the former regime in path-dependent ways (Stark 1996).[14] Since the ruins of Communism vary, as do the paths of extrication, postsocialist transformations can hardly be expected to evolve toward a singular and uniform end point. Rather, a variety of capitalist arrangements is expected to emerge in postsocialist Europe, all as viable forms of capitalist organization, since there is no evidence that one single and uniform set of economic institutions is superior in its efficiency.

From a social-constructivist viewpoint, either explanation seems incomplete. While Communist institutions cannot vanish over night so they can be replaced with a neoliberal blueprint, it is also difficult to imagine how significant economic change is possible if the past commands the future. Likely, it is both new and old institutions that shape economic transformations. Indeed, if we analyze the changes after socialism as an instance of reconfiguration of one substantive variety of economic embeddedness (socialist redistribution) to another (capitalist markets), we become interested in *how and why* new and old institutions matter for postsocialist transformations. We study, on the one hand, the more or less rapid dismantling of centralized command over production and redistribution and, on the other hand, the establishment of new economic institutions of private property and market exchange. We see a more or less radical shift in the distribution of power among economic actors, with the Communist Party losing its despotic throne and supranational bodies, such as the European Union and international financial organizations, assuming substantial control over national economic matters. These changes are accompanied by a more or less extensive legitimization of new economic priorities of profit maximization and self-interest over socialist concerns with job security and other social protections. The process of change is characterized by fundamental uncertainty, and actors, maneuvering the shifting economic space, need to be practical rather than rational. They may learn to adapt to new formal market institutions, but their learning will be shaped by the informal taken-for-granted rules and practices that accompanied socialism, which are most resistant to change (North 1990, 1993). Vestiges of socialism not only hamper learning the new rules of the game, and therefore limit efficiency, they also enable actors, as they face novel challenges, to create solutions that lead to innovative change. Hence, institutions of postsocialism, old and new, do not merely constrain self-interested behavior, as proposed by an instrumentalist perspective, but also enable practical economic actors to manage uncertainty and articulate their interests.

Finally, what are the implications of the constructivist approach for economic development? When we describe the substantive varieties of embeddedness, we identify specific configurations of social structures, power distributions, and cultural understandings that congeal into distinct forms of economic organization (cf. Whitley 1992a, 1992b; Dobbin 1994a; Guillén 2001b). Such investigation into the social organization of the economy elucidates a variety of potentially viable paths of economic performance because "effectiveness" and "rationality" have multiple instantiations. Concretely, this implies that free-market economies are not naturally superior to state-socialist systems. Both are socially, culturally and politically defined. Both reside on some notion of organizational effectiveness, such as insuring full employment in the socialist system, or pursuing profitability in capitalism. Both systems are governed by a particular power structure, either the Communist Party or neoliberal elites and international organizations. And both systems have established institutions that hold their cultural and political structures in place.

Embeddedness of Economic Action

The notion of substantive varieties of embeddedness elucidates the broad macro patterns of economic organization and transformation, but the social-constructivist perspective also has implication for our understanding of economic action.[15] On the one hand, the instrumentalist view is clear on the theory of action: economic actors are rational utility-maximizers. This means that they know what they want and they decide how to get it in a way that is most efficient, that is, incurs lowest costs for maximum benefits. All this implies known and stable goals, and exogenously given, stable, and transitive preferences. On the other hand, from the constructivist viewpoint, uncovering social foundations of economic action exposes the limits to the rational actor model because it highlights *substantive varieties of rationality* and *procedural variation in the logic of economic action*, going beyond profit maximization and beyond rational means-ends calculations, respectively.

As regards buying, selling, producing, and exchanging in markets, the traditional economic account privileges the understanding that firms strive to maximize profits. This is primarily because most of such work assumes behavior in contemporary competitive Western-style markets. However, if social forces constitute economic preferences, then there may be other likely and legitimate goals of economic action, resulting in different substantive varieties of rationality. To isolate one such goal, Neil Fligstein proposes that we "replace profit-maximizing actors with people who are trying to promote the survival of their firm" (2001a, 17). Firms may also explicitly target shareholder value, or market share, and not simply the highest profits. Moreover, when states act as economic actors, they may aim at political power or job protection. In the case of FDI in Central and Eastern Europe, decisions could also be informed by value rationality, whereby certain investment locations, such as a country to which one maintains affiliate ties, will be preferred on normative grounds and the conviction that one should do good for that country. In the case of East European émigrés or their children investing in their home countries, economic action may have an ideological basis, such as building capitalism after the fall of Communism. Consequently, not all market activity should be seen as profit-maximizing. Likely, the conception of economic action that encompasses substantive varieties of goals and preferences has more empirical utility. Moreover, while the instrumentalist perspective treats economic motives as exogenous, the social-constructivist focus can contribute significantly to the understanding of goals and preference formation, by tracing their social construction.

Still, strictly speaking, any substantive variety of rationality can be subsumed under the rational-action perspective. As a matter of fact, in the formulations of rational action that go beyond allocative efficiency within a market setting, a claim that an act is rational refers less to its substance than to its procedural means-ends logic. The means-ends schema implies internal coherence of decision-making whereby actors have clear fixed goals and stable preferences, and they decide upon the means to reach goals in a way that maximizes their utility, whatever the components of their utility function may be.

However, if economic processes have social foundations, the influence of social networks, cultural understandings, and politics on economic activity will also shape the procedural logics of action, resulting in behavior that is quite different from rational means-ends calculations. Distributions of power and political interests may lead people to strongly identify with certain strategies of action or solutions to problems, so that they may be unable or unwilling to switch to alternatives, even when they are recognized as more cost efficient. In these cases, means-to-act are independent of goals, and goals are often identified only as a consequence of committing to certain means.[16] Moreover, shared understandings (or lack thereof), which develop during the course of action between transaction partners, create emotionally charged circumstances that can compel actors to change their initial goals or modify their preferences. Likewise, new information that comes to actors via their social networks may induce them to change their preferences as transactions unfold. All this suggests that social forces not only constitute actors' preferences and goals but also affect their stability, and hence the procedural logic of decision-making.

In addition, different types of economic arrangements or processes in different temporal and spatial contexts encounter more or less environmental uncertainty, such as changes in the legal and political environment or economic crises that commonly occur during postsocialist transformations. Under conditions of uncertainty, rational means-ends schemas can be difficult to identify, much less implement, as actors will shift their goals or strategies to reach them. Indeed, their final goals will likely be articulated on-the-fly during the process of action itself. Therefore, the goal they reach at the end of the transaction may be quite different from that which they wanted in the beginning. If means and ends of economic action are not fixed at the beginning of transactions, but emerge out of situations themselves, actions are better conceived as creative rather than rational (Joas 1996).

The traditional economic account of clear fixed goals, stable preferences and cost minimization strategies is monolithic. Uncertainty, and the resultant embeddedness, can render situations in which economic action does *not* follow from straightforward, means-ends calculation. Rather, economic action can be based on commitment (where goals are articulated as a consequence of the choice of means); it may reflect muddling through[17] due to situational contingencies (where ends and means articulated at the beginning differ from those achieved in the end because preferences change during the process); or it may resemble improvisation (where both ends and means evolve during the process of action itself). Paying attention to different kinds of social forces and degrees of uncertainty, we can identify conditions when means-ends schema can be usefully retained, but also those where practical actors employ alternative economic action strategies.

• • •

Rather than rational asocial systems in which agents pursue their universal self-interest, I suggest that economies are socially constructed institutional arrangements where practical economic action is constituted by social structures, power relations, and cultural understandings. But it is an empirical question whether uncovering the social foundations of economic organization and action really helps us better understand economic processes in times of change. Hence, in the second part of this introduction, I explicate the details of the empirical case that will be used to examine the explanatory power of the social-constructivist perspective—the case of foreign direct investment in postsocialist Europe.

THE EMPIRICAL CASE: FOREIGN DIRECT INVESTMENT IN POSTSOCIALIST EUROPE

Globalization, the intensification of cross-national flows of goods, services, people, technology, and capital that create the compression of time and space, is distinctly marked by the recent unprecedented rise in FDI. World FDI flows, which increased more than twenty-fold over the past twenty years, were valued at $1.4 trillion in 2000 (UNCTAD 2002). In fact, the activities of multinational corporations (MNCs), mostly U.S.-based firms investing in other developed countries, started to make a significant impact on the international economy as early as the 1950s (Gereffi 2005, 164). A couple of initial MNC studies examined these trends, highlighting the benefits of U.S. FDI for host economies (Dunning 1958; Safarian 1966). Among the earliest attempts to extensively study MNCs was the Multinational Enterprise Project, started in 1965 by Raymond Vernon, an economist at the Harvard Graduate School of Public Administration who focused on the strategies of MNCs, highlighting the role of the product cycle in determining foreign investment decisions (Vernon 1971, 1999). Whether interested in macro international capital flows or micro firm-level behavior, these first studies of MNCs were all grounded in neoclassical economic theory, analyzing corporate strategies as examples of rational profit-maximization and transnational investment as beneficial to global welfare (Kindleberger 1970; Stopford and Wells 1972; Knickerbocker 1973; Hymer 1976).

New research approaches emerged in the 1970s, primarily among sociologists, who questioned the proclaimed positive spillovers of MNC activities and emphasized the uneven power relations between Western core nations that provided the source of FDI and underdeveloped peripheral countries that were the destinations. Concerned with how worldwide expansion of capitalism leads to dependency in Third World countries, the dependency school argued that MNCs, as instantiations of the uneven link between developed and underdeveloped countries, create dependencies because they hurt the ability of the Third World countries to build domestic industries controlled by locally owned firms (Cardoso and Faletto 1979; Gereffi 1978, 1983; Evans 1979).[18] With a similar focus on the political economy of FDI, world systems theorists have argued that foreign investment serves primarily the investors from developed core states and thus retards the development of poor countries on the periphery (Wallerstein 1974; Chase-Dunn 1975; Bornschier and Chase-Dunn 1985). The deleterious effects of foreign investment, these researchers posit, result because the entry of MNCs distorts a nation's forces of production such that it relies on low-wage and unskilled labor to produce goods at low levels of technological sophistication. This creates few opportunities for beneficial "spillover" effects such as research and development, industrial services, or differentiation and constrains economic growth (Galtung 1971; Bornschier and Ballmer-Cao 1979; Bornschier and Chase-Dunn 1985). Furthermore, heavy dependence on foreign capital promotes an uneven distribution of capital intensity across sectors and geographical regions in the receiver economy. This concentrates income in (typically more productive) outward-oriented sectors, increasing overall income inequality (Frank 1967; Stack 1980). In addition, foreign capital penetration limits the production of human capital within the receiver economy and constrains the development of bureaucratic skills necessary for a highly functioning business sector (Bornschier and Ballmer-Cao 1979; Evans and Timberlake 1980; Bornschier and Chase-Dunn 1985). Scholars also argue that foreign capital penetration encourages inequality by influencing the distributive capacity of nation-states. Increases in global capital flows tend to produce a "race to the bottom" in which governments in developing nations seek to attract foreign investment by implementing policies that lower the bargaining power of labor, eliminate provisions that encourage full employment and wage enhancement, such as job training and local purchasing requirements, and thus remove institutional constraints on rising income inequality (McMichael 1996; DeMartino 1998; Ranney 1998; Beer and Boswell 2002).[19]

Nonetheless, arguments about the positive effects of liberalization and foreign investment reemerged in the 1980s as part of the "Washington consensus," advocated by international development agencies like the IMF and the World Bank (Gore 2000). John Williamson, who coined the name *Washington consensus*, argued that its principles of stabilization, liberalization, privatization, and deregulation constitute "the common core of wisdom embraced by all serious economists" (1993, 1334). Indeed, the Washington consensus—also referred to as neoliberalism—is closely related to neoclassical development economics, and a basic tenet is that growth in the stock of capital is the primary driver of economic expansion (Solow 1956; Swan 1956; Barro and Sala-i-Martin 1995). According to this view, for underdeveloped countries with dearth of domestic capital, the inflow of foreign investment increases the stock of capital and stimulates domestic economic growth (Balasubramanyam, Salisu, and Sapsford 1999). In addition to propelling capital accumulation, investment by MNCs also has positive spillover effects, including job creation, skill upgrading, and the transfer of technological and managerial know-how to domestic firms (Markusen 1995; Blomstrom and Kokko 1997; Markusen and Venables 1999; Javorcik 2004). But how do these expectations square with empirical research that finds negative impacts of FDI for economic growth and equality? They don't.

There is very little consensus in the literature on the role of FDI in development. In fact, scholars working in different theoretical or disciplinary traditions propose contradictory effects. How to adjudicate between these diverse findings? In my view, the only way to better comprehend the *consequences* of economic globalization is to first understand the *causes and processes* of actual foreign direct investment activities. We need to know what structures FDI flows and what shapes firms' decisions on foreign investment. Contributing to this effort, my study of FDI in Central and Eastern Europe is particularly valuable because it provides a natural experiment setting. As table 1.2 shows, FDI was restricted before 1989 and diffused into the region in subsequent years. Hence, tracing the trajectories of FDI flows in postsocialist Europe offers an excellent opportunity to examine the evolution of FDI markets. While initial flows into the region were minimal in absolute numbers, FDI has grown significantly over the past fifteen years, leading to substantial FDI stock when considered relative to the size of these transition economies. As shown in table 1.2, since 1995 average FDI stock as a percentage of GDP for Central and Eastern Europe has been higher than the world average; by 2004, it was almost twice as high.

Explicating the determinants of FDI is also significant for understanding postsocialist economic transformation. It is precisely FDI that has been advocated by prominent international organizations as an engine in the transition to market and a powerful force for integration of this region into the global economy (IMF 1997; UNCTAD 1998). Many experts have suggested that "without massive inflows of foreign capital, successful transition [from planned to market economies] in Central and Eastern Europe is unlikely" (Schmidt 1995, 268). As a catalyst in the transition from state socialism, FDI would affect key macroeconomic indicators, such as the balance of payments and employment. Moreover, foreign investors would bring financial, managerial, and technological resources to induce corporate restructuring in formerly state-owned enterprises (Meyer 1995, 1998; Lankes and Venables 1996; OECD 1998c; Bevan and Estrin 2004).

Sociological research on postsocialist transformations has only begun to recognize the crucial role of foreign investment. In a recent review of

TABLE 1.2
Foreign Direct Investment Trends

	FDI Inflows ($ billions)[a]		Average FDI Stock as % of GDP[b]	
	CEE[c]	World	CEE	World
1970	0	13	0	
1980	0	55	0	5
1981	0	69	0	5
1982	0	59	0	6
1983	0	57	0	6
1984	0	59	0	6
1985	0	58	0	7
1986	0	87	0	7
1987	0	140	0	7
1988	0	165	0	7
1989	<1	193	<1	8
1990	<1	208	2	8
1991	2	161	2	8
1992	3	169	5	8
1993	4	228	7	9
1994	4	259	9	9
1995	10	341	10	9
1996	9	393	12	10
1997	10	488	16	12
1998	18	701	19	14
1999	19	1,092	23	16
2000	21	1,397	27	18
2001	22	826	31	20
2002	25	716	35	21
2003	17	633	37	22
2004	28	648	39	22

Source: UNCTAD 2006.

[a] Cumulative FDI inflows in a particular year.

[b] Average for the region/world.

[c] CEE includes Bulgaria, Croatia, Czech Republic, Estonia, Hungary, Latvia, Lithuania, Poland, Romania, Slovakia, and Slovenia.

the post-communist economies, King and Szelényi (2005) write that the most advanced among them have been successful because they have built capitalism from "outside," with foreign capital, and that foreign investors constitute the new ruling elite in Central and Eastern Europe (cf. Eyal, Szelényi, and Townsley 1998). If foreign investors participate in the transformation of property rights *as well as* formation of new class structures, then their relevance for the creation of capitalism in postsocialist Europe could not be greater. Still, scant attention is paid to how foreign investors

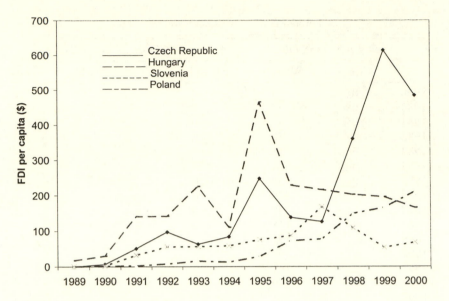

Figure 1.2. FDI Inflows in Select Central and East European Countries, 1990–2000

come to be involved in the creation of market processes in postsocialist Europe, and why the extent of their presence differs in individual countries.

Indeed, despite its alleged key role in postsocialist economic transformations, empirical data show substantial cross-national variation in FDI flows (figure 1.2). For instance, in the period from 1995 to 1997, foreign investment levels in Hungary and Latvia reached over 6 percent of GDP in comparison to 2 percent for Slovenia and Lithuania. Foreign direct investments in Poland and Slovakia were less than the 1997 regional average of 3.3 percent, while the Czech Republic and Estonia attracted above-average FDI levels (UNCTAD 1998). By 2000, FDI stock in Latvia amounted to only about $2 billion, while in Poland it was almost fifteen times higher. But it is not only the size of the economy that matters: Estonia, with a population of 1.5 million, attracted about $2,500 per capita in FDI stock by 2000, while for Romania, fourteen times larger, this figure was $300.

FDI is not only highly variable across individual Central and East European countries and over time, but *within* countries. There are differences in who invests where. By 2000, Germany and the Netherlands were the biggest investors in the region. Both countries invested substantially in Hungary and Slovakia, but while Dutch investment was significant in the Czech Republic and Poland, Germany invested more in Bulgaria and

Latvia. U.S. investment featured prominently in Croatia and Lithuania. Among smaller investors, Estonia received more than three-quarters of Finland's investment in the region and almost 50 percent of FDI in Slovenia came from Austria. Australia invested some in Poland, Croatia, and the Czech Republic, but Asian and Latin American investments in the region were negligible.

Variation in FDI also exists at the level of firms. Some attempts at FDI are successfully realized to the mutual satisfaction of all parties involved. Many FDI attempts are modified in scope or in mode of entry during the process of negotiation with host governments or targeted firms. An investor company might attempt to acquire a 100 percent ownership of an existing company, but then forms a joint venture with the host firm, or perhaps ends up establishing a completely new entity in that country (so-called greenfield investment). Furthermore, some attempted FDI transactions (albeit very difficult to track down) fail to materialize. Investor firms may encounter resistance, if not outright rejection, at local sites and decide to withdraw their investment offers. Host firms actively looking for a foreign partner may also be unsuccessful in their search. Moreover, many opportunities for FDI are never even considered.

In short, FDI in Central and Eastern Europe varies across countries over time, within countries by the investor's country of origin, and across organizational cases. What explains this variation? What determines FDI flows and transactions in postsocialist Europe?

Economics and Political Economy of Foreign Direct Investment

Economists have studied FDI extensively and built their explanations around a central thesis: FDI, like other economic behavior, reflects independent economic agents responding to freely determined prices in pursuit of utility maximization. In particular, MNCs consider the profitability of alternative investment strategies and decide to engage in foreign direct investments because this minimizes their transaction costs and promises high returns. Most analyses of FDI flows at the country level examine the effects of economic opportunities generated by the demand and costs associated with the supply at the investment site (Basi 1963; Aharoni 1966; Agarwal 1980; Dunning 1980; Grubaugh 1987; Alter and Wehrle 1993; Welfens 1993; Schmidt 1995; Jun and Singh 1996; Markusen 1995; Meyer 1995, 1998; Billington 1999). Demand is estimated by market potential in terms of size and growth. Key cost factors include the availability, skill, and cost of labor; macroeconomic stability; and development of infrastructure.

Several studies by political economists add political risks, government policy, and the level of democratic development of host countries to this list of cost factors that investors should consider in their calculations of risk and return. This research hypothesizes that political hazards add to investment risks and therefore discourage FDI (Kobrin 1982, 1984; Gastanga, Nugent, and Pashamova 1998; Delios and Henisz 2000; Henisz 2000, 2002; Wei 2000; Henisz and Delios 2001). In addition, researchers argue that foreign investment policies of host countries, which provide incentives to investors in the form of tax holidays or exemptions from import duties, have an impact because they deflect costs at investment sites, while protectionist policies increase them (Bhagwati, Dinopoulos, and Wong 1992; Brewer 1993; Blonigen and Feenstra 1996; Ellingsen and Wärneryd 1999; UNCTAD 2002). Investigating a relationship between democracy and FDI, in a recent comprehensive study Nathan Jensen (2006) finds that democracies attract more FDI, arguing that this is because democratic governments can more credibly commit to market-friendly policies than can authoritarian regimes. Earlier studies, however, found no effect of the political regime (Oneal 1994; Alesina and Dollar 1998) or found evidence of a negative relationship between democracy and FDI (Li and Resnick 2003).

Whether it is because of promising economic conditions or political stability or tax incentives for investors, this research uniformly concludes that those countries which promise highest returns and minimum costs will attract the most FDI. The prosperity and the stability of the economy will have a positive effect on FDI, while political risks and high tax costs will reduce it. But do these trends hold for the uncertain and transforming postsocialist Europe? For instance, Slovenia, a country considered as the most advanced in the transition process, with little investment risk, has seen comparatively small FDI flows. Latvia and Lithuania, two Baltic states quite similar in their economic and political development, have attracted significantly different FDI amounts. For Poland, the country with the largest domestic market in the region, FDI stock has represented a much smaller share than for Estonia, which has the smallest domestic market in the region. Moreover, if uniform country characteristics are key determinants of FDI flows, how can we explain variations in the investor country of origin?

Existing studies of FDI transactions at the firm level focus on why and how firms decide to undertake direct investments abroad. Research suggests that firms, as profit-maximizing agents, are motivated to exploit their own advantages, such as access to patented technology, specific management or marketing skills, or ownership of brand names, and to exploit institutional and productive factors of the target setting (Hymer 1976; Vernon 1971; Stopford and Wells 1972; Dunning 1981, 1995; Wheeler and Moody 1992). Minimization of transaction costs, or strategic behavior aimed at maximization of profits, guides firms' choices about the form of internationalization (direct investment abroad, trade, or licensing) and the form of FDI entry, such as greenfield investment, joint ventures, or mergers and acquisitions (Williamson 1975, 1985; Buckley and Casson 1976; Hennart 1982; Vernon 1983; Vickers 1985; Anderson and Gatignon 1986; Hill, Hwang, and Kim 1990; Oxley 1997; Sun 1999). Enhancement of learning and technological capabilities may also be important goals (Kogut 1988; Kogut and Chang 1991; Kogut and Zander 1993).

Focusing on the motives of foreign investors, this research is strangely silent about the host side of FDI transactions. What happens when foreign direct investment efforts, identified as cost-efficient and profitable by investors who attempt them, are resisted by host firms or the host country's government?

Sociology of Foreign Direct Investment

Research that emphasizes the potential profitability of investment locations and minimization of transaction costs as key determinants of FDI rests on two assumptions. First, such analyses are investor-centered and either ignore the role of the hosts or treat them as passive receivers of investment. Second, this research adopts the instrumentalist view of economic life, assuming that economic processes are largely asocial and that economic outcomes are a straightforward result of instrumentally rational calculation of risk and return, and efficiency.

Instead of treating hosts as passive recipients of foreign investment and investors as efficiency maximizers, I adopt a social-constructivist perspective and conceptualize and empirically analyze FDI as a relational, socially constituted process. Why relational? By definition, investment flows from an origin (investor) to a destination (host). Thus, FDI results from a relation between two parties to an economic exchange. Consequently, the causes of FDI must likewise be traced to the actions of both investors and hosts and the relations between them. In doing so, we can examine how not only Western foreign investors but also hosts on the periphery importantly influence the FDI process by making it a site for the assertion of local interests and possible resistance to globalization (cf. Guillén 2001a, 2001b, 2002a).

Why social? Because FDI involves actors who are oriented to each other in their behavior, attribute meaning to economic exchanges, are influenced by power dynamics, and rely on networks and institutions to practically navigate economic interactions. Social structures, distributions of power, and cultural understandings constitute any economic action, and FDI is no exception. In fact, some exemplary studies that pay attention to the role of social forces have found that national culture influences the mode of foreign entry (Kogut and Singh 1988), that investors embedded in interorganizational networks imitate behavior of their peers (Delios and Henisz 2000; Henisz and Delios 2001; Guillén 2002a, 2002b), and that institutional distributions of power structure the frequency of hostile takeovers as an FDI strategy (Schneper and Guillén 2004). I build on these studies to bring to the fore the social foundations of cross-border investments. I expect that the variability in FDI across countries and across organizational cases in transforming Central and Eastern Europe will have more to do with institutions, social networks, politics, and culture than objective risk-and-return indicators.

To test the explanatory power of this argument, I empirically examine in this book the following questions about the determinants of FDI at three different levels of analysis:

1. What accounts for the differences in country-level FDI trajectories since 1989? In particular, how do postsocialist states, international and regional organizations, such as the IMF and the EU, and domestic nationalist discourse influence the creation of FDI markets?

2. What explains the cross-sectional variation in national FDI flows? In particular, what is the significance of political, economic, and cultural relations between investor and host countries for determining which countries are more or less integrated into transnational capital flows?

3. What determines the realization of foreign investment attempts at the firm level? In particular, what is the role of institutions, social networks, power struggles within firms, and cultural understandings of economic partners, strategies and goals, in shaping the practice of FDI transactions in conditions of high uncertainty?

After setting the stage with chapter 2, which provides a general overview of the socialist system and the larger context in which postsocialist economic changes occur, I take up the first empirical question outlined above in chapter 3, which examines the proliferation of FDI exchanges in eleven postsocialist countries from 1989 to 2000. Theorizing market transition, the orthodox economic perspective stipulates that markets will emerge spontaneously once the control of the Party state is abolished and an incentive structure is put in place for self-interested actors to exchange and maximize utility. But what my analyses show is that economic incentives and stabilization in host countries explain little about FDI flows to eleven Central and East European countries in the first ten years after the fall of the Berlin Wall. Rather, the findings show that the efforts of postsocialist states to institutionalize and legitimize FDI make the crucial difference. It is in those countries where FDI is encouraged by privatization policies, by a political commitment of postsocialist government to liberalization, and by concrete state actions to increase the legitimacy of FDI practice that we see the highest foreign investment inflows. These results suggest that it is the involvement of the postsocialist states rather than their withdrawal from the economy that facilitated the marketization of Central and Eastern Europe in the first decade after 1989. Moreover, contrary to the instrumentalist view suggesting that economic efficiency is the key reason for states to encourage FDI, I find that host states' decisions to legitimize FDI depend most upon the legacy of previous policies, mimetic and coercive pressures from the international environment, and efforts to protect domestic ownership in the newly established states. This means that postsocialist states construct markets in ways that reflect institutionalized alternatives for action available to political actors, which are themselves shaped by existing cultural repertoires and international power relations.

But how do FDI markets operate? The second set of questions outlined above focuses on what structures cross-national capital flows across countries and provides the basis for chapter 4. FDI flows to postsocialist Europe reveal substantial within-country variation by investor country of origin. Basically, there seems to be a pattern in who invests where, suggesting that a set of relations between individual postsocialist countries and world investor countries can be more important than a postsocialist country's economic prosperity or political turbulence. The empirical analyses of FDI between investor-host country pairs substantiate that FDI flows between countries that have established political, migration, trade, and cultural relations, underscoring the fundamentally relational aspect of cross-border transactions.

The weakness of standard risk-and-return indicators to explain macro-level FDI flows implies that, at the micro level, economic actors involved in FDI transactions may not maximize profits. While preexistent business and personal ties forged through trade and migration flows between nations likely decrease transaction costs, established connections, personal affiliations, and cultural conceptions may also lock actors into a limited number of alternatives. Moreover, these macro-level analyses point to a possibility that local actors at investment sites interfere with investors' efforts to maximize profits by modifying investors' original intentions, and sometimes by rejecting them altogether. However, what happens at the level of firms can only be inferred from macro-level analyses, and it is more effective to directly examine organizational decision-making. I do that in chapter 5. The empirical question here is this: What determines the realization of FDI transactions? Instrumentalist explanations of FDI make these exchanges seem very straightforward and unilateral. The investor weighs costs and benefits and decides to invest abroad because FDI is less costly than other forms of internationalization, such as trade or licensing. Calculating transaction costs, firms first decide on the mode of foreign entry (e.g., joint venture, greenfield investment, or acquisition), and on the investment location. And then they realize their investment. Investigating a number of concrete FDI attempts in transforming Central and Eastern Europe shows that the practice of FDI is not as straightforward as the economic model portrays it. To understand why certain FDI efforts pan out while others don't, we need to go beyond efficiency calculations of investors, and examine how the organizational behavior of both investor *and* host firms is shaped by the social structures, cultural understandings, and power relations in which they are embedded.

In keeping with the neoinstitutionalist perspective in organizational analysis (Powell and DiMaggio 1991), case analysis of organizational behavior in FDI transactions demonstrates that FDI decisions by Western firms can be often characterized as jumping on the East European bandwagon, since the behavior of peer firms is followed more frequently than objective evaluations of alternative strategies. In addition, social networks matter because investors use the information they get from their business partners or colleagues to make decisions about investment targets, and they are often swayed by personal ties to a particular country or company. For both investors and hosts, conceptions of different nations and cultures influence the evaluation of potential partners. The ability to build shared understandings during the negotiation process often seals or breaks the deal. Furthermore, economic exchanges are in no way isolated from issues of power and control between stakeholders, nor from the interventions of political elites. In firms, political coalitions often form to resist or champion particular FDI attempts. Finally, transactions are structured by state policies and institutional arrangements of the host country. These policies do not just regulate investment and impose constraints on investors. The institutional makeup of postsocialism, especially nontransparency and ambiguity, frequently also represents a resource by means of which economic actors on both sides of the transaction pursue their preferred strategies of action.

"Foreign investment in Central and East European countries is based too much on emotional prejudices and daily political needs and is far from rational economic considerations," lamented John Dunning (Dunning and Rojec 1993, 12), one of the most prominent economists of FDI. Chapter 6 is motivated by my observation that his words capture well the empirical reality of FDI in postsocialist Europe, though I do not share his sense of discouragement. I argue that to understand socially embedded economic action in situations of high uncertainty, we need to step outside of the confines of the rational action model. In conditions of high uncertainty—in times when cultural ideas of valued economic goals are changing, when new economic and non-economic institutions are being built hastily, and when sudden changes among ruling political elites are commonplace—FDI transactions are not a matter of rational profit maximization of economic agents because not all uncertainty can be turned into risk (Knight 2002). Rather, the uncertainty and resultant social embeddedness of economic processes contribute to substantive and procedural variability in economic action. Substantively, there are many competing ideas as to what valuable economic goals should be. In particular there are great differences between goals emphasized during socialism, such as full employment, and those promoted in the postsocialist period, such as shareholder value. Procedurally, because of cognitive and situational uncertainty, and resultant structural, political, and cultural embeddedness, economic actions based on commitment, muddling through situational contingency, and improvisation are more common than rational means-ends calculations.

In the concluding chapter, I make the case that understanding economic processes is greatly enhanced by a constructivist sociological perspective. Social forces are not mere constraints on profit maximization, because somehow the "true nature" of markets is to be void of social influences. Rather, social structures, distributions of power, and cultural understandings are integral components of market organization, as they constitute every economic transaction. Discussing the implications of this study for theory building in economic sociology, I underscore the social-constructivist view, which pays attention simultaneously to the three key mechanisms that structure economic organization and action—repeated patters of social interactions that manifest themselves in institutions and social networks, allocations of power, and cultural understandings.

Finally, I consider how this research contributes to the empirical study of market transition and what its implications are for the varieties of postsocialist capitalism. Transformation from redistributive socialism to market capitalism implies that redistributive arrangements are replaced with self-regulated market exchange. With the fall of Communist regimes, many analysts expect the social, political, and cultural forces in the economy to easily give way to the profit-maximization market imperative and considerations of efficiency. Instead, a comparative sociological approach—one that draws on a variety of data sources and methods of analysis—substantiates the embedded, socially constructed character of postsocialist economies, shaping the multiple paths to economic development in Central and Eastern Europe.

• • •

How are markets created and how do they operate? A fundamental transformation of economic systems in Central and Eastern Europe offers ideal opportunities to reconsider the assumption that markets are asocial and that actors are always profit-maximizers. Using empirical analyses of foreign direct investment in postsocialist Europe, I argue that our understanding of economic organization and action will be greatly limited if it ignores the interrelationships between social structures, power distributions, and cultural understandings, which do not merely constrain economic life but make it possible.

Chapter 2

FROM SOCIALISM TO POSTSOCIALISM

THE FALL OF THE Berlin Wall on November 9, 1989, was a watershed in twentieth-century history. The destruction of the concrete fixture that separated the Eastern socialist part from the Western capitalist part of Berlin will forever remain a symbol of the collapse of Communism, the lifting of the Iron Curtain, and the end of the Cold War. The concrete(ness) of the Berlin Wall and its swift destruction promote the illusion that social change is about the efficient dismantling of the past in a few fervent days, leading to a bright borderless future. Although the events in 1989 and early 1990s were momentous and revolutionary, leading to shifts in political power in all Central and East European states, the transformation from socialism to postsocialism was much more gradual and complex. Unlike the consistent concrete structure of the Berlin Wall, the socialist system was a dynamic institutional configuration whose character, although uniform in principle, was varied in practice and had changed over time. It was characterized by a particular set of social structures, distributions of power, and cultural understandings, which could not be erased overnight. While it is common to hear that Communism "fell" in 1989, it is important to remember that several of the initial transfers of power in Central and East European countries were negotiated (Welsh 1994), and that in many instances Communists reformed into political constituencies that were part of the democratizing political process, even winning elections (Orenstein 1998; Grzymala-Busse 2002). Existing socialist networks of economic relations were not just broken up but reconfigured and used to hedge the uncertainties of social change (Stark 1996; McDermott 2002). And while many formal economic institutions were substantially changed (most obviously, collective ownership was turned into private property), this process was complex, negotiated, and uneven (Stark and Bruszt 1998; Spicer, McDermott, and Kogut 2000; Verdery 2003). Above all, informal institutions, or cultural beliefs and everyday practices that were taken for granted during socialism, were resistant to change, suggesting that economic actors do not automatically, naturally, respond to a new set of economic incentives but must come to understand alternative strategies of action as plausible and appropriate (Kogut and Zander 2000).

From this perspective the challenge of economic change in Central and Eastern Europe is about transforming one institutional configuration, in its principle and lived form, into another. Capitalism does not emerge automatically, by letting nature take its course. It is not an immediate consequence of quickly dismantling centralized production systems and allocating private property rights, leading to spontaneous bargaining and exchange that is economically efficient. Rather, the proliferation of new forms of economic activity, such as foreign direct investment, requires the social construction and institutionalization of new rules of economic behavior and macro-level structures that support it, a process largely structured by the available capabilities and resources.

Because economic activity is embedded in society, we need to situate economic changes in the broader historical context of Central and Eastern Europe. Therefore, this chapter first outlines the character of the socialist system and paths of extrication, and second, presents the structural, political, and cultural contours of the transforming postsocialist landscape.

SOCIALISM

Socialism,[1] a socially constructed institutional system characterized by the rule of the Communist Party, an ideology of Marxism-Leninism, and collective ownership of productive assets and a centrally planned economy, developed in Central and East European countries after the World War II.[2] During the war, all of these countries were either occupied by Nazi Germany or allied themselves with the Nazi regime. Near the end of the war, Soviet troops invaded and occupied Bulgaria, Czechoslovakia, Hungary, Poland, and Romania, freeing them from German control and installing Communist governments. In Yugoslavia, the Communists led the struggle against Nazi Germany and liberated the country with limited help from the Soviet Red Army. Hence, the country remained independent from Moscow, and the Yugoslav Communist regimes after the war were not externally imposed.

The Basic Features of the Socialist System

The basic institution in the power structure of socialism was the Communist Party, which, in a single-party regime, had autocratic power. The Party apparatus selected the members of the legislature, the state administration, and the judiciary. Practically, this meant that the state was subordinate to the Party; that is, it was a Party state. The tight coupling between the Party and the state also implied that no state affairs were free of politics. Indeed, all aspects of society were subordinated to the politically valued goals of Communism.

The ideology of Marxism-Leninism provided distinct values to guide the political, economic, and social organization of the socialist system. This ideology maintains that history advances by means of class struggle and that at the end of history awaits a Communist system in which the working class has ultimate power (Marx and Engels 1978). The extant socialist system is a transient stage on the way to this ultimate phase; the working class is represented by the Party as its vanguard, destined to lead society to Communism, to freedom, justice, and equality.

While Marx envisioned that Communism would follow as the last stage after advanced capitalism (Marx 1974), the Communist parties took power in economies that were characterized by a "backwardness of largely precapitalist nature, poverty, striking inequality, brutal oppression, war, and . . . a deep crisis in society" (Kornai 1992, 28). In these conditions the promises of the Communist parties resonated powerfully: on the road to Communism, to a state of abundance, equality and free choice, a socialist economic system would catch up to and surpass capitalism. It would do away with the inefficiencies and injustices of capitalism. It would accomplish large-scale industrialization. There would be food, subsidized housing, social protections, and a constitutional right to work (Kornai 1992, 54).

To industrialize, Communist parties established large-scale factory production with an emphasis on extractive and manufacturing industries. "One Nation, One Factory" was the vision of the socialist system (Róna-Tas 1997). To facilitate large-scale production, the Party developed elaborate bureaucracies and imposed factory discipline on the entire population. Three major institutions were needed to assure that end. First, *private property had to be abolished* because it was an impediment to large-scale production. All production assets were nationalized, becoming the property of "the whole of the people" or "the whole of society" (Kornai 1992, 71).[3] Second, mechanisms were established to eliminate the inefficiencies associated with capitalism. Thus, instead of relying on market competition, the economy was organized as a redistributive system based on *central planning*. Party-appointed economic planners fixed output targets and prices, and consequently "[made] decisions about production, investment, income and careers" (Walder 1994, 297). Party-appointed managers, or better yet administrators,[4] controlled the execution of the plan. Third, the whole adult population was needed to achieve large-scale industrialization. *Universal state employment* was a solution on several grounds: it would help concentrate production, eliminate the inefficiencies and injustices of labor markets, and fulfill the promise to the people by guaranteeing jobs.

While from the perspective of capitalism the design of the socialist economy may seem irrational, such an assumption misunderstands its purposes. In fact, planning and control were put in place to achieve rationality and to undo the inefficiencies associated with market fluctuations.[5] Nevertheless, there were clear differences between the rationality of the socialist redistributive system and that of market capitalism (Szelényi, Beckett, and King 1994). The most explicit difference was the proclaimed goal of economic activity. While profit is extolled in capitalism, redistribution and equality were valued in socialism. Because of these different goals, firms operated under different conditions. As economist János Kornai (1980, 1986, 1992) characterized it, the key difference was in the budget constraints. Because private firms strive to maximize profits, they operate under "hard budget constraints." If they lose money, they go out of business. State-owned firms operate under "soft budget constraints"; if costs are higher than revenues, firms can continue to operate, since the state will bail them out. The state does so to insure that the whole system functions. Any enterprise in a socialist economy is highly dependent on others for industrial production, and redistribution eliminates competition. Large state-owned firms, the most important socialist property form, are largely monopolies, and the system cannot tolerate the failure of any particular entity if it wants to advance the general interest (Kornai 1980). This principle is an instantiation of the grander cultural logic of the socialist system where collective interest supersedes self-interest. The case for socialism is thus made on both economically rational and moral grounds. The structures and politics of socialism cement the particular cultural logic of the socialist system, that is, the shared understandings of what we value, how we do things, and what we believe is right and what wrong.

The Practice of Socialism

Centralized planning of the economy implies that uncertainties in economic production are largely eliminated since all activities are carefully planned and controlled. However, in practice large-scale production proved to be too inflexible, and plans too rigid, for the economy to meet the expectations of the planners and those of the people. While the central committees designed five-year plans, the targets set sometimes changed, and supplies and raw materials needed for production would often not arrive on time or in right amounts. Hence, the administrators of state-owned enterprises would often negotiate the received plans with redistributors, what East European economists described as a "plan-bargain" (Bauer 1983). To manage uncertainty, administrators padded budgets and hoarded materials. All this resulted in chronic shortages (Kornai 1980, 1992; Szelényi, Beckett, and King 1994; Verdery 1996b).

Unlike in the capitalist economies, where producers struggle to create new demand niches to sell products and make profits, the challenge in the socialist economy was supply. Because of shortages, it was customers who had to be innovative, relying on interpersonal networks to get what they needed. A second economy—the production, consumption, distribution, and exchange of goods outside of the state regulation—developed, contributing to the consolidation of two distinct spheres, the official and the nonofficial. Indeed, the decoupling of formal and informal spheres was part of everyday life and one of the core features of lived socialism (Verdery 1996b; Creed 1998; Böröcz 2000). The institution of the second economy was accompanied by a practical logic: in order to achieve economic goals, one is best served by circumventing the official rules. Indeed, the official rules were more or less ceremonial, and even those who were supposedly their guardians, such as officials in public offices or administrators in enterprises, were themselves aware of widespread informality. The meaning of the "open-door day" in the former Yugoslavia nicely illustrates the consensual nature of the informal economy. Officially, open-door days were special occasions when guests, community members, and pupils could visit a firm to experience the spirit of the socialist economy. However, the term acquired quite a different unofficial meaning: From time to time, the doorman in the booth at the entrance to the factory, supervising who entered and who left, would conveniently disappear from his post so that workers could take out raw materials and equipment and use them for home improvement or in small-scale private ventures run from their homes as part of the second economy.

Varieties of the Socialist System and Reform Efforts

Socialist systems in Central and Eastern Europe were premised on similar ideological grounds, held by the Communist Party in each state. However, the actual experiences of socialism in its political and economic aspects, the reforms to centralized planning, and the paths of extrication from the system were different in each country. In particular, two factors contributed to the variety in the European socialist systems: the source of political power and the character of economic organization.

In terms of politics, we should remember that the birthplace of Communist Party rule was the Soviet Union and that the installation of Communist parties in Bulgaria, Czechoslovakia, Hungary, Poland, and Romania was controlled by the Soviet Union, after it had occupied these states near the end of World War II, having freed them from German control. The Soviets held a strong hand over the political systems in these countries, which functioned like the Soviet satellite states. The trajectory of Communist Party rule in Yugoslavia, however, was different. There Communist rule was not imposed by the Soviet Union, but resulted from domestic political struggles after the defeat of fascism. The Communist Party in Yugoslavia rose under the lead of Marshall Josip Broz Tito, who, because of his divergent political views, and perhaps also because of a clash of personalities (Campbell 1980), defied Stalin and declined the Soviet shield.

In terms of economics, the major difference within the region was the distinction between redistribution and central planning in Soviet satellite states, and workers' self-management in Yugoslavia. The latter entailed decentralization of economic planning and decision-making, but retained collective ownership of assets, although it replaced state ownership with social ownership. In principle, decentralization and social ownership meant that the economy was governed by so-called "communities of work" (Horvat 1976). That is, in each enterprise workers' councils were entrusted with management responsibilities. They set broad production goals, supervised finances, and encouraged participatory decision-making at the lower levels of the hierarchy. Although central authorities outlined general guidelines, rather than imposed mandatory targets, it was still the Party state that appointed directors of enterprises (who had veto power over councils' decisions) and controlled the allocation of investment resources, thereby retaining considerable de facto control over the economy (Horvat 1976). Analysts argue that one of the main reasons that Yugoslavia adopted a system other than centralized planning was the political dispute between Tito and Stalin, and Tito's need to legitimate the Yugoslav kind of socialism (Szelényi, Beckett, and King 1994, 246).

Workers' self-management, in a sense, represented a reform of the socialist economic system. In addition to decentralization of control and reform of economic planning, the Yugoslav state also freed some prices to fluctuate according to supply and demand. In the reforms of 1988–89, Yugoslavia also made provisions for foreign ownership of enterprises.

Other Central and East European states had also reformed their economic systems before 1989. Hungary, for example, pursuing a market socialism (Kornai 1992, 479), beginning in 1968 granted greater scope of operation to private enterprises and allowed for the second economy to flourish. The passage of the Law on Enterprise Councils in 1984 also introduced a self-management system into large and medium-sized enterprises and increased the role of managers, rather than state officials, in the governance of these enterprises (Frydman and Rapaczynski 1994). In 1988 Hungary adopted Act XXIV on the Investment of Foreigners (World Trade Organization 1998).

In Poland, following demonstrations against the price hike introduced at the end of 1970, Edward Gierek was appointed as head of the Communist Party. Gierek introduced a new economic program based on large-scale borrowing from the West to buy technology that would upgrade

Poland's production of export goods—without, of course, importing the capitalist system. The program brought an immediate rise in living standards and expectations, but it faltered unexpectedly because of worldwide recession following the 1973 oil crisis (Ekiert 1996). In response Gierek increased prices and slowed the growth of wages. This provoked labor protests and strengthened the Solidarity labor union, which, along with calls for greater freedom, pushed for workers' participation in the management of socialist enterprises (Frydman and Rapacynski 1994, 104). Among the reform efforts of the late 1980s, Poland also adopted the Joint Venture Law in 1986, permitting joint ventures with foreign investors under certain conditions. This was replaced by the 1988 Law on Economic Activity with the Participation of Foreign Parties in Poland (GATT 1992), which lifted the limit on the share of foreign capital.

Economic reforms were limited in Czechoslovakia. Changes were attempted during the so-called Prague Spring of 1968, when revolts led by Alexander Dubček united opponents of the regime under the slogan "Socialism with a Human Face." Dubček pushed to have directives from the central plan replaced by plans drawn up by individual enterprises or associations of enterprises. However, Prague Spring was brutally repressed by the Red Army, and Dubček's reform program was discounted. Hence, in contrast to developments in Hungary and Poland, state officials maintained their commanding role in Czechoslovak socialist enterprises. They continued to appoint managing directors, approve the compensation of all employees, and retain the right to interfere with production decisions (Frydman and Rapaczynski 1994, 105) until December 1989, when Communists in Czechoslovakia capitulated.

Reform efforts in the Baltic republics of Estonia, Latvia, and Lithuania, which were part of the Soviet Union, followed Gorbachev's perestroika program, which he laid out in the June 1987 plenary session of the Central Committee of the Communist Party of the Soviet Union. Thereafter the Supreme Soviet passed the Law on State Enterprise, which allowed state enterprises to determine output levels based on demand from consumers and other enterprises, and curtailed the government's role in supporting soft budget constraints. This law also shifted control over the enterprise operations from ministries to elected workers' collectives. The Law on Cooperatives, enacted in May 1988, permitted private ownership of businesses in the services, manufacturing, and foreign-trade sectors. In addition, regional and local organizations and individual state enterprises were permitted to conduct foreign trade. Perestroika reforms also brought the Soviet Joint Venture Law, which allowed foreigners to form joint ventures with Soviet enterprises, though limiting foreign shares to 49 percent and requiring that Soviet citizens occupy the positions of chairman and general manager.

In Bulgaria, where economic problems during the 1980s were chiefly caused by the rising cost of energy imports, the reforms were actually prompted by Gorbachev as part of the perestroika program. In 1987 the Bulgarian Communist Party officially endorsed perestroika and glasnost. However, administrative and economic reforms were haphazard and did not result in substantial changes. In Romania, instead of economic reform to increase the welfare of the population, Ceauşescu embarked on an austerity program, pledging to repay the country's staggering foreign debt of $10.5 billion, which, amid food shortages and widespread power cuts, he in fact achieved by 1989 (Karatnycki, Motyl, and Graybow 1999).

The Collapse of Socialism

By the end of 1980s, Communist rulers in most Central and East European countries introduced some economic reform, which included experimentation with economic decentralization and liberalization. While there were economic reasons for changes, we need to emphasize that calls for reforms had political and moral foundations. An important political fact is that the Communist Party had become more fragmented over time. After Stalin's death in 1953, the old-line Stalinist leaders in the Soviet satellite states were soon gone as well, and the Communist parties in these countries opened up to "technocratic intelligentsia . . . skilled or highly skilled professionals who did not feel comfortable ruling the old way" (Szelényi and Szelényi 1994, 226). This prepared ground for intra-Party conflict between old-timers and newcomers, and ultimately led to an inability to reproduce the political legitimacy of the system.

In addition, the socialist system was critiqued on moral grounds by intellectuals and other voices for freedom and democracy. For example, the slogan of Prague Spring, "Socialism with a Human Face," signaled a call for greater individual freedoms. However, the socialist system was not able to establish democratic institutions. Indeed, with the restrictions imposed on individual self-expression (Verdery 1996b), socialism was moving further and further away from the proclaimed Marxist goals of freedom, equality, and social justice, and its legitimacy was getting weaker and weaker.

Multiple internal factors—economic, political, and cultural—eroded the legitimacy of the socialist system, but were they responsible for the regimes' ultimate demise? It is ironic that, as Walder put it,

> economic stagnation and consumer deprivation, deeply eroded commitment to official ideology and the growth of widespread cynicism, the corruption and weakening of the apparatus of rule, and the gradual enlargement of autonomous, self-organized spheres of social and

intellectual life . . . were only recently [i.e., before 1989] treated as evidence of the remarkable comparative *stability* of the communist regimes throughout the world in the last half-century. (1994, 297; emphasis added)

If so, then internal tensions cannot be the only reason for the system's collapse. For Verdery (1996b, 30), to explain why socialism failed, "properties of the internal organization need to be linked with the properties of its external environment." Next to the internal tensions, we need to consider a set of forces exogenous to the system, which added to the complexity of the historical situation that culminated in 1989.

Although it tried to close itself off from the rest of the world and hide behind the Iron Curtain, the socialist system could not remain isolated from the economic and political forces that affected the rest of the world. In particular, the explosion of oil prices after the OPEC crisis, and developments in Western economies, which were moving away from heavy industry to information technology and services, were key economic factors. Faced with pressures to restructure their industries, in addition to internal tensions, the socialist economies started borrowing heavily from the West and soon were drowning in foreign debt.

The economic and political crises, aggravated by a constellation of domestic and international forces, induced grassroots mobilization and mass protests. Very important in this regard is that after Mikhail Gorbachev's accession to leadership of the Soviet Union in 1985, the USSR would not militarily intervene in the satellite states to repress revolts, as it had done in Hungary in 1956 and in Czechoslovakia in 1968. In fact, under the pressures of a military arms race with the United States, during Gorbachev's rein the Soviet Union itself began the program of domestic reform known as perestroika, which was accompanied by glasnost, political reforms that increased freedom of speech and decreased the Party's grip on the media. Gorbachev's unwillingness to use military power to curtail unrest in the satellite states was consistent with glasnost.

A significant large-scale mass mobilization began in Poland in 1980, when the Solidarity workers' movement, founded in Lenin Shipyards in Gdansk, mobilized an estimated ten million members (Jenkins and Benderlioglu 2005), about one-third of the Polish adult population. One of the key reasons for Solidarity's popularity was the strong support it received from the Catholic Church and Pope John Paul II, a native of Poland. Although Polish Communist leader General Jaruzelski, under pressure from the Soviet Union, declared martial law to ban Solidarity and stifle antiregime protests (Ash 1984), it was suspended in 1982, and Solidarity leader Lech Wałęsa was released from prison. Protests continued, emboldened by Gorbachev's unwillingness to intervene, and culminated in a round of strikes following the government's decision to close the Lenin Shipyards, the birthplace of the Solidarity movement. In February 1989, the Polish government announced formal roundtable talks with Solidarity, with the Catholic Church mediating. The Polish Communist Party agreed to semifree elections, facilitating what turned out to be a negotiated transition from Communism (Welsh 1994). After six weeks of negotiations, a historic accord was reached in April 1989. Solidarity was relegalized, opposition political associations were sanctioned, legal rights were conferred on the Catholic Church, the Party's media monopoly was lifted, and a new constitution, based on socialist and pluralist principles, was drafted. In the subsequent elections, held in June 1989, the Communists were defeated and Solidarity took over the government. Based on a previous agreement negotiated at the roundtable talks, Jaruzelski was elected president in July 1989. In Poland's first free parliamentary elections, which were held in 1991, more than one hundred parties participated, representing a full spectrum of political views (Karatnycki, Motyl, and Graybow 1999).

A negotiated transition happened also in Hungary. In early spring of 1989, talks began, with the "second funeral" of Imre Nagy (a leader of the first large-scale anti-Communist protest in Hungary in 1956) conferring symbolic significance to the demand for change. By then the Hungarian Communist Party was split into two rival wings, and with the opposition forces present at the roundtable, the negotiations were marked by political competition (Welsh 1994, 386). In the March 1990 national elections, the first multiparty elections since 1945, the Hungarian Democratic Forum (MDF) won, and József Antall, its leader, was elected prime minister.

Following a wave of protests throughout the region, mass demonstrations organized by the New Forum ultimately brought down the Berlin Wall on November 9, 1989. It was also in November that Civic Forum, a proreform movement led by dissident playwright Václav Havel, was formed in Czechoslovakia, after the Communist police violently broke up a peaceful prodemocracy demonstration. Inspired by successful protests in Poland and Hungary, the initially weak Czechoslovak opposition grew rapidly, mobilizing large-scale protests in a Velvet Revolution. Increasing internal defections within the Communist Party prevented the total imposition of violence on protestors. Faced with overwhelming popular rejection, the Communist Party capitulated in December 1989. A coalition government, in which the Communist Party had a minority of ministerial positions, was formed. Václav Havel was appointed the president of Czechoslovakia on December 29. The first free elections in the country since World War II took place in June 1990. Havel's Civic Forum won a landslide victory. In 1992, negotiations about the new federal constitution deadlocked over the issue of Slovak autonomy, and in the latter half of

1992, agreement was reached to peacefully divide Czechoslovakia. On January 1, 1993, the Czech Republic and the Slovak Republic were simultaneously and peacefully founded.

In Bulgaria and Romania, the Communist parties resorted to preemptive moves by staging internal revolts to remove longtime leaders. In Bulgaria, on November 10, 1989, after several months of plotting and secret meetings, party reformers mounted an internal coup, removing a longtime leader Todor Zhivkov, who resisted Soviet-style perestroika and glasnost. Protests by Bulgarian demonstrators occurred after the internal coup, demanding democratic reforms. The reform Communists announced plans to amend the constitution and permit multiparty elections, which were announced for early 1990. Their goal was to exploit their advantage against a weak and divided opposition and remain in power. They also resorted to force and fraud to control the election results. In June 1990 elections, the ruling Communist Party, which renamed itself the Bulgarian Socialist Party (BSP), won the majority. Following a period of social unrest and passage of a new constitution, the first fully democratic parliamentary elections were held in 1991, in which the United Democratic Forces, a post-Communist party, won with a tight majority.

The situation in Romania was largely similar to that in Bulgaria. The reform-minded Party officials and grassroots opponents were largely nonexistent due to the neo-patrimonial nature of the Ceauşescu regime (Jenkins and Benderlioglu 2005). When protests in Poland began, Ceauşescu was the only Communist leader who openly criticized Gorbachev for not using military power to curtail demonstrations against the Communist Party. Not surprisingly, he himself resorted to force and mass arrests to contain protests that emerged in Romania after strict rationing was put in place to repay the foreign debt and after his controversial "villagization" program to resettle more than eight thousand rural villagers in new agro-industrial cities. These measures were criticized by some Party officials. At the end of 1989, Party officials bent on removing Ceauşescu launched a coup, or "scripted revolution" (Condrescu 1992), staging protests and armed clashes. The army was on their side and Ceauşescu was soon captured and, together with his wife, executed on December 25, after a summary trial in which he was charged with corruption and human rights abuses by the National Salvation Front Party, led by Ion Iliescu, the former secretary of the Communist Party who formed a provisional government after Ceauşescu's execution. The National Salvation Front declared an end to the Communist monopoly and announced multiparty elections for spring 1990. Despite demonstrations against Illiescu in the period leading up to the election, he and his party won amidst widespread irregularities.

Events in Yugoslavia followed their own logic, and were complicated by the dissolution of the federal state and civil war. After Tito's death in

1980, the Yugoslav presidency became a collective post rotated between nine elected members from different republics. The federal system of six autonomous republics and two semiautonomous regions, Kosovo and Vojvodina, was hard to maintain because individual republics envisioned different futures. While Slobodan Milošević, a Serbian nationalist who became the Serbian Communist Party leader in 1987, was eager to revive a vision of a "Greater Serbia,"[6] the northern Yugoslav republics, Slovenia and Croatia, saw their future in European integrations. In early 1989, Serbia, which is largely Greek Orthodox, under the leadership of Milošević rescinded the semiautonomy of the Kosovo region and sent in troops to suppress the protests of Kosovo's largely Albanian Muslim population. This action was not approved of by Slovenia or Croatia, which, influenced by events throughout the region, elected non-Communist governments in the early 1990. They demanded greater autonomy and threatened secession from Yugoslavia.

In the case of Slovenia, tendencies for pluralization and democratization, strengthened at the end of the 1970s and the beginning of 1980s, caused political fragmentation and gave rise to opposition movements. In September 1989, the Slovenian parliament amended the constitution to allow multiparty elections. The change of political regime was largely possible because of the reform-oriented League of Communists of Slovenia and the Slovene democratic movements. Remaining within the Yugoslav federation was less and less desirable, and Slovenia declared its independence on June 25, 1991. Immediately after the declaration of independence, an armed conflict broke out in Slovenia as the Yugoslav federal army (controlled largely by Serbs) occupied the Slovenian international border crossings, which led to a ten-day civil war. Largely due to the ethnic homogeneity of Slovenia and international recognition of the country's independence, by the end of July 1991, all Yugoslav military forces had left Slovenia. The country held multiparty elections in December 1992. The center-left Liberal Democratic Party emerged victorious, and its leader, Janez Drnovšek, one the former post-Tito presidents of Yugoslavia, became prime minister. Milan Kučan, the leader of the reformed Slovenian League of Communists, became the country's first president.

Croatia held its first multiparty elections since World War II in 1990. The Croatian Democratic Union (HDZ), a nationalist party, won a majority, and its leader, longtime Croatian nationalist Franjo Tudjman, was elected president. Like Slovenia, Croatia declared its independence on June 25, 1991, and was subsequently invaded by the Yugoslav army. But unlike the short military conflict that followed Slovenia's declaration of independence, the fighting in Croatia turned into a civil war between Croatian forces and the federally backed Serbs from Serbian areas of Croatia, between Croats and Bosnians for the territory of Bosnia and Herzegovina populated by ethnic Croats, and between Serbians and Bosnians for the Bosnian territory populated by ethnic Serbs. After rampant bloodshed, the December 1995 talks in Dayton, Ohio, convened by American arbitrators, led to a peace accord among Bosnia, Croatia, and Serbia, although the violence of Serbs toward Bosnians and Albanians from the Kosovo region continued until 1999, when NATO forces bombed Yugoslavia. Subsequently, in June 1999, Milošević agreed to withdraw from Kosovo. After manipulating the electoral system and invalidating election results in favor of his opponent, he was finally ousted at the end of 2000.

The fight for state sovereignty also marked the extrication of the Baltic republics of Lithuania, Latvia, and Estonia, which declared their independence from the Soviet Union in 1990. The formal dissolution of Soviet Union happened in 1991; while politically intense and violent, the process did not escalate into a civil war. The pursuit of national sovereignty in Estonia, Latvia, and Lithuania was emboldened after Gorbachev's declaration of perestroika and glasnost. Elites in these Soviet republics defected from Moscow's umbrella and enjoyed great popular support. Protests against Communist Soviet domination were closely coupled with the Baltic people's expressions of nationalism and pride.

Lithuania established a multiparty system in 1990. Under the leadership of Sajudis, the anti-Communist and anti-Soviet movement for independence, which won a majority in Spring 1990 elections, it proclaimed its renewed independence on March 11, 1990, the first Soviet republic to do so. Moscow reacted with an economic blockade of Lithuania, keeping Red Army troops in the country, purportedly to secure the rights of ethnic Russians. In January 1991, clashes between Soviet troops and Lithuanian civilians occurred, leaving twenty dead. This further weakened the Soviet Union's legitimacy, internationally and domestically. In the first Lithuanian multiparty elections in 1992, the Democratic Labor Party, led by the former Communist Party boss Algirdas Brazauskas, received a plurality of votes and a clear majority of parliamentary seats (Karatnycki, Motyl, and Graybow 1999).

Latvia's goal of independence was formalized on July 28, 1989, when the Supreme Soviet of the Latvian Soviet Republic adopted a "Declaration of Sovereignty" and amended the constitution to assert the supremacy of its laws over those of the USSR. Pro-independence Latvian Popular Front candidates gained a two-thirds majority in the Supreme Council in the March 18, 1990, democratic elections. On May 4, the Council declared its intention to restore full Latvian independence. In January 1991, Soviet political and military forces tried unsuccessfully to overthrow the legitimate Latvian authorities by occupying the central publishing house in Riga and establishing a "Committee of National Salvation" to usurp governmental functions. Seventy-three percent of all Latvian residents confirmed their strong support for independence in a nonbinding "advisory" referendum on sovereignty. A large number of ethnic Russians living in Latvia also voted for the proposition. Latvia claimed de facto independence on August 21, 1991. In 1993, Latvia held its first parliamentary election in the post-Communist period. The Popular Front, which led the Latvian independence movement and won a 75 percent majority in the parliamentary elections in 1990, did not gather enough support to qualify for representation. The centrist Latvia's Way party received one-third of the votes and joined with the Farmer's Union to head a center-right coalition government (Karatnycki, Motyl, and Graybow 1999).

Estonia, the Soviet republic with the smallest population and the highest level of GDP per capita, adopted its own constitution in 1988, with a power of veto on all Soviet legislation. The new constitution allowed private property and placed land and natural resources under Estonian control. An Estonian Popular Front was established in 1988 and campaigned, with mass rallies, for democratization, increased autonomy, and eventual independence. On March 30, 1990, the Estonian Supreme Council declared that the Soviet power in Estonia since 1940—the year when Estonia, together with Latvia and Lithuania, was annexed to the USSR—had been illegal, and started a process to reestablish Estonia as an independent state. In August 1991, in the midst of the attempted anti-Gorbachev coup in the USSR, during which Red Army troops came into Tallinn and the Soviet navy blocked the Estonian main port, Estonia declared its full independence and outlawed the Communist Party. On September 6, 1991, Estonia, together with Latvia and Lithuania, was recognized by the Soviet government. The first postindependence elections in Estonia took place in September 1992, and the right-of-center Pro Patria Union, with a market reform agenda, emerged victorious.

In sum, the paths out of socialism, while influenced by the regional momentum that started with Solidarity protests, nevertheless differed across individual states. They were influenced by the strength or fragmentation of the final Communist regimes as well as the timing and nature of the mass protests (Jenkins and Benderlioglu 2005). In Poland, Solidarity and Communists negotiated a way out of the system. In Hungary, strong division within the Communist Party was crucial for the early emergence of party competition. In Czechoslovakia, after the popular protests, negotiations with Communist rulers led to their capitulation. In all these countries, roundtable talks brought together the (more or less) fragmented Communist elite and representatives of civil society who were able to agree on a relatively quick and not particularly contentious shift in the political order. In Bulgaria and Romania, the Communist parties resorted to preemptive moves by staging internal revolts to remove longtime leaders, resulting in weakly reformed Communist governments in the first few years after 1989. Extrication from Communist rule in the Baltic states of Estonia, Latvia, and Lithuania was marked by the will for national independence, as was the case in Slovenia and Croatia. The first elected governments of all these countries harbored nationalist tendencies, but these were the strongest in Croatia, the only of these countries where transition came with the violence of a civil war.

In retrospect, the collapse of socialisms and the fall of the Communist Party may seem inevitable, and this is the popular view. However, social scientists by and large did not see the change coming (Przeworski 1991; Lipset and Bence 1994; Szelényi and Szelényi 1994). Therefore, for many the question of socialism's collapse—whether inevitable because of the internal contradictions of the system or caused by historical contingencies beyond the system's control—is still not settled. Largely, the answer depends on one's understanding of what socialism was. If socialism was an inefficient detour on the universal road to capitalism, then its fall was inevitable. But if socialism was a socially constructed configuration, that is, a particular institutional order with concomitant cultural and political logics, then the major reason for the crisis of a system is the weakening of the legitimacy of its core institutions, not inherent inefficiencies of command economy or autocracy. From this perspective, it was the weakening of legitimacy—caused by contingent historical events—that reduced capacities to maintain order and led to a system's collapse (cf. Szelényi and Szelényi 1994).

CHALLENGES OF THE TRANSFORMATION: SHOCK THERAPY VERSUS GRADUALISM

The collapse of Communist regimes throughout Central and Eastern Europe meant the transformation of socialist economies. Neoliberal economists from the West who offered advice largely argued for rapid changes, "shock therapy," a "big bang," with the goal of quickly creating markets by eliminating state command of the economy and its supposed irrationalities of redistribution. These economists emphasized that the most efficient form of economic organization is a self-regulated market. Socialist economies needed to quickly create a private property rights regime, which could be achieved by mass privatization. Prices and currency controls needed to be dissolved, state subsidies withdrawn, and trade liberalized. These reforms would give rise to a *depoliticized* economic system (Boycko, Shleifer, and Vishny 1996) coordinated through market prices and competition, with a clear incentive structure that would induce efficient corporate governance and rapid restructuring of firms (Sachs 1989; Lipton and Sachs 1990; Sachs and Lipton 1990; Blanchard et al. 1991;

Fischer and Gelb 1991; Aslund 1992, 1995; Sachs 1994; Blanchard, Froot, and Sachs 1994; Shleifer and Vishny 1994; Boycko, Shleifer, and Vishny 1996).

By the mid-1990s the superiority of a shock-therapy transition was accepted by the international policy circles.[7] As then president of the International Monetary Fund, Michel Camdessus, emphasized in a 1995 speech:

> First, and most important, the most appropriate course of action is to adopt a bold strategy. Many countries . . . have by now proven the feasibility of implementing policies of rapid—*and I stress rapid*—liberalization, stabilization, and structural reform; and such policies have indeed been shown to provide the key to successful transition and economic recovery—more so than a country's starting conditions, natural resources, or external assistance. (Qtd. in Spicer, McDermott, and Kogut 2000, 631; emphasis added)

The neoliberal view largely understands history as a natural course of progression from one stage to another, with socialism an unnecessary detour before capitalism. In this view, capitalism, proven to work in the West, is a clear end point of the journey. Hence, to achieve market transition, postsocialist elites could take advantage of the "great void [that] opened up" (Aslund 1992, 16) and rely on a proven market blueprint. As shock therapy prescribed, erasing the old institutions of a command economy and putting in place private property rights would give rise to markets that would allocate resources efficiently.

In contrast, evolutionary economists, political scientists, and sociologists approached the postsocialist challenge from a different position, supposing that, in principle, the paths after the fall of Communist regimes were multiple and uncertain, and that initial conditions—in sharp contrast to what the IMF's Camdessus claimed—do matter (Murrell 1992, 1993; Poznanski 1993; Stark 1992, 1996; Grabher and Stark 1997; Spicer, McDermott, and Kogut 2000). If so, social change in Central and Eastern Europe is not about a transition but a *transformation* of social, political, economic and cultural forces that configured a socialist system. Consequently, social change should be seen "not as a transition from one order to another but as transformation—rearrangements, reconfigurations, and recombinations that yield new interweavings of the multiple social logics that are a modern society" (Stark and Bruszt 1998, 7). This perspective, also known as "gradualism" in policy circles, focuses on *path dependency*, the ways in which structures inherited from before and during the state-socialist period influence transformation processes, so that transformations occur out of the ruins of the former regime and often result in reproduction rather than social change (Seleny 1991; Stark 1992;

Szelényi and Kostello 1996; Stark and Bruszt 1998). Advocates of the gradualist approach criticized shock therapists for assuming an institutional vacuum after the fall of socialism, and they doubted market institutions could be successfully designed at a systemic level (Stark 1992; Murrell 1992). They argued that economic change is a gradual process of institution building. It depends on experimentation and evolutionary learning, requires the participation of the state, and incorporates existing social and economic networks and forms of practice (Kogut 1996; Stark 1992, 1996; Stark and Bruszt 1998; Kogut and Zander 2000; Spicer, McDermott, and Kogut 2000; McDermott 2002).

Neoliberalists countered that gradualism would require a negotiated reform process that would include a plurality of interests springing up in newly democratizing states, and would likely lead to a political stalemate over reform (Lipton and Sachs 1990, 297). In addition, gradualism would maintain the inefficient state sector (Frydman and Rapaczynski 1994, 202) and give rise to "spontaneous privatization," whereby insiders (managers or state bureaucrats) would appropriate formerly state-owned assets for personal gain (Boycko, Shleifer, and Vishny 1995; Kaufman and Siegelbaum 1997).

From a theoretical standpoint, a focus on institutional path-dependence limits our understanding of significant economic change, which undoubtedly occurred after 1989. The vast possibilities of bricolage, of rearrangements, reconfigurations, and recombinations (Stark and Bruszt 1998), provide so many alternative paths that it is difficult to assess why certain ones are taken over others. In response to these critiques, sociologists Eyal, Szelényi, and Townsley proposed a theory of transition called "trajectory adjustment," which combines the perspectives of blueprint capitalism and path dependency to argue that "evolutionary adjustment to new challenges and the path-dependent transformation of previous institutions/behaviors occur *simultaneously*" (1998, 8; emphasis added). Using this theory to explain the role of various elites in building capitalisms in Hungary, the Czech Republic, and Poland, the authors suggest that old institutions shape the dispositions of individuals, who in turn contest and transform those institutions, which leads to individual trajectory adjustment. Applying this perspective at the country level, we might expect that historically shaped country trajectories would adjust in response to the implementation of new institutions. Hence, it is likely that both new and old institutions will shape transformations in Central and Eastern Europe. Empirical investigations of the persistence of old institutions, how new policy agendas are set, and what their effects are for economic change, can provide important insights into post-1989 economic transformations.

This book aims to contribute to this debate by examining the creation of new forms of market-based behavior, specifically foreign direct investment, in eleven Central and East European states in the first decade after 1989. From a social-constructivist perspective, which is aligned with gradualism and the trajectory adjustment approach, I argue that postsocialist economic transformations involve a reconfiguration from one kind of embedded economy to another. For a market order to be established, new formal and informal institutional rules need to be put in place, which requires a change in cultural understandings, a reconfiguration of networks, and shifts in power structures. This means that new forms of market-based economic activity, such as foreign direct investment, do not emerge spontaneously. The extent of FDI will depend on its level of institutionalization and legitimization, that is, the degree to which it becomes accepted as the appropriate and desirable strategy of economic action. This institutionalization and legitimization will not occur *de novo* but will be shaped by the domestic and international actors' recombination and renegotiation of existing capabilities and interests, a process embedded in structures, political interests, and ideas. Hence, before we proceed with the details of the empirical case of foreign direct investment, we need to pay attention to the broader social context of postsocialism, which provides the framework for understanding the evolution and practice of FDI in postsocialist Europe.

The Context of Transformation

The gist of the postsocialist transformation is *the simultaneity of privatization, democratization, regionalization, and globalization* processes. This presents postsocialist Europe with challenges unlike those accompanying economic and political transformation in East Asia, Latin America, or China. Unlike the East Asian societies, which started with democratization only after they already established links to the global economy (Evans 1995), East European political transformations are congruent with liberalization of economies. And while economic and political transitions in Latin America were undertaken at the same time, these reforms did not involve a fundamental transformation of property regimes, as is the case in Central and Eastern Europe. Postsocialist Europe also differs from China. While the socialist past creates commonalities, the fact is that China has not (yet) democratized or substantially privatized (Walder 1995).

Simultaneity of privatization, democratization, regionalization, and globalization implies that a multitude of societal forces—structural, cultural, and political—will shape economic transformations, and that they will exert their influence from different levels: the level of the nation-state, the European region, and the world society.

Privatization

The first challenge of the postsocialist economic transformations was privatization—the conversion of a system without private ownership to one where economic actors have property rights—a bundle of claims related to the ownership and control of assets. Property rights are necessary for market transactions, as they empower people to engage as sellers or buyers on the market.

How best to privatize and how quickly were questions integral to the debate over shock therapy versus gradualism. The advocates of shock therapy argued that rapid mass privatization would be the economically optimal solution. Such privatization would involve distribution of vouchers (quasi company shares) to the population. Then, via auctions, those who held vouchers (individuals or investment funds) would invest these "shares" in specific firms, which would thus become joint-stock companies with individual owners. Subsequently, these owners could strike efficient bargains and exchange shares at will, which would lead to consolidation of shares in the hands of strategic investors willing to engage in the restructuring of firms, contributing to improved economic performance (Shleifer and Vishny 1994; Boycko, Shleifer, and Vishny 1995).

It is important to note that mass privatization was not advocated only on economic grounds. As David Lipton and Jeffrey Sachs saw it,

> The real risk in Eastern Europe is not that the privatization process will be less than optimal, but that it will be paralyzed entirely. We believe that unless hundreds of large firms in each country are brought quickly into the privatization process, the political battle over privatization will soon lead to stalemate in the entire process. (1990, 297–98; cf. Boycko, Shleifer, and Vishny 1995)

Those who espoused gradual transformations were skeptical about the viability and benefits of rapid mass privatization. These observers emphasized the deeply social character of the privatization process, and the political and moral questions that it raised (Stark 1992; Stark and Bruszt 1998; Verdery 2003). Who should the beneficiaries of privatization be? Should privatization entail the distribution of free certificates to citizens, which they could subsequently exchange for ownership stakes? Or should a system be devised that would require citizens to pay a nominal fee for such vouchers? Instead of a "voucher privatization," should assets simply be auctioned off to the highest bidder? Should privatization encourage domestic or foreign ownership of a country's assets? Should it allow for dispersed or concentrated ownership?

Sifting through this myriad of questions, Stark and Bruszt (1998, 84–88) proposed that privatization entailed decisions on three central issues. First is how one evaluates the assets to be privatized. This could be done by administrative or market means. That is, the state could appoint agencies to assess the economic viability of firms, and decide which to privatize. Alternatively, assets could be auctioned off, so that competitive bidding would determine the selling price. The second important question about privatization, according to Stark and Bruszt, concerns the actors who acquire assets. If governments want to involve citizens as beneficiaries of privatization, they will act differently than if they target corporations and distribute property rights to incorporated units. The third issue in privatization concerns the resources exchanged for ownership rights. Money, credit, or other financial resources are clear possibilities, but, in economies that formerly prevented the accumulation of personal wealth, positional resources were also important, and some privatization schemas were designed to accord privileges to managers or employees of privatizing firms (Stark and Bruszt 1998, 87).

In practice, postsocialist countries chose among alternative paths to private property. Despite the wide support for rapid mass privatization from international policy elites (Spicer, McDermott, and Kogut 2000), this strategy was not implemented across the Central and East European region. Even if we define mass privatization conservatively as a program that converted at least 25 percent of all large state-owned enterprises over a period of two years (King and Hamm 2006), then mass privatization happened in the Czech Republic, Latvia, Lithuania, and Romania, but not in Bulgaria, Estonia, Hungary, Poland, Slovakia, or Slovenia.[8]

The specific strategies that postsocialist countries chose to allocate private property were diverse. Each country selected a unique combination of policies, which can be broadly characterized as voucher privatization, direct sales, or management/employee buyouts (EBRD 2001b). In the end, individual Central and East European countries implemented different combinations of these strategies (Dallago, Ajani, and Grancelli 1992; Earle, Frydman, and Rapaczynski 1993). Table 2.1 provides a summary. For example, the allocation of property rights in the Czech Republic was achieved largely by the distribution of vouchers to citizens over the age of eighteen, who were asked to pay a nominal fee. Each person could receive vouchers equal to one thousand investment points and could exchange them for shares in the enterprises offered for sale in auctions or invest them in investment privatization funds (Hanousek and Kroch 1998). The equity of enterprises was distributed in auctions. As for the three issues in privatization outlined by Stark and Bruszt (1998, 91), "The Czech strategy is an exemplary case of evaluating assets directly by the market, involving participation on the basis of citizenship and utilizing monetary resources."

Slovenia adopted a gradualist approach to privatization designed by domestic academic economists who largely rejected the advice of Western

TABLE 2.1
Privatization Strategies

Country	Methods of Privatization[a]	Openness to Outsiders[b]
Bulgaria	MEBOs, direct sale, vouchers	++
Croatia	MEBOs, vouchers	+
Czech Republic	vouchers, direct sale	+++
Estonia	direct sale, vouchers	++++
Hungary	direct sale, MEBOs	++++
Latvia	direct sale, vouchers	+++
Lithuania	vouchers, direct sale	+++
Poland	direct sale, MEBOs, vouchers	+++
Romania	MEBOs, direct sale, vouchers	++
Slovakia	vouchers, direct sale, MEBOs	++
Slovenia	MEBOs, vouchers	+

Source: Adopted from EBRD 2001b, national accounts for Croatia.

[a] Methods are listed in order of importance. MEBOs are management employee buyouts.

[b] Coded by the author based on privatization strategies, where the prevalence of direct sales signals the greatest openness to outsiders, followed by vouchers, with MEBOs signaling the lowest outsider openness.

experts advocating shock therapy.[9] Most companies were privatized through the free distribution of vouchers (called ownership certificates) to citizens, who could exchange these for shares in the privatizing company, either directly or via private investment funds. Twenty percent of the shares of each large company that was being privatized were allocated to governmental funds (Simoneti, Rojec, and Gregorič 2004, 231). In addition, Slovenian policy encouraged management and employees to invest their ownership certificates in the companies they worked for. This not only maintained insider control but limited purchases by foreign investors.

In Hungary, the privatization process was administered by the State Property Agency, which sold the rights to lead and manage privatization of specific enterprises to international investment banks and consulting firms (Stark and Bruszt 1998, 97). Hence, the primary method of privatization was direct sale of companies in auctions, with assets sold to the highest bidder. In the absence of domestic capitalists (Eyal, Szelényi, and Townsley 1998), this strategy often put formerly state-owned assets in the hands of foreign investors (Antal-Mokos 1998). Moreover, Hungarian legislation allowed formation of joint-stock companies by dividing state enterprises into numerous corporations, which became new legal entities owned partially by the founding state enterprise, by top and midlevel managers, and by other joint-stock companies. This resulted in interesting cross-ownership ties across Hungarian postsocialist enterprises that David Stark (1996) refers to as "recombinant property."

Individual postsocialist countries chose among the multitude of privatization strategies, but their choices were not random. As Stark and Bruszt (1998) convincingly argue, these choices depended on possible means of extrication from the Communist system. For example, the strategies adopted in Poland were possible because regime change involved negotiations between the old and the new elite, while in Hungary the end of Communism was marked by political party competition, and in Czechoslovakia Communist leaders capitulated. Privatization strategies also depended on the type of socialism. For example, Slovenia and Croatia, where socialism was based on workers' self-management, implemented management and employee buyouts as their primary privatization strategies. Because the Yugoslav self-management system privileged decentralized control of workers councils, decisions to allow insiders to acquire ownership stakes seem consistent with the spirit of self-management.

If management and employee buyouts favored insiders, direct sales opened the door to outsiders. This distinction is relevant for the analysis of FDI patterns. If new institutions influence subsequent economic outcomes, we should see that the type of privatization strategies adopted, in particular their openness to outsiders, will have an impact on the extent of FDI penetration into particular countries.

Overall, privatization in Central and Eastern Europe has been a complex process, captured well by Janusz Lewandowski, the Polish privatization minister, who characterized it as a process in which "someone who doesn't know who the real owner is and doesn't know what it is really worth sells it to someone who doesn't have any money" (qtd. in Verdery 2003, 1). More importantly, the complexity and uncertainty of privatization shows that it is not an objective economic problem to which the "right" solution is obvious. Rather, privatization is a socially driven process because it implicates moral issues concerning rightful beneficiaries and is entangled in the web of political relations. Furthermore, privatization is a policy *idea* diffused across national borders as part of world culture. Examining what determines whether a country launches a privatization program, Kogut and Macpherson (2003) found that rapid and widespread privatization has a lot to do with the number of U.S.-trained, and particularly Chicago-trained, economists in a country, showing the role of ideas, and not just objective economic conditions, in economic policy. In their recent study of the worldwide diffusion of neoliberal market reforms in the infrastructure sectors, specifically telecommunication and electricity privatizations, Henisz, Zelner, and Guillén (2005, 871) find robust evidence that countries implement these reforms not only because of domestic economic and political factors but also because of "international pressures of coercion, normative emulation and competitive mimicry." For example, whether a country decides to privatize its telecommunications or energy sectors significantly depends on the country's exposure to the World Bank and the IMF (which espouse the neoliberal credo) and competition with, and imitation of, peer countries.

Democratization

The challenge of transformations in Central and Eastern Europe involves not just a change in the economic system but also a fundamental shift in the political order, from authoritarian one-party rule to democracy. The collapse of Communist regimes after 1989 was quite sudden from the point of view of external observers, who failed to anticipate such dramatic changes. Only a few years before 1989 Samuel Huntington concluded that Eastern Europe was *less* likely to democratize than other parts of the world (Huntington 1984). Indeed, only in retrospect have scholars tried to understand how the Communist downfall came about, and what determines the different outcomes in different countries within the region.

Examining how the transitions from Communism occurred, many scholars have relied on a central theoretical claim that the mode of transition influences the resulting regime type (O'Donnell, Schmitter, and Whitehead 1986). Based on the experiences of the third-wave democratization in Latin America and southern Europe, scholars hypothesized that transitions after socialism resulted from the negotiation of power-sharing arrangements between different elite factions (Linz and Stepan 1997). Some empirical studies found support for this pacted-transition hypothesis (Welsh 1994), but others disagreed. For instance, McFaul (2002) argued that when we take into account the whole socialist region, including those former Soviet bloc countries that have been less successful at democratization, and examine persistence of dictatorship as well as emergence of democracy, we see that noncooperative, rather than negotiated, transitions were most effective. It was a simple power game: "Democracy emerged . . . in countries where democrats enjoyed a decisive power advantage" (McFaul 2002, 212). In addition to the importance of power shifts among elites for the collapse of Communist regimes, researchers have also paid attention to the role of the masses and protest (McSweeney and Tempest 1993; Jenkins and Benderlioglu 2005) and to external influences, such as the political opportunity for oppositional challenges created by the loosening of the Soviet grip on the satellite states once Gorbachev came to power (Niklasson 1994; Bunce 1999), and the power of the "demonstration effect," whereby circumstances in other countries influenced domestic behavior (de Nevers 2003).

Early democratic developments in post-1989 Central and Eastern Europe have been marked by a plethora of political parties. In one of the most extreme cases, almost 100 political parties competed in Polish parliamentary elections in 1991, and "the vote was divided among some thirty parties, none of which won more than 12 percent of the total vote" (Mason and Kluegel 1995, 5). Results of elections where multiple parties vie for power have frequently resulted in coalition governments, which were often unstable, resulting in early elections, or new prime minister appointments during a single election period. One unexpected feature of the postsocialist political scene was the regeneration and persistence of Communist parties after 1989. In Poland, Hungary, Lithuania, and Bulgaria in the second or third round of elections, former Communist parties were returned to power (Orenstein 1998; Grzymala-Busse 2002). In addition, in all postsocialist European countries, with the exception of Hungary, nationalist parties had widespread appeal (Verdery 1996a) and often won representation in government. In Croatia during Tudjman's presidency and in Slovakia under Mečiar, nationalists had the ruling majority.

How about the relationship between economy and democracy? While most scholarship on democratization has been interested in how economic conditions affect the nature of democratic consolidation (Lipset 1959; Jackman 1973; Bollen 1979; Haggard and Kaufman 1995; Przeworski and Limongi 1997; Przeworski et al. 2000), some analysts of the postsocialist transition argue for the reverse effect—that the establishment of democratic institutions assists marketization (Bartlett 1997) and that economic change after socialism is intertwined with political developments (Campbell 1996). If so, we need to pay close attention to the political rule and ideological orientations of the post-1989 governments to understand economic policy choices and outcomes. In terms of FDI, more or less political stability may influence investment risks and hence foreign investors' choices. Also, if politics and state actions are integral to market building, then it makes a difference for foreign investment whether governments in power are more or less committed to rapid economic liberalization and marketization and whether they take actions that institutionalize and legitimize FDI as a developmental strategy.

Nationalism

Postsocialist developments have been marked also by the salience of nationhood and nationalism, which in their most tragic form resulted in rampant bloodshed in the former Yugoslavia. Some observers suggest that the national question was revived in Central and Eastern Europe after the collapse of Communism because it had been suppressed, first by the occupation of the region by imperial powers, the Habsburg Monarchy, the Ottoman Empire, or czarist Russia, and after World War II, by the Communist regimes (Caratan 1997). Others argue that socialist systems in fact promoted national consciousness and institutionalized nationhood and nationality as "basic cognitive and social categories" (Brubaker 1996, 8). This view is supported by a few studies that actually document expressions of nationalism and national identity during socialism (Gal 1991; Verdery 1991; Molnár 2005). But even if national questions were prominent during socialism, other scholars contend, they have become especially vital during the postsocialist period because the fall of the Soviet rule, which kept nationalism in check, provided an impetus to recover state sovereignty and national independence (Zubrzycki 2001).

Moreover, the "nation" became salient for communities from the formerly multinational states of Yugoslavia and the USSR, where the fall of socialism was accompanied by legal assertions of state sovereignty and independence. In these circumstances, as Klaus Offe put it well, "at the most fundamental level a decision [had] to be made as to who 'we' are, i.e., a decision on identity, citizenship, and the territorial as well as social and cultural boundaries of the nation-state" (1991, 869). Here, nationalism can be seen as an integral part of the consolidation of the identity of a new state.

Whatever the causes, the fact is that after the end of the Communist Party rule, the world witnessed a proliferation of national movements and national sentiments in postsocialist Europe (Calhoun 1993; Verdery 1998; Harsanyi and Kennedy 1994). Nationalism was used as a tool of political mobilization and support so that in a number of countries, "the rhetoric and symbols with the greatest electoral appeal were national(ist) ones" (Verdery 1998, 294). Nation-oriented idioms had a prominent place in the cultural repertoires of actors making sense of postsocialist transformations. They were "widely available and resonant as a category of social vision and division" (Brubaker 1996, 21). It is also important to note that extreme versions of nationalism were a cause of civil war in the former Yugoslavia, under the Milošević and early Tudjman regimes. Kennedy (2002) suggests that one of the reasons why other Central and East European states embraced Western capitalism so quickly may have been precisely the effort to distance themselves from such violent alternatives.

How is nationalism relevant for the economy? If economic action is embedded in political and cultural understandings, as I argue, then nationalism, and cultural understandings more generally, will influence how postsocialist nations embark on market building and what alternatives of economic development they see as desirable and appropriate. The increased salience of the national question may take the form of economic nationalism, where governments enact policies to protect domestic industries and retain ownership of assets in domestic hands. Even if they do not enact policies, political elites may show economic nationalist stances in their handling of economic affairs. These are not limited to Eastern Europe. A recent example of "economic patriotism" was the action of

French prime minister Dominique de Villepin, who preempted the attempt of an Italian investor to take over Suez, a French utility company, by brokering a merger between Suez and Gaz de France, a gas giant. The event was greeted with approval by the French public but frowned upon by the international economic elites who thought it inappropriate in the age of globalization and liberalization (*The Economist* 2006, 65).

Some evidence of the salience of economic nationalism in postsocialist countries can be found in the 1995 International Social Science Program's survey on national identity, which included seven postsocialist states: Bulgaria, the Czech Republic, Hungary, Latvia, Poland, Slovakia, and Slovenia. One question addressed attitudes toward foreign ownership. Respondents were asked to indicate their agreement or disagreement with the following statement: "Foreigners should not be allowed to own land in (respondent's country)." Large majorities in postsocialist countries strongly agreed or agreed. As table 2.2 shows, on average, Bulgarians, Czechs, Hungarians, Latvians, Poles, Slovaks, and Slovenes were twice as likely to oppose foreign ownership as people from other surveyed countries, including, among others, the United States, Germany, Italy, Japan, and Sweden. Moreover, Central and East Europeans who expressed their strong opposition to foreign ownership of land were also significantly more likely to report feeling close to their own country, agreeing that it is important to be a citizen of their country and speak its main language. They also expressed pride in their country's history and agreed that people should support their country even if it is in the wrong, or when doing so leads to conflict with other nations. Moreover, these respondents were very likely to agree that their country should limit the import of foreign products in order to protect its national economy.

Overall, an analysis of FDI in Central and Eastern Europe needs to take into account the cultural embeddedness of this economic process. Values and beliefs about economic strategies shape a country's economic policy not only because they inform political interests of nationalist groups but also because they constitute understandings among the general public about the desirability of foreigners in national economies. Moreover, nationality affiliations may shape the types of commitments that actors will want to realize through FDI attempts, and cultural conceptions of nationality may influence the evaluation of potential partners in economic transactions.

EU Integration

While privatization, democratization, and nationalism provide the domestic context for the investigation of the proliferation of FDI markets in postsocialist Europe, this process is also structured by regional forces. In

TABLE 2.2
Public Attitudes toward Foreign Ownership of Land

	Percentage Opposed to Foreign Ownership of Land
Australia	42
Germany-West	16
Great Britain	32
United States	33
Austria	49
Italy	24
Ireland	35
Netherlands	21
Norway	39
Sweden	36
New Zealand	50
Canada	28
Japan	28
Spain	29
Average	33
Bulgaria	81
Czech R.	61
Hungary	77
Latvia	70
Poland	57
Slovakia	60
Slovenia	70
CEE average	69

Source: International Social Survey Program, National Identity Module 1995 (author's calculations).

particular, the role of the European Union is crucial. Immediately follow-ing the shifts in political power in Central and Eastern Europe, the post-Communist states began their integration into the community of Euro-pean states. The EU integration may very well have been "one of the least controversial issues on the political agenda" (Grabbe and Hughes 1998, 71) in these transforming societies, and perhaps Mitchell Orenstein (1998, 480) was right to assert that "the transition as we know it will end when these countries do qualify for membership in the EU," adding that "Europe is the *telos* of transition." Indeed, for some postsocialist states, the integration with Western Europe provided the impetus to break from Communism and old political structures. "Europe, now!" was the slogan of Slovenia's independence movement. During the Velvet Revolution, Ha-vel's Civic Forum rallied with "Return to Europe." Moreover, EU mem-

bership was thought to benefit postsocialist countries in multiple ways.
As Kurtz and Barnes (2002, 549) summarized,

> Economically, member states gain access to a lucrative European
> market, as well as direct financial assistance. In political terms, EU
> membership means symbolic acceptance into the "Western world,"
> a completion of the "return to Europe.". . . EU accession is [also] in
> the private interest of political leaders in the region—their electoral
> fortunes can only improve by delivering their citizens material bene-
> fits, labor mobility to the wealthy West, and the increase in national
> stature that membership implies.

To affirm their desire to integrate into the EU, in December 1991 Poland and Hungary were the first among the postsocialist states to sign the
so-called Europe Agreements. Marking the beginning of a country's path
toward EU integration, the Europe Agreements provided a bilateral institutional framework between EU member states and postsocialist countries, covering trade, political dialogue, legal harmonization, and other
areas of cooperation, including industry, environment, transport, and customs. These EU Agreements also required the abolition of most tariffs and
the adaptation of the country's regulatory framework to EU rules (Meyer
1998). Following Poland and Hungary, Romania and Bulgaria signed the
agreements in spring 1993. The Czech Republic and Slovakia, after the
dissolution of the federal state, each separately signed in October 1993.
The three Baltic states followed in June 1995, and Slovenia in June 1996.

Preparing for the eastern enlargement, the EU also put in place specific
instruments to assist restructuring in Central and Eastern Europe. The
Poland and Hungary: Action for the Restructuring of the Economy
(PHARE) program was one such instrument. Initially created to facilitate
reforms in Poland and Hungary, PHARE has since included most of the
Central and East European countries. As the EU website states, objectives
of PHARE include

> strengthening public administrations and institutions to function ef-
> fectively inside the EU, promoting convergence with the EU's exten-
> sive legislation (the acquis communautaire). [PHARE also promotes]
> the *functioning of the market economy* and helps build the capacity
> to cope with competitive pressure and market forces within the EU,
> which is key to fulfilling the obligations of membership. Consider-
> able investment is required to ensure that the enterprises and infra-
> structure in candidate countries comply with Community standards,
> as well as to establish an appropriate institutional and regulatory
> context. (European Union 2006; emphasis added)

Clearly, the EU accession has left an important mark on the restructuring of Central and Eastern Europe. Through various instruments and requirements to adopt the EU legislation (*acquis communautaire*), an altogether uncertain process marked by power asymmetry between the full members and applicants (Grabbe 2003), the EU has structured the development of market-based institutions and, by making it a condition of membership, promoted the liberalization of postsocialist economies. In May 2004, eight of the postsocialist states, the Czech Republic, Estonia, Hungary, Latvia, Lithuania, Poland, Slovakia, and Slovenia joined the EU in what marked an unprecedented enlargement of this regional association. Romania and Bulgaria joined in January 2007.

Globalization

Next to domestic and regional processes, postsocialist transformations were greatly affected also by forces that have been changing the character of the world society. In fact, postsocialist transformations and intensification of globalization happened simultaneously, and the two processes affected each other. The rise in FDI after the 1980s, one of the key indicators of the intensity of global interactions (Guillén 2001a), and "one of the most stable and economically important of the international capital flows" (Jensen 2006, 23), has been spectacular (figure 2.1). The collapse of Communist regimes and the liberalization of Central and Eastern Europe provided plenty of opportunities for foreign investors. Emphasizing the importance of the simultaneity of the two processes, some observers consider the penetration of foreign capital after the collapse of state socialism to be "the most momentous structural force in the transformation process" (Böröcz 2001, 1163).

Although the phenomenon of cross-country exchanges in capital, people, ideas, and technology is not novel (Sklair 1991; Sassen 1996; Lechner and Boli 2000), the term *globalization* appeared in the early 1970s, and debates in the popular press and in academic discourse have grown exponentially ever since (Fiss and Hirsch 2005). Indeed, one would be hard pressed to find a person who denies that in the recent decades the world has witnessed "a compression of time and space" (Harvey 1989) and "greater interdependence and mutual awareness (reflexivity) among economic, political, and social units in the world, and among actors in general" (Guillén 2001a, 236). Analysts are urged to consider the global economy, polity, and culture when studying what have traditionally been considered domestic affairs (Evans 1997; Berger 2000; Guillén 2001a; Brady, Beckfield, and Seeleib-Kaiser 2005; Gereffi 2005). But whether globalization is "civilizing, destructive or feeble," as Mauro Guillén (2001a) asks in a review of the literature, remains an open question. From

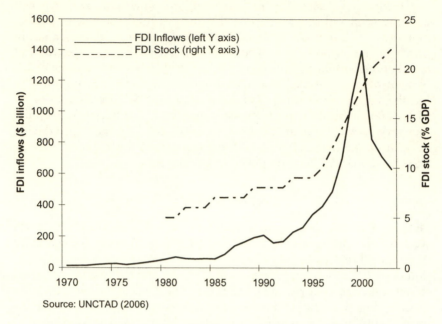

Figure 2.1. World FDI Trends, 1970–2003

a practical standpoint, it is unlikely that we can characterize such a diverse and multiplex process, captured under the umbrella term of globalization, in a uniform way. The effects will be different for different substantive phenomena: cities (Sassen 1991), the welfare state (Brady, Beckfield, and Seeleib-Kaiser 2005), democracy (Schwartzman 1998; Wejnert 2005), science (Drori et al. 2003), social movements and activism (Keck and Sikkink 1998; della Porta, Kriesi, and Rucht 1999; Guidry, Kennedy, and Zald 2001), labor (Silver 2003), environment (Frank, Hironaka, and Schofer 2000), and economy (Hirst and Thompson 1999; Chase-Dunn, Kawano, and Brewer 2000; Dicken 2003; Gereffi 2005), among others.

While the first generation of globalization studies was primarily concerned with how to define it and understand its character (Harvey 1989; Giddens 1991; Robertson 1992; Beck, Giddens, and Lash 1994; Featherstone and Lash 1999), more recent discussions have been concerned with its consequences. One of the central issues is whether the increased intensity of cross-national exchanges undermines the authority of nation-states. As many have noted, global processes seem to be controlled by multinational corporations more than by national governments, which are losing their regulatory power (e.g., Vernon 1971; Kennedy 1993; Sakamoto 1994; Cox 1996). In addition, one of the key consequences of globalization has been the rise of global cities, such as New York, London, and Singapore, whose role and stature transcend the nation-state in which they happen to be located (Sassen 1991; Choi, Park, and Tschoegl 1996). Hence, globalization leads to an "attenuation of the state" (Waters 1995, 96–123), not in the least because neoliberalism as globalization's associated ideology opposes intervention by the state (Evans 1997, 82–87). From this viewpoint, power in the global world is moving from states to markets (Strange 1996; Mishra 1999; Huber and Stephens 2001; Jessop 2002).

On the other hand, some scholars argue that globalization reinforces the role of the state, because global processes entail competition between states for economic, military, and political supremacy (Wallerstein 1974; Tilly 1992). Arguing a similar point but from a different theoretical perspective, John Meyer and colleagues (1997, 157) write that "globalization certainly poses new problems for states, but it also strengthens the world-cultural principle that nation-states are the primary actors charged with identifying and managing those problems on behalf of their societies." In addition, scholars note that global pressures provoke responses from states to engage in regionalization and protectionism (Gilpin 1987; Berger 2000). If anything, globalization may be more about "reorganizing" than bypassing states (Panitch 1996, 84), and states in the era of globalization are not defenseless and passive but rather "adapting, whether out of necessity or desire" (Ó Riain 2000, 205). So globalization may bring transformation of the state rather than its diminution. Hence, in keeping with the focus on embedded economies in this book, the relevant question is not whether states matter but *how* they matter. If my story is correct, we should see that the lifting of the Iron Curtain, one of the key events facilitating globalization, does not mean the diminishing of the Central and East European states but the transformation of their role in the economy. Indeed, as I will argue for the case of FDI, postsocialist states will play a crucial role in building open market institutions and facilitating global integration of the region with the rest of the world.

Whether increasing international movement of capital, people, and culture makes the world more homogenous is another central issue addressed in globalization studies (Lechner and Boli 2000). Empirical work conducted on the subject has found divergent results. Research in the world-society tradition has found increasing convergence in institutional arrangements across countries and organizations (McNeely 1995; Meyer et al. 1997). Other scholars report that over the past decades national value differences have persisted (Ingelhardt and Baker 2000) and that in order to cope with globalizing forces, countries and organizations strive to be different and emphasize their unique economic, political, and social advantages (Guillén 2001b). With regard to the presence of multinational corporations, empirical evidence suggests that foreign and local interact to produce hybrid practices (Watson 1997) or Creole cultures (Hannerz 2000).

Resisting the formulation of the question about globalization's consequences for the economy as "convergence vs. divergence," Viviana Zelizer
(1999, 212) proposes that

> the economy operates at two levels: seen from the top, economic
> transactions connect with broad national symbolic meanings and in-
> stitutions. Seen from the bottom, economic transactions are highly
> differentiated, personalized and local, meaningful to particular rela-
> tions. No contradiction therefore exists between uniformity and di-
> versity; they are simply two different aspects of the same transaction.

Hence, it is likely that both convergence and divergence operate simultaneously, albeit at different levels of analysis and for different aspects of
this diverse phenomenon that we call globalization. If so, detailed investigations attending to the process of globalization simultaneously at national and organizational levels of analysis, such as my research on FDI
in Central and Eastern Europe, may reveal that formal national policies
align with universalizing neoliberal reforms, but embedded economic
practices in local settings result in a great variety of actions and, ultimately, in the particularization of global forces (Bandelj 2003).

Neoliberalism

Amid a myriad of ideas about how globalization is relevant for changes
in Central and Eastern Europe, I think it is most important to keep in
mind that globalization has not only structural but also cultural manifes-
tations. Increases in cross-border exchanges of financial capital, goods,
and people are accompanied by a diffusion of ideas about appropriate
economic strategies. The last two decades of the twentieth century saw a
rise in the market deregulation and economic liberalization on a global
scale (e.g., Lash and Urry 1987; Albert 1993; Przeworski 1995; Campbell
and Pedersen 2001). While many welcome these developments as evidence that the market is finally freed to select the most efficient policies
(Posner 1986; Williamson 1990), others consider these changes the result
of a political project—neoliberalism—promoted by international organizations and domestic political forces, such as the Reagan and Thatcher
governments (Meyer et al. 1997; Gore 2000; Babb 2001; Campbell and
Pedersen 2001; Carruthers, Babb, and Halliday 2001; Brune, Garrett, and
Kogut 2004; Henisz, Zelner, and Guillén 2005).

What is neoliberalism? As Henisz, Zelner and Guillén (2005, 873)
summarize:

> [Neoliberalism] proposes to reduce the role of politics and the state
> in the economy so that markets may function unhindered. . . . [It]
> proposes to encourage entrepreneurship, investment, and long-run

economic growth through reductions in subsidies, tax reforms, tax cuts, stabilization of the money supply, the free flow of trade and capital and . . . market-oriented reform of state-owned industries. Dozens of countries adopted elements of market-oriented reform between 1980s and 1999. Whereas in 1980s only 10 countries had adopted such an element in telecommunications and 44 had done so in electricity, these figures had respectively increased to 124 and 94 by the end of 1999.

Some note that the codification of the neoliberal agenda, explicitly aimed at developing countries, appeared in the so-called Washington consensus (Williamson 1990, xiii). This consensus advocated liberalizations of trade and foreign direct investment regimes, and privatization of state enterprises as vehicles to prosperity in developing countries. According to Charles Gore,

> The introduction of the Washington Consensus involved not simply a swing from state-led to market-oriented policies, but also a shift in the ways in which development problems were framed and in the types of explanations through which policies were justified. Key changes were the partial globalization of development policy analysis, and a shift from historicism to ahistorical performance assessment. (2000, 789)

In 2000, Gore also predicted that "the demise of the Washington Consensus is inevitable because its methodology and ideology are in contradiction" (2000, 789).

Whether neoliberalism is just a trend in economic policymaking that will soon be replaced with another set of ideas about the right path to economic development, or an indication that markets are finally let free to achieve allocative efficiency, it undoubtedly has had an impact on postsocialist Europe. "After communist regimes in Eastern Europe collapsed in 1989, the new postcommunist governments have embarked, at various speeds, on neoliberal economic reforms designed to bring about rapid liberalization, macroeconomic restructuring, and, ultimately, privatization" (Bockman and Eyal 2002, 310). While socialism was a closed system that shied away from international interactions, as soon as the Iron Curtain was lifted, Central and East European countries opened up to international influences, including neoliberal policy prescriptions promoted by international organizations such as the IMF, the World Bank, the European Bank for Restructuring and Development (EBRD), and the Organization for Economic Cooperation and Development (OECD). The shock-therapy reforms discussed earlier in the chapter align with these neoliberal prescriptions.

Furthermore, immediately after 1989, postsocialist states sought membership in such international organizations as the World Trade Organization (WTO) or signed international agreements with the IMF, which imposed common standards and obligations in line with the association's philosophy of liberal economic development. For instance, signing Article VIII of the IMF agreement meant that members agreed not to "impose restrictions on the making of payments and transfers for current international transactions," thus facilitating cross-national financial flows (IMF 2005a, 1). Table 2.3 summarizes the integration of Central and Eastern Europe in international institutions.

It is important to acknowledge that integration into international organizations has consequences for distributions of political power. Decision making at the level of the nation-state can be substantially constrained because of a country's integration into transnational structures. However, we should not equate such integration with the ultimate loss of state power. The influence of international organizations is stronger in the case of states on the periphery of the world system that cannot assert their interests as vehemently as core states can. Because postsocialist states were emerging from the periphery, they were structurally in weak positions to negotiate with international institutions. In particular, international organizations provided loans and other financial resources for economic restructuring after state socialism and could tie obligations to this assistance. As is stated on the IMF's website, "An IMF loan is usually provided under an 'arrangement,' which stipulates the specific policies and measures a country has agreed to implement in order to resolve its balance of payments problem" (IMF 2006). Should countries stray, the IMF exerts pressures to put them back on track. Like a scolding parent, "IMF *warned* Romania that progress in disinflation and consolidation of the external position will require wage and financial discipline in the state-owned enterprises, continued fiscal consolidation, and prudent monetary policy" (EBRD 2001a; emphasis added). Countries bound by IMF loans are also tied to the institution's prescriptions for economic development.

Last but not least, it is important to acknowledge that the role of neoliberalism in developments in postsocialist Europe is not just a manifestation of an imbalance of power and thus an externally imposed pressure. In an insightful analysis, sociologists Johanna Bockman and Gil Eyal (2002) propose that neoliberalism's success in East Europe is in large part due to transnational dialogue between American and East European economists in which neoliberal ideas were worked out prior to the collapse of Communism. For example, to facilitate this dialogue, the Ford Foundation had established exchanges during the Cold War with Poland (signed in 1957), Yugoslavia (1959), Hungary (1962), Romania (1965), Czechoslovakia (1968), and Bulgaria (1968). Participants in such dialogues were

TABLE 2.3

Integration of Central and East European Countries into International Institutions as of 2005

Country	Europe Agreement Signed	Europe Agreement in Force	Application for EU Membership	Negotiations Begin	Negotiations Concluded	Accession to EU	IMF Article VIII	GATT/WTO
Bulgaria	March 1993	February 1995	December 1995	October 1999	December 2004	January 2007	September 1998	December 1996
Croatia	October 2001[a]	February 2005[a]	February 2003	October 2005	not yet	not yet	May 1995	November 2000
Czech Republic	October 1993	February 1995	January 1996	March 1998	December 2002	May 2004	October 1995	January 1995
Estonia	June 1995	February 1998	November 1995	March 1998	December 2002	May 2004	August 1994	November 1999
Hungary	December 1991	February 1994	March 1994	March 1998	December 2002	May 2004	January 1996	January 1995
Latvia	June 1995	February 1998	October 1995	October 1999	December 2002	May 2004	June 1994	February 1999
Lithuania	June 1995	February 1998	December 1995	October 1999	December 2002	May 2004	May 1994	May 2001
Poland	December 1991	February 1994	April 1994	March 1998	December 2002	May 2004	June 1995	July 1995
Romania	February 1993	February 1995	June 1995	October 1999	December 2004	January 2007	March 1998	January 1995
Slovakia	October 1993	February 1995	June 1995	October 1999	December 2002	May 2004	October 1995	January 1995
Slovenia	June 1996	February 1999	June 1996	March 1998	December 2002	May 2004	September 1995	July 1995

Source: EU 2005 and IMF 2005b.
[a] Stabilization and Association Agreement.

economists who later championed neoliberal reforms in their home countries, like Václau Klaus from the Czech Republic or Leszek Balcerowicz
from Poland. Hence, Bockman and Eyal counter research and perceived
wisdom, which sees neoliberalism as simply exported by Western advisors
and international economic agencies, and instead emphasize the active
role of East European reformers who embraced neoliberalism long before
1989 because they participated in a transnational dialogue. Bockman and
Eyal's point about the relational nature of global economic processes is
well taken. Postsocialist states cannot be regarded as passive receivers of
external influences and blind imitators of world culture. While external
forces are crucial in the global environment, often it is domestic actors
and their interests that channel these forces and shape the extent to which
countries embark on neoliberal development paths.

Conclusion

To understand the rise of FDI in postsocialist Europe as a socially constructed economic process, we need to understand the historical background of transformations from socialism to postsocialism. This chapter
outlined the character of the socialist systems and paths of extrication,
and presented the broad context in which the reconfiguration of socialist
command economies as market-based institutions took place. Legacies of
the past, as well as the simultaneity of privatization, democratization,
regionalization, and globalization, have characterized social change in
Central and Eastern Europe. Likewise, FDI in postsocialism needs to be
understood in the context of property rights transformation, the establishment of a democratic political order, and the prominence of nationalism.
It also should be seen as influenced by integration into the European
Union, by international financial institutions, and by the spread of neolib-
eral economic principles, which are part and parcel of globalization.
Against this backdrop, the next chapter empirically examines the rise of
FDI in Central and Eastern Europe after 1989.

Chapter 3

INSTITUTIONALIZATION OF FDI IN POSTSOCIALISM

THE CHANGES IN Central and Eastern Europe after the fall of the Communist regimes have provided social scientists with an unprecedented social laboratory. Analysts of economic changes in postsocialism have plunged into theorizing and examining the East European "emerging markets," not only to produce voluminous scholarship but also to shape economic policy. The label *emerging markets*, coined by the International Finance Corporation in 1981, as applied to Central and Eastern Europe, implies spontaneity, naturalness, or inevitability. In this sense, do markets "emerge"? The question is not only rhetorical. The label *emerging markets* epitomizes an understanding of market exchange as a natural structure of economic organization, which will emerge as soon as the (unnatural) control of the Party state is abolished. In the absence of state intervention, self-interested market actors will be free to exchange and maximize utility. As one observer stated, "If given the presence of rational, self-interested actors and the absence of government interference, market exchange takes place of its own accord, market economies should emerge automatically" (Koslowski 1992, 674). Or in the words of a prominent economist Jeffrey Sachs (1994, xii), who served as advisor to many postsocialist governments, "Markets spring up as soon as central planning bureaucrats vacate the field."

In sharp contrast to the view that markets reflect the natural outcome of individual human activity, and spring up spontaneously, political economists and economic sociologists have long argued for the social and political foundations of markets. This research builds on the classical work by Karl Polanyi (1944). Tracing the great transformation of nineteenth-century England into a liberal market economy, Polanyi showed that free markets were neither natural nor inevitable: "There was nothing natural about laissez-faire; free markets could never have come into being merely by allowing things to take their course. . . . Laissez-faire itself was enforced by the state" (1944, 139). Therefore, markets should be understood as "instituted," that is, as "embedded and enmeshed in institutions, economic and non-economic" (Polanyi 1957, 248).

In line with Polanyi, and consistent with the constructivist perspective on embedded economy adopted in this book, I argue that market-based activity in Central and Eastern Europe—including foreign direct investment as its integral element—could not just emerge "by allowing things to take their course," but had to be constructed as a new system of socio-economic organization in the process of institutionalization of markets. To advance this argument, this chapter first explicates the institutional conditions for FDI in postsocialist Europe, paying special attention to how postsocialist states create the demand for FDI by legitimizing FDI practice. In the second part, I present empirical evidence for the importance of institutional conditions on the volume of FDI in postsocialist Europe.

FDI as Instituted Process

The social-constructivist perspective implies that proliferation of FDI needs to be understood as part of an *institutional* transformation: from one type of embedded economy, based on institutional rules of central planning and redistribution, into another kind of embedded institutional system, where the bulk of economic activity is performed by private actors exchanging property rights on the market. Markets and FDI should not be expected to emerge spontaneously, but need to be institutionalized.

What does institutionalization encompass? One of the earliest definitions was given by Shmuel Eisenstadt:

> The institutionalization of any social system means that certain norms, sanctions and organizations must be set up, and that policies through which these norms can be upheld and applied to a relatively large and complex variety of social situations must be implemented. (1964, 245)

According to Eisenstadt, institutionalization is incited by institutional entrepreneurs who are in "strategic positions" to stimulate change (1964, 245). For a system-wide change in any Central and East European country, the actor who can set up rules and policies to uphold those rules is the postsocialist state, but its actions will be influenced by domestic politics and interest groups as well as by transnational forces (Van Rossem 1996; Meyer et al. 1997; Campbell 2004). This means that an analysis of FDI in Central and Eastern Europe needs to pay close attention to how postsocialist states negotiate domestic interests and external pressures to create institutional conditions for market exchanges that involve domestic actors selling property rights to foreign investors. Such an analysis aligns with the perspective in political economy that sees states not as an unnecessary intervention in self-regulating markets but as a force that facilitates their functioning (Campbell and Lindberg 1990; Block 1994; Evans 1995; Evans and Rauch 1999; Fligstein 2001a; Chibber 2002; Block and Evans 2005).

Furthermore, as we can infer from Eisenstadt's definition, central to the institutionalization processes are norms, sanctions, and policies, or rules called institutions. While there is little agreement on a common definition of an institution (Hollingsworth 2003, 88), many analysts follow Nobel Laureate economist Douglass North's (1990, 3) formulation: institutions are the rules of the game that constrain behavior. Most institutional economists emphasize that such rules emerge because they are efficient (Williamson 1985), but North questioned this assumption (1990, 6). North nevertheless emphasized that institutions *constrain* autonomous behavior, as part of the context in which people act, and did not explicitly point to the socially constructed character of institutions. This aspect is emphasized by sociological neoinstitutionalists, who define institutions as "socially constructed, routine-reproduced (ceteris paribus), program or rule systems" that "operate as relative fixtures of constraining environments and are accompanied by taken-for-granted accounts" (Jepperson 1991, 149). This definition highlights that institutions are treated by actors as objective fixtures because they come to be taken for granted, and their social origins are gradually forgotten (Schutz 1962; Berger and Luckmann 1967). Moreover, like any social structure, institutions simultaneously constrain and enable actors (Giddens 1984; Sewell 1992). They "involve mutually related rights and obligations for actors, distinguishing between appropriate and inappropriate, 'right' and 'wrong,' 'possible' and 'impossible' actions and thereby organizing behavior into predictable and reliable patterns" (Streeck and Thelen 2005, 9). Hence, institutional rules of the game are accompanied by cultural accounts of what is appropriate or not in any social situation, what we often refer to as *legitimacy*. "Legitimacy is a generalized perception or assumption that the actions of an entity are desirable, proper, or appropriate within some socially constructed system of norms, values, beliefs, and definitions" (Suchman 1995, 574). Newly institutionalized rules must be legitimized if they are to have an effect on behavior. If, on the other hand, institutionalized rules lack legitimacy, deviations from them, that is, the decoupling of institutional rules and actual practice, will follow (Meyer and Rowan 1977).

From this brief conceptual discussion we can infer that proliferation of FDI in postsocialist Europe will depend on the extent to which this economic behavior is *institutionalized and legitimized*, that is, turned into rule-like behavior that is appropriate and desirable and reproduced through practice. But how, precisely, is the institutionalization of market-based FDI achieved after very different economic institutions of centralization and redistribution have prevailed for forty years? Such a fundamental economic transformation requires implementation of new formal and informal institutions that support the open market system, as a macro-structural arrangement, and FDI behavior, as a firm-level organizational action. As such, the institutionalization and legitimization of FDI is a political and cultural project.

In the opening of a previously closed socialist system, FDI will always depend on the actions of the state, which will make domestic assets more or less available to foreign investors, and to differing degrees encourage domestic actors to seek out foreign partners. Hence, the institutionalization of FDI is a political project, in which a state puts in place formal institutions, policies, and laws that encourage or discourage FDI.

One of the key institutions that the postsocialist states had to establish to facilitate market-based economic activity was private property rights. Since property rights are rules that define ownership and control of assets, and consequently specify what people can withhold or grant to another person, they are a necessary condition for market exchange. In order for foreign investors to participate as market players in a postsocialist economy, they must be allowed to acquire property rights of assets they pay for, and thus rights to dispose of these assets at their will. Moreover, if postsocialist actors are to sell ownership stakes in domestic firms to foreign buyers, then ownership structures of these firms need to be clarified. Who owns what must be clearly specified. Volkswagen cannot exchange with "the whole of the people" who collectively owned automobile manufacturer Škoda in the Czechoslovak command economy, but with economic actors who hold private property rights to Škoda's assets, and can decide to sell them to Volkswagen in a market transaction.

As discussed in chapter 2, allocating property rights in the process of privatization was one of the major goals of postsocialist governments, and one of the most hotly debated issues by those who advocated shock therapy or a gradualist approach to postsocialist transformation. The process of privatization would have two kinds of consequences for FDI. First, the sheer extent of privatization in any country would structure the demand for FDI by determining the quantity of assets to be sold to foreign buyers. Second, different privatization strategies would enable different kinds of involvement of foreign investors in the process. Direct sales of assets, as were common in the Czech Republic, Hungary, Estonia, and Latvia, were advantageous for foreign investors because few domestic investors had the means to bid for assets in auctions. On the other hand, privatization that relied on management and employee buyouts precluded the involvement of foreign investors, because it privileged domestic economic actors already involved in companies.

Besides instituting private property rights to facilitate market exchange, including FDI, postsocialist states also needed to put in place governance structures and rules that define relations of competition, cooperation, and organization (Fligstein 1996, 2001a). Changes in laws and policies regulating economic activity since 1989 (and even earlier in countries that experimented with reforms during socialism) have been tremendous. Consider the schematic report provided by the European Bank for Reconstruction and Development (EBRD) about major areas of liberalization, stabilization, and privatization in the Czech Republic between 1991 and 1998, including enterprise, infrastructure, financial, and social reforms:

> 1991: exchange rate unified, fixed exchange rate regime adopted, most prices liberalized, most foreign trade controls lifted, small-scale privatization begins, restitution law adopted; 1992: treasury bills market initiated, first wave of voucher privatization begins, EFTA Agreement signed; 1993: Czechoslovakia splits into Czech and Slovak Republics, VAT introduced, income tax law adopted, new currency (koruna) introduced, first Czech Eurobond issued, CEFTA founded, stock exchange begins trading, bankruptcy law amended; 1994: second wave of voucher privatization begins, first pension fund obtains license, first corporate Eurobond issued; 1995: WTO membership granted, full current account convertibility introduced, OECD membership granted, bad loan provisioning regulation adopted, energy law adopted, telecommunication privatization begins, mortgage banking law adopted; 1996: exchange rate band widened, BIS capital adequacy regulation enacted, securities law amended, competition agency established; 1997: austerity package announced, managed float exchange rate regime adopted, second austerity package announced; 1998: bankruptcy law amended, independent securities regulator established, law on investment funds adopted, EU accession negotiations commence, investment incentives adopted, banking law amended. (EBRD 2003, 136–37)

To consider so many changes in law and policy in the brief span of seven years, recording each formal decision that might influence FDI in multiple countries, is a task for a book of its own. However, what suffices for our purposes is recognition that any institutional change designed to attract foreign investors and facilitate their business in postsocialist countries is predicated on political commitment by the ruling government to market reform. Opening borders to foreign investment and supporting market exchanges with foreign investors seems necessarily a sign of a postsocialist state's commitment to advancing market reform. This implies that postsocialist governments that did not put market reform at the top of their political agenda were stalling the process of FDI institutionalization. This proposition is consistent with studies that point to the role of politics, coalition building, and balances of power in fostering institutional change (Abolafia 1996; Fligstein 1996; Roy 1997; Mizruchi and Fein 1999; Perrow 2002; Schneiberg 2005).

Furthermore, it is important to emphasize that institutionalization of FDI is not just a political but also a cultural project. Selling domestic assets to foreign investors needs to be legitimized as an appropriate and desirable economic activity. Admittedly, any FDI policy signals the state's attitudes toward FDI; however, there is a distinction between rules on paper and those that are legitimized also in practice. In particular for Central and Eastern Europe, understanding *legitimization of FDI practice*, not just institutionalization or legalization in formal rules, is critical. With the substantial institutional change that the postsocialist period brought, many rules were written in law or policy but not all were implemented in practice (O'Toole 1997; Bandelj 2004; Schimmelfennig and Sedelmeier 2005). Therefore, it is especially important to consider concrete actions by states to legitimize the practice of FDI. This follows from the understanding advanced in this book, that economic actors primarily act practically: they learn the rules of market behavior not so much through incentives put in place by formal institutions as through observing each other's behavior, imitating and learning from each other. Hence, we would expect legitimization of FDI practice to be more consequential than formalization in policy.

Legitimization of FDI Practice

Postsocialist states play a crucial role in instituting FDI by helping legitimize exchanges with foreign investors as an appropriate economic behavior, as FDI will not occur "naturally." Adam Przeworski captures this point well:

> [The] assumption that if individuals internalize the costs and benefits of their decision everyone will respond to price stimuli is nothing but an article of faith. Powerful cultural barriers must be broken and well-entrenched habits must be eroded if people are to behave like market actors. . . . Modernization, the process by which individuals became acculturated to market relations, took decades or longer in Western Europe. Moreover, whereas, as Lenin once remarked, any cook can be taught to administer a socialist economy, the market economy is a world of accountants, stockbrokers, investment planners, and financial wizards. It takes time for cooks to become MBAs. (1991, 158)

If legitimization is required to facilitate FDI, how does it occur? In his explication of the concept, Mark Suchman (1995, 600) lists several legitimization strategies, including producing proper outcomes, embedding in institutions, offering symbolic display, proselytizing, popularizing and

TABLE 3.1
Foreign Direct Investment Agencies in Central and Eastern Europe

Country	Name of Agency	Established
Bulgaria	InvestBulgaria Agency	1995
Croatia	Croatian Investment Promotion Agency	1996
Czech Republic	CzechInvest	1992
Estonia	Estonian Investment Agency	1994
Hungary	Hungarian Investment and Trade Development Agency (ITDH)	1993
Latvia	Latvian Development Agency	1993
Lithuania	Lithuanian Development Agency	1995
Poland	Polish Agency for Foreign Investment (PAIZ)	1992
Romania	Romanian Agency for Foreign Investment	1997
Slovakia	Slovak Investment and Trade Development Agency (SARIO)	2000
Slovenia	Trade and Investment Promotion Agency	1995

Source: National accounts; interviews with agency officials.

standardizing new models, and professionalizing operations. The latter is emphasized also by neoinstitutionalists, who focus on the importance of professionalization for disseminating practices within organizational fields, which structure the behavior of firms within those fields. In particular, organizations adopt those practices that are disseminated by professionals and professional organizations in the process called normative isomorphism (DiMaggio and Powell 1983). Hence, in the case of FDI in postsocialism, establishing professional organizations that stimulate and promote FDI transactions is an important legitimization effort, influencing the behavior of firms. State FDI agencies can play this role. The key purpose of these governmental bodies is to promote a country as a destination for foreign investment and to serve the needs of foreign investors. For example, the Polish Information and Foreign Investment Agency "exists to increase the inflow of foreign direct investment (FDI) in Poland, by encouraging foreign corporations to invest [there]. It serves to help them deal with all the administrative and legal procedures encountered during the investment process" (Polish Information and Foreign Investment Agency 2005). Likewise, "[The] Bulgarian Foreign Investment Agency [is] a one-stop shop institution for foreign investors. . . . It provides to prospective investors up-to-date information on the investment process in the country, legal advice, identification of suitable Bulgarian partners, [and engages in] co-ordination of the investment policy with other institutions" (InvestBulgaria Agency 2005).

Table 3.1 shows that the first two Foreign Direct Investment Agencies, in Poland and the Czech Republic, were established soon after the collapse of communist regimes, in 1992. Hungary, Latvia, and Estonia followed suit in the next two years. By 2000 all Central and East European countries had established an FDI agency, as a separate organizational entity supported by and reporting to a state body, usually the Ministry of Economic Affairs.

The staff and financial resources of these FDI agencies vary greatly, as do the number of FDI transactions they facilitate. Between 2001 and 2003, I visited and talked to officials in six Central and East European FDI Agencies and corresponded over email with five others. My efforts to get information that would help me gauge the power, and hence contribution to legitimization efforts, of each of these FDI agencies were variously successful. I would have preferred to examine their budget, staff, scope of their activities, the number of FDI efforts they facilitated, and the number they realized. My respondents were generally quite reluctant to give out budgets and performance indicators. Surprisingly, some said that they do not have these data readily available. The agency that was most forthcoming with the information was CzechInvest. Its representative was proud to tell me that CzechInvest had twice received an award for the best foreign investment agency worldwide. Its annual reports looked similar to those of multinational corporations, and the agency willingly provided estimates of the worth of the FDI transactions that it facilitated. CzechInvest has a large number of branches in foreign countries, including those in Chicago, Silicon Valley, Brussels, Hong Kong, Yokohama, Cologne, London, and Paris (CzechInvest 2005, 35). While one cannot prove that CzechInvest is responsible for the high levels of FDI in the Czech Republic, its prominent role is evident.

Despite significant differences in the scope of their activities, the services that these FDI agencies provide are free of charge for potential foreign investors, and as state institutions, they are financially supported by their respective governments. Hence, the establishment of a foreign direct investment agency signals at least a minimum level of state commitment to attracting FDI, contributing to the legitimization of FDI practice in a particular postsocialist country.

In addition to establishing professional organizations, states also legitimize FDI by "producing proper outcomes" (Suchman 1995, 600), that is, taking part in FDI transactions. Such involvement was frequent in Central and Eastern Europe, where large-scale privatization and liberalization occurred simultaneously. During privatization, many states granted ownership rights to their citizens and firms via voucher schemes. However, in some cases states themselves (via state agencies) directly negotiated the sale of property to foreign buyers. This happened most frequently with large state monopolies, including public utilities and banking enterprises, because they involved strategic control, national sovereignty, and large sums of money. Table 3.2 lists the first sales to foreigners of formerly state-owned monopolies in telecommunications and banking for the eleven Central and East European countries.

Noting the timing of state actions related to FDI, we can see that in some countries, such as Estonia, Hungary, and Latvia, legitimization of FDI practice started earlier than in others, such as Croatia, Slovakia, and Slovenia, which seem to have been more reluctant to welcome foreign investors in the first decade after 1989. The first sale in the banking sector to foreigners in Slovenia, for example, happened only in 2001, when one-third of the largest Slovenian bank, Nova Ljubljanska Banka, was sold to Belgian KBC Bank (Bandelj 2006).

Why these differences? What determines the timing of the decisions in postsocialist states to act so as to increase the legitimacy of FDI practices? To answer this question, we need to take into account the broader context of transformation to a market-based economy outlined in the previous chapter. In particular, we need to understand the FDI-related actions of postsocialist states as embedded and enmeshed in domestic politics, marked by the struggle between neoliberal ideals and nationalist protectionist sentiments, and by preexisting institutions that shape which strategies political actors take to be more or less plausible. In addition, we need to pay attention to the external transnational pressures on state actions, which arise because of the efforts of these states to join the EU, the power of IMF to influence the scope of reform, and, not the least, the strategies observed in peer countries.

Interests and Politics

If economic behavior is influenced by issues of power and control, as political economists take for granted, then postsocialist states' decisions related to FDI are not a matter of straightforward calculation of the efficiency of various policy alternatives. After all, selling strategic monopolies and attracting FDI might be an obvious choice for a state that needs to service foreign debt or patch a growing budget deficit. In contrast, decisions related to FDI in postsocialist Europe have been plagued by fears of losing control and surrendering national economic (and political) sovereignty. For states emerging from decades-long domination by Soviet rule, allowing domestic assets to be acquired by foreigners has been a particularly sensitive issue. This is how economist Hans-Werner Sinn and colleagues explained the "surprisingly low demand for FDI" in Central and Eastern Europe and the "mixed feelings . . . about the role of FDI" (Sinn et al. 1997, 182). These authors reported that, five years into the transition, Central and East European countries

TABLE 3.2
First Sales in the Telecommunications or Banking Sector to Foreign Investors Prior to 2001

Country	Year	Host Company	Investor (country of origin), Acquired Share
Bulgaria	1997	United Bulgarian Bank	EBRD (UK), 35%, Oppenheimer & Co. (US), 29.63%
Croatia	1999	Hrvatski Telekom	Deutsche Telekom (Germany), 35%
Czech Republic	1999	CSOB Bank	KBC Bank (Belgium), 65.69%
Estonia	1992	Eesti Telefon	Baltic Tele AB (Finland and Sweden), 49%
Hungary	1993	Matav Telecommunications	Deutsche Telekom (Germany) and Ameritech (US), 30.2%
Latvia	1994	Lattelecom	Tilts (Finland), 49%
Lithuania	1998	Lietuvas Telekomas	Ambereleholdings (Finland and Sweden), 60%
Poland	1993	Wielkopolski Bank Kredytowy	EBRD (UK), 28.5%
Romania	1998	RomTelecom[a]	OTEROM (Greece), 21.21%
Slovakia	2000	Slovak Telekom	Deutsche Telekom (Germany), 51%
Slovenia[b]			

[a] In addition, in 1998, Société Général acquired 42.16% of the Romanian Development Bank.
[b] No sale before 2001.

fear that FDI makes a country vulnerable to foreign influence, a partial loss of sovereignty, and that national treasures are sold at low sale prices to the West. Czech Prime Minister Vazlau [sic] Klaus asked foreign investors to wait until privatization is finished; his government has explicitly warned against selling the "family silver." In Hungary, opposition to privatization through foreigners has been growing. Polish privatization Minister Gruszecki warned against giving foreigners too much preference in the privatization process; Former Prime Minister Pawlak argued that he had tried his utmost to prevent foreign investors taking over Polish companies. Polish trade unions accuse foreign investors of employing "slave labor" and taking away the "family silver." (182)

On the other hand, political groups in these countries that took to heart the importance of expedient reform and trusted the invisible hand of the market to optimize the transition argued for the benefits of FDI. The conflict of interests was settled in a game where those groups with the most power and political resources, that is, the ones who ruled the government, ultimately decided the course of action. This is what a conflict perspective on state choice would predict: the extent of legitimization of FDI practice by postsocialist states would reflect the interests of political parties in power. As reported in the previous chapter, postsocialist governments have been more or less eager to restructure their economies, following (or not) a shock-therapy approach. This attitude had implications for their willingness to offer national assets to foreign investors. Governments committed to reform would be more likely to legitimize FDI by selling strategic monopolies to foreign investors, while successors of (insignificantly reformed) Communist parties or nationalist governments would have other political agendas. In fact, during the Mečiar government, Slovakia instituted a law that excluded strategic monopolies from privatization, a law revoked when a new government took charge in 1998. Two more years passed before Slovakia established an official FDI agency and sold the first strategic monopoly to foreigners, the telecommunications purchase by Deutsche Telekom (EBRD 2001b). Slovakia was among the last countries in the region to make such a sale.

In contrast, the Hungarian state adopted a welcoming attitude toward foreign investment early on. During the last months of Hungarian Communism under Károly Grósz, the government showed great interest in attracting foreign investors:

In a press conference on January 31, 1989 . . . the Minister of Industry mentioned a list of 51 Hungarian state enterprises marked for sale to foreign buyers. Within days, reporters were following the story of how Minister of Commerce Tamas Beck was traveling throughout

Western Europe with this same list to look for buyers for enterprises constituting about one-quarter of Hungarian industrial production. (Reported in Stark and Bruszt 1998, 54)

Consistent with this proactive stance, whose proponents saw the sale of state enterprises to foreigners as a sure way to generate hard currency that could be used to reduce foreign debt (Stark and Bruszt 1998, 55), the first Hungarian post-Communist government adopted measures that welcomed foreign investors. The ruling political party from 1990 to 1994, the Hungarian Democratic Forum (MDF), was quite favorable to FDI. Its representatives argued that FDI was good for the country because it created jobs, brought in technological know-how that spreads to domestic firms, and helped integrate Hungary into the world economy (King and Varadi 2002). Moreover, in the words of Peter Boross, Hungarian prime minister in 1994, "FDI improves Hungary's prestige abroad" (*MTI Econews* 1994). This stance on FDI was not shared by all political interest groups (e.g., Workers' Party, Independent Small Holders' Party, and Christian Democratic People's Party), which voiced opposition to FDI. Their arguments were that well-organized multinational corporations had strong lobbying power in Hungary and that MNCs would weaken cultural cohesion in Hungary, usually representing an Americanizing influence on lifestyles by bringing in shopping malls, fast food, and anti-union attitudes (King and Varadi 2002). However, parties opposed to FDI held a minority representation, or were not even in the parliament (for example, the Workers' Party). Hence, the dominant position by the ruling majority—in favor of FDI—prevailed, and the postsocialist Hungarian state quickly established an FDI agency in 1992, and sold a stake in the Matav Telecommunication monopoly to a consortium of German and American investors already in 1993.

Nationalism and FDI

To a large extent, "political resentment" of FDI in the Central and East European countries (Sinn et al. 1997, 179) found fuel in the prevalence of nation-based idioms and nationalist sentiments, constituting a particular political-cultural environment in which state decisions about FDI took place. If economic transactions are not outside of the cultural domain, and can be understood and acted upon only once they are interpreted with available cultural frames, then we would expect nationalist discourse to importantly shape decisions about foreign ownership. Because of their cultural significance, the consequences of FDI efforts for the national economy can be interpreted variously. One of the popular interpretations of FDI in postsocialist Europe has centered on its detrimental effects for a country's national sovereignty; hence the sense that countries should avoid foreign takeovers and privilege domestic ownership.

For example, beginning in mid-2000, decisions about privatization of the banking sector in Slovenia triggered a public debate. The question was whether selling Slovenian strategic assets to foreigners was in the national interest. Many argued for protection from foreign capital and foreign ownership, which were seen as threats to the economic, political, and cultural sovereignty of the Slovenian state. One of the prominent intellectuals who helped draft the first Slovenian constitution claimed, "If the function of foreign capital, as is evident now, is takeover of Slovenia, then it is perfectly clear that such a takeover is detrimental" (qtd. by Natlačen 2002). Thus, proper protections should be put in place, observers argued, to constrain inflows of foreign capital and privilege domestic ownership. For Zoran Janković, then CEO of the biggest retail chain in Slovenia, it was clear what was in the national interest: "I can define national interest: If there are two contenders for a takeover, a domestic and a foreign one, under the same conditions, the domestic contender must get the approval for the takeover." It follows that "it is always better that, given the same conditions, [ownership] goes to Janez instead of Johann or Giovanni" (reported by Križnik 2002).[1] Most often this "protectionist" stance was justified by references to Slovenia's past and, in particular, the fact that until 1991 Slovenians had never had their own independent nation-state and thus were "servants to foreign masters," an idiom perpetuated in Slovenian literature and poetry. Calls for "a right dose of healthy nationalism" were made and for "strategic support of domestic capital" (Seljak 2002).

Appeals to protect national ownership were present in other countries as well. As reported in chapter 2, in an international survey that included questions on foreign ownership, citizens of Central and East European countries were significantly more likely to say that ownership should be protected from foreign influences and that domestic economic actors should be given priority. By 2000, all Central and East European countries had in place protections against foreign ownership of land (EBRD 2000b). Nevertheless, it may be that in those countries where nation-building accompanied the economic transformation, and, indeed, was integral to collapse of Communism—Estonia, Croatia, Latvia, Lithuania, Slovakia, and Slovenia—ceteris paribus, efforts to legitimize FDI practice were less intense than in other countries with a longer history of national sovereignty.

Institutional Path-Dependence

When considering the forces that shape actions of postsocialist states, we also need to pay attention to the path dependency of institutional choices. No institutionalization happens de novo, on a blank slate. Rather, "institutions are historically rooted and there is a great deal of path dependency in the way various institutional components evolve" (North 1990;

Steinmo, Thelen, and Longstreth 1992; Thelen 1999i; Hollingsworth 2003, 105). Hence, as many observers who argued for the gradualist transition to market emphasized, our understanding of the institutionalization of markets in Central and Eastern Europe needs to take into account the institutional configurations of the socialist system and how previously existing rules and practices were incorporated into novel institutional arrangements.

In fact, almost all research in sociology and political science on postsocialist transformations recognizes some form of path dependency (Seleny 1991; Stark 1992; Hausner, Jessop, and Nielsen 1995; Campbell and Pedersen 1996; Szelényi and Kostello 1996; Róna-Tas 1998; Smith and Pickles 1998; Stark and Bruszt 1998; Ekiert and Hanson 2003). This literature most often focuses on the ways in which structures inherited from before and during the socialist period influence the transformation processes, so that transformations are incremental and often reproduce existing institutions (Szelényi and Kostello 1996). This may be because "institutional legacies of the past limit the range of current possibilities and/or options in institutional innovation" (Hausner, Jessop, and Nielson 1995, 6). Because previously existing institutions, formal and informal, constrain the range of institutional alternatives from which actors choose, actors are locked into certain courses of action that may be difficult to reverse (North 1990).[2]

Others note that the conception of path dependency does not condemn actors to simple repetition or retrogression (Stark 1992; Stark and Bruszt 1998; Spicer, McDermott, and Kogut 2000). It is unrealistic to expect that in the presence of a significant external shock, such as the revolutions of 1989, actors will stay locked into certain paths of behavior. Nevertheless, it is likely that the established understandings of how the world works and institutions that cement these cultural accounts may leave a mark on the creation of subsequent institutional forms. In this sense previous institutions structure the trajectory of future change. When adoption of new rules is being considered, existing logics of action set a range of options that are available and considered appropriate (Dobbin 1994b). Hence, novel economic processes, such as FDI in formerly socialist countries, will be predicated upon the previously legitimated understandings even when institutional rules that created those understandings are no longer in place.

In light of this discussion, legitimization of a novel economic practice, such as FDI, will depend on two kinds of institutional path-dependence. First, it is likely that new institutions aligned with a market-based economy will be legitimized earlier in those economies that embarked on reform of their socialist command systems before 1989. The decisions to encourage foreign investment transactions after the fall of Communist

regimes might be dependent on the place of market-based activity in socialist economies. Socialist Yugoslavia, Hungary, Poland, and Estonia
(Watson 1994) experimented with decentralization of economic activity
before the fall of their Communist regimes. Such openness to markets,
albeit limited, and practical experience with market-based activity should
expedite market reform after the collapse of Communist regimes. Legitimization of FDI can be considered part and parcel of these efforts. Because of path dependency, we should see it being embraced more readily
in those countries that started reforming their economies before 1989.

Second, because of institutional complementarities (Amable 2000; Hall
and Soskice 2001), path dependency may have its effects also because
FDI legitimization efforts are aligned with other kinds of institutions that
are being set up. Privatization, that is, turning collective ownership into
private ownership, as one of the key institutional changes set in motion
after 1989, is likely to have an impact on many policy decisions. In particular, the consequences for FDI are quite different if a state willingly makes
its assets available for purchase through open auctions and direct sales to
anyone who offers the highest price, than if it encourages insider management and employee buyouts or allows assets to be grabbed by the former
Communist elite who convert their political capital into economic wealth.
If states harbor insider preferences, they will also consider the inclusion
of foreign investors in national economies a less appealing alternative.
The preference for insiders in the privatization process, most prominent
in those countries that opted for management-employee buyouts, such as
Slovenia or Croatia, should be associated with less eager legitimization
of FDI.

Transnational Pressures

In the previous three sections I have tried to show that actions of postsocialist states are deeply intertwined with domestic political processes, and
grounded in newly emergent but also path-dependent understandings of
what is appropriate economic action in the period after a command economy. But it is important to move up the level of analysis and consider
how FDI legitimization efforts by postsocialist states are shaped by *supranational* forces. Work of Stanford sociologist John Meyer and his colleagues emphasizes that

> [nation-states] are more or less *exogenously* constructed entities—
> the many individuals both inside and outside the state who engage
> in state formation and policy formulation are enactors of scripts [sup-
> plied by global culture and associational processes] rather than they
> are self-directed actors. (Meyer et al. 1997, 150; emphasis added)

Consequently, state action may not be primarily oriented toward efficiency but instead toward external legitimacy; state actors may make choices that are defined as most legitimate, that is, those that enhance the cultural standing and membership of a particular society in the community of nation-states (McNeely 1995).

More generally, as proposed in a widely influential article by Paul DiMaggio and Walter Powell (1983), coercive, mimetic, and normative pressures from the external environment influence action. Actors adopt strategies of action because (*a*) they are influenced by powerful organizations that impose particular structural and cultural forms (referred to as coercive isomorphism), or (*b*) they mimic the behavior of their peers (mimetic isomorphism), or (*c*) they yield to pressures from, and adopt guidelines provided by, professional organizations (normative isomorphism). Although DiMaggio and Powell constructed their theory with organizations as actors in mind, their framework is also applicable to states (cf. Henisz, Zelner, and Guillén 2005). For example, states adopt certain strategies because they need to meet the requirements for membership in international institutions. As summarized in table 2.3, all of the Central and East European states under scrutiny in this analysis sooner or later applied for membership in the EU, and this required aligning their institutions with *acquis communautaire*, common European legislation. They all signed IMF Article VIII (IMF 2005a), which required liberalization of financial capital flows. Many relied on loans and concessions by the IMF and EBRD, and underwent structural changes as a quid pro quo for financial assistance. Furthermore, in many of these countries the World Bank's Foreign Investment Advisory Service (FIAS) was commissioned to write reports and make recommendations for providing incentives and lifting administrative barriers to foreign investors. In these ways international institutions either (*a*) coercively required liberalization to foreign capital as a condition of membership or financial assistance, or (*b*) promoted neoliberal development policies and legitimized the attraction of foreign investors as a desirable strategy. It is likely that yielding to international pressures meant opening up economic sectors to foreign investors that postsocialist states would have preferred to keep in domestic hands. After all, even in the capitalist West many "strategic" sectors are retained in largely domestic ownership, for example, German banks, French telecommunications, and American utility companies.

Besides coercive and normative pressures, Central and East European states may have also adopted certain action strategies because they imitated the behavior of their peer states in the region. Mimetic behavior requires that actors perceive themselves as similar to those whom they emulate (Strang and Meyer 1993). Although individual postsocialist countries differ from one another and have idiosyncratic characteristics, because of their common Communist past and more or less simultaneous extrication from it, they are all grouped—and they group themselves—into one single category, the "East European transition countries." Following the revolutions of 1989, observers and international media reported on "Eastern Europe," not so much on Estonia or Romania or Slovakia. Most explicitly, with the "Eastern Enlargement," the EU decided to treat postsocialist applicants as one big category and did not admit individual countries on a case-by-case basis. Thus, individual postsocialist countries would look to each other, compare themselves to one another, and be treated by the international community as belonging to one category.

The consolidation of the "East European" category encouraged mimetic behavior between these states, something that came across in my interviews with officials in FDI agencies. My respondents frequently described their country's FDI strategies (or their agency's activities) in comparison to those in other postsocialist countries. Respondents demonstrated great awareness of what others were doing to attract FDI. These officials began with the stipulation that investors were interested in the East European region and would choose between individual countries. This meant that the FDI agencies in these countries saw other countries (other FDI agencies) as their competitors, and wanted to match or surpass their efforts.

In sum, state action is structured by supranational pressures in many ways. Following this reasoning, we expect to see that the decisions of postsocialist states to implement activities that increase the legitimacy of FDI will be significantly shaped by the process of EU integration, participation in IMF programs, and FDI legitimization activities in peer states.

Economics of State Actions

In keeping with the conception of embedded economies, the previous sections outlined the social-structural, political, and cultural foundations of economic policymaking. Nevertheless, it is important to consider the alternative explanation that ignores embeddedness and focuses on the economics of state actions. From the instrumentalist perspective, which holds that universal economic laws structure social systems, all action evolves toward solutions that maximize utility. Thus, in the case of policymaking, action aims at maximization of "the common good." Nation-states, as real, rational, and purposive actors, make choices about FDI with a goal of ultimate efficiency. They take actions that will most likely reduce the economic costs relative to the benefits gained. Thus, the instrumentalist perspective stipulates that the establishment of FDI agencies and the sale of strategic monopolies happen when state actors judge that these acts will be most efficient for the national economy. This may be when the state needs money to patch its budget deficit or service its external debt or when the economy is in a poor shape and needs additional capital for growth. This means that regardless of prevailing institutions, it is really economic necessity that is key in determining state actions.

Indeed, most analysts of the Hungarian transition suggest that the country opened its state-owned enterprises for sale to foreigners precisely because it faced a huge external debt and needed to repay it (Stark and Bruszt 1998; King 2001). However, if we compare Hungary with other East European countries, we can see that large external debts (which many of these countries started to accumulate after the 1973 oil crisis) were dealt with in a variety of ways. As Dora Piroska summarizes:

> Poland successfully lobbied for debt relief at the Paris Club, Bulgaria defaulted on its foreign obligations, Slovenia managed to reduce its share of the Yugoslav foreign debt by a relatively high portion, while Hungary refinanced the whole part of its giant debt in due time. . . . [The] Baltic states denied any sort of Soviet debt financing. (2002, 2–3)

Debt management was probably most drastic in Romania, where Ceauşescu decided that the way to repay debt was to ration food and fuel, slash vital imports, and export everything possible to earn hard currency. By 1989, Romania indeed had paid off a foreign debt of about $10 billion, but at what price? Ceauşescu's choice of foreign debt management, in no way inevitable, was devastating for the Romanian people and catastrophic for the economy. Moreover, despite scholars' claim that Hungary needed to service its foreign debt by opening its door to foreign investors, early in the transition period some domestic and international observers argued that "the most valuable form of 'aid' for Hungary would be *debt relief*" (Hare and Révész 1992, 228; emphasis added).

Therefore, to test economic efficiency arguments we need to conduct empirical analysis that includes a sample of postsocialist countries to determine whether, *ceteris paribus*, economic factors, such as foreign debt, are significantly linked to legitimization efforts of FDI practice. The constructivist expectation is that state decisions will not be straightforwardly related to "objective," "unilateral," and "absolute" economic necessity. While economic conditions are certainly relevant, ideas shape the perception of their importance and plausible solutions (Campbell 1998), and struggles for political power put them high or low on the agenda of state priorities.

Empirical Analysis of FDI Legitimization

Explicating the social-structural, cultural, and political embeddedness of state action, I identified several factors that have a potential influence on the extent to which postsocialist states engage in the legitimization of

FDI practice. In brief, these can be clustered in three broad categories: international pressures, domestic political and cultural forces, and institutional path-dependency. In addition, we should consider relevant factors that underpin the economic necessity of state choices. The goal of the empirical analysis is to investigate whether these factors were consequential for the legitimization of FDI practices in the eleven postsocialist states in the first decade after the fall of Communist regimes (1990–2000). As a conservative measure of the extent of legitimization of FDI practice (as opposed to formal rule), which is the dependent variable to be explained in this analysis, I constructed an indicator that scores from 0 to 2 and incorporates the two previously discussed practical actions of postsocialist states with regards to FDI: establishing an FDI agency and privatizing strategic monopolies by means of sales to foreigners. More details about the operationalization of variables, data sources, and analytic technique are provided in the appendix. Table 3.3 reports the results, which strongly support the embedded nature of economic policy.

If states are instrumental actors maximizing efficiency, FDI-related decisions should reflect economic conditions in postsocialist states. Countries and time periods with greater economic welfare (higher levels of GDP per capita) should exhibit lower legitimization, while greater foreign debt and greater budget deficits should increase legitimization efforts. However, the analyses (which check for the robustness of results using various model specifications appropriate for the time series data structure and for selection effects) show the contrary: objective economic conditions have weak relations to legitimization of FDI practice. Instead, internal and external social and political factors account best for the state's attitudes toward FDI.

The set of external pressures factors shows that states are influenced by the transnational environment in the choices they make about FDI. As years pass, and more and more postsocialist countries establish FDI agencies and begin selling their strategic monopolies to foreigners, any particular state is going to strengthen its FDI legitimization efforts in response to peer pressure.[3] Countries converge in their legitimization of liberal markets over time, a result consistent with the spread of neoliberalism, advocated as the appropriate development policy by international elites during this period.

Moreover, the EU integration process exerts a significant effect on the FDI legitimization efforts of postsocialist states. The years after the countries sign the EU agreement are associated with higher legitimization scores. As noted in chapter 2, through various instruments and requirements to adopt EU legislation (*acquis communautaire*), the EU has affected the development of market-based institutions in postsocialist countries. Indeed by making openness to foreign capital a condition of membership, the EU has exerted significant pressures on postsocialist states to commit to FDI in practice, not just on paper.

TABLE 3.3
Predictors of the Extent of Legitimization of FDI Practice by Postsocialist States, 1990–2000

	Model 1 PCSE[a]	Model 2 PCSE	Model 3 PCSE	Model 4 PCSE	Model 5 FE[b]	Model 6 2SLS[c]
Economic necessity						
GDP/capita	-.065	-.003	-.034	-.070	-.275	-.225
	(-0.37)	(-0.04)	(-0.59)	(-1.05)	(-0.78)	(-0.74)
Foreign debt	-.003	.001	.001	.001	.003	.001
	(-0.76)	(0.14)	(0.70)	(0.65)	(0.66)	(0.67)
Budget deficit	-.002	-.006	.009	.010	-.022	.018
	(-0.09)	(-0.27)	(0.41)	(0.45)	(-1.14)	(1.04)
External pressures						
EU Agreement		.347***	.278***	.253***	.312***	.279***
		(5.45)	(5.09)	(4.03)	(3.86)	(3.11)
IMF Program		.045	.041	.058	.124	-.046
		(0.62)	(0.70)	(0.89)	(1.00)	(-0.09)
Mimetic isomorphism		.465***	.512***	.471***	.431***	.497***
		(7.52)	(11.10)	(6.68)	(3.83)	(5.10)
Political/cultural forces						
Political commitment to market reform			.356**	.208*	.239*	.239*
			(2.23)	(2.10)	(2.36)	(2.35)
Left government			-.101	-.083	-.186	-.095
			(-0.94)	(-0.74)	(-1.49)	(-0.88)
Newly established state			-.285**	-.283**		-.299*
			(-2.81)	(-2.80)		(-2.23)
Institutional path-dependence						
Insider preference in privatization			-.357***	-.323***		-.336***
			(-5.23)	(-3.63)		(-3.45)
Reform before 1989			.234*	.233*		.292^
			(2.07)	(1.99)		(1.67)

TABLE 3.3 (cont.)

Predictors of the Extent of Legitimization of FDI Practice by Postsocialist States, 1990–2000

	Model 1 PCSE[a]	Model 2 PCSE	Model 3 PCSE	Model 4 PCSE	Model 5 FE[b]	Model 6 2SLS[c]
Controls						
Previous FDI				.074 (0.76)	.109 (0.93)	.066 (0.51)
Time trend[d]	.208*** (6.03)					
Country fixed effects					Included	
Constant	.504 (0.38)	1.156*** (7.51)	1.849*** (6.49)	2.007*** (7.74)	3.106 (0.99)	3.869 (1.43)
R^2	.130	.166	.643	.645	.814	.738
N	97	92	92	92	92	92

Note: t-values in parentheses.

[a] Ordinary least-squares estimation with panel corrected standard errors and autocorrelation (AR1) adjustment.

[b] Fixed effects specification with HC3 standard errors; since it is equivalent to adding the set of country dummies to the analysis, it must omit all time-invariant variables from the analysis to avoid perfect collinearity.

[c] Two-stage least squares with robust standard errors: Instrumented: EU agreement, IMF program; instruments: GDP/cap, foreign debt, budget deficit, mimetic isomorphism, political commitment to market reform, left government, newly established state, insider preference in privatization, reform before 1989, previous FDI, GDP/growth, and share of other countries bound by EU agreement.

[d] Because time trend and mimetic isomorphism are correlated at .934 level, combining the two in the analysis creates disturbances due to multicollinearity. Hence, for Models 2–6, mimetic isomorphism variable performs the function of a time trend.

^p < .10. * p < .05. ** p < .01. *** p < .001. (Two-tailed tests.)

On the other hand, the results show that being under the influence of an IMF program, that is, receiving a loan from the IMF and agreeing to the IMF's conditions, does not have significant effects on FDI legitimization activities, although the sign of the coefficient is in the expected positive direction. It is important to note that, first and foremost, the IMF "assists countries in restoring economic stability" (IMF 2006), which means that the IMF's requirements in transition countries usually involve "basic" corrective policies of stabilization and privatization, and do not specify that borrowers show actual (as opposed to professions on paper) commitment to opening borders to foreign capital.

As for the influence of domestic politics on FDI legitimization efforts, political commitment to market reform by governments in power proves to be quite important. Those postsocialist governments that focused on market reform and economic liberalization were more likely to legitimize FDI in the first decade after 1989. It is important to note that because of the plurality of political interests springing up in postsocialist Europe, parties and party coalitions in favor of market reform may have been of left or right ideological persuasion (the correlation between left ideological orientation and proreform political commitment is a very weak −.13), which attests to the observation that favoring market reform is not necessarily a component of a rightist or leftist political persuasion. Some scholars might argue that left-leaning governments would halt the legitimization of FDI, but the results do not support this claim. Rather, they show that it is not the ideological orientation of the government but its pragmatic stance toward fostering market transition that matters for legitimizing FDI practice.

Further, we see that ideas and cultural understandings play a role in economic decisions of the state. In particular, patriotic sentiments and nationalist discourse is influential in postsocialist Europe. Since the prevalence of nationalism is extremely hard to measure, I try to capture it with a proxy that indicates whether a country under consideration is a newly established state. This choice is based on the reasoning that those countries for which the breakup of socialism also meant the breakup of multinational federations engaged in nation-building projects, which were often also integral to their extrication from Communist regimes. Indeed, the results show that, all else being equal, newly established states are not as willing to offer their national assets to foreign ownership or control as states with longer histories of independence.[4]

The analysis also tries to capture the path dependency of institutions. Arguments about the path-dependent nature of postsocialist transformations abound, but it is really an empirical question: Which old institutions will have an impact on future outcomes, and in what fashion and for how long will their impact persist? In the present analysis, I check whether those countries that embarked on significant reform before 1989 were more open to decisions in line with market liberalization. As the results show, there is some tentative evidence that this was the case, although this factor is sensitive to different model specifications. We should keep in mind that reforms during socialism were of different kinds, and that some may have been more in keeping with establishing a hybrid socialist market economy than full-fledged liberal markets. Hence, even if a country were open to market reform before 1989, the speed with which it embraced liberalization afterwards may have varied. Reform before 1989 could have led states to expedite liberalization or to gradually continue with what they had started. Consequently, the relationship between previous reform experience and subsequent legitimization of FDI is not as strong as one might expect.

On the other hand, institutional complementarities have a strong and robust effect. Those countries that adopted policies that allowed outsiders to participate in privatization, also more readily established FDI agencies and decided early to sell strategic monopolies to foreigners. In other words, the institutionalized preference for insiders during the privatization process made the presence of foreign investors in national economies a less plausible and accessible economic alternative in the reorganization of economies in postsocialist Europe. Privatization policy decisions adopted right after the exogenous shock of Communism's collapse set grounds for the subsequent state choices about economic development, which turned out to be largely consistent with those initial decisions.

The explanation of the weakness of traditional economic factors deserves further elaboration. It would be inappropriate to interpret these results as saying that economic conditions are irrelevant to state decisions about FDI. Foreign debts, economic decline, and budget deficits are issues seriously considered by any government. However, what this analysis suggests is that there is no general pattern in how these issues are approached by individual postsocialist states. That is, economic conditions are not sufficiently objective to prompt states to respond in a uniform and unilateral manner. Rather, because they are socially constituted, economic decisions play out differently in different political and cultural environments. For example, the need to patch budget deficits is a strong argument that political elites make in favor of sales of strategic monopolies to foreigners. After all, these sales involve substantial amounts of money that represent revenues for the state, and many of these states are under pressures from the EU or the IMF to lower their budget deficits. Nevertheless, results presented here suggest that the size of the budget deficit is not the immediate, and unquestionable, reason for offering domestic assets to foreign investors. But it can certainly be a very compelling justification to do so for those interest groups who see selling to foreigners as being in their political or ideological interest. That is, interpretation of economic conditions, the setting of priorities, and visions of effective strategies of action all happen in a political and cultural context.

• • •

FDI in Central and Eastern Europe is a socially constituted process. It is instituted and legitimized by postsocialist states. As such it is a political and cultural project: path dependent and embedded in domestic politics, nationalist discourse, and supranational pressures. To what extent actions of postsocialist states influence *actual FDI flows* to Central and Eastern Europe after 1989 is a related but, nonetheless, quite different question. Are institutionalization and legitimization efforts consequential for the size of the FDI flows to postsocialist countries? The next part addresses this point directly. But first, let's review in more detail the FDI trends in individual countries.

FDI Trends since 1989

The Central and East European region attracted virtually no foreign investment before the fall of the Berlin Wall in 1989 because of the closed economic policy of the communist regimes. As part of their socialist reform, Hungary, Poland, and former Yugoslavia put in place laws that allowed formation of joint ventures with foreign firms after 1985. By 1988 these states, followed by the Baltic countries that were moving in parallel with perestroika in the Soviet Union, legalized full foreign ownership of firms. Czechoslovakia, Bulgaria, and Romania enacted such laws only after the fall of Communist regimes. De facto liberalization happened by 1989, when we observe first flows of FDI to the region (see table 1.2).

In the first few years after 1989 the regional inflows were quite minimal compared to global FDI. The mean inflow for the countries for which 1990 data are available (Bulgaria, the Czech Republic, Hungary, Poland, and Slovenia) was only $7 per capita in 1990. With global FDI expanding, 1995 marked the year of the first substantial surge of foreign investment in the Central and East European region; flows grew by 80 percent over the prior year, amounting to $108 per capita on average for the eleven countries studied here.

The initial growth trend leveled off somewhat by 2000 and picked up again by 2002. The average per capita FDI inflow increased to $191 in 1998, subsided slightly to $185 in 2000, and increased again to $315 in 2002. In absolute terms, by 2000, the eleven countries analyzed here attracted about $100 billion in FDI stock, while this figure was up to almost $180 billion in 2003. As a proportion of entire economies, on average, FDI stock represented only about 2 percent of GDP in 1990, but ten years later this figure stood at 27 percent, which was above the average for developing and developed countries. By 2004, the average share of FDI stock in GDP for these Central and East European countries hit 39 percent, which is almost twice as much as in the developed and developing world in total, and much higher than in China, one of today's premier foreign investment locations, which accumulated 15 percent of FDI stock as a share in 2004 GDP (UNCTAD 2006). In terms of sectoral composition, most FDI in Central and Eastern Europe has been in categories specified by their two-digit level of ISIC classification as trade; financial intermediaries, transport, storage, and communications; and business activities. Among the top fifty world MNCs in 2000 (UNCTAD 2002), Vodafone, Shell, Philip Morris, Volkswagen, Siemens, Nestlé, IBM, Unilever, and Philips have presence in multiple postsocialist countries. Among the financial institutions, German insurance company Allianz, French bank Société Général, American Citibank, Austrian Creditanstalt and Raffeisen banks, as well as Dutch ING and ABN Amro banks are all strongly represented in Central and Eastern Europe. (See table A.4 in the appendix for more detail.)

Despite a general growth trend across Central and Eastern Europe, individual country trajectories exemplify a variety of paths, differing in the timing of the initial increase in FDI inflows, and in the size and frequency of the peaks in the series (figure 3.1). Hungary, for example, has a most noticeable increase in FDI inflows right after 1989. With an average inflow at $7 per capita across the five postsocialist European countries for which 1990 data are available, Hungary attracted $30. However, after 1998 inflows to Hungary have stagnated at the regional average level.

Like Hungary, the Czech Republic, Estonia, and Latvia already recorded comparatively high FDI inflows a few years into the transition period. In the Czech Republic, inflows have continued to increase, putting this country at the top of Central and East European FDI destinations. In 2002, the Czech Republic received record yearly inflows of almost $8.5 billion. Poland has also attracted significant FDI in absolute numbers because of its sheer size (i.e., almost 40 million inhabitants). But measured as per capita inflow, or stock as a percentage share in GDP, Polish inward FDI has stayed below the regional average throughout this period. Among those countries that have experienced small FDI inflows in the early period but were able to attract above-average inflows later are Croatia and Slovakia. In particular, Slovakia registered a major increase in FDI after 1999. Several other countries, including Bulgaria, Lithuania, and Romania, stagnated at the bottom for several years before they showed any growth in

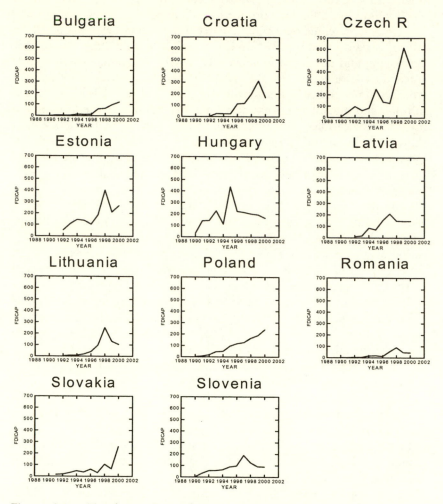

Figure 3.1.   Trends in FDI Inflows in Individual Postsocialist Countries, 1990–2000

FDI inflows. Slovenia, the wealthiest among these eleven Central and East European countries, was right at the average FDI levels up until 1997. For the next few years its inflows remained substantially under the regional average, but picked up in 2001 and 2002 because of sizable banking privatizations to foreigners and a foreign takeover of a major pharmaceuticals company (Bandelj 2006). In 2003 and 2004, the flows were again below the regional average.

How can we explain these varied levels of FDI in individual Central and East European countries and within countries over time?

Explaining FDI Inflows across Countries over Time

Traditional economic explanations of FDI highlight the importance of economic prosperity and political stability, which create incentives for profit-seeking investors. This accords with shock-therapy economic prescriptions that emphasize the withdrawal of the state from the economy so that the invisible hand of the market can create an appropriate incentive structure for market players who want to engage in cross-border transactions. In contrast, I argue that FDI is not a mere matter of risk-and-return calculations at the discretion of investor companies, which simply wait for the postsocialist states to stop interfering with the economy. Rather, FDI is a socially constituted relational process that reflects negotiations between investors and hosts, and thus heavily depends on the institutionalization and legitimization efforts of postsocialist states.

Institutional Foundations of FDI Flows

As argued previously, one of the key institutions to foster FDI in Central and Eastern Europe after 1989 was the establishment of property rights as a precondition of market exchange. In the absence of clearly defined property rights, buyers would have no guarantee of de facto control over purchased assets, and they would most likely not want to engage in such transactions. Moreover, the larger the private sector in a particular country, the more opportunities for foreigners to acquire assets there. We should see a positive correlation between the size of the private sector in a country and FDI inflows.

In addition to private property rights, states also need to show political commitment to building markets, which will result in the implementation of other rules and laws governing private sector activity that are necessary for fully functioning markets. Based on this perspective, market activity, including FDI transactions, is not a result of arbitrage outside of an institutional context, but deeply dependent on the institutional order that sustains markets. Similarly, the proreform commitment of postsocialist states is likely to have an effect on potential investors, which might prefer states that in light of tremendous uncertainty following the collapse of communism show a commitment to instituting rules and policies that govern private sector activity, and oversee their implementation. Hence, political commitment to market reform by ruling governments should have a positive effect on the proliferation of FDI because it facilitates both domestic and foreign actors' involvement in FDI transactions.

The role of postsocialist states in legitimating the practice of FDI as an appropriate means of economic engagement in a market-based economy will also matter for the proliferation of FDI markets. If individuals have a natural propensity to exchange, then legitimization processes are irrelevant, because as soon as economic conditions are stable enough and promise good returns, agents will engage in FDI exchanges. However, if individuals need to learn FDI behavior, and need to be socialized into the benefits of open-market rationality, then professional organizations (i.e., FDI Agencies) and powerful institutional actors (i.e., states) will need to disseminate desirable practices and set examples by producing desirable outcomes for others to emulate.

In the case of FDI, as discussed in the first part of this chapter, establishment of FDI agencies and states' decisions to start selling strategic national assets to foreigners signal an important shift in the state's official attitudes toward economic liberalization and, importantly, toward foreign investment *practice*. This influences other business actors in the home economy as well as potential foreign investors. Once a precedent is set in a highly visible transaction that legitimizes selling to foreigners by a powerful actor such as the state, other domestic business actors in that country more readily see FDI as an appropriate and desirable economic strategy and engage in market transactions with foreign investors as well, contributing to a higher volume of FDI inflows. In addition, legitimization also affects foreign investors. Recognition that a country offers its strategic assets for sale to foreign buyers, an event often internationally publicized because of the great monetary value of such transactions, highlights the country as an investment destination in the eyes of potential buyers and encourages them to look for opportunities in that country. Furthermore, having an established FDI agency helps increase FDI because the agency acts as a middleman and provides help to foreign investors to realize their investment goals. In addition, the agencies' primary objective is to promote their country as an investment location and actively search for potential investors. Based on all of these consequences, we can expect that the more extensively postsocialist states legitimize FDI practice, the greater the subsequent FDI inflows.

Investors' Risk and Return Considerations as Determinants of FDI

Other research privileges the importance of investors' risk-and-return considerations as determinants of FDI. From this instrumentalist view, it is the incentive structure for rational exchange that is crucial for the proliferation of FDI markets, not the involvement of states. Provided that prices are liberalized and private property rights are quickly allocated to efficiency-maximizing economic agents, foreign investors will engage in transactions in Central and Eastern Europe by identifying and pursuing those possibilities (investment options) that maximize their profitability.

The first chapter reviews the research that focuses on FDI as a matter of risk-and-return calculations by foreign investors, research that offers many economic and political factors that will encourage or deter MNCs from any specific foreign investment. Based on this research, we should expect both economic potential and economic risk significantly to impact the proliferation of FDI exchanges. Most commonly used as a general indicator of economic performance, GDP per capita also captures the size of the potential market for a foreign investor (Chakrabarti 2001, 96). The economic argument stresses the importance of incentives for market exchange. *Ceteris paribus*, if it is objective economic conditions promising high returns that attract investors, then higher GDP levels should encourage more FDI. Alternatively, if inflation is high and prices significantly increase from year to year, this is a sign of instability that signals higher risks to potential investors. Thus, a higher inflation rate should be negatively associated with FDI inflows.

There are several other factors that investors consider important when making investment decisions, including policy environment, corruption, and other economic factors that affect the general levels of risk. For investors' reference, professional agencies, such as Institutional Investor or Euromoney, compile credit ratings for individual countries, which indicate the expert assessed risk of default on investment for a country. These credit ratings include not only economic potential for revenues but also an evaluation of the general investment climate and thus provide an overall assessment of country risk. Based on the profit maximization thesis, we should expect that the lower the assessed risk (and the higher the credit rating score), the greater will be the FDI inflow.

In addition to economic factors, political economists have suggested that risk-and-return calculations of investors also include considerations of political risk (Kobrin 1982, 1984; Gastanga, Nugent, and Pashamova 1998; Delios and Henisz 2000; Henisz 2000, 2002; Wei 2000; Henisz and Delios 2001; Li and Resnick 2003; Jensen 2006). In Central and Eastern Europe political risks could be gauged by the ideology of the government in power. Investors may tend to avoid countries where (more or less reformed) post-Communist parties return to power because they pose greater risk of state involvement in economic activity and policies that might hurt MNCs. In addition, low levels of democracy may be associated with lower levels of FDI. As researchers argue, weak democracy implies weak property-rights protection (North and Weingast 1989; Olson 1993, 2000; Bates 2001; Li and Resnick 2003) and a lesser commitment to market-friendly policies (Jensen 2006). Both would discourage MNCs from investing in weakly democratic countries.

Furthermore, signing the EU agreements may signal lower political risks to investors, and opportunities for higher returns associated with access to the whole European market once full membership is in place. This should make those countries that sign the EU agreements early more attractive to foreign investors. Likewise, involvement of the IMF when a country is under its loan program could signal to investors lower risks because these programs are expected to improve both the current account balance and the overall balance of payments in a country (Haque and Khan 1998). Alternatively, as Jensen finds, participation in IMF programs could have a negative impact because "IMF conditionality might cause an underprovision of market-enhancing public goods" (2006, 144).

Empirical Analysis of Overtime FDI Flows

We can assess the role of different explanatory factors by conducting multivariate regression analysis, which allows us to simultaneously test the influence of multiple factors on the outcome of interest. In particular, I am interested in comparing the relative importance of economic incentives that structure the risk-and-return calculations of profit-maximizing investors (as FDI determinants identified by the instrumentalist perspective) with the institutional foundations of FDI, and the different ways postsocialist states create FDI markets in Central and Eastern Europe in the first decade after 1989. (To account for the industrial structure of the economy, which necessarily has an impact on foreign direct investment because foreign investors are interested in the services and manufacturing sectors and not in agriculture, a variable that captures the size of the agricultural sector is added as a control, with the expectation that countries and time periods with greater employment in agriculture will receive less FDI.) The appendix provides details of data, measurement, and analysis. The results are reported in table 3.4.

The first model presented in table 3.4 examines the thesis that FDI proliferates when the "objective" incentive structure is put in place for actors to conduct exchanges in the market, provided that private property rights are allocated. As expected, the results show that the greater the privatization of the economy, the higher the FDI, affirming that instituting private property rights is a necessary condition for economic liberalization. On the other hand, the results show that the influence of economic factors, in particular of economic potential as measured by GDP per capita and economic stability, as captured by the level of inflation, is not significant.[5] Because a country's credit rating reflects the expert-assessed risk in a country based on a combination of all relevant economic factors that may

TABLE 3.4
Predictors of FDI Inflows over Time, 1990–2000

	Model 1 PCSE[a]	Model 2 PCSE	Model 3 PCSE	Model 4 PCSE	Model 5 FE[b]	Model 6 2SLS[c]
Economic incentives						
GDP/capita	.027	.044	.141^		.023	.154
	(0.32)	(0.59)	(1.79)		(0.15)	(1.23)
Inflation	-.002	-.003	-.003		-.004	-.001
	(-0.62)	(-1.12)	(-1.42)		(-1.39)	(-0.24)
Country credit rating				.014^		
				(1.66)		
Institutional foundations						
Extent of privatization	.020*	.248**	.198**	.191**	.246**	.135
	(2.26)	(2.90)	(2.40)	(2.23)	(2.40)	(0.71)
Legitimization of FDI practice		.426***	.418***	.375***	.363***	.610**
		(3.46)	(3.74)	(3.30)	(3.67)	(3.25)
Political commitment to market reform	.696**	.880***	.918***	.676**	1.449**	
	(2.99)	(3.91)	(3.82)	(2.41)	(2.85)	
Controls						
Democratization			-.191*	-.227**	.103	-.731**
			(-2.06)	(-2.42)	(0.93)	(-2.69)
Left government			-.241^	-.153	.120	-.170
			(-1.95)	(-1.19)	(0.78)	(-0.83)
EU agreement			.101	.102	.117	.173
			(0.87)	(0.77)	(1.11)	(0.75)

Table 3.4 (*cont.*)
Predictors of FDI Inflows over Time, 1990–2000

	Model 1 PCSE[a]	Model 2 PCSE	Model 3 PCSE	Model 4 PCSE	Model 5 FE[b]	Model 6 2SLS[c]
Controls						
IMF program			.347^	.321^	.184	.038
			(1.89)	(1.84)	(1.02)	(0.17)
Share of labor in agriculture	−.491**	−.410***	−.518***	−.449***	−.931***	−.613***
	(−2.64)	(−3.44)	(−4.92)	(−3.70)	(−3.48)	(−4.90)
Time trend	.096^	.035	.171	.194		.145
	(1.64)	(0.75)	(1.47)	(1.52)		(0.79)
Country fixed effects					Included	
Constant	2.786***	3.667***	4.787***	4.393***	3.903***	7.796***
	(8.96)	(11.69)	(8.69)	(5.96)	(4.72)	(5.48)
R^2	.471	.616	.697	.678	.862	.705
N	88	88	88	86	88	88

Note: t-values in parentheses.

[a] Ordinary least-squares estimation with panel corrected standard errors and autocorrelation (AR1) adjustment.

[b] Fixed effects specification with HC3 standard errors; does not include the time trend because with such low degrees of freedom the model with both country fixed effects and year variable is overdetermined and cannot be estimated.

[c] Two-stage least squares with robust errors: Instrumented: privatization, legitimization, political commitment to market reform, democratization; instruments: GDP/cap, inflation, left government, EU agreement, IMF program, percentage labor in agriculture, time trend and country fixed effects.

^p < .10. * p < .05. ** p < .01. *** p < .001. (Two-tailed tests.)

affect default on investment, I also present a model that includes a country risk credit rating.[6] The relationship between FDI and country risk rating is in the hypothesized positive direction, but it is not statistically significant, and explains only a minor proportion of the variance.

In contrast, the institutionalization and legitimization of FDI by postsocialist states turns out to be highly consequential for the inflows of FDI. Proreform commitment of the government makes an important difference. Years when the host government in power makes market transition reform a priority show substantially higher FDI flows to that country. Furthermore, legitimization of FDI practice is one of the most significant and robust predictors. More than any other factor, it is the legitimization of FDI practice in postsocialism that encourages FDI inflows in the first decade after 1989.

The significance of institutionalization and legitimization of FDI, as evidenced in the analysis, points to the importance of rules and understandings that support FDI as an appropriate and desirable market-based activity. Socialist economies were predicated on a particular set of rules and a cultural logic of collective interest. Transformation to markets involves establishing new institutions that facilitate market-based exchange. Thus, we see that states do not only *constrain* economic processes if they remain involved in economic activity, but *enable* market-based transactions by legitimizing and promoting them as the appropriate economic strategy—by constructing an open-market rationality.

I conducted checks for the robustness of institutionalization and legitimization effects. Controlling for the left orientation of the government, speed of democratization, and external pressures from participation in an IMF program or EU integration process does not substantively alter the previous findings of the role of state actions.[7] Results also remain substantively similar if we apply a stringent fixed-effects model, which takes into account *any* possible country-specific characteristic and thus controls for any potentially omitted country-level variables, or if we conduct a 2SLS estimation, which accounts for potential endogeneity. (See the appendix for further explanation.)

The results from these alternative model specifications confirm the robustness of the key findings: stimulating FDI in Central and Eastern Europe after 1989 is heavily dependent on the actions of postsocialist states that create demand for FDI by institutionalizing and legitimizing it as a desirable economic strategy. On the other hand, in all model specifications, the economic indicators perform rather poorly and explain very little of the variance in FDI flows across postsocialist countries over time.

How to explain this poor performance of economic indicators as predictors of FDI flows to postsocialist Europe? When examining the data in more detail, we see clearly that all countries during the period captured in this analysis experienced economic volatility, with inflation levels up to 240 percent and severe net declines in GDP per capita. They suffered huge economic shocks and saw skyrocketing prices. The economic environment in postsocialist Europe was very uncertain.

Unanticipated sudden changes in the external environment can make an investment location that looks promising today look very unattractive tomorrow. The fact that actors involved in FDI transactions must contend with great environmental uncertainties—shifts in political power, policy changes, and economic crises—is indeed a serious challenge. This kind of environmental and situational uncertainty cannot be anticipated precisely in advance and measured as a probability to be used in rational calculations of risk and return (Knight 2002). Our results suggest that in conditions of high uncertainty, foreign investors and postsocialist hosts act practically: they rely on social and political clues, such as following opportunities in countries where they already have contacts, pursuing options that they hear about from their networks, and judging prospects based on political commitments by the government in power, even though economic conditions may not be very promising. It also seems that some investors may engage in FDI by retroactively responding to offers that come to them from domestic actors directly or via FDI agencies. Hence, the challenges to profit-maximization efforts of investors are exacerbated by the fact that foreign direct investment exchanges are always relational, involving two sides to the transaction.

In brief, the complexities caused by the relational nature of FDI transactions and high uncertainty that actors have to contend with in societies undergoing fundamental social, political, and economic change likely interfere with profit-maximizing efforts and hence obscure the relationship between economic indicators and FDI at the aggregate level. To provide further evidence for these claims, I explicate the consequences of the relational nature of transactions and the effect of uncertainty on economic outcomes in chapters 5 and 6.

Finally, a cautionary note is in order that qualifies the generalizability of the importance of institutionalization and legitimization effects on FDI. Although these effects are strong and robust to different model specifications and testing for selection effects, we need to keep in mind that this analysis reflects processes in the initial phases of FDI in postsocialist Europe, as it captures only the first ten years after the fall of Communist regimes. It is quite likely that institutionalization and legitimization are crucial particularly in this stage of market building. Once market exchange becomes "normal" economic behavior, that is, become fully institutionalized so as to be taken for granted—when, in Przeworski's words, actors become "acculturated to market relations" (1991, 158)—processes of institutionalization and legitimization may not be so visible. This suggests that creation, stabilization, or possible decline in markets may each require a different explanatory framework because they are distinct stages of economic organization that involve different social processes (cf. Fligstein 2001a).

How Postsocialist States Create Markets

The basic feature of a socialist system was state control of the economy, leading to the characterization of these societies as "command economies." For many analysts, the key to economic transformation, development, and prosperity in Central and Eastern Europe was ending control by the state and its inefficient redistributive arrangements. This view was based on the reasoning that free-market exchange is only possible with the state's withdrawal from the economic sphere. Prominent economist Lawrence Summers echoed this conviction by emphasizing that "the invisible hand is more powerful than the [hand of the government]. Things will happen in well-organized efforts without direction, controls, plans. That's the consensus among economists" (qtd. in Yergin and Stanislaw 1998, 150–51). Is that so?

Observers of economic transformations in Central and Eastern Europe agreed that establishing property rights was a necessary condition for market exchange to proliferate. However, they disagreed on how establishing them was best accomplished, and what the role of postsocialist states in the economy should be beyond privatization. Those aligned with the instrumentalist, neoliberal perspective focused on the importance of liberalization and stabilization to establish the incentive structure for rational market actors. Except for these unavoidable interventions, states should remove their influence from the economy and allow the "invisible hand" of the market to do its job and insure efficient allocation of resources. Indeed, should the states remain involved, they would interfere and constrain free-market activity.

On the other hand, the constructivist approach highlights markets as institutionalized and continuously shaped and structured by the state and political institutions: "State action *always* plays a major role in constituting economies . . . [so] it is not useful to posit states as lying outside of economic activity" (Block 1994, 696). States' involvement in the economy should not be understood as a mere constraint through intervention but as facilitation of economic processes and creation of markets (Evans, Rueschemeyer, and Skocpol 1985; Campbell, Hollingsworth, and Lindberg 1991; Block 1994; Hollingsworth, Schmitter, and Streeck 1994; Evans 1995; Fligstein 1996, 2001a; Hollingsworth and Boyer 1997; Fligstein and Stone Sweet 2002). From this perspective, ever removing the state from the economy is implausible.

Conceptually, the neoliberal view separates sharply markets from states, while political economy and economic sociology denounce the demarcation into two separate spheres, arguing that markets are embedded and enmeshed in institutions. The implication of the "separate spheres" argument is that any state involvement in the economy is an interference, contaminating the purity of economic exchange and rendering it inefficient.[8] On the other hand, the view of state-market embeddedness emphasizes not only the constraining force of states, but their constitutive influence on the economy. Consistent with this view, this chapter empirically examined how state actions facilitated FDI, and therefore market-based exchange, in postsocialist Europe.

Other sociologists have paid attention to the role of postsocialist states in societal transformations in this region. In one of the key books on postsocialist developments, David Stark and László Bruszt envisioned the following role for the postsocialist states:

> [W]ithout directly intruding on enterprise affairs, the [postsocialist] state can facilitate decentralized institutions that constrain the networks to take into account long-term dependencies. It should not regulate *content*, but it can regulate the *context* of enterprise governance through legislation that weakens or strengthens the ability of social actors to negotiate about these interdependencies. Not by issuing directives or by setting substantive targets but by shaping the environment of procedural rights, the state can facilitate the deliberations that lengthen time horizons. (1998, 200)

The analyses presented in this chapter show that the role of postsocialist states after the fall of the Communist regimes went beyond setting up legislation and procedural rights that Stark and Bruszt underscore. Instituting formal laws and policies, as a context for transformation, does not adequately encompass the state's role in all aspects of marketization. Fundamentally, the unprecedented challenge for states in postsocialism on their way to markets was to legitimize free-market rationality. In case of FDI examined here, the states instituted professional agencies to support foreign investors and, as market actors themselves, engaged in FDI exchanges by selling large state monopolies to foreign buyers. Market-based processes in Central and Eastern Europe after 1989 did not simply *emerge* in the presence of rational profit-maximizing actors and the absence of central control. In fact, the notion of *emerging* markets is misleading. There is little that is spontaneous or natural in the transformation from a command economy to a system of market exchange. It is more empirically correct to describe the proliferation of market-based activity as a process *created* by postsocialist states, which negotiated domestic and international political and cultural forces.

The expectations based on the economic theory of market exchange imply that economic incentives are the most important determinants of exchanges between buyers and sellers since they create conditions for self-interested actors to maximize profits. In contrast, the present analysis shows that economic prosperity and stabilization of a country do not exert a significant influence on the initial phases of FDI penetration. Rather, it is the actions of host country states, political choices, and structures inherited from the socialist times that shape this economic activity most significantly.

Last but not least, while the analyses presented here show that in the first decade after 1989 the influence of postsocialist states was crucial, it remains an empirical question *what kind of role* postsocialist states will have over time, once they sell off most of the formerly state-owned assets. The wording is intentionally precise here. The empirical question for future research is not whether the role of the state will persist over time, but what qualitatively this role will entail. Judging from the experiences in advanced capitalist countries, there are multiple possible state-economy relations, which induce more or less "productive synergy between states and markets" (Block and Evans 2005, 507). The test of time will show what kind of state-market embeddedness will characterize developments in Central and Eastern Europe in the next decades.

CONCLUSION

This chapter examined the actions of postsocialist states to legitimize and institutionalize FDI, and the consequences of these efforts on actual proliferation of FDI in postsocialist Europe in the first decade after 1989. The empirical findings provide strong support for the institutional underpinnings of FDI and for the need to examine how host states create the *demand* for FDI and not only how opportunities for profit-maximization enlarge the *supply* of interested investors, privileged in previous studies. The strong effects of the state's involvement in the economy, shaped by the path-dependent patterns of economic organization, suggest that policy recommendations emphasizing state withdrawal from the postsocialist economy, if liberal markets are to be achieved, are off the mark. Moreover, postsocialist states facilitated FDI inflows not only by establishing the legal framework of property rights and rules of exchange, but more importantly, by legitimizing FDI as the appropriate and desirable strategy of market behavior. In the context of economic policy formulation, these legitimization activities were shaped by previous institutions, domestic political interests, and shared understandings in favor of preserving national assets in domestic ownership. They are also influenced by external pressures, in particular by peer states and by the EU, which makes economic liberalization a condition for the EU accession. Ultimately, these analyses indicate the importance of social forces in constituting FDI. They show that this economic process is influenced as much by interests of investors as by actions of hosts. The next chapter scrutinizes further this social relational nature of FDI, by examining how embedded relations between investor and host countries structure the aggregate FDI flows between them.

Chapter 4

CROSS-COUNTRY PATTERNS IN FDI FLOWS

CHICAGO'S POLONIA is the largest local community of Polish Americans (Lopata 1994, xxi). Established in the late 1860s (Granacki 2004, 9), it is home for many of the almost 10 million Americans who report some Polish ancestry (Erdmans 1998, 16). At the end of 1970s and in the early 1980s, many of those who wished to escape the political turmoil of the last decade of the Communist rule in Poland emigrated to Polonia. Some of these immigrants were university-educated men and women who had been involved in the Solidarity movement. Even if their involvement had been minimal, they found little professional opportunity in their home-land after the Communist government banned Solidarity. Bogdan Pukszta was one such man. As a young intellectual in his thirties, with a diploma in American literature from the University of Silesia, Pukszta in 1982 left a life he characterized as "very depressing" to come to Chicago, where his parents and other relatives already lived. Chicago was "a place he had long dreamed of going, ever since he had written his thesis in Poland on the Chicago renaissance in American literature. Soon, he was another all-American immigrant success story" (Ungar 1998, 230–31).

After the collapse of Polish Communism in the spring of 1989, Pukszta helped launched the Polish American Economic Forum, and became its president in 1992. The goal of this organization was promotion of private foreign investment in Poland. Erdmans (1998, 173) points out that the Forum's objective was entangled with the social and political ties that new immigrants and ethnic Polish Americans had with Poland:

> New immigrants created Forum to show support for the new Solidar-ity government by promoting and facilitating foreign investment in Poland's private market. . . . New immigrants were eager to show their support by helping the new government develop a new market economy. Forum leaders who were immigrants defined economic support of the private market in Poland as a political act. Investment dollars were cast as a form of political demonstration. One leader said, Forum "is nothing more than an idea to make another demon-stration—only without the rotten eggs." The political theme of Forum was its emphasis that investment dollars would contribute to the collective good—an economically stable Poland.

The establishment of the Polish American Economic Forum in Chicago after the fall of the Communist regime is a telling example of how foreign investment in Central and Eastern Europe is shaped by social, political, and cultural forces. Moreover, it clearly indicates the relational nature of foreign investment processes. The Forum was not just a collection of profit-minded investors searching for the best investment opportunities, comparing one country in Central and Eastern Europe with another (and to others in Asia and Latin America), and then deciding on the one that promised the highest profits. Instead, the Forum—a result of long-term migration ties between two countries—was an economic entity that promoted *American* FDI in *Poland*.

The more general question, then, is how webs of relations between investor and host countries shape FDI in postsocialist Europe. If foreign investment is a socially constituted relational process, as I argue in this book, then images of profit-maximizing investors moving seamlessly across national borders, indifferent to any concern but the highest return, are misleading. The investment process is better captured by a focus on practical actors who use their social and political ties, and bring their cultural affiliations to bear, in their investment business. If that is so, then we should see that at the macro level, FDI flows through a network of preexisting relations between countries that provide social channels for economic transactions. The goal of this chapter is to elaborate and empirically test these claims.

From Country Characteristics to Relations between Countries

The spectacular rise in world FDI since the 1970s may be one of the most dramatic indicators of the intensity of cross-border exchanges that increase transnational dependencies. What drives these capital flows? How can we understand which countries attract more or less FDI? Most analyses of FDI build on the general equilibrium theory in economics, which identifies two central motivations for multinational enterprises—access to markets and access to low wages (e.g., Helpman 1984; Markusen 1984). Hence, these analyses focus on the economic attributes of host countries, such as the size of the domestic market, economic growth, and labor costs, as stimuli for FDI inflows. Another set of FDI studies highlights the host country's policies (or lack thereof) designed to make the country attractive to multinationals. Many scholars believe that states are engaged in a "race to the bottom" in which competition over investment capital leads to the loosening of regulatory standards (in particular, environmental protections and labor standards), so as to attract MNCs (London and Ross 1995; Robinson 1995; Rodrik, Bradford, and Lawrence 1997; Mosley 2003; Monks and Minow 2004). Among those skeptical of this claim is prominent economist Jagdish Bhagwati (2003, 58), who counters that "we have little evidence that governments actually play the race (choosing to attract investment) by offering to cut [labor and environment] standards or that multinational corporations actually are attracted by such concessions and thus are competing in such a race." Bhagwati does suggest that a "race to the bottom occurs in tax concessions offered by governments to attract multinationals" (59). In one of the most recent FDI studies, political scientist Nathan Jensen (2006) tested how tax policy affects FDI and found little support for the claim that governments "must slash spending and taxation in a race for the neoliberal bottom" (55). Instead, Jensen emphasizes that FDI goes to those countries that offer political stability and hence lower political risks to investors.

Whether emphasizing the importance of labor costs, market potential, labor and environmental standards, or political risks, existing research commonly focuses on country characteristics as key determinants of FDI flows. If government actions and country characteristics are key (because they serve as cues to profit-minded investors about potential risk and return), then the Polish American Economic Forum is an exception to the rule, and we should see little evidence that FDI flows to a country are affected by its relationship with the investor country. However, a detailed examination of trends in Central and Eastern Europe after ten years of market liberalization shows just the opposite (table 4.1).

While the United States is the world's leading investor, Germany holds the top place in Central and Eastern Europe, although German MNCs are more prevalent in Bulgaria, the Czech Republic, Hungary, Poland, Romania, and Slovakia than the three Baltic states of Estonia, Latvia, and Lithuania. In 2000, U.S. investment was about 20 percent of FDI stock in Croatia but less than 5 percent in economically more advanced and politically more stable Slovenia, a fellow former Yugoslav republic. Estonia receives the great majority of all Finnish investment in the region. The biggest investors in Lithuania and Latvia are Denmark and Sweden, which are much less prominent in Hungary, the Czech Republic, and Poland, the countries that receive the bulk of FDI in the region. Greece, a country with minimal FDI outflows, has an established presence in Bulgaria, as does Cyprus, which invests notably in Romania. Australians hold some investments in Poland and Croatia, but Asian and Latin American investments in the region are negligible. How can we explain these trends? If economic and political characteristics of countries matter because they signal risk and return to investors, then the investing country's FDI should be relatively similar across host countries. Those countries considered more economically prosperous and politically stable should receive more investment from world's top investors. This does not seem to be the case.

TABLE 4.1
FDI Stock by Investor Country of Origin

Host Country	Investing Country	US$ Millions	Percentage of Total Stock
Bulgaria			
	United States	258	12
	United Kingdom	238	11
	France	59	3
	Germany	417	19
	Hong Kong	0	0
	Cyprus	208	10
	Russian Federation	145	7
	Belgium/Luxembourg	134	6
	Austria	121	6
	Greece	95	4
	Other	485	22
	Total	2,160	100
Croatia			
	United States	1,108	21
	United Kingdom	110	2
	France	99	2
	Germany	1,160	22
	Hong Kong	0	0
	Austria	1,307	25
	Belgium/Luxembourg	333	6
	Netherlands	209	4
	Italy	126	2
	Slovenia	118	2
	Other	623	12
	Total	5,193	100
Czech Republic			
	United States	1,401	6
	United Kingdom	750	3
	France	926	4
	Germany	5,522	26
	Hong Kong	0	0
	Netherlands	6,508	30
	Austria	2,409	11
	Belgium/Luxembourg	1,159	5
	Switzerland	872	4
	Sweden	294	1
	Other	1,803	8
	Total	21,644	100

TABLE 4.1 (*cont.*)
FDI Stock by Investor Country of Origin

Host Country	Investing Country	US$ Millions	Percentage of Total Stock
Estonia			
	United States	132	5
	United Kingdom	53	2
	France	26	1
	Germany	79	3
	Hong Kong	0	<1
	Sweden	1,058	40
	Finland	794	30
	Norway	106	4
	Denmark	106	4
	Netherlands	53	2
	Other	230	9
	Total	2,645	100
Hungary			
	United States	1,830	8
	United Kingdom	229	1
	France	1,601	7
	Germany	5,946	26
	Hong Kong	0	0
	Netherlands	5,260	23
	Austria	2,744	12
	Belgium/Luxembourg	1,144	5
	Italy	686	3
	Switzerland	457	2
	Other	2,973	13
	Total	22,870	100
Latvia			
	United States	188	9
	United Kingdom	104	5
	France	0	0
	Germany	229	11
	Hong Kong	21	1
	Sweden	271	13
	Estonia	229	11
	Denmark	208	10
	Finland	125	6
	Russian Federation	125	6
	Other	584	28
	Total	2,084	100

TABLE 4.1 (*cont.*)
FDI Stock by Investor Country of Origin

Host Country	Investing Country	US$ Millions	Percentage of Total Stock
Lithuania			
	United States	233	10
	United Kingdom	163	7
	France	23	1
	Germany	163	7
	Hong Kong	12	0.5
	Denmark	420	18
	Sweden	397	17
	Estonia	140	6
	Finland	140	6
	Norway	93	4
	Other	548	23.5
	Total	2,334	100
Poland			
	United States	3,240	9
	United Kingdom	1,131	3
	France	4,172	12
	Germany	6,482	19
	Hong Kong	0	0
	Netherlands	8,432	25
	Italy	1,478	4
	Russian Federation	1,344	4
	Sweden	1,182	3
	Austria	1,100	3
	Other	5,666	18
	Total	34,227	100
Romania			
	United States	339	7
	United Kingdom	241	5
	France	313	7
	Germany	541	11
	Hong Kong	2	<1
	Netherlands	583	12
	Cyprus	387	8
	Italy	352	7
	Austria	245	5
	Turkey	196	4
	Other	1,517	33
	Total	4,716	100

TABLE 4.1 (*cont.*)
FDI Stock by Investor Country of Origin

Host Country	Investing Country	US$ Millions	Percentage of Total Stock
Slovakia			
	United States	256	7
	United Kingdom	119	3
	France	124	3
	Germany	1,064	29
	Hong Kong	0	0
	Netherlands	908	24
	Austria	539	14
	Czech Republic	218	6
	Hungary	182	5
	Belgium/Luxembourg	65	2
	Other	258	7
	Total	3,733	100
Slovenia			
	United States	109	4
	United Kingdom	102	4
	France	299	11
	Germany	351	12
	Hong Kong	1	<1
	Austria	1,280	46
	Italy	152	5
	Czech Republic	105	4
	Switzerland	102	4
	Netherlands	83	3
	Other	225	8
	Total	2,809	100

Source: World Investment Report (UNCTAD 2001) computed by author, data for 2000, except for Bulgaria (1999). The data for Romania are from Romania Factbook (2005), and pertain to 2002.

Note: The first five investors listed for each host country, the United States, United Kingdom, France, Germany, and Hong Kong, are world's first through fifth largest investors for 2000.

Moreover, as table 4.2 shows, the top investors in Central and Eastern Europe are not the same as the top world investors. Based on total stock of investment in the region as of 2000, Germany and Netherlands rank above the United States. The United Kingdom and France rank second and third in the world but have a less significant presence in Central and Eastern Europe. Hong Kong is the world's fifth largest investor but did

Table 4.2
Top Investor Countries in 2000

World	Central and Eastern Europe
1. United States	Germany
2. United Kingdom	Netherlands
3. France	United States
4. Germany	Austria
5. Hong Kong	Sweden

Source: UNCTAD 2001
Note: Rankings are based on outward FDI stock as of 2000.

not have any investments in most postsocialist countries by 2000. On the other hand, Austria and Sweden were very prominent investors in the region, ranking fourth and fifth, but on the list of the world investors in 2000, they lag in the twenty-third and thirteenth places (UNCTAD 2001).

This preliminary evidence suggests that the focus on host country characteristics as determinants of FDI flows inadequately captures the trends in internationalization and liberalization in postsocialist Europe. This is because economic actors do not make decisions independently (atomistically), as FDI theories assume, but are embedded in a web of intercountry relations. Nation-states are connected to each other through political relations, migration and trade flows, and associational alliances, all of which influence the choice of where to invest and how much.

Bringing to the fore the importance of historically embedded relations between countries as foundations for FDI in postsocialist Europe is in line with the constructivist approach adopted in this book and with an understanding of FDI as a socially constituted relational phenomenon. However, the constructivist perspective emphasizes not just the relational nature of FDI but also loosens the assumption that investors act only to maximize profits, an assumption that underlies research that tries to explain FDI flows by examining countries' characteristics. Ultimately, general equilibrium economic models and the race-to-the-bottom thesis assume atomistic markets in which capital flows to the most profitable opportunities. By contrast, the constructivist approach emphasizes the embeddedness of economic action, which may or may not lead to profit maximization. Although relying on preexisting social relations may increase profits by reducing search and communication costs, ties between investors and hosts may also limit options. In addition, the social relational focus pays attention to circumstances in which hosts may interfere with the investor's profit-maximizing efforts by resisting certain investors in favor of others with whom they are connected.

SOCIAL RELATIONS AS DETERMINANTS OF FDI FLOWS

Economic sociologists have elaborated on the relational, rather than atomistic, decision-making of economic actors. In a classic manifesto for the new economic sociology, Mark Granovetter (1985, 481–82) stated that "[economic] behavior and institutions . . . are so constrained by ongoing social relations that to construe them as independent is a grievous misunderstanding." According to Granovetter, most economic analyses portrayed an "undersocialized," or atomized, economic actor, while those focusing on the influence of social structure ended up with an "oversocialized" conception of action. With a focus on ongoing systems of social relations, or social networks, Granovetter positioned himself between the two poles.

Inspired by Granovetter's work, the network perspective has become the dominant approach in economic sociology (Krippner 2001). This important research examines a variety of individual and organizational level network outcomes, such as job search (Granovetter 1974; Fernandez, Castilla, and Moore 2000; Yakubovich 2005), consumption (DiMaggio and Louch 1998), entrepreneurship (Aldrich and Waldinger 1990; Portes, Haller, and Guarnizo 2002; Aldrich 2005), interlocking directorates (Galaskiewicz et al. 1985; Mizruchi and Stearns 1988; Lang and Lockhart 1990), and strategic alliances and interfirm cooperations (Gulati 1995; Gulati and Garguilo 1999). Walter Powell and his collaborators have argued that in some industries, such as biotechnology, network organization is the common organizational principle that encourages learning and innovation (Powell, Koput, and Smith-Doerr 1996; Powell et al. 1999; Powell et al. 2005).

Another important strand in network research has dealt with the consequences of the network positions of firms for their economic performance. Advancing the concept of "structural holes," Ronald Burt (1992) has argued that the more structurally autonomous firms (i.e., with fewer redundant ties leading to the same alters) obtain larger profits. Uzzi (1996, 1997) explicated the relationship between network ties and efficiency. In his work on the New York garment industry, he found that firms employ both "embedded" and "arm's length" ties, and that relying on a mix of both kinds of ties improves a firm's probability of survival. Based on this finding, Uzzi pointed to "the paradox of embeddedness," suggesting an inverse-U relationship between a firm's performance and its reliance on embedded ties: network embeddedness has positive effects on performance up to a certain threshold, but overembeddedness has its downsides.

Examining the role of social networks in economic processes has stimulated a rich body of research, which provides a powerful antidote to atomistic explanations of economic exchange (for a review see Smith-Doerr and Powell 2005). Nevertheless, research on network embeddedness raises additional empirical and theoretical questions. Despite strong evidence for the effects of social connections on the economic life of individuals and organizations, the influence of network embeddedness on macroeconomic activity at the level of nation-states remains unexamined (Ingham 1996). Research in the world-systems tradition investigates the effect of structural positions of countries on their economic growth in order to explain the *development of individual countries* (for a review see Chase-Dunn and Grimes 1995). However, few studies investigate how institutional, political, and cultural relations between nations shape *patterns of economic exchange between them*.

From a social constructivist perspective, a focus on the influence of network ties on exchange is incomplete because it largely ignores the influences of politics, culture, and institutions.[1] A way to integrate these factors into the relational analysis is to study the effects of *different substantive varieties of social relations* (political, cultural, institutional) on economic exchange. Such an investigation necessarily takes into account a whole range of social forces but integrates them into a relational framework. Moreover, it helps us advance research on networks by paying attention to the substantive content of ties. While previous studies suggest that social ties among economic actors are consequential for economic outcomes, all of them need not be. Which kinds of relations matter for what kinds of economic exchange is an empirical question. Within this framework, it is the analyst's job to develop testable propositions about the effects of substantively different social relations on economic activity.

Which kinds of social relations are important for explaining FDI flows to postsocialist Europe? As I stated earlier, economic exchange between countries is likely rooted in political state relations, international exchanges of goods and people, and national identity. First, nation-states as political actors forge formal institutional and political alliances with other states. Second, countries build contacts with each other through exchanges of people and goods via trade and migration flows. Third, nationality as a form of identity has particular cultural understandings and meanings, and those meanings shape contacts between actors from different nations. With these mechanisms in mind, we expect to see that institutional arrangements, political alliances, business and personal networks, and cultural ties between investor and host countries influence FDI flows between them. In the following sections, I describe each of these social relations and develop testable propositions about their specific effects on FDI flows.

Institutional Arrangements between Investors and Hosts

State institutions are often seen as a fundamental force in economic processes (Polanyi 1944, 1957; Campbell and Lindberg 1990; Perrow 1990; Allen and Campbell 1994; Block 1994; Fligstein 2001a; Block and Evans 2005). From a constructivist perspective, state institutions themselves are interdependent and embedded in a global environment (Meyer et al. 1997; cf. Fligstein 2005). In an analysis of FDI between countries, it is critical to incorporate the relational character of institutions because specific institutional arrangements between investors and hosts may have an impact on investments between them. In this vein, we go beyond understanding how single institutions regulate economic processes to focus on how the interdependence of states and international political institutions shapes cross-border investment flows.

Institutional arrangements between states may have different effects on FDI. If institutions are central to the governance of contractual relations, states may institutionalize foreign ties to minimize international transaction costs (Williamson 1981, 1985, 1994). That is, institutional connections could affect economic relations between countries by routinizing transactions and therefore reducing uncertainties and costs associated with international business. The transaction cost perspective thus predicts a positive relationship between institutional arrangements and FDI flows between countries.

Alternatively, international business theories suggest that minimizing transaction costs may actually reduce FDI (Dunning 1981; Rugman 1981). This is because in these more favorable conditions, firms simply service foreign markets through exports or licensing agreements with domestic firms and opt to forgo the costs and risks of FDI. Following this reasoning, we would expect see that the institutional ties between states negatively affect FDI flows.

During the first decade after the fall of Communist regimes, two kinds of institutional relations regulated FDI flows between investor countries and Central and East European host countries: bilateral investment treaties (BITs) and EU agreements. BITs specifically regulate FDI and the activities of transnational corporations, and could be considered a means to help corporations reduce transaction costs. They are designed for the promotion and protection of investments between countries that sign a treaty. For instance, a prototype treaty between the U.S. government and other foreign governments specifies that U.S. investments abroad will be treated as domestic investments, that foreign investments will "not be expropriated or nationalized," and that all transfers relating to foreign investments (such as profits, compensation, or dividends) will be "made freely and without delay into and out of [a host country's] territory" (UNCTAD 1996a). Texts of

German and Swiss BIT prototypes specify very similar provisions between investor and host countries, and UNCTAD provides these treaties as examples for other countries to emulate (UNCTAD 1996a).

Furthermore, the post–Cold War period has witnessed increasingly formalized international regimes that establish rules regulating international economic activity (Block 1994). The dominant European example is, of course, the EU. As I described in chapter 2, all postsocialist countries included in this study signed EU agreements after the fall of the Communist regimes, and thus expressed their intention to join the EU. Poland and Hungary signed in 1991, Bulgaria, the Czech Republic, Romania, and Slovakia in 1993, Estonia, Latvia, and Lithuania in 1995, and Slovenia in 1996; Croatia signed the equivalent to an EU agreement in 2001. EU agreements provide a bilateral institutional framework between EU member states and a partner country, covering trade-related issues, political dialogue, legal harmonization, and other areas of cooperation, including industry, environment, transport, and customs. The agreements require the abolition of most tariffs, and the regulatory framework in the signatory country must conform to EU rules (Meyer 1998). If institutionalized agreements between investor and host countries reduce transaction costs in investment exchanges, then profit-maximizing investors will choose host countries that are bound by such institutional agreements, and the effects of BITs and EU agreements on FDI will be positive. Alternatively, if economic actors prefer informal to formal institutional channels as a means to manage uncertainty, these institutional agreements will have little influence on FDI flows.

Political Alliances between Investors and Hosts

BITs and EU agreements are institutional provisions designed to regulate foreign investment activity. But nation-states are also connected to each other through less formal political alliances. Sachs reports that "in 1989, post-communist Poland desperately needed a fund to stabilize the exchange rate . . . [and while] the IMF mission to Poland dismissed the idea of a stabilization fund . . . the Poles were able to lobby the United States directly" (1998, 4). The United States helped established the złoty stabilization fund and prevent hyperinflation. Hostile to the Communist regime in Poland, the United States supported Solidarity with political and financial assistance:

> After the Round Table Agreement of mid-1989, the United States moved quickly to encourage democratic processes and assist economic reform in Poland. Toward this goal, President Bush initially promised some US$100 million in economic assistance, and a three-

year package totaling US$1 billion was proposed later in the year. In November Wałęsa visited Washington and addressed a joint session of the United States Congress, which greeted his unprecedented speech with promises of additional economic assistance. . . . The privately managed Polish-American Enterprise Fund (PAEF) was created in May 1990 to provide credit for Polish entrepreneurs to start businesses. . . . In 1990 the United States led an international effort to create the US$200 million Polish Stabilization Fund, which was instrumental in making the złoty convertible with Western currencies. (U.S. Library of Congress 2006)

This case illustrates that those Central and East European countries that forge ties to rich and powerful states secure benefits from their political alliances. In addition to financial aid, these alliances encourage political visits and facilitate exchanges of information between countries. In the postsocialist period, such information may concern privatization-related investment opportunities. As Stark and Bruszt (1998, 54) report, "On June 21, 1988, Károly Grósz [Hungarian reform Communist leader] remarked in a meeting to business leaders in San Francisco: 'We would be very pleased if perhaps you would purchase some of our enterprises . . . even if they became 100 percent foreign owned.' "

Disbursements of official aid signal the nature of political alliances between two countries; more aid will be disbursed to countries with which donors have closer political connections. Certainly, some countries have large foreign aid budgets but generally less political influence in the global arena, such as Sweden or Denmark, while other countries, such as the United States, have a proportionally small foreign aid budget but more political influence. However, for this analysis, the political influence is not considered in absolute terms but relationally. Aid flows thus show political patronage by donors of recipient countries, and I argue that these political connections shape international economic exchange. In this vein, aid flows from a donor to a recipient country should have a positive effect on future FDI between that country pair.

Personal and Business Networks between Investors and Hosts

In addition to political ties, two countries can have established networks of personal and business connections. Two types of such networks might influence the choice of FDI sites: organizational networks between foreign firms and companies in a host country, and personal networks among affiliates of a specific host country and foreign investor firms. A potential investor firm can have established ties in a foreign country because it had previous trade relations with that country. Consider Glaxo, a large UK pharmaceuticals manufacturer that decided to invest in the Czech Republic in 1993.

> Glaxo had had a representative office in Czechoslovakia for 15 years prior to the decision to establish a subsidiary. Although this was only a small office and sales were not large, this prior experience was beneficial when the subsidiary was established, both as the office already had some knowledge of the country and the market, and as Glaxo already had an established image and its name and products were known to some extent in the country. (Reported in Estrin, Hughes, and Todd 1997, 71)

Consistent with this example, Rojec and colleagues (2001) report that almost all large FDI investment efforts in Slovenia were a result of previously existing business cooperation between the investor and host firms. In addition, a survey of foreign investors in Slovenia found that links between companies were one of the key factors in the choice of investment locations (TIPO 1998). Generally, these examples give us good reasons to expect that established business ties between investors and hosts will have a positive effect on FDI between them.

A decision to invest abroad can also be influenced by personal networks. De Mortanges and Caris's (1994) study of individual cases of Dutch investment in Central and Eastern Europe identified promoters within a firm as very influential in foreign investment decisions. These people promoted FDI in a particular country because they had personal or other affiliate ties to it. Such ties are often a result of immigration or shared ethnic origin (Dobosiewicz 1992). The investments facilitated by the Polish American Economic Forum, described in the introduction to this chapter, were affected by such ties.

Although, the notion of an "Iron Curtain" implies that the border between the Communist East and capitalist West was impenetrable, some of the socialist countries maintained contacts with their Western neighbors. Watson (1994, 83) reports on such relationship between Estonia and Finland:

> The independent Estonian Republic had already enjoyed an intimate relationship with Finland during the interwar period. From the 1960s onwards, the diplomacy of Finnish president Urho Kekkonen facilitated a resumption of contacts. A regular ferry service between Helsinki and Tallinn brought a steady flow of Finnish tourists, lending a cosmopolitan flavour to the Estonian capital. During the same period, access to Finnish television opened up an "electronic window on the West" for the residents of northern Estonia.

Similarly, the northernmost republic of socialist Yugoslavia, Slovenia, had negotiated an arrangement with neighboring Austria about special border-crossing privileges. Those Slovenians who lived in the proximity of the Austrian border had special permits, which allowed them more frequent crossing of the border and granted them lower custom tariffs for goods purchased in Austria. As an informant told me, some of the permit holders used this privilege to do work in Austria, or to sell goods, which they manufactured in their small businesses, to get valuable foreign currency, or to deposit their savings in Austrian banks.[2]

Why would expatriate links and contacts developed during a history of business and personal exchanges influence FDI in postsocialist Europe? Importantly, affiliates to host locations can facilitate information flows and lobby potential investors. They can offer knowledge about home countries' political, economic, and legal systems, make business contacts, and facilitate transactions as middlemen. These activities help interested foreign investors deal with the tremendous uncertainty that has plagued Central and Eastern Europe in its economic transformation. As there had been no history of FDI in these countries, formal mechanisms for gathering information were underdeveloped (Estrin, Hughes, and Todd 1997). Many firms thus amassed information about investment opportunities through business or personal ties. These ties may have had an even more pronounced role for investments in countries considered politically risky, such as Croatia. Because political conflicts and civil war subsided in that country only in 1995, it is surprising to see investments there, particularly from the United States and Australia, since the early 1990s. One explanation is the sizable Croatian immigrant communities in the United States and Australia. Emigrant Croats maintain strong links to their home country, evidenced by the high level of remittances sent back to Croatia (IMF 1999). It is thus likely that Australian and U.S. investments in Croatia were initiated through personal networks based on ethnic ties between host country immigrants and investor firms. Information from a personal interview with a consultant to the Croatian Investment Promotion Agency supports this interpretation.[3] Based on these illustrations, we can expect that aggregate personal ties between a country pair facilitate information flows and build trust, and thus should encourage FDI flows between the two countries. At the aggregate level, we can capture these processes through established trade and migration flows between an investor and host country, and test their effect on the subsequent FDI within the pair.

Cultural Ties between Investors and Hosts

Economic behavior is culturally embedded because shared collective understandings of economic strategies, goals, and actors influence economic outcomes. As Max Weber (1978) emphasized, any economic exchange is constituted by the meaning that parties ascribe to observable (or imagined) behavior. For an economic exchange between social actors to happen, all parties involved must make sense of the transaction, that is, they must attribute meaning to it. In this process, people rely on culture, that is, "a set of publicly shared codes or repertoires, building blocks that structure people's ability to think and to share ideas" (Eliasoph and Lichterman 2003, 735). These repertoires (also called schemas, frames, typifications) help people make sense of the various phenomena around them, to perceive them, interpret them, and act upon them (Berger and Luckmann 1967; DiMaggio and Powell 1991).

Cultural embeddedness is especially important for understanding transnational processes and making cross-national comparisons (Zukin and DiMaggio 1990, 19). When partners from different countries engage in economic transactions, as by definition happens in FDI exchanges, nationality becomes salient, as investors are differentiated on the basis of their country of origin. Such differentiation came across in a remark by one of my informants, a retired judge from Croatia, who reported: "Our Office of External Affairs would quickly issue all the necessary investment documents to German or Swiss investors, no problem, but, you know, that wouldn't be the case for Italians." The statement implies that Italian investments are different from, and less desirable than, German and Swiss ones. The informant went on to say that "Italians just want to buy the whole of [Croatia's] coast" and that Croatians "shouldn't allow that to happen."[4]

In the case of FDI, cultural ties influence economic activity because the exchange involves the transfer of a lasting interest in an acquired company, which implies a significant degree of influence by the investor on the management of the host company (Dunning and Rojec 1993). Knowing that management practices are not universal but culturally specific, we can infer that a host and an investor may to varying degrees share conceptions of management and work organization (Bendix 1956; Lincoln, Hanada, and Olson 1981; Boltanski 1990; Guillén 1994). On these grounds, hosts may welcome investments from those they consider closer to their cultural values and practices, and resist those that are perceived as distant.

The reception of an attempt by an American household appliances manufacturer to buy a majority share in a Slovenian company illustrates the point. Perceiving "the American way of doing business" as indifferent to the welfare of workers and merciless in cutting costs, middle management of the targeted firm mobilized workers and launched a news campaign, labeling the American effort "a hostile takeover."[5] The Americans did not want to be perceived as having hostile intentions, so they withdrew their offer. Half of this Slovenian company was later acquired by a German multinational, with a style of management much more familiar to Slovenes because of a history of connections between the two countries. This case illustrates that investment flows are imbued with cultural significance; their place of origin is relevant to a host's willingness to accept them.

Management theory has acknowledged the role of culture in international business, suggesting that investors prefer locations that are culturally and linguistically similar to themselves (Davidson 1980; Kogut and Singh 1988; Benito and Gripsrud 1992; Agarwal 1994; Mead 1994). Most of this research builds on Geert Hofstede's (2001) influential studies of the differences and similarities among national cultures. Based on a large-scale survey distributed to subsidiaries of IBM in sixty-four countries, Hofstede proposed that countries differ along the following dimensions: power distance (the extent to which people accept and expect that power is distributed unequally); individualism versus collectivism (the degree to which individuals in a society are integrated into collectivities); masculinity versus femininity (the prevalence of assertive and competitive versus modesty and caring values); and uncertainty avoidance (the society's tolerance for uncertainty and ambiguity).[6] Hofstede coded various countries along these dimensions, making it possible for researchers to measure the effect of cultural distance (for a review and critique see Shenkar 2001).[7]

While this research acknowledges cultural influences, it defines culture in terms of coherent values-based national character and treats it largely as essentialist. In contrast, contemporary cultural sociologists argue that we should understand culture not as essential national values but as historically institutionalized cultural repertoires (Lamont and Thevenot 2001; cf. Swidler 1986; Cerulo 1997; DiMaggio 1997). This view is in line with the constructivist perspective adopted in this book. From the constructivist standpoint, it is not inherent commonalities between investors' and hosts' national cultures (in the form of language, religion, and deeply ingrained shared values) that encourage FDI transactions between them. Such a formulation of culture's consequences would be static and inflexible. In fact, for a successful transaction to occur, it may be sufficient if both exchange parties possess cultural knowledge of each other that allows for cultural matching: a process in which each party to the exchange comes to understand the other as a trustworthy partner (cf. Collins 1981; DiMaggio 1993). While common language or religion most likely facilitates trust, it is *cultural matching*—in contrast to cultural similarity—that provides a more flexible definition of cultural effects. It highlights the constructivist rather than essentialist properties of culture. It allows us to anticipate the bridging of supposed differences and therefore account for successful transactions between partners whose national cultural background may not seem very similar.[8] Rather, cultural matching emphasizes the role of knowledge and understanding of the other, acquired through repeated interactions and common experiences. At the macro level, we would consider two countries with a history of such inter-action to share a cultural tie. Consequently, we would expect investors and hosts that share historical-cultural ties to be involved in more FDI than those who do not.

In a quantitative macro analysis it is extremely difficult to capture cul-tural ties. In the context of Central and Eastern Europe, I believe that the presence of national minorities in a foreign country is a good proxy for historical-cultural ties.[9] Presence in the investor country of national mi-norities from the host country contributes to historical experiences and interactions between the two nations, which create tacit knowledge about each other's cultures and affirm cultural ties between them. National mi-norities in European countries are either remnants of historical divisions of territory, such as Prussia or the Austro-Hungarian Empire, which do not correspond to current national boundaries, or are traces of historical migration dating back to medieval Europe. The presence of German eth-nic minorities in Central and Eastern Europe is a notable example.

> From the thirteenth century onwards German communities mi-grated eastward, establishing settlements, sometimes with the active encouragement of local lords and monarchs. By the start of the twen-tieth century there were German speaking communities spread across Eastern Europe . . . and sizeable settlements within the Aus-tro-Hungarian empire (in what was to become Hungary, Romania and Yugoslavia). . . . In many of these societies the German speakers occupied prominent positions as landowners, clerics, officials, whilst others were farmers and artisans. Remnants of these communities survive in many of these countries today. (Prauser and Rees 2004, 3; cf. Wolff 2000)

The historical presence of an ethnic minority creates cultural knowl-edge and affinities that may influence contemporary economic links. Writ-ing about the German minority in Romania, Wolff (2000, 229) observes that "the Romanian government has long recognized the 'value' of its German population in order to attract foreign investment and to establish mutually beneficial bilateral relationships with Germany." Scholars have written extensively about the influence of colonial ties for political, cul-tural, and economic relations between Western nations and their former colonies. For East European countries, the links created through national ethnic minorities, in particular Germans, are akin to colonial ties.

Empirical Analysis of Cross-Country Patterns in FDI Flows

To investigate the effects of social relations, I use country dyads, host-investor pairs, as units of analysis.[10] Hosts are the eleven countries of postsocialist Europe, while investors are the twenty-seven countries that together contributed 94.2 percent of the total world FDI stock in 1997 (UNCTAD 1998). The sample thus captures the population of the world's investor countries. The appendix details the sampling strategy, data sources, measures, and analytic techniques.

While previous research focuses on the influence of host country characteristics on FDI, I have argued that a variety of social relations between host and investor countries should have a stronger effect on determining FDI flows between them. First, I consider institutional relations, which are captured by BIT treaties and EU agreements between country pairs. In particular, I am interested in whether these formal arrangements have a significant effect on FDI flows. Second, I check for the influence of government aid between a country pair to capture political state relations and patronage between the two countries, which facilitate information flows about investment opportunities and lead aid recipients to favor investment attempts from their donor countries. Third, I examine how previously existing migration and trade flows between a country pair affect subsequent FDI between the two countries. Finally, I capture the notion of cultural matching by looking at how historical-cultural ties established by the presence of national minorities influence FDI.[11]

In addition to social relations, we should also take account of the factors that previous research has identified as important in structuring FDI. Thus, I include a measure of geographical distance between countries, which follows the gravity theory adopted by some economic research on FDI (e.g., Linneman 1961; Bergstand 1985, 1989; Summary 1989; Feenstra, Markusen, and Rose 2001), which predicts that trade flows between a country pair will depend on the sizes of the two economies (often measured as GDP) and the geographical distance between them. Applying this logic to FDI, researchers have stipulated that two countries that are geographically closer will tend to have higher FDI flows, mainly because shorter distances lower transaction costs (Brainard 1997; Hejazi and Safarian 1999; Buch, Kokta, and Piazolo 2003; Bevan and Estrin 2004). If so, in the present analysis geographic proximity should be associated with higher FDI flows between a country pair. Some gravity models also consider shared language a sign of lower transaction costs between investor and host (Brainard 1997). Therefore, I also check for the influence of language similarity, indicated by the investor and host belonging to the same language group, for example, Italy and Romania or Finland and Estonia.

Most importantly, I also consider a variety of host and investor country characteristics privileged in previous research. First, there are economic factors such as GDP, GDP per capita, GDP growth, inflation rate, infrastructure development, unemployment rate, level of skill of the workforce, and labor costs. Combining all of these indicators in a single model that tests their influence on FDI creates measurement difficulties since many of these economic factors are highly correlated with one another and reflect the overall economic performance and level of development of a country. Following previous research, I use GDP per capita as a general indicator of economic performance.[12] (I also conduct robustness checks with other economic measures as well as a fixed-effects specification, which includes a set of country dummies and thus controls for any host country characteristic.) Second, political economy research has identified political stability as an important influence on likely return on investment and therefore a factor that should play a significant role in determining the locations of investments. Third, I consider research on the "race to the bottom" to see how the policy environment in a host country affects FDI. All analyses also take into account the general propensity of individual investor countries to engage in FDI in Central and Eastern Europe.

Table 4.3 reports the results of regression analyses predicting FDI flows between country pairs. These findings are consistent with the expectations elaborated earlier. As anticipated, political, network, and historical-cultural ties between countries have a significant influence on FDI flows between country pairs and provide strong support for the hypothesized positive effects of embeddedness on FDI.

Geographical distance between countries has a generally negative effect on FDI, although this finding is not as robust as for political, migration, trade, and cultural-historical ties. Perhaps surprisingly, a shared language does not seem to matter for this set of countries. But there are only a few country dyads in the sample that belong to the same language group: Romania scores on this variable in pairs with all other Romance language countries; and Estonia and Hungary share a language tie with Finland because all belong to the Finno-Ugric group. In addition, Latvian and Lithuanian are the only two Baltic languages, which form their own distinct branch of the Indo-European languages. All the other host countries are Slavic.[13] From a constructivist perspective, we would expect that the effect of culture is not the result of some essential similarity or distance that decreases or increases transaction costs. Instead, what matters is cultural matching and familiarity between nationals from different countries, which is a result of a history of interactions and exchanges that builds common knowledge. Transaction partners can draw upon this tacit knowledge to develop sympathy and trust, which (all else equal) increases the likelihood of a successful negotiation of FDI. I provide further evidence for this point in the next chapter.

Based on these findings we can also assess the importance of economic, political, and policy country characteristics for FDI. Contrary to the general equilibrium theory and race-to-the-bottom thesis, my analyses show that individual host country characteristics, such as economic potential and growth, political stability, and the policy environment, explain

TABLE 4.3
Predictors of FDI Flows in Investor-Host Country Dyads

	Model 1 OLS[a]	Model 2 OLS	Model 3 OLS	Model 4 OLS	Model 5 FE[b]
Host country characteristics					
GDP/capita	.037			.034	
	(1.65)			(1.65)	
Political stability	.080*			.054^	
	(2.23)			(1.78)	
FDI policy	.021			.003	
	(1.40)			(0.24)	
Investors' propensity to invest					
Total FDI from Investor	.005***	.003***	.003***	.004***	
	(8.70)	(6.47)	(6.62)	(6.86)	
Institutional arrangements					
Bilateral Investment Treaty		.161*	.125^	.122	.044
		(2.42)	(1.79)	(1.64)	(0.52)
EU agreement		.136**	.115*	.104*	.009
		(3.24)	(2.69)	(2.38)	(0.16)
Political alliances					
Foreign aid		.060***	.057**	.057**	.051**
		(3.32)	(3.13)	(3.16)	(2.79)
Networks					
Migration		.203**	.205**	.215**	.192*
		(2.84)	(2.88)	(3.03)	(2.42)
Export		.002***	.001***	.001**	.001*
		(3.86)	(3.69)	(2.76)	(2.10)
Cultural ties					
Historical-cultural ties		.243*	.254*	.275**	.240**
		(2.32)	(2.37)	(2.59)	(2.58)

TABLE 4.3 (*cont.*)
Predictors of FDI Flows in Investor-Host Country Dyads

	Model 1 OLS[a]	Model 2 OLS	Model 3 OLS	Model 4 OLS	Model 5 FE[b]
Gravity model controls					
Geographical distance			-.027^	-.031*	-.328**
			(-1.87)	(-2.10)	(-2.71)
Language			-.216^	-.215^	-.020
			(-1.71)	(-1.73)	(-0.17)
Fixed effects[b]					
Host country fixed effects					Included
Investor country fixed effects					Included
Constant	-.122	.087^	.186**	-.082	2.623***
	(-0.76)	(1.71)	(2.65)	(-0.61)	(4.36)
R^2	.259	.515	.526	.547	.712
N	261	261	261	261	261

Note: t-values in parentheses. Outcome is FDI flow/capita between investor and host country, measured as average for the period 1995–97; predictors measured as averages for the period of 1992–94.

[a] Ordinary least-squares with Huber-White robust standard errors.

[b] Fixed effects specification; equivalent to adding the set of investor and host country dummies to the analysis, so it must omit all host and investor country characteristics from the analysis to avoid perfect collinearity.

^p < .10. *p < .05. **p < .01. ***p < .001. (Two-tailed tests.)

relatively little of the variation in flows between pairs of countries. Political risk is the only significantly influential host characteristic in one analysis, but its effect disappears once the relational predictors are taken into account. This indicates that political volatility in the postsocialist Europe is mediated by social relations. Those investors that receive information about possible investment locations from their networks may decide to pursue investments even if broad country indicators point to a prohibitive political risk.

The insignificant effect of FDI policy is surprising, but there may be large differences between official policy and its practical application (cf. Calavita 1992). Information from a personal interview with a high-ranking official of the Central and East European Privatization Network supports this interpretation.[14] Negotiations of investments in Central and Eastern Europe are often handled case by case at the level of the firm; in this way interested investors can bypass some of the legal regulations in the host country. This implies that relational measures may be better than official policy at identifying FDI determinants.

However, not all country relations are consequential. In the most conservative analysis, where *any* possible characteristics associated with investor and host countries are considered (presented in the last column of table 4.3), the institutional arrangements of BIT and EU agreements lose their significance for bilateral FDI. Therefore, we should consider that standardization of the institutional environment between countries, and lowering of transaction costs through routinization of exchanges, may not have a direct effect on actual FDI flows. That is, formal institutional frameworks may not be as influential in concrete practice as their advocates propose. In fact, actual transactions may be substantially decoupled from formal provisions. A simple counting of the number of BIT agreements signed by country pairs makes me even more dubious about the effect of these international agreements. For instance, Romania, which is the country that receives *the least* FDI among the Central and East European states, had signed *the most* treaties by 1999—a staggering seventy-five. For comparison, the world's largest investor country, the United States, had signed only forty-two BITs by 1999. The dates of BITs show that postsocialist countries embarked on a BIT crusade after the Iron Curtain was lifted. Signing economic agreements may have been a way to reestablish links to the rest of the world after Communists relinquished their rein. Nevertheless, the lack of a correlation between actual FDI flows and institutional agreements to facilitate them indicates that signing BITs has been a political gesture rather than an economically relevant practice.

In addition, the relative insignificance of institutional arrangements for FDI in postsocialist Europe points to the pervasiveness—and, indeed, usefulness—of informality in times of social change. Foreign investors contemplating investment possibilities in the region after 1989 could have been paralyzed by radical uncertainty: economic crises, political instabilities, cultural unfamiliarity, lack of institutional guarantees, and so on. The findings from the country-level quantitative analyses indicate that if these investors wanted to do business, they needed to rely on informal channels: on information from their networks, on previous business ties, on personal connections, on cultural affinities. If host firms wanted to attract foreign investors, they would contact those with whom they already had personal or organizational contacts.

On the one hand, the weakness of formal institutional guarantees and the insignificance of general host country characteristics may seem surprising, countering much research on the link between macroeconomic factors and FDI flows. On the other hand, these findings, coupled with the strong relevance of social relations between countries as determinants of FDI between them, make perfect sense as macro-level indications that FDI is a social process, in which social relations are used to constitute economic transactions, and economic actors need to be first and foremost practical, rather than purely rational, in maneuvering the uncertain economic space of international exchange.

Embeddedness and Globalization

The contemporary economic landscape is characterized by massive flows of capital across national borders, but some countries are able to establish strong connections to transnational corporations, while others remain less integrated into the world economy. What patterns do cross-border economic exchanges show? Asking this question, I examined in this chapter sources of FDI in postsocialist Europe between investor and host country pairs. The findings strongly support a relational approach to explaining FDI. Foreign investors and hosts are not independent from each other but situated in different kinds of relational settings, which shape macroeconomic exchange between them. Strong effects of political alliances, migration, trade, and historical and cultural ties between investors and hosts on FDI prompt serious reconsideration of previous studies emphasizing the market potential and political environment of individual host countries as key FDI determinants.

The analyses presented in this chapter align well with the main thesis of the book concerning the multiplex social embeddedness of economies, wherein structures, power, and culture all influence FDI. I argued that we need to examine these social forces concurrently and integrate them in a single analysis. Such a research strategy paid off. By considering the effect of several substantively different kinds of social relations on cross-border exchanges, I found that not all types of relations matter, an impression one may derive from reading the extensive literature on networks and economy. Different economic processes exhibit different substantive varieties of embeddedness. It is the task of a researcher to specify what consequences various kinds of social relations have for different economic phenomena in different socio-historical settings.

In my analysis, I found that political alliances, cultural ties, and the presence of migration and trade networks between countries encouraged FDI flows to turbulent postsocialist Europe. However, formal institutional arrangements between countries do not seem to have a significant influence, implying that institutionally reduced transaction costs are not consequential for FDI. Both BITs and EU agreements are official rules or formal contracts. They attempt to regulate what is often a very situation-specific practice, in which formal provisions between a country pair are overridden by informal considerations, such as cultural knowledge, political connections between hosts and investors, or the presence of personal and business networks that facilitate information flows and promote certain investment opportunities over others. This finding—that economic actors in uncertain environments engage in transactions supported by previously existing personal and business ties rather than those guaranteed by formal institutional channels—is consistent with research in economic sociology on risk reduction in economic exchanges (e.g., Uzzi 1997; DiMaggio and Louch 1998; Ingram and Roberts 2000; Guseva and Róna-Tas 2001). An emergent generalization is that in conditions of high uncertainty, people reduce risk not just by relying on institutional guarantees, but by channeling economic transactions through previously existing social relations. This strategy may reduce uncertainty and cost, increase knowledge of the other party and third-party guarantees, but it may also have negative effects on economic efficiency (Portes and Sensenbrenner 1993; Uzzi 1997).

Differentiation between formal-legal regulations and actual FDI flows may also support propositions in neoinstitutional theory (Meyer and Rowan 1977; Edelman 1992; Sutton et al. 1994; cf. Powell and DiMaggio 1991). Claiming that institutionalization of certain formal-legal arrangements between countries is driven by legitimization and world-society myths (Meyer et al. 1997), neoinstitutionalists would expect the effects of institutional arrangements to be rather symbolic than actual. Hence, formal-legal arrangements would not have much impact on the actual practice of macroeconomic exchange and would lead to what scholars call "decoupling" between formal rules and practice (Meyer et al. 1997;

Bandelj 2003). Concretely, signing of the BITs between countries may be a result of worldwide legitimization of foreign investment as appropriate and beneficial to societies, consistent with the spirit of neoliberalism that fuels the debate about the alleged "race to the bottom" whereby countries ferociously compete for foreign investment flows. In light of this, not only would countries have to lower taxes to woo MNCs, but they would also hasten to form bilateral agreements with particular countries to signal privileged investor status. The findings of previous research on the influence of low taxes and liberal FDI policies on actual FDI flows are inconsistent, with the most recent evidence casting doubt that these really matter (Jensen 2006). If treaties and formal policy arrangements are put in place largely for ceremonial reasons to go with the rhetoric of neoliberalism, then a discrepancy between formal rules and grounded practice is not surprising.

For postsocialist Europe, the significance of informal over formal processes may not be surprising for additional reasons. Historically, highly bureaucratized and regulated socialist systems fostered opportunities to escape control through informal mechanisms (Lomnitz 1988; Stark 1996; Verdery 1996b; Böröcz 2000). Thus, reliance on personal networks and political alliances were more plausible economic strategies than following formal institutional arrangements. Since the social organization of an economy is deeply rooted in collective understandings and practices, it is resilient to changing cultural circumstances (Biggart and Guillén 1999). This explains why economic practices established during socialism persist after the regime's fall and points to the continuity of institutions and practices from the socialist into the postsocialist period. Informality, indeed, may be one of the most resilient legacies of socialism. This practical logic of how to negotiate everyday life may have permeated the societal tissue in Central and Eastern Europe so thoroughly that it will take much more than a decade to subside.

Finally, what does this story from postsocialist Europe tell us about the process of economic globalization? Some may be skeptical that the robustness of the embeddedness perspective is very specific to postsocialism. But it is quite unlikely that the specificity of transformations in Central and Eastern Europe is the sole reason for the significant effects of social forces and weak effects of standard risk-and-return indicators. More broadly, these results point to departures from profit maximization in inherently uncertain cross-border exchanges because social relations in which FDI is embedded *may or may not* lead to maximization of profits. Global exchanges are patterned by social, political, and cultural relations. And while preexisting business and personal ties forged through trade and migration flows between nations likely decrease transaction costs, established connections may also lock actors into a limited number of alternatives, constraining efficiency.

Moreover, because cross-border exchanges are relational processes, the local actors at investment sites may interfere with the investors' profit-maximizing efforts. Despite the overwhelming focus in extant research on what investors want or do with FDI, we should recognize that the reception of foreign investment attempts, and other global pressures for that matter, is not an unproblematic process. As I elaborate in the next chapter, economic actors at investment locations sometimes show outright resistance to FDI efforts, particularly when they do not have preexistent knowledge of the potential investor, when they want to protect their positions of control, or when they have certain cultural preconceptions about the investors based on their countries of origin. By resisting certain FDI attempts and favoring others by those with whom they are connected, hosts can determine who the foreign investors are, and thus actively influence global economic exchange. Certainly, the extent of local actors' involvement in global processes is varied; some are more and others less well positioned to shape global forces by countering the efforts of powerful MNCs.

This also speaks to the issue of whether interconnectedness of the world creates convergence to global models or whether divergence persists, a debate that has provoked great attention. Based on my findings, I can say that we need more comparative research that systematically links different levels of analysis to examine which conditions facilitate local reactions and assertions of local interest, and which induce homogenization. I found that while all countries more or less uniformly open their borders to the penetration of global capital in formal policy (i.e., their policies are becoming more and more similar), there is significant variation in how much policy matters in practice and from which investor countries FDI comes. Because economic processes are structurally, politically, and culturally embedded, investors differentiate between hosts, and hosts in turn differentiate between investors on the basis of their preexisting networks, political alliances, and cultural affinities. Economic actors rely on differentiated ties (Zelizer 2000) and particularize the global investment process. They sustain diversity at the level of economic practice in a world that is increasingly similar in terms of macro-level institutions. Ultimately, "Does globalization cause convergence or divergence?" is a wrong question to ask. More fruitful avenues of inquiry focus first on identifying where and how the world is becoming more and more similar *as well as* where and how it is remaining differentiated. The next task for globalization researchers is to use comparative tools, and to explicate the mechanisms behind these trends and processes that sustain—concurrently— diversity and homogeneity.

CONCLUSION

In accord with my argument that FDI is a socially constituted relational process, this chapter presented a relational analysis of FDI flows in postsocialist Europe. Paying attention to who invests where, I suggested that a set of social relations between investor and host countries may be more influential for FDI flows than country characteristics such as economic prosperity, political stability, or attractive FDI policy. The analyses of FDI between country pairs showed that FDI flows between countries that have political, migration, trade, and historical-cultural relations. Highlighting discrepancies between formal institutions and actual transactions, these findings exposed the social nature of FDI business, where social relations are used to constitute economic transactions, and where economic actors need to be first and foremost practical, rather than instrumentally rational, in maneuvering through the uncertain economic space of international exchanges. It is time now to step down one level of analysis and venture into the embedded worlds of organizational FDI attempts that will help us explicate the organizational processes underlying macro-level trends. I take on this challenge in chapter 5.

Chapter 5

EMBEDDEDNESS OF ORGANIZATIONAL
FDI ATTEMPTS

THE MACRO-LEVEL evidence presented in the previous two chapters points to the inadequacy of traditional accounts of FDI, which emphasize economic efficiency. Standard economic and political risk indicators do not predict well which postsocialist countries receive more and which less investment. Rather, analyses of cross- and within-country variation in FDI bring to the fore the relevance of institutions, networks, politics, and culture for understanding FDI flows.

Nevertheless, because they treat FDI in the aggregate, as *flows* of foreign capital, those analyses cannot fully specify what shapes the realization of FDI attempts at the *level of firms* that participate in these transactions. Macro-level analyses show strong associations between social forces and FDI. Still, to provide further evidence for the argument about the socially constructed relational nature of FDI, it is important to more concretely identify how social networks, cultural understandings, power divisions, and institutional arrangements influence decisions of firms engaged in FDI transactions. With this goal in mind, this chapter shifts the analysis of FDI in postsocialist Europe to the organizational level and examines FDI attempts between investor companies, usually from the West, and host firms from Central and Eastern Europe. I first present a detailed case study of FDI attempts involving an American MNC, a German MNC, and a Slovenian firm. Analyzing this case, I lay out the variety of ways in which social forces influence FDI attempts. I trace the concurrent influences of structures, power, and culture on economic action. Doing so, I show how social forces not only serve as a context for instrumental decision-making or act as a constraint on economic action, but how—by constituting actors' preferences, goals, and strategies—they provide social foundations of economic transactions.

INVESTED TRANSACTIONS: THE INTRICACIES OF FDI ATTEMPTS

Slovan, a manufacturer of components used in electrical appliances, grew out of a metalworkers' manufacturing cooperative, which was founded in a small town in the northwestern part of the Yugoslav republic of Slovenia in March 1946. The factory grew over the years, and in 1958, when Tito's self-management socialism permitted more decentralization, it began exporting its main product to the United States. In the early 1960s, the company merged with several other similar firms into a state-owned holding company, which established a trading office in the United States. Through this office, Slovan developed a relationship with AmeriCo, a U.S.-based electromechanical products manufacturer that was developing into a multinational corporation. In keeping with these expansion efforts, AmeriCo approached Slovan to establish joint production in the early 1970s. However, during these socialist times, FDI in former Yugoslavia was restricted, and Belgrade did not approve AmeriCo's request for cross-border cooperation. As one of Slovan's managers put it, "They [officials in Belgrade] said that we as a socialist country couldn't mix with the capitalists." Nonetheless, the two companies remained in contact. According to one of the top managers of Slovan:

> If we visited the U.S., we also visited AmeriCo. I knew the vice president well. His father was from the Czech Republic and his mother was a Slovenian. He actually wanted to find out about his ancestors in Slovenia. . . . I even tried to look up some things for him. . . . And there was also another person [in the top management of AmeriCo] who was Greek by origin and his wife was from Serbia. She would always serve us slivovitz and real Turkish coffee.

Ties that developed over the years between the top executives of both companies were of a personal character, going beyond strictly business relations.

With the fall of socialism and the breakup of Yugoslavia in 1991, Slovan separated from the satellite company and started a process of privatization. Consistent with the most common strategy in Slovenia, Slovan decided on a management-employee buyout (MEBO). As explained in chapter 2, postsocialist countries implemented a variety of privatization strategies. Reflecting the socialist self-management tradition and reluctance to sell assets to outsiders, MEBOs were a common practice in Slovenia. Via this privatization method, Slovan employees and management acquired a 53.11 percent ownership share by investing their own privatization certificates. (Underlying MEBOs was a voucher privatization scheme where each Slovenian citizen received certificates that could be exchanged for an equity share in firms. Citizens did not have to pay fees for them.) The other owners of Slovan were the old cooperative that initially established the company (which received its share because of the denationalization/restitution law adopted in Slovenia as another strategy of privatization), two state-owned investment agencies (which, as stipulated in the Slovenian Privatization Law, kept ownership of about one-third of the company), and a few private investment funds.[1] As such, the ownership of Slovan after privatization was very dispersed.

From AmeriCo's point of view, the fall of socialism presented new investment opportunities in Central and Eastern Europe, well in line with the company's strategy of growth through strategic acquisitions and alliances; in 1996 it had thirty-three subsidiaries abroad. Only a few years after the Communist downfall, Slovan strengthened its position as a player in Europe and by 1996 held about 20 percent of the European market in sales of electronic motors. AmeriCo, which controlled about 50 percent of that market, saw Slovan as one of its main competitors, as all the other players had relatively insignificant shares. Therefore, as one of AmeriCo's managers commented, "To acquire Slovan made sense. [AmeriCo] was pursuing two parallel strategies: to increase market share and to lower production cost. With Slovan, we could do both at the same time."

Once it started considering the acquisition of Slovan, did AmeriCo conduct formal analyses to compare opportunities in Eastern Europe in order to choose the most profitable location? No. According to the person assigned to lead AmeriCo's foreign investment effort in Slovenia, the company had been familiar with Slovan for a long time as a player on the market, and the fall of socialism opened up an opportunity for AmeriCo "to do something about it":

> We were very aware that Slovan was a competitor, a significant competitor, who was disturbing the market. And AmeriCo was interested to do something about it. Looking at Slovan, it was considered an interesting prospect for acquisition. So talks developed in this way. . . . Talks go on even with competitors, especially with competitors, all the time, and these talks were oriented toward the acquisition to the point when the visits were made. . . . The process of knowing your competitors is something which is well understood by AmeriCo. . . . We have always been very close to the market, very close to the customers, very close to our competitors. We want to know what's happening. We understand that the information is the way to win wars.

In the summer of 1996 the top management of AmeriCo started negotiating the acquisition by talking to the top management of Slovan, including someone who had maintained personal ties to AmeriCo since the 1970s. Another Slovan manager involved in negotiations was interested in the cooperation between a global company and Slovan because "he saw further. He was, compared to the other managers, a worldly person. The others were rather stuck in their local town and couldn't see further. He used to be in charge of the representative office of the holding [state-owned firm to which Slovan belonged until the privatization] in Switzerland. He was from Ljubljana [the capital of Slovenia]." The majority of managers and workers were originally from the town in which the company is located. They have lived and worked there all their lives.

As a next step in the acquisition process, AmeriCo sent an Englishman working for AmeriCo's subsidiary in Italy to conduct due diligence. The top management of AmeriCo also visited Slovan to make their objectives clear at a town-hall meeting that they convened with Slovan's top and middle managers. Slovan representatives were also invited to visit AmeriCo's subsidiary in Italy. In fact, the general manager of the Italian subsidiary, an Italian by origin, visited Slovan together with AmeriCo's delegation from headquarters in the United States. The Americans believed that the Italian could speak about the benefits of AmeriCo's acquisition. They also expected Slovan to learn from the Italians. However, as it turned out, some Slovenes perceived the Italian's presence as a signal that the Italian subsidiary would be in charge of their firm after acquisition, a prospect they did not like.

What was the key argument of Slovan's top management in favor of the sale? According to one manager,

> It's hard to say what the key argument was. There were many arguments. There was an opportunity for Slovan to become a powerful manufacturer in Europe. . . . AmeriCo promised to bring the technology up to world standards, as in Italy [in AmeriCo's subsidiary] and in the United States. And we went to see the production in Italy and it was really very good. . . . They said they would invest 50 million German marks. . . .

When asked whether the company conducted any formal analysis of the advantages and disadvantages of the acquisition offer, the answer was no. According to the CEO, the main argument was that "this American multinational has thirty-three firms around the world, and all of them, after the acquisition, in a few years increased their sales two and a half times. They promised to double the sales in our company within five years."

And how did AmeriCo decide on the mode of entry? Why were they interested in acquiring a 100 percent share of Slovan, as opposed to forming a joint venture or buying a minority stake in the company, for instance? The AmeriCo manager who led the acquisition effort explained, "It had to be a majority share. A 100 percent share is much easier to operate for a multinational. The word which came down [from the board of directors] was, 'You can go ahead, talk about acquisition, but if you are talking about less than 50 percent, then forget about it, don't waste your time.'" Asked why that was the requirement, he answered,

> Because of control, and because we were extremely aware that another American company invested in [another company in Slovenia], and we heard, we were told, that [the American company] acquired

the majority 51 percent but [the company they acquired] was still competing with the mother company on the European market and [the mother company] couldn't exercise management control. And for AmeriCo this was totally an impossible situation. We were talking to people in the market about what was happening in [this other Slovenian firm]. So we were very wary of not getting into a situation like that.

Because of the company preference for a controlling share, and because it was aware of another American MNC's experience, AmeriCo was interested in acquiring a 100 percent share in Slovan. However, the shares of the firm privatized in a MEBO, via restitution, and by allocation to state investment funds were in several hands, and AmeriCo found it quite difficult to get all the stakeholders in favor of the acquisition. In fact, when AmeriCo made a formal offer to Slovan, Slovan's middle management organized a coalition against the sale. According to a person who led the opposition group, the main argument against the sale was that

AmeriCo had a 50 percent share of sales in Europe. This already smelled like a monopoly. If they took us over, they would have a 70 percent share. And how would the market react? It would prepare another player. . . . The market was scared of a potential AmeriCo monopoly. The market showed clearly that it needs at least two strong producers in Europe. That was the tipping point. If you have the market behind you, which allows you to grow. . . . We knew that we could only increase our current 20 percent share, to help reach some balance on the market.

The fact that this person was so concerned about the welfare of "the market" as opposed to the opportunity to become part of a monopoly hardly makes sense in the framework of self-interested economic action. Wouldn't being part of a global company—and getting 70 percent of the European market, achieving economies of scale, and gaining opportunities for expansion to non-European markets where AmeriCo was already present—lead to higher profits? In fact, when a journalist talking to another representative of the opposition asked him if it is not obvious that Slovan would benefit from the acquisition and substantially increase sales, he did not want to comment.[2]

The perspective of one of Slovan's managers in favor of the acquisition was different:

The leaders of the opposition group were afraid for their jobs. It's clear. And also, they knew that if they took things in their hands and succeeded [in rejecting AmeriCo's offer] that they would get to the top positions; from middle managers they would become top managers. . . . It was clear that the top management that supported the foreign takeover would be overthrown if the opposition gathered the majority owners on their side.

AmeriCo's manager commented on the negotiation process:

When we first started talking with Slovan, just prior to my going there, [Slovan had a] general manager [who] was just going into retirement. He was what we would consider an old-school general manager. He was part of the old regime. He was not going to be a success in the market as we see it today. He had a group of top managers who ruled by committee, and he was strong with them. He controlled them and it was accepted. When I arrived, he went into retirement, and the finance manager moved up into the general manager position, and he wasn't a strong leader, and he didn't have the kind of leadership which was needed in that transition. We saw that the company was trying to move out of the socialist situation. But the privatization process was still going on, so there wasn't this experience of what owners and what employees do, and who does what, and what the roles are. This was for us not clear in Slovan. So what we found was new not-so-strong management, the group of top managers who were used to having somebody who was putting the power there, who were happy to let the old general manager be the spokesperson and be the key figure. But the problems started when the new general manager was not that [kind of a] figure and the rest of the company started questioning what role, what right, they had as shareholders of the company. . . . There wasn't a strong management there to say, "Be good, we are the managers, you are workers. You do that job. When we have something to discuss about the company we will do it in the town hall meeting. But we will not do it every afternoon at four o'clock."

As it turns out, middle managers who led the opposition group got on their side the local cooperative, which had been given an ownership share of Slovan in the property restitution process because they owned the company before communists nationalized it. The comments voiced by the cooperative representatives reflected a strong desire to maintain domestic ownership of Slovan and, in particular, "to keep the integrity" and "assure the prosperity of [the local town]" in which Slovan was founded and grew into a distinctive presence over a half century. The American investment was seen as destructive to this integrity and image. As one person present said, "We are not going to be the buriers of the industry in our local town. . . . We shouldn't consider numbers of how much everyone will get [for their shares if they sold them to AmeriCo], but think with a clear head." Another person reasoned, "We can't sell. Look at the many craftsmen [who collaborate with Slovan]. We can't go walking around asking the Americans if they are going to give us [any work]." According to another who spoke, "If we are against the sale, we are working for the good of the local people." Speaking on behalf of many like her, one woman, who had worked in the firm all her life and recently retired, said with fervor: "We who used to work in the firm, we were with our hearts and souls in the firm. Even if I don't get anything [for the shares], I am for the existence of this firm!" She implied that American ownership would change the company so that it would not be "old Slovan" and would lose its character (and value).

The opposition also lobbied the government to stop the state privatization agencies from selling their 20 percent share of Slovan to the Americans. According to a journalist who followed events, the Slovenian minister for economic affairs was inclined to oppose the acquisition [by asking the state privatization fund not to sell to AmeriCo] because his hometown was close to Slovan.[3] It should be also noted that the general policy toward FDI in Slovenia in the mid-1990s was relatively passive and the government, unlike those in several other postsocialist states, did not push FDI as a desirable strategy. Nevertheless, the AmeriCo representative who visited government officials to lobby for the purchase said he believed state authorities supported AmeriCo's entry into Slovenia.[4]

The opposition group of middle managers also managed to get the workers on their side, emphasizing widely that the acquisition by Americans would bring the loss of jobs. The opposition repeatedly reminded everyone that AmeriCo did not want to sign a written statement promising to keep the jobs, mentioning that in other cases of foreign investment in Slovenia, such statements were signed. One of Slovan's top managers said, "AmeriCo said they would work to keep the jobs, but they didn't want to put this in writing. That was a big mistake."

The events surrounding the acquisition of Slovan were also widely publicized, and the media helped frame Americans' intentions as hostile by publishing stories about "the American danger,"[5] calling the American company a "foreign firm-hunter"[6] and its attempt a "hostile takeover."[7] In these circumstances, pressured by strong opposition from the company's small shareholders, that is, the cooperative, middle management, and workers, one of Slovan's top managers who was initially in favor of the sale—the same person who actually had personal contacts with the executives at AmeriCo—switched sides. Despite his ties to AmeriCo, he was also a native of the town in which Slovan is located, a neighbor to many Slovan workers, former employees, and representatives of the cooperative. In addition, as it turned out, he had ambitions to become the firm's CEO.

After the public outcry against its potential investment, AmeriCo withdrew from their FDI attempt after more than a year of negotiations. According to one of the negotiators,

> When we sensed such hostility on the part of the workers and middle
> management, we asked ourselves, "Do we really want to acquire this
> company?" We knew of a case in Italy where workers went out on a
> walkout because they disagreed with the sale. It would have been too
> expensive for us [should something like that happen in Slovan].

The AmeriCo representative most heavily involved in the negotiations
admitted that the company, and he personally, did not expect such a reaction from Slovan's employees. But at the same time, he was of the opinion
that there was nothing that AmeriCo should have done differently.
AmeriCo tried its utmost and had the best intentions.

How can this sequence of events and the final outcome be explained?
Those involved in the acquisition attempt offered different accounts, but
everyone mentioned the impact of the Italian manager from AmeriCo's
subsidiary. The involvement of Italians was not welcomed in Slovenia,
which has had a history of conflict with Italy. The Slovenian view is that
after World War I, Italians unjustifiably expropriated a large portion of
Slovenian territory, subsuming about one-fourth of all Slovenian nationals within the Italian state (Premik 2005). Some middle managers from
the opposition believed that if the acquisition succeeded, Slovan would
be subordinated to the Italian subsidiary, or at least that "there will be
a great rivalry between Slovan and the Italians." The involvement of
the Italian counterpart was a decisive negative factor, according to one
manager:

> If AmeriCo hadn't involved the Italians in the negotiations, and the
> acquisition were led directly from the United States, perhaps the re-
> sult would have been different. I dare say that it would have been—
> because we, the Slovenians, have this problem; we think of Italians
> differently.

Or as another Slovenian put it, "We think it is a disgrace for us to be
under the Italians."

Listing other causes of the outcome, another of Slovan's managers
commented,

> One of the reasons was that in such a tight-knit local environment,
> a foreign firm has no chance. Then, the middle management took
> advantage of the situation to climb up [the career ladder], and they
> knew how to attract others to their side; many of those were not in
> favor because of the first reason [concerns in a tight-knit commu-

nity]. Also, AmeriCo did not provide any guarantee for keeping the jobs. And, come to think of it, the top management [of Slovan] didn't have a real strategy. They thought that they are going to see this transaction through very easily. And in the end, they were not unanimous. One member of the top management switched sides. And perhaps that was a decisive factor that enabled the opposition to be in the majority, because, in the end, when the shareholder meeting was called, the vote against the acquisition was relatively tight. If that person hadn't switched, it would have been very tight. Maybe they wouldn't have had the majority.

When asked whether the nationality of investors was an issue, this manager said,

If the investors were Germans that would have been better. We trust Germans. And to have Italians involved had a negative influence. They should have kept the negotiations on the Slovan-U.S. relation. That was one of the big mistakes. But overall, the biggest factor was the local setting, the tightness of the community and their involvement with the firm. Negotiating in such an environment—that might have worked only if the firm were really bankrupt.

Reflecting on events five years after the fact, Slovan's top manager, who in the end switched the sides, quipped, "I think AmeriCo's attitude was, 'We are going to eat you for breakfast.'. . . Investors study the local conditions too carelessly. Beside economics, there should be some psychology." It was also the case that the Slovenian opposition kept insisting that AmeriCo's attempt was a hostile takeover, even though AmeriCo's representative repeatedly emphasized, in statements for the press and official correspondence with Slovan, that the company did not have any negative intentions and there was no secrecy in the process. One AmeriCo manager involved in the negotiations claimed that the company did pay attention to the local culture.

As expected, a very different perspective on the company's effort was offered by the AmeriCo manager in charge of conducting due diligence.

I found out that in Slovan the delineation between ownership, management, and other roles was not as clear as I was used to. I had an impression that there was no clear distinction between employees and owners. Often they were the same people. And their management did not have a clear strategy to lead the corporation. They were meeting with the stakeholders on a daily basis and followed their advice in an *ad hoc* manner. There was no strong manager and people felt as if they were losing their independence, which they just gained [after the fall of socialism]. I think they wanted to know what it feels like to be owners, and they were sufficiently competent to do that. And they are doing well now, but sometimes I wonder if they perhaps wouldn't have been even better off with AmeriCo.

Looking back after five years, this person was of the opinion that

the timing for the acquisition was not right, because for both compa-nies this capital alliance would have been painful. Because of the stock market, AmeriCo is pressured to continuously increase the profits. The profits cannot suffer because of acquisitions. If the Americans managed to acquire Slovan, they would be very hard pressed to keep the profitability up. They wouldn't be able to meet the demands of the shareholders.

To enhance shareholder value was sacred for AmeriCo. The company's mission statement asserted, "[AmeriCo's] objectives are double-digit an-nual percentage growth in earnings per share over the business cycle and superior return on total capital." While AmeriCo's objective was aggres-sive growth so as to offer superior return on investment, Slovan's vision for the company was defined more broadly. As its mission statement put it, "The mission of [Slovan] is to increase its value for customers, employ-ees and shareholders." This shows that Slovan put the relationship with its customers and the satisfaction of its employees before immediate share-holder concerns. Maximization of profit is not the only and foremost goal of such a business, as traditional economic accounts would have it. In-stead, rationales for economic action can vary substantively.

AmeriCo's withdrawal from Slovenia ended the intricacies of FDI nei-ther for AmeriCo nor for Slovan. After the Slovan acquisition failed, AmeriCo set up a production plant in the Czech Republic as "part of a strategy to get low-cost production." The AmeriCo manager that I spoke to did not know exactly how the company decided to invest there or about any other countries that were considered.

In the Czech Republic, we looked around there for some time with-out a lot of success. In the moment when we found somebody local that could help us with the greenfield operation, then we said yes, this is a way to go.

When I asked him why that decision was made, he replied, "Networks. Networks are certainly important."

Networking was consistent with the company's efforts at "being close to the market." With the help of business connections, a firm producing electrical components in the Czech Republic proposed to AmeriCo that it buy out one of its empty facilities. In AmeriCo's view, "There was an opportunity and we took it." As this was a greenfield operation, establishment of a wholly new business entity, there were no problems with employees and a multiple stakeholders, as in case of Slovan. AmeriCo primarily had to deal with local authorities and the administrative paperwork required for establishing a new foreign-owned firm. Since the Americans utilized the help of a local person, who mediated the transaction, the process worked smoothly. In fact, according to the AmeriCo manager, having a local person's help was crucial for the success of this FDI effort. By 2003, AmeriCo's Czech subsidiary was operating very well, having increased its production about fourfold in the six years since its establishment.

The continuation of the Slovan side of the story is more complex. A year after the unrealized acquisition by AmeriCo, one part of Slovan that functioned as a relatively independent unit was acquired by a German multinational. This was not completely unexpected. According to one manager,

> Germans sent down [to Slovenia] one manager in 1993 or 1994 [i.e., before the negotiations with Americans started], because they were interested in buying a part of our company that was pretty much producing a high-specialty product for them exclusively for the past ten years. As soon as there was an opportunity to acquire firms in Slovenia, they were interested. But our firm wouldn't sell because the management didn't think that was of any advantage to us.

After AmeriCo's acquisition attempt failed, the German firm let Slovan know that it continued to be interested in buying part of the company. In fact, according to one observer, the Germans "pressured" Slovan into selling by reducing their orders from Slovan "to the critical limit. . . . They were the only buyer and they said they could find another supplier. They talked about going to Poland."

But how real was this threat? Did Slovan really have to sell out of economic necessity? Just as the Slovenians were bound to the Germans, the Germans were also tied to the Slovenians, since the Slovenian company was the only supplier of highly specialized products, which were custom-made and technologically highly advanced. It is not clear, therefore, that the Germans could have shifted to another producer as quickly as the manager portrayed. In fact, there may be other reasons why Slovan sold relatively quickly to the Germans.

I should note that in the effort to counter AmeriCo's acquisition, the opposition group in Slovan led by middle management managed to sway to their side shareholders with a majority of shares. After AmeriCo withdrew, this coalition had enough votes to overthrow the top management in Slovan that had favored the acquisition. The coalition selected a new CEO, a young salesperson and relative newcomer to the firm, who, according to one observer, "was selected almost by coincidence. They needed someone quickly, and he was ambitious and ready to do it and said yes." Such an inexperienced CEO was not well received by the person from the former top management who had switched sides on the American acquisition deal. After putting up with the new CEO for several months, he successfully lobbied the board to replace the new CEO with himself. This action was regarded as unacceptable for the employees in Slovan who had expressed support for the man who was ousted. How was this situation resolved?

> These two people [who had held the position of CEO], together with the board, reached a Solomon solution. They decided that the part of the company wanted by Germans would be sold to the Germans and the former top manager who switched sides would become a CEO of that part. The other person would regain the position of CEO of the remainder of the company.

Not surprisingly, the person who assumed the CEO position in the now German-owned part of the company gave very different reasons for the sale: "The German company was interested in buying because they were afraid that another investor might come, after AmeriCo, and they would have to pay a greater price [for the products they were buying from Slovan] than they did in the negotiations with Slovan." This person did not mention the Germans' pressuring the Slovenians into selling, as did others. According to him, "There were no problems with the acquisition. People supported it."

Indeed, everyone I talked to listed several arguments in favor of the deal with the Germans. First, the Germans were their buyers for ten years, and that part of the company depended on German cooperation. As mentioned earlier, some said that the deal had to happen because the Germans were decreasing their orders in order to "pressure" the Slovenians into selling. Nobody raised concerns about this transaction. There were no implications of hostile intentions on the part of the Germans. There were no fears voiced about losing jobs, although the Germans, like AmeriCo, did not sign a promise that jobs would be protected.

Last but not least, in light of the conflict between different coalitions within the firm about the CEO position, selling to Germans seemed a crafty way to solve the dispute. To do so, the negotiation with Germans had to be expeditious, without internal divisions, without media attention. Appointing the Slovenian manager who wanted Slovan's CEO position as the head of the operation was not obvious choice, unless the appointment was part of the negotiations.

When asked to compare the divergent outcomes of the two FDI attempts, one manager said that being bought by a competitor and being bought by a trade partner are very different. In addition, the two attempts were different because of people's conceptions about American versus German capital:

> The American mentality is to completely focus on profit, as opposed to the mentality of Germans. If we compare how quickly a firm can be opened, closed, how quickly you can be dismissed with a smile ... Such an approach, this 100 percent focus on profitability and self-sufficiency, such narrow-mindedness, also has a lot of negative effects. If we consider these threats, which were present, should we have accepted American capital? And on the other side, [there was] German capital. These threats were much smaller with the Germans. The German mentality is different. There are long-term alliances, partnerships, open relations, a search for a common ground that satisfies both partners. These differences in mentalities, national characteristics, surely influence the amount of risk. Because American capital, simply, if it doesn't reach the required profit margin, it moves on. There is no sentimentality. But it is a question whether this is an optimal approach. I am not sure. Again, I absolutely support the market and the rules of the market, but still there are different possible alternatives.[8]

What Determines FDI Transactions?

The presented case illustrates the complexities of FDI efforts in postsocialist Europe. How can we understand the events that took place? How can we explain the processes and outcomes of FDI transactions?

Previous research, primarily by economists and business scholars, has been concerned with why and how investor firms decide to undertake direct investments abroad. Stephen Hymer (1976), one of the first to study why firms go abroad, claimed that firms are motivated to increase their profits by exploiting their inherent advantages in other countries. These ownership advantages include access to patented technology, specific management or marketing skills, and ownership of brand names. Building on Hymer's work, economist John Dunning refined the importance of ownership advantages and developed one of the most influential theories for the study of FDI transactions, the *ownership, location, and internalization* (OLI) framework for investment by multinational enterprises (Dunning 1979, 1980, 1981, 1995). What became known as the eclectic paradigm postulates that undertaking FDI is determined by realization of three groups of advantages for the investor firm: *ownership* (whereby firms benefit from characteristics specific to the company, such as intangible assets, technological capacities, or product innovation); *location* (whereby firms exploit institutional and productive factors of the target setting); and *internalization* (whereby firms draw upon capacities of a firm to lower transaction costs by coordinating activities internally in the value-added chain).

With respect to FDI, transaction cost economics focuses on the fact that there are several strategies through which firms may exploit their ownership, location, and internalization advantages. Besides direct foreign investment, firms may also export their products or license their technology to lower transaction costs. When trade or licensing is too costly as a form of internationalization, firms choose FDI (Rivoli and Salorio 1996, 341). Transaction costs also explain multinationals' choice of mode of FDI, whether joint venture, greenfield investment, or acquisition of existing companies (Williamson 1975, 1985; Buckley and Casson 1976; Rugman 1981; Hennart 1982; Teece 1985; Anderson and Gatignon 1986; Hill, Hwang, and Kim 1990; Oxley 1997; Sun 1999; for a review see Caves 1996).

The transaction cost economics approach to FDI is based on a set of assumptions about the nature of economic agents. First, firms are considered unitary coherent rational actors interested in exploiting their advantages to maximize profits. In order to do so, firms use means-ends schemas to calculate the costs and benefits of different economic strategies, in light of their capabilities and market opportunities. They adopt strategies based on their relative profitability. The goals that companies choose are set in advance and do not change during the process. Their preferences are exogenous and remain stable throughout the transaction process. Second, this instrumentalist perspective assumes that it is primarily the activities of investor firms that determine FDI transactions. The perspective is strangely silent about the host side of FDI transactions and does not take into account the possible reactions and interventions from the target sites that might shape FDI and co-determine the outcomes of FDI attempts. Overall, the economic transactions are viewed as relatively separate from social influences, and the impacts of social structures, power allocations, and cultural understandings on economic actions are largely ignored.

If we consider the Slovan-AmeriCo case, neither of the two sets of assumptions just outlined seems realistic. The selection of investment sites and mode of entry is not always determined by an explicit calculation of transaction costs, not to mention that precise quantification and calculation of costs is often extremely difficult. Company goals and means to reach them might emerge during the process as actors respond to particularities of immediate situations. It is also not obvious that decisions by economic actors are always made with maximization of profitability in view. In fact, companies (and individuals within them) may have different goals that guide their actions. Even so, firms may not be able to select the optimizing strategy to reach their goals. Besides the fact that they have to deal with uncertainty, lack of information, and time pressure, firms' behavior is influenced by the fact that organizations are rarely coherent units but are instead coalitions of actors whose interests may not converge. Furthermore, as the Slovan-AmeriCo case shows, considering only the intentions of investors in FDI transactions misses a crucial part of the process, which is profoundly social and heavily influenced by networks, culture, power, and macro-institutions. Let us now examine in more detail how these social forces shape firms' FDI transactions.

NETWORK EMBEDDEDNESS

How does integration of business actors into networks of social relations influence economic action in foreign investment transactions? Firms are influenced by ties they have to peer firms in their home environment and the ties they have to various actors in the country where they attempt to conduct business. Networks are also consequential because of personal connections that decision makers in firms have with individuals at home or abroad. In addition, firms also use their existing connections to establish new ties, as for example when they rely on their contacts to act as mediators in FDI transactions.

The selection of foreign investment sites is often influenced by direct or indirect business ties between foreign firms and actors in a host country. Many firms get clues about what investment locations to pursue through ties with their peers. For example, when asked how his firm decided to invest in the Czech Republic, Herr Junger, general manager of a midsize German firm, answered that he decided to invest there because he "already knew some other local [German] entrepreneurs who had invested there and was aware that a number of SMEs [small and medium enterprises] from Bavaria had already invested in the Czech Republic" (Estrin, Hughes, and Todd 1997, 97). Quantifying such trends in their study of foreign investment behavior of Japanese multinational firms, Henisz and Delios (2001) found that the probability of locating a plant in a given country is greater the greater is the number of prior plants owned by other firms in the investor country, particularly from the same business groups and the same industry, which makes the existence of network ties more likely.

Firms also consider particular investment locations because they follow their suppliers, or their customers in their foreign investment efforts. For example, British Vita, a multinational chemical company based in the United Kingdom, established a wholly owned subsidiary in Poland primarily because it wanted to follow its German customers who relocated there (Estrin, Hughes, and Todd 1997). Very often, Western firms use their previously existing trading ties and turn them into foreign investments. In the Slovan case, the fact that the German company had a previously existing trading connection with Slovan was the main reason why they even considered and eventually bought an equity share in it. They transformed the trading connection into an investment relationship. In fact, according to a survey of foreign investment firms in Slovenia, prior business cooperation provided an impetus to invest for more than two-thirds of the representative sample of the Slovenian enterprises with foreign investment share (Trade and Investment Promotion Office 1998). One-third of the surveyed companies also mentioned that the decision was initiated through a contact with a foreign firm or a host firm. Decisions based on the market analysis were listed by less than 1 percent of the investors, and they were never listed as a sole reason for investment. As Rojec and coauthors write, "A handful of large (for Slovenian circumstances) FDI projects *as a rule* emerged out of previous co-operation between foreign investors and Slovenian companies" (2001, 10; emphasis added). Foreign investors, who had long-term business connections with the managers in the formerly state-owned enterprises, had an advantage over those without networks. Through long-term business cooperation both sides of the transaction accumulated relatively extensive knowledge of the other and established trust relations. Preexistent business ties were crucial also because hosts would more likely accept those investors with whom they had been connected.

Ties to business partners or professional colleagues can be a trusted source of information that influences FDI transactions. It is commonplace in the contemporary business world that "managers utilize the information gathered through extra-organizational, interpersonal networks to make decisions on how to relate to other organizations in their task environment and achieve organizational ends" (Galaskiewicz and Wasserman 1989, 454). Signore Marti, an Italian manager whose company invested in Romania, told me that they relied on professional ties to establish contacts at the investment site:

> We know a consulting company, an Italian company, with a specialization in Eastern countries, mostly Romania. They gathered the information and organized the opportunity to have a meeting with the major stakeholder of the Romanian firm. . . . Our top manager knew the manager of this consulting company. They have known each other for a long time and the company had a good reputation, so we followed their advice.[9]

Mark Granovetter's (1974) famous study on finding jobs showed that people obtained the information that landed them a new job through their networks, rather than formal channels, such as job ads or direct application. In fact, Granovetter's important point was about "the strength of weak ties" because the job information received from weak ties to acquaintances and distant relatives is less redundant than the information one most likely already has from frequent contacts with close kin and close friends. But not all information can be treated similarly. Business efforts that involve high stakes are quite different from a recommendation about a job. In the case of FDI tips, one will more likely trust and act on this information if it comes from a close, trustworthy source rather than a distant acquaintance. As Signore Marti said, the manager that made a decision about their firm's investment in Romania knew the person who recommended the source "for a long time," implying a level of confidence that comes with a relationship that has persisted over years.

Much research substantiates the importance of trust in business transactions. Gulati and Westphal (1999), for instance, found that the likelihood a firm would form a strategic alliance was stronger when the board and CEO cooperated in strategic decision-making because this promoted trust. On the other hand, in cases where CEO-board relations were characterized by an independent board, there was less trust. Obviously, not all network ties should be assumed as trustworthy relationships, so besides understanding the differences in the strength of ties, it is also very important to examine the effect of the content of ties on different kinds of outcomes.

In addition, the fact that members of organizations have multiplex ties has to be taken into account. Although network ties will generally be influential, when demands based on substantively different types of ties (e.g., friendship, family, business ties) come into conflict, ties that are linked to the aspect of identity that is more salient to an actor in a particular situation will be more consequential. For example, one of the top managers in Slovan had a friendship tie to an AmeriCo executive, which may have influenced his positive attitudes toward AmeriCo's acquisition attempt. However, this same person was also strongly integrated into the local community. Once these two qualitatively different types of ties were pulling him in different directions, he had to choose between them. In that situation, it was the friendship to the AmeriCo executive that took the back seat to the community tie. The decision was not so difficult. After all, the AmeriCo contact was not directly part of the negotiations, and though the tie was of a personal character, the two men were not the closest of friends. Hence, the community ties to the neighbors that he would face in everyday interactions prevailed.

Utilizing network ties to local people, who act as mediators in transactions, influences the ability of investors to realize their FDI attempts. In Volkswagen's investment effort in Poland, managers reported that

> a major advantage in the negotiations was the local Polish spokesman or representative of the local regional authorities. He was very welcoming and positive to the Volkswagen negotiations and dealt with both the regional and national governments to try to assist the deal. (Estrin, Hughes, and Todd 1997, 199–200)

The presence of mediators in FDI transactions is important for several reasons. First of all, people with local knowledge are valuable sources of information for foreign investors, and they help them navigate an unfamiliar environment. Because these actors are situated between the two parties in the transaction, they can serve as "translators."[10] Sometimes they have to translate literally, but more frequently they present one party's perspective in the other party's language, that is, in ways that the other party can understand and find meaningful. The mediators help the two parties establish a common ground, a shared understanding, which helps both of them envision their cooperation and contributes to the success of the FDI negotiations. This is why immigrants can often serve as great mediators between investor firms they know in their immigrant country and hosts in their homeland. Having the knowledge of both sides puts them in a strong position to bridge between them.

While most research on bridging ties emphasizes the advantages that come with a position between two alters who are not connected by the third, so-called *tertius gaudens* (Burt 1992, 2004), the role of mediators in economic transactions highlights the potential benefits brought to the two unconnected parties linked by the third person between them. Thus, we should not assume that the actor who bridges two parties who are not connected will always strategically guard the structural hole from which she or he can benefit. In contrast, often those in positions to do so strive to bridge connections and facilitate a new tie, advancing what Obstfeld (2005) innovatively calls the *tertius iungens*—the third who joins—orientation.

Overall, the importance of social networks for economic transaction is widely acknowledged. Much research in economic sociology has found that personal contacts can be useful in helping actors overcome uncertainty (DiMaggio and Louch 1998; Ingram and Roberts 2000; Guseva and Róna-Tas 2001). Many business scholars and economists have integrated the role of networks in their analyses, arguing that economic actors rely on social ties because doing so enhances efficiency. Others have countered that position. According to Macauley (1963), it may be less cost effective in the short run to do business with a friend or acquaintance, but managers will absorb the short-term cost so as to maintain a long-term and trustworthy relationship with the buyer or seller. In addition, the relationship between embeddedness in social relations and firm performance may not be linear. That is, as Uzzi (1997) finds, more network integration does not yield greater efficiency. In fact, there are negative effects of relying too strongly on social relations in business transactions, leading to suboptimal performance. There also may be other downsides to network embeddedness (Portes and Sensenbrenner 1993). Hence, it is important to consider that while actors may use their networks to gain strategic benefits, they more often rely on their ties because of trust and cooperation, rather than efficiency maximization. Indeed, if actors merely opportunistically exploited their networks, they would soon find themselves shunned.

Cultural Embeddedness

Economic behavior is culturally embedded because shared collective understandings of economic strategies, goals, and transaction partners influence economic actions (Zukin and DiMaggio 1990, 19). In particular, cultural understandings influence FDI in postsocialist Europe because shared values define desirable goals that actors choose to pursue, and shape a repertoire of plausible strategies of action. Cultural affinities also influence the types of commitments that actors will want to realize through FDI transactions. Cultural conceptions that actors have about other nationals influence the evaluation of potential partners in economic transactions.

Socially constructed and intersubjectively shared values define the desirable goals and preferences of economic action. How do firms decide to engage in FDI as a business strategy? From an instrumentalist standpoint, actors try to maximize profit and minimize transaction costs. However, many sociologists have argued that it is not immediate efficiency but rather cultural conceptions, that is, intersubjectively shared understandings, of how firms *should* operate that influence organizational actions. Defining what valued goals companies should pursue is influenced by powerful actors such as states, normative pressures from professional associations, and observing and mimicking the actions of peers (DiMaggio and Powell 1983).[11] From this perspective, companies' decisions to invest in Central and Eastern Europe after the fall of socialist regimes can be seen as a sort of jumping onto the postsocialist bandwagon, investing because everyone else was investing, which created a sense of urgency, whereby firms would try to get to East European markets before others to claim their share of the new pie. This means that the rise of foreign investment in postsocialist Europe may be as much due to calculations of how to best minimize transaction costs as due to adopting behavior that has become "fashionable" in the post–Cold War period, when economic globalization and corporate strategies of international expansion, mergers, and acquisitions have become the order of the business day.

Beside the preferences for FDI as a firm strategy, profit maximization as the most valued goal of any economic action should also be viewed as a product of a cultural context of modern capitalism. The pursuit of profit maximization in the contemporary world is legitimized to the extent that it appears as a natural economic goal. But this goal is not inherently natural. Rather it can be seen as a product of a long-term rationalization of society, which can be traced to historical changes in social structure and culture (Meyer et al. 1997). As Frank Dobbin (1994b, 123) underscores, "Instrumental rationality emerged for identifiable social and historical reasons that merit examination, rather than because as a meaning system, it more accurately represents the nature of reality than mysticism, religion or philosophy." That profit-maximization is not a natural goal of economic action is evident when we consider socialist economies, where economic activity was not aimed at maximizing profits. In fact, a concept of profit played no role in the functioning of state enterprises (El Kahal 1994). Rather, economic actors' primary goal in state socialism was to maximize the amount of surplus over which they exercised control (Kornai 1959; Szelényi, Beckett, and King 1994).[12]

The Slovan-AmeriCo case illustrates the variability in the goals of economic action. AmeriCo's managers (and the company website) emphasized the company's desire to maximize profits by increasing market share and decreasing the cost of production, with an overarching goal to provide better value (higher stock prices, higher dividends) to shareholders. On the other hand, Slovan's managers emphasized several other values, such as commitment to community and job security, which were pronounced because of the company's socialist legacy, and because of the structural organization of a management- and employee-owned firm. The two mission statements of the companies reflected these differences, pointing to different substantive rationalities that can guide economic behavior. In the postsocialist context, one of the key complexities of economic transformation is precisely the fact that economic goals valued during socialism are quite opposite to those valued in capitalism. Hence, restructuring firms find themselves facing mutually exclusive alternatives, as maximizing social security and maximizing shareholder value can rarely be pursued simultaneously.

Available cultural repertoires are repositories of shared knowledge about available strategies of action in foreign investment transactions. Contemporary business communities possess a body of knowledge about how to conduct foreign investment transactions in general and investments in Central and Eastern Europe in particular. These are articulated in many published investment guides to Eastern Europe, in seminars offered to potential investors, and in advice rendered by professional agencies. As one of my interviewees remarked, "There are plenty of consultants, more than happy to offer their services."[13] This compilation of knowledge offered by consultants and professionals is not some objective truth about the fundamental nature of foreign investments but is a cultural product, transmitted through educational institutions and professional organizations. Learning in business schools, in executive training programs, and in meetings organized by professional management organizations equips a businessperson with a cultural repertoire of available economic strategies that can be drawn upon when engaging in foreign investment transactions.

According to DiMaggio and Powell (1983), managers are often guided by norms and standards held by their professional associations. These norms determine the kind of practices that are considered appropriate and acceptable for certain kinds of problems. These practices are institutionalized insofar as they are communicated to managers in schools, workshops, seminars, and consultations. They are also perpetuated and reproduced. As managers change jobs, they take the repertoire of solutions with them and apply them in other settings. After certain strategies are repeatedly used, they become routinized and habitually relied upon in the future.

Pieces of such cultural knowledge acquired in educational or associational settings are, for example, the types of formal analysis firms should conduct before engaging in FDI, and the factors that they should consider important. SWOT analysis is a commonly used tool, whereby actors are urged to examine the (S)trengths, (W)eaknesses, (O)pportunities, and (T)hreats of their business strategies. Firms also develop their own matrices for formally evaluating new investments. For example, the U.K.-based McVitie's Group, an operating division of United Biscuits, European second-largest producer of biscuits, developed an internal three-stage decision-making model that was used in all of their investment efforts. The model outlined the following considerations and actions:

> [first] a country screening process (gathering information on size of population, net wealth of population and income distribution, stability of government, level of corruption, bureaucracy involved in foreign investments, future expropriation of property); [second] an evaluation of the market (i.e. of market stability, competitiveness, number of competitors, eating habits of the population, availability of ingredients and costs of importing . . .) [and third,] consideration of market entry options (e.g. exporting, setting up a sales venture,

manufacturing, existence of import tariffs . . .). (Reported in Estrin, Hughes, and Todd 1997, 148–49)

Conducting formal analysis is not a "natural" way to proceed in FDI transactions, although it may appear so because of heavy promulgation of formal analysis as a business tool in management programs. Rather, tools of formal analysis are acquired knowledge only available to those that have learned them. Many firms in postsocialist Europe looked for foreign partners to help them restructure their socialist firms. Rarely did they conduct formal analysis of the market to identify the best partners, especially in the early stages of restructuring, when management education was rudimentary. In one instance, a Hungarian firm decided to post an ad on bulletin boards in Hungarian embassies abroad as a way to find a foreign strategic partner (Estrin, Hughes, and Todd 1997), an unorthodox way to conduct business for Western MNCs. As we have seen in the Slovan-AmeriCo case, Slovan did not engage in any formal analysis of AmeriCo's investment. It did not formally calculate the costs and benefits of accepting AmeriCo's offer, which a fresh MBA would take to be an integral part of any business negotiation.

On the other hand, we should not assume that if a firm conducts a formal analysis to choose an FDI location, this is necessarily a clear sign that an organization is rationally approaching its decision-making. Ann Langley (1989), who examined the use of formal analysis in organizations, found that it is not only used for information gathering, but also for communication, direction, and control, and for symbolic purposes (cf. Meyer and Rowan 1977). One of Langley's respondents commented: "We didn't really do [formal analysis] for the profitability but for other reasons. The study . . . was just because we had to have economics of it for the Board. We had to have something to support the decision" (quoted in Langley 1989, 605). In this case, formal analysis seems to have been conducted for a decision that had already been made (Kerr 1982; Meyer 1984).

The participation in foreign investment transactions in postsocialist Europe is often influenced by cultural affiliations to a specific host country. Tom Kovac, an American citizen and professional lobbyist whose grandparents were Slovenian, had a vested personal interest in attracting American companies to Slovenia because of his personal affiliation with the country. Kovac met representatives of Telcomp, an American telecommunications company, through his lawyer's office, which also served Telcomp. He suggested that the company look into investing in Slovenia. Telcomp was at that point considering several other investment sites and decided to look into the opportunities in Slovenia based on Kovac's recommendation and willingness to get involved and gather additional information about this opportunity. Since any foreign investor entering the Slovenian telecommunications sector needed to apply for an approval with the authorized state agency, Kovac called on his friendship with Jan Perko, a Slovenian state official with plenty of connections, to help complete the necessary documents. In my conversation with Perko, he was certain that Telcomp had no chance in its foreign investment without relying on an insider like him. He also said that he got involved primarily because of his personal connection and friendship with Kovac, whose interest in attracting investment to Slovenia (and not Hungary or Croatia, for instance) was clearly shaped by the affinity to his grandfather's homeland.[14]

In a survey of Dutch companies that invested in Eastern Europe, de Mortanges and Caris (1994) found that internal promoters within investor firms were frequently mentioned as important influences on investment decisions. These promoters often had a personal attachment to a specific host country, either because of their ancestry or because they had a personal relationship with someone from that country. Based on their commitment and affiliation to particular countries, they promoted them within their firms as host locations. An Italian manager whose mother was Slovenian admitted in an interview that he was particularly interested in the possibility his firm would invest in Slovenia because of his connection to that country.[15] Such behavior where ethnic identities and personal affinities shape actors' engagement in economic transactions is not uncommon. Others report of several cases where after the fall of the Berlin Wall, people with East European ancestry started investing in their homeland because they wanted to help their home countries restructure (Estrin, Hughes, and Todd 1997). As Erdmans (1998) reports, many of the members of the Polish American Economic Forum established in Chicago in 1989 by Polish immigrants and Polish Americans to facilitate FDI in Poland had a "political theme":

> The political theme of Forum was its emphasis that investment dollars would contribute to the collective good—an economically stable Poland. However strongly these economic objectives were emphasized, immigrants maintained that Forum was also a political organization and that supporting the new economy was a political act. In a questionnaire completed by 98 of the 170 people who attended Forum's inaugural meeting, 70 percent of the respondents said they became involved in Forum for political reasons. . . . For example, one respondent said, "It's our responsibility to bring help to our nation"; other respondents echoed this sentiment, describing their membership in Forum as a "duty" and "obligation" in order "to help" Poland "our fatherland." In my survey of 109 Forum members, 73 percent of the respondents indicated that they had joined Forum "to help Poland." (Erdmans 1998, 173)

Cultural understandings and conceptions influence the evaluation of potential partners in economic transactions. Because economic action is influenced by cultural understandings, those engaged in investment transactions are also influenced by cultural conceptions they have about potential transaction partners. In particular, for business situations that involve participants from different countries, actors differentiate between investors and hosts on the basis of their country of origin. Such conceptions and shared understandings are a likely influence on international economic transactions, leading to differentiation between investors as more or less likely partners in FDI transactions.

One of my informants was explicit about the differences between German and Italian investors:

> German people and German investments are perceived as precise, orderly, trustworthy. Against Italians, there are always some suspicions—that their money is dirty, that things will get screwed up, that there is some iffy business involved, that these are unreliable people—while, on the other hand, Germans and Austrians are elevated and treated as hyperorganized, orderly, trustworthy.[16]

As we saw in the Slovan-AmeriCo case, participants in the transaction drew sharp distinctions between Germans, Italians, and Americans. As one of them said, "The American mentality is to completely focus on profit. . . . The German mentality is different. There are long-term alliances, partnerships, open relations, a search for a common ground, which satisfies both partners." It is hard to isolate the effect of cultural conceptions on FDI attempts because transactions are also heavily embedded in networks, power, and institutions. Nevertheless, conceptions of different nationals and their management practices were frequently mentioned in interviewees' explanations of the economic outcomes, and we should acknowledge their role in shaping how friendly or unfriendly actors were toward FDI attempts.

Actors can also have a certain set of conceptions and shared understandings of what a particular business firm represents or stands for. These conceptions may lead to differentiation between potential investors, some being evaluated as more, and others as less, desirable partners. Such evaluation is likely based on affective and normative grounds rather than instrumental rationality. This comes across in a statement by a representative of the owners of the Slovenian Krek Bank, which was sold to the Austrian Raiffeisen Bank:

> Raiffeisen is a person after whom their bank is named. This person was a role model for Mr. Krek [the name of the person after whom the Slovenian bank is named]. Mr. Raiffeisen established savings and

loans banks with social intentions for local needs and to protect the small people from big capital, just as did Krek in our country. So there exists an ideological affinity. . . . [Similar goals] were also the reason for establishing the Krek bank. The circumstances, that Mr. Raiffeisen was a model to Mr. Krek, also somewhat diminished the guilt associated with the sale of the Krek bank to foreigners, because it provides a moral guarantee that our local interests and intentions will be respected.[17]

This person emphasized the great importance of the ideological affinity between the investor and host, which played a significant role in bringing the two parties together and contributed to the successful realization of the FDI attempt.

In sum, cultural conceptions can both facilitate and deter an FDI effort. Actors will always try to make sense of an unfamiliar situation by assigning those with whom they interact to preexistent categories (DiMaggio 1997). Invoked cultural schemas shaped by cognitive processes will contribute to the presence or lack of cultural matching between those who engage in interactions. This in turn will lead to the presence or lack of positive inclinations and, in the end, trust between two parties. But it is important to note that cultural conceptions and typifications of the other are not static ideas that derive from some general stereotypes that people of a particular country hold about other nationals. This would be an essentialist understanding of nationality, which cultural sociologists eschew (Lamont 1992; Lamont and Thevenot 2001). Rather, cultural evaluations are significantly influenced by people's experiences in actual interactions. People will strive to align what they already know with what they experience, and this will either reinforce the beliefs that they hold based on upbringing, literature, media, and folklore, or induce them to change those typifications.

POLITICAL EMBEDDEDNESS

Political embeddedness of FDI points to the role of power in structuring organizational activities (Pfeffer and Salancik 1974, 1978; Fligstein 1990; Fligstein and Brantley 1992; Roy 1997). Many argue that political alliances and distributions of power are an especially prominent influence on economic activity in postsocialist settings, as yet another form of institutional legacy: a vestige of the socialist system where polity and economy were deeply intertwined. As evidence these observers bring up the notion of political capitalism: a phenomenon in which, upon the fall of Communist regimes, the old Communist elite used their cadre positions, their political capital, to gain an economic advantage by privately appropriating state assets (Staniszkis 1991; Frydman, Murphy, and Rapaczynski 1996; King 2001).

However, it would be incorrect to assume that economic processes are not politically embedded in settings without socialist legacy. FDI transactions always implicate issues of power since, by definition, they involve acquiring or letting go of an ownership stake—and thus control—in a firm. What may be particular to the postsocialist case is the frequent ambiguity about ownership rights and their dispersion across different stakeholders, including the state. This leads to certain kinds of political embeddedness of FDI that may be less common in other settings. FDI transactions that involve sales of formerly state-owned enterprises to foreigners provide ample opportunities for the involvement of political elites in the process because by default the state and state agencies are major stakeholders. Politicking within firms is also common. Especially when multiple stakeholders are involved (i.e., national governments, local governments, management groups, worker's councils, trade unions) the opportunities to form political coalitions are great and potential complications with FDI attempts multiple.

Interventions of state actors and political elites shape FDI transactions. The offer of an Italian bank to acquire a 100 percent ownership share in the Slovenian Bank Koper is a case in point. Although the three corporate partners owning the majority of the bank's shares were willing to sell to Italians, the foreign investment attempt was publicly interpreted as an exercise of control by Italians over a region of Slovenia. A civil society launched a public call on the front page of a major national newspaper:

> To the Slovenian government and Attorney General: to protect its public, state, and national interest, and to prevent the supervisory board of the Slovenian Port [a major corporate shareholder in the Koper Bank] from usurping a public good, and from estranging strategic assets in the Koper Bank to Italians. The Koper Bank has to remain in Slovene hands since the inhabitants of the Primorska region do not want another Rapal contract.[18]

The Slovenian Port, together with other corporate shareholders, responded in a public advertisement titled "The Bank of Koper will remain in Slovenian hands,"[19] reassuring the public that even if the corporate shareholders sold their shares, "banks located in Slovenia will remain Slovenian; they will conduct business in accordance with the Slovenian law." The Port also promised to keep 30 percent of the ownership and remain the decision maker in the bank. In the ad, the Port also noted that "the highest price is not the most important criterion in this bank transaction," and that it would not sell shares in a financial company Fidor, part of the Bank of Koper, which owned vineyards and agricultural land in the region.

Because of the public polemics about this foreign investment transaction, the National Bank of Slovenia took a full three months to reach its decision about granting approval.[20] It finally granted approval with the provision that the Italian investor's 62 percent share translate into just 32.9 percent of the voting power. The three corporate owners kept altogether 30 percent of shares and signed a binding agreement not to sell those shares for at least four years.

One could argue that Slovenians are simply reluctant to sell their banks, which they consider as strategic national assets. However, in another case, a French investor smoothly acquired a 100 percent ownership share in a similar Slovenian bank. No public calls against the transaction were raised, nor was there any media discussion or outcry against the investment. Another similar bank was sold to Austrians. Thus, the fact that the investors were Italian was of crucial importance. Negative historical experiences resonated in the collective memory of Slovenians and raised issues of power and control.[21]

In a Spanish attempt to invest in Poland, the presence of multiple stakeholders with divergent interests led to failure:

> Following a tender, the Voivod (provincial governor) selected Compania ROCA Radiadores of Spain for exclusive negotiations concerning the takeover of ZWS in Wroclaw, Poland in December 1995. Employees and management, however, favored the alternative proposed by a Dutch investor, and thus tried to undermine negotiations with the Spanish firm. Employee protests were widely reported in the local press, culminating in escalating demands for higher wages. The Spanish wanted to negotiate the purchase of controlling interest in the firm with Voivod, who was representing the state as owner. They found themselves, however, confronted with three parties interfering with the negotiations: the Voivodship bureau, the management, and the trade unions. The Spanish negotiators observed that the management of ZWS were more busy having conflict with ROCA and the Voivodship bureau than running the company which they found unacceptable. After 6 months of arduous negotiations, ROCA withdrew. (Reported in Meyer 2002, 268)

Furthermore, a case of a Belgian FDI in a Slovenian brewery illustrates how political and business elites' interests influence economic activity. Once the Belgians announced their takeover intentions and made a public offer to acquire the majority share, a competing offer was made by Pivovarna Laško, a Slovenian company. Anton Končnik, president of the para-state-owned Capital and Indemnity Fund, which held 12.2 percent of the brewery's shares, decided single-handedly, without consultation with the fund's board, to sell these shares to Pivovarna Laško, as opposed to the Belgians. It so happened that Končnik was associated with the Slovenian People's Party, a centralist conservative party, which favored protection of strategic industries by means of domestic ownership. The leadership of Pivovarna Laško also had political allegiance to that party. The government, which immediately ordered Končnik's resignation, was a liberal coalition government, pushing its promarket (pro-FDI) reform agenda. The three governmental representatives of the Slovenian People's Party were against the order.[22]

Political coalitions formed within organizations influence FDI transactions that these organizations are engaged in. In the Slovan-AmeriCo case, political alliances and power fights were clearly an important influence on the outcome of the American attempt. In the end, it was a matter of which group (either those in favor or those against the AmeriCo offer) would sway more small shareholders to its side, and thus exercise its majority at the decision-making table. And ultimately, the desire for power by particular individuals within the firm facilitated the successful transaction with the German investor.

As much organizational theory suggests, firms should not be viewed as coherent units, uniform in their goals and preferences. The coalition model of organization (Cyert and March 1963) views members of a firm as having divergent values and objectives. Conflict among members is thus widespread, and the decisions are made by those who have power in a particular context. "Power, rather than what is optimal for achieving some organizational objective, becomes an important decision variable" (Pfeffer and Salancik 1974, 136).

From this perspective, individuals or groups within organizations have their own interests that they want to protect, and they act according to their own needs and perceptions. In a decision situation, the involved parties focus on those aspects of a problem that they perceive as affecting their own particular interests. Thus, it is less likely that the individuals involved in making a decision will accomplish the task by rationally choosing the optimal outcome to maximize organizational welfare. In the end, parties that emerge as key decision-makers engage in a power struggle in order to get their favored outcome. Often this process also involves each party trying to sway others to adopt its viewpoint and influence the final decision (Allison 1971; Lyles and Thomas 1988).

Furthermore, decisions become a matter of internal politics when uncertainty abounds. Complete information is not available, nor is the best alternative obvious. In fact, information is often withheld in order to advance a particular interest. When interests are fierce, positions on a certain matter are articulated even before the problem-solving properly begins:

> There is a sense in which the political game turns a decision-making process around back to front. Interests in its outcome are already there before the process begins, insofar as most of those whose interests may be implicated know their objectives, their preferences and their logiques d'action irrespective of which topic arises. Thus solutions exist before problems arise, and the game is to find a problem to which you can attach your solution. (Hickson 1987, 173)

As was obvious in the Slovan-AmeriCo case, members of organizations do not necessarily align to support a single course of action. In Slovan, roles were multiplex: individuals were simultaneously employees, firm owners, members of the local community, and Slovenian nationals. In addition, multiple stakeholders were involved who could potentially align with different political coalitions. In such a context, people with social skill (Fligstein 2001b) maneuvered by emphasizing the roles of owners over the roles of employees, and the roles of members of the local (or national) community over the roles of business actors guided by profit. Individuals who may have been interested in personal survival or gain pushed their self-serving objectives by articulating them as beneficial to larger constituencies in order to sway members of the organization to their side. This suggests that the more uncertain and ambiguous a situation, the more multivocal it is—it can be framed and interpreted in multiple plausible ways. Forming power coalitions, then, depends on the ability to concentrate on particular aspects of people's fragmented identities and to provide arguments that resonate with them and justifications that appeal to them.

MACRO-INSTITUTIONAL EMBEDDEDNESS

The network, cultural, and political embeddedness discussed so far largely points to the role of social influences on interactions within and between organizations. But organizations also operate in a broader macro-institutional environment that shapes economic processes, and much research in sociology shows how macro-institutions provide a fundamental context of economic action (Polanyi 1944, 1957; Campbell and Lindberg 1990; Perrow 1990; Allen and Campbell 1994; Block 1994; Campbell and Pedersen 2001; Fligstein and Stone Sweet 2002; Nee 2005).

For the case of FDI, it is important to consider the effects of foreign investment policies and other features of the legal and administrative environment in Central and Eastern Europe. These institutional features often constrain investors and hosts, but in many cases they also enable them because they can be used as resources in pursuit of preferred strategies of action. Hence, just like other social forces, institutional arrangements can constrain and facilitate, depending on a situation and actors' position.

Macro-institutional policies regulate FDI activity in postsocialist Europe. At the national level, FDI policies signal a country's official response to foreign investment. Content analysis of FDI provisions in Central and Eastern Europe reveals that the official policies reflect the negotiation between two extremes: freely opening borders and providing incentives to foreign capital, on one hand, and closing borders and discouraging foreign investment, on the other hand (UNCTAD 1996a). The former is rationalized by neoliberalism and the alleged benefits of FDI for economic growth: Namely, the prosperity of a transition country is greatly enhanced with inflows of foreign capital, transferred technological and managerial know-how, and the integration of a transition economy into the web of MNCs. The other end of the spectrum is fueled by nation-oriented discourse, which emphasizes the preservation and protection of national assets, and is grounded in opposition to the exploitation by the rich West.

Situating itself between the two poles, a state can adopt a variety of official measures that more or less regulate FDI, impose restrictions over it, or actively encourage it. For example, states can greatly intervene if they review every FDI effort and require approval for every transaction from a domestic state agency. By identifying sectoral restrictions, states can prevent investment in those strategic activities that should be preserved in national control, such as natural resources, military production, or media. States can also regulate FDI by setting limits on repatriation of profits.

On the other hand, states can solicit FDI by offering incentives that render the locations within their national territory more attractive than alternatives in other countries. In particular, states can offer tax holidays or tax breaks or can exempt investors from paying customs tariffs. Moreover, privatization schemes in the transition countries can also facilitate FDI by giving foreign investors rights to buy state-owned enterprises equal to the rights belonging to domestic investors.

How do states decide which policies to adopt? From the instrumentalist perspective, public action aims at utility maximization. States as rational and purposive actors select the policy that will ensure the most efficient outcomes. On the other hand, a social-constructivist account proposes that the adoption of FDI policies is a process through which a state institutionalizes its attitudes toward foreign investment. If (*a*) the public at large is against selling national property to foreigners, or (*b*) protectionist attitudes are also in line with formal nation-building processes accompanying the establishment of a new state, or (c) political parties with populist (nationalist) attitudes have a majority, it is likely that a country's official FDI policy will reflect protectionist attitudes and discourage or restrict foreign investments. Moreover, such policies are not stable. In particular, we can see that formal FDI policies in Central and East European countries have become more liberal over time (Bandelj 2003). To understand these changes, we have to go beyond national borders and consider the global context of neoliberal reform and how associational memberships in WTO and OECD and links to the World Bank, IMF, or EBRD promote it (Meyer et al. 1997; Carruthers, Babb, and Halliday 2001; Henisz, Zelner, and Guillén 2005).

Policies are also converging because of mimetic isomorphism (DiMaggio and Powell 1983). Central and East European states often compete for similar FDI opportunities from the West. Hence, they are very aware of FDI provisions in other countries and strive to emulate them. For instance, officials in the Slovenian Trade and Investment Promotion Agency expressed their opinion that Slovenia should adopt additional incentives and further liberalize its legislation in order to compete for foreign investments with the other Central and East European states. They remarked that other countries are continuously improving their investment climate and are providing additional incentives to foreign investors. Slovenia should follow suit.[23]

Overall, official institutional provisions regulate economic transactions and impose concrete restrictions on economic exchange. These provisions are not objectively given and they change over time, responding to transnational pressures and domestic interests.

Institutional arrangements can be used as resources for participants in FDI transactions to pursue their preferred strategies of action. A Dutch petroleum company wanted to build a gas station on land it bought in Slovenia. However, national regulations mandated that after land is acquired, investors, be they domestic or foreign, need to apply for a location permit and a building permit before they start construction. At the completion of construction, the investor needs to get an operation permit. Acquiring all these permits is a highly bureaucratized procedure. For example, the location documentation (i.e., all the documents submitted to get a location permit) involves multiparty clearances by up to twenty-two local and state authorities and substantial documentation by investors. The process takes several months. An operation permit requires a minimum of thirty documents and again takes several months to be issued (FIAS 2000). Such a redundant and often poorly coordinated procedure is very uncertain and allows for many grounds (relevant or irrelevant) for authorities to refuse issuing the permit, which is precisely what happened to the Dutch company. After the local authorities denied its documentation several times and thus prolonged the process for several months, the investor decided to sell the land and find a location in another country.[24] It is hard to pinpoint precisely why the Dutch investor ran into so many bottlenecks and procedural hurdles. It is possible, but of course not publicly acknowledged, that the major Slovenian petroleum company used its political alliances in the local administration that was handling the Dutch investment case, and thus drove off the competition.

As the Slovan-AmeriCo case illustrated, as a part of a macro-institutional environment, the privatization strategies available to Slovenians and the MEBO option crucially determined how the American attempt to acquire Slovan evolved. Should the country not allow this privatization strategy, the small shareholders among the middle management and employees would not have such a powerful say in negotiations. This case also showed that the influence of institutions is intimately bound up with the distributions of power that structure FDI transactions.

EMBEDDEDNESS: STRUCTURES-POWER-CULTURE CONFIGURATIONS

The previous four sections outlined the different ways that social forces—structures (networks and institutions), culture, and power—influence economic processes. In fact, distinguishing those influences is a hard task. Different kinds of embeddedness—network, political, cultural, and macro-institutional—are analytical devices that simplify the complex reality of transactions. However, delineating different types makes little sense if we want to understand the outcome of FDI efforts, since all social forces jointly influence economic outcomes, and they are all always, albeit in different substantive ways, implicated in economic transactions. For example, focusing only on the role of social networks in FDI efforts is insufficient. As the Slovan-AmeriCo case shows, both the American and the German investors had preexisting business and personal ties with managers of Slovan. Still, the AmeriCo acquisition failed, and this was largely due to how cultural framings and distributions of power shaped the salience of particular network ties. Therefore, it is only by treating embeddedness in its thick multidimensional version that we can understand any specific economic outcome. We need to pay attention to all three social forces concurrently and examine their constellations and interrelations. In this sense, it is empirically most useful if we conceptualize embeddedness as a structures-power-culture configuration.[25]

With this perspective in mind, let's summarize the outcome of the Slovan-AmeriCo case. Beginning at the macro level of analysis, we need to acknowledge that the action of a foreign company to invest in Slovenia was made possible by a state decision to lift restrictions and liberalize the economy, as part and parcel of economic reforms embraced by the Communist elite in the late 1980s (Slovenia was then still a republic of Yugoslavia). Moreover, state institutions and policies related to privatization in Slovenia really set the stage for the transaction to unfold. It was because of the preferred MEBO privatization strategy (with legacies in Yugoslav self-management socialism) that Slovan employees and managers could acquire equity in their company and thus a voice at the decision-making table. In addition, the consequences of state privatization decisions that required 20 percent of equity of any firm to be deposited in state funds also left significant room for the influence of state agencies and, therefore, political elites.

The interest of the American investor in this particular Slovenian firm was a result of the interactions between them as players in the same organizational field, which led to establishment of social ties between them. Likewise, the interest of the German investor in buying a part of Slovan was a result of a previously existing business connection. The initial talks about the possibility of strategic acquisition of Slovan by AmeriCo were probably facilitated because of personal connections that a few Slovan top managers had with two executives of AmeriCo. These grew out of initial business ties, which deepened because of shared cultural affinities with Slovenia or Yugoslavia because of ancestry and marriage ties.

The acquisition attempt from Americans was supported by the top management in Slovan because managers saw that it could advance their personal and the company's interest. For some it was an opportunity to sell their shares of the company for a relatively high price. For others, especially those with more experience in international business, it was an opportunity to receive an influx of fresh capital to restructure the firm and get access to new markets. At the same time, others interpreted this same economic action quite differently. They considered the American FDI attempt as a direct threat to their interests. Middle managers who were the leaders of the opposition most likely feared for their own positions or saw an opportunity to increase their power in the organization, or both. Others followed value-laden interests in preserving jobs or local community relations.

Like any social action, this FDI attempt was imbued with symbolic meaning and therefore could be framed and interpreted in many different ways. Those who were opposed to AmeriCo's acquisition latched on to a particular set of meanings that could be associated with an American FDI attempt. They framed the effort as destructive for employees and the local community, emphasizing that Americans are known for downsizing, and disregarding local relationships because they think only about profit.

This cohort of opponents used these cultural resources to advance its political interests, in a small-scale collective action.

The opposition's arguments resonated (were perceived as "right" and "believable") with several constituencies, including workers, the local cooperative, several middle managers, and the one top manager who in the end switched alliances. These people supported the framing of the Americans' effort as destructive because this interpretation aligned with the aspects of their identity that became salient in the situation. Workers (who were simultaneously owners of shares) pushed their self-interested owner identity aside and ignored how much money they could get for their shares if they sold them to AmeriCo. Rather, their identity as workers, afraid for their jobs, was made salient, although in reality there was no objective reason to believe that jobs would be lost *because* interested investors were Americans. (As it turns out, the company laid off workers later because of financial difficulties. We can only speculate, but capital and market expansion brought by AmeriCo's investment might have made layoffs *less* likely). Those community members who were part of the local cooperative, which owned a portion of Slovan shares, and those retired Slovan employees-owners who had lived in the local town for all of their lives, sided with the opposition group. Not surprisingly, they trusted those who led the opposition because they had all lived in the same close-knit community. They also felt that AmeriCo would destroy cherished Slovan-community relationships, which they strongly valued. Some middle managers joined the opposition because they felt insecure about their own positions and opportunities for advancement, and many workers joined because their friends joined, without much deliberation or articulated self-interest. In addition, many with strong Slovene patriotic attitudes didn't like the fact that Slovan might be subordinated to AmeriCo's Italian subsidiary. Potential Italian control added fuel to the opposition effort. Finally, for the top manager who switched sides, changing his position appeared a calculated strategy that could bring more personal gain, that is, a CEO position. But it is also important to acknowledge that in addition to material interest, there was an attempt to save face. He was the only one among the top managers who had lived in the local community all his life, and whose neighbors, and people he would run into in church, the local pub, or a shop were largely against the acquisition because they believed that it would ruin the highly valued character of the local community.

The Slovan-AmeriCo case was a situation where power was diffuse and interests were manifold. An issue was at stake with which top managers had very limited experience. None of these managers ever worked in a firm that had to decide on an FDI offer. Also, the CEO and the top management of Slovan were not in the position to counter the opposition effectively and mobilize stakeholders on their side. They failed to do so also because they did not convincingly articulate what they believed were the benefits of AmeriCo's acquisition for all shareholders and stakeholders. Further, it was not at all helpful that they could not unanimously stand behind their decision and that one member switched sides in the end. And according to the reasoning of the AmeriCo manager, the current CEO was reluctant (not willing? not able?) to exercise the power given to him by his position of authority.

When the German firm appeared on the scene as a potential investor, no opposition was mobilized. There were no fears of foreign owners ruining the tight-knit community character, no worries about downsizing. This economic action was interpreted as greatly beneficial to the company, in fact as the only way of saving the company from losing one of its most important trading partners. In addition, the German investment was also a solution to an intraorganizational political problem of two candidates fighting over the CEO position. And it certainly didn't hurt that there were no Italians involved in the process.

On the whole, paying attention to the structures-power-culture configurations elucidates the nuances of economic transactions. Like any other type of social action, economic exchange occurs in a network of social relations, is shaped by a broader institutional environment, is imbued with meaning, and provides terrain for power struggles. More precisely, economic actors are located in a network of social relations that have different structural properties, and influence actions through strength of ties, density of networks, or centrality of position.[26] But any economic action also has cultural significance because it is constituted by the meanings that parties ascribe to observable or anticipated behavior. It is these meanings that can be articulated as valued interests to pursue in exchanges, and have consequences for the distribution of power.[27] Moreover, any position in the network of relations requires attendant frameworks of understanding that enable actors to make sense of their role position. At the same time, any single position in the structure of social relations comes with differential power resources vis-à-vis actors in other positions, which enables actors to take certain actions but not others. Thus, every economic exchange will be simultaneously influenced by social structures, cultural understandings, and distributions of power.

Additionally, each of these social forces interacts with the other two. Exemplifying the link between culture and networks, we see how shared understandings or commitments based on identities influence the formation (or not) of network ties. In turn, network ties are important venues through which actors get new ideas that shape their cultural understandings. Network positions imply allocations of power, while changes in the distribution of power reconfigure the network structure. Interests that actors decide to pursue are based on cultural conceptions and interpretations. And if individuals can push their interests by getting support from others, they will increase their relative power. The other way around, power holders can use their power to legitimize new courses of action and valued goals and thus change prevalent cultural understandings.

Uncovering the interrelationships between structure, culture, and power in economic exchanges shows that social forces are not only a context for economic actions, and hence unnecessary friction (transactions costs) that rational actors need to minimize when pursuing self-interest maximization. The notion of the social as a "context" implies a clear delineation between purely (objectively) economic action, on the one hand, and exogenous social forces that impinge on this action as constraints on instrumental behavior, on the other hand. In contrast, from a social-constructivist, embedded-economies perspective, the relationship between economic action and social forces can be metaphorically likened to a figure/ground relation where the background is an integral part of the figure, the image, the action. In fact, without the ground(ing), the figure (action) would not manifest itself. Analogously, social forces in which economic action is grounded not only provide the context but, above all, constitute economic action.

CONCLUSION

What determines the realization of FDI attempts? Instrumentalist explanations make these exchanges seem straightforward and unilateral. The investor first weighs costs and benefits and decides to invest abroad because FDI is less costly than other forms of internationalization (e.g., trade, licensing). Having calculated transaction costs, firms then decide on the mode of foreign entry (e.g., joint venture, greenfield investment, or acquisition), and on the investment location, all with the goal of minimizing costs and maximizing revenues. Finally, the investors go to the chosen location and invest.

In contrast, investigating a number of concrete FDI cases showed the intricate social nature of economic practice. To understand why certain FDI efforts realize while others do not, we needed to go beyond efficiency calculations of investors and examine how organizational behavior of both investor *and* host firms is shaped by social structures, cultural understandings, and power relations in which they are embedded. The findings show that FDI decisions by Western firms can often be characterized as jumping on the East European bandwagon. Namely, investors and hosts more frequently follow the behavior of their peers than objective evaluations of alternative economic strategies available. Social networks also matter because investors use the information they get from their business partners or professional colleagues to make decisions about investment targets, and they are often swayed on the basis of personal affiliate ties to a particular country or company. FDI transactions are also culturally embedded because socially defined goals and strategies shape courses of action, and cultural conceptions of different nationals influence the evaluation of potential partners. The ability to build shared understandings during the negotiation processes, to reach a common ground, seals or breaks the deal. In addition, FDI transactions in postsocialist Europe are plagued with issues of power and control between stakeholders, and are often targets of interventions by political elites. In firms, political coalitions form to resist or champion particular FDI attempts. Furthermore, macro-institutional embeddedness leaves its mark on FDI transactions because state policies and institutional arrangements of a particular host country significantly influence the process of foreign investment. State policies, however, do not merely constrain investors through regulation. The institutional makeup of postsocialism, especially nontransparency and ambiguity, frequently also represent resources for economic actors to pursue their preferred strategies of action.

On the whole, paying attention to social structures, culture, and power in how they enable and constrain economic processes gives us analytical leverage that improves our explanations of actual economic transactions. Including all these social forces in one analysis—where they are not simply considered part of a context peripheral to the economic sphere—also reveals important interrelations between these three mechanisms that structure economic life and, consequently, provides sharper insights into why each of them makes a difference.

Chapter 6

UNCERTAINTY AND THE PRACTICE
OF FDI TRANSACTIONS

"UNCERTAINTY IS one of the fundamental facts of life. It is as ineradicable from business decisions as from those in any other field" (Knight 2002, 347). What to do and how to do it are issues that an economic actor needs to address in any situation. Sometimes finding answers may be extremely difficult. Just imagine Mr. Investor, arriving at the airport in Sofia or Ljubljana, Budapest or Riga in the early 1990s, during "a very chaotic time," venturing into a "loose environment [with] no infrastructure for investors," trying to understand Lithuanian or Romanian, or the legal system, which "is changing so rapidly it is difficult to keep abreast of all the changes," not knowing whether the tenuous post-Communist coalition government will falter next week or in six months, or if the thirty-something pieces of paperwork he just handsomely paid for (plus a "handling fee" to the bureaucrat in the office) will turn out to be completely useless or just (still) insufficient to acquire the assets he is interested in . . . among other adventures of doing business in postsocialist Europe.[1]

If Mr. Investor approached the foreign investment process rationally, provided that he already knew that he wanted to invest in Central and Eastern Europe, and was now at the stage of selecting a particular location (neither of which is straightforward to determine, but let's be kind and limit the scope of his task), Mr. Investor would have to calculate the transaction costs associated with each possible investment alternative (out of the permutations of all possible country/town/mode-of-entry options), and compare them with the estimated short-term and long-term benefits of the investment, and then choose the one that maximizes his utility. It sounds very straightforward—choose the investment that maximizes your goals—but how would Mr. Investor (who may even hold an MBA from Harvard Business School) do this *in practice*? Even if he smartly recognized that he had limited information, and narrowed the search to a few investment alternatives, how would he choose between them? For instance, when calculating transaction costs, is overcoming the communication gap with employees who only know how to work in a socialist firm, which hoards surplus and relies on state subsidies, worth $500,000 in costs? Less? More? What is the value of time spent on getting the whole set of official documents and approvals before any activities can begin . . . let's say $140,000? (Well, if he gets the head of the local administration office on his side, this would speed up the process tremendously, and might bring his cost down to about $40,000.) Let's not be fastidious! Mr. Investor can consider these costs in some general estimation of overhead (whatever that may be). But here is a tough one: How does he estimate the costs of buying an enterprise when the sale price is not announced ahead of time, because, let's face it, in the complex process of privatization, nobody knows what the price should be. How does he evaluate the heavy state involvement in private investment transactions when one cannot know whether politicians will be strongly supportive (because that is how they see their self-interest) or will fight against the foreigner who wants to "steal the country's family silver"—even if he offers loads of money for it? How would Mr. Investor conduct negotiations with the owners over the (undetermined) sales price when the owners are also managers and workers with a multitude of other concerns beyond that of maximizing share price? Not to mention that he would attempt to do so in an environment that is going through complex transformations—political, economic, cultural, legal, and so on.

I don't think I exaggerate if I conclude that in the face of such radical uncertainties, Mr. Investor would be simply overwhelmed. The idea of FDI as a result of "rational calculation of risk and return" in such circumstances seems meaningless. Moreover, should Mr. Investor attempt to calculate, he would have to pretend to know things that are to be learned only after the decision is made, and would have to commit to certain procedures that would sacrifice flexibility. Indeed, in such a situation, Mr. Investor can proceed with his business and realize his FDI *only if* he acts practically—relies on social networks, uses political alliances, and draws on available cultural conceptions to make sense of the situation. Social forces transform the uncertain, complex mess into a manageable transaction. They provide the answers to the issues of what to do and how to do it.

This chapter focuses on the practice of FDI transactions to suggest how the always present uncertainty in economic processes forces actors to behave practically rather than rationally. In the next sections, I first review different conceptualizations of economic action, discuss the concept of uncertainty, and then elaborate on the practical actor model by distinguishing between different substantive rationalities and procedural varieties of economic action. As illustrations, I describe instances of FDI attempts in postsocialist Europe.

RETHINKING INSTRUMENTAL RATIONAL ACTION

This book has advanced the idea that social structures, cultural understandings, and distributions of power are constitutive of economic exchanges and are not just part of the context exogenous to economic action. This social-constructivist perspective has consequences for our understanding of the microfoundations of economic processes, and FDI transactions in particular. Those who adopt an instrumentalist position, conceptualizing the economic and social spheres as separate, and thus treating social forces as exogenous variables mitigating, in a calculable fashion, quantifiable transaction costs, conclude that economic actors' main motivation is to minimize transaction costs and maximize profitability. However, if we adopt a constructivist stance and conceptualize social forces as endogenous to economic action, that is, if we consider that social structures, culture, and power are constitutive elements of economic situations, then we need to rethink the dominion of rational action and profit maximization as given logics of economic behavior. Within the constructivist framework, no particular principle of action can be assumed as natural; they are all socially constituted, and they acquire their taken-for-granted properties through institutionalization. Admittedly, this constructed character of economic action is rarely obvious in times of stability in contemporary capitalism, but it does come to the fore when social order is disrupted and uncertainty and ambiguity prevail.

As far as FDI goes: when the meaning of FDI as a strategy of profit maximizing is intersubjectively established as the most valuable goal in cross-border economic pursuits, and when political and institutional bases that support the capitalist system are relatively stable, rational action with a goal of profit maximization is undertaken by practitioners and assumed by observers. In this case, the fact that economic action is socially embedded is rather hidden below the surface of things, as it rests in taken-for-granted social, political, and cultural structures. This pattern reverses in times of social change. With economic change, especially the kind stimulated by large-scale transformations in Central and Eastern Europe after the fall of Communism, the meanings of valuable goals and strategies are shifting, institutions are being redesigned, and political instability is paramount. In such turmoil, social embeddedness of economic action comes to the fore, and the influence of cultural understandings, networks, institutions, and politics on economic life is made visible.

In light of this, we should not be surprised that one of the most prominent economists of FDI, John Dunning, when analyzing foreign investment in the first few years after 1989, concluded, "Foreign investment in Central and East European countries is based too much on emotional prejudices and daily political needs and is far from rational economic considerations" (Dunning and Rojec 1993, 12). Because Dunning's assumption was that rational calculation is the natural principle for conducting FDI exchanges, he implied that economic behavior in postsocialist Europe is somehow an anomaly. I disagree. From a constructivist perspective, economic life is fundamentally uncertain, and while stable institutions can help turn uncertainty into calculable risk in some situations, in most complex economic transactions there remain forms of "true uncertainty . . . not susceptible to measurement and hence to elimination" (Knight 2002, 232). In light of this character of economic worlds, profit maximization is only *one of the possible action principles* in economic transactions, and rarely manifested, albeit often intended. Because of "true uncertainty," which necessitates reliance on social forces, economic action is *substantively and procedurally variable* and not limited to the profit-maximization imperative and means-ends calculations. Therefore, in conditions of high uncertainty and ambiguity, such as those accompanying social change, it is the practical actor model that has more empirical utility than the commonly assumed rational actor approach. To establish the contrast between these two conceptual models, let us first review ideas of economic action proposed by different theoretical schools.

Synoptic Rationality of Homo Economicus

The model of action advanced by neoclassical economic theory presupposes that economic actors are independent in their decision-making, possess complete information in conditions of perfect competition, and have fixed preferences and preference ordering, which fulfills the condition of transitivity (Becker 1957; Dow 1985; Weintraub 2005). As Frank Knight put it, rational actors

> are supposed to "know what they want" and to seek it "intelligently." Their . . . acts take place in response to real, conscious, and stable and consistent motives, dispositions, or desires; nothing is capricious or experimental, everything deliberate. They are supposed to know absolutely the consequences of their acts when they are performed, and to perform them in light of the consequences. . . . People are formally free to act as their motives prompt in the production, exchange, and consumption of goods. They "own themselves"; there is no exercise of constraint over any individual by another individual or by "society"; each controls his own activities with a view of results which accrue to him individually. Every person is the final and absolute judge of his own welfare and interests. (2002, 77)

According to neoclassical rational actor model, the primary objective (or the end goal) of firms is to maximize profits. To do so, they gather information about all possible courses of action that would help them achieve their goal. They determine the costs and revenues associated with each course of action and decide on the one that maximizes profits. In case of FDI, profit-maximizing agents figure out that investing outside of their home country yields more profits than investing domestically. Moreover, comparing all possible foreign investment locations and modes of entry, they are able to choose the one that objectively minimizes transaction costs and maximizes profitability. Actors follow a rational means-ends approach and make decisions deductively by first determining their goals, then evaluating the potential strategies to reach goals based on the information at hand and, finally, choosing the alternative that yields the highest profits.

Bounded Rationality

While the neoclassical rational action model used to be widely accepted as a theoretical framework, most scholars today find that actual business decision-making deviates from the model's assumptions. They attribute this to limited cognitive capacities of humans, which prevent economic actors from synoptic rationality. In 1957, Herbert Simon conceptualized these limitations as "bounded rationality":

> The limits of rationality have been seen to derive from the inability of the human mind to bring to bear upon a single decision all the aspects of value, knowledge, and behavior that would be relevant. The pattern of human choice is often more a stimulus-response pattern than a choice among alternatives. Human rationality operates, then, within the *limits of a psychological environment*. (108; emphasis added)

Because of imperfect cognitive abilities, "limits of a psychological environment," people cannot access all information, know all action alternatives, nor the exact outcome of each, and they lack a complete preference ordering for those outcomes. This limits the extent to which actors can make a fully rational decision, and they are forced to make decisions by "satisficing," that is, finding satisfactory—"good enough"—instead of "maximizing" solutions to problems. In a sense, actors simplify a decision problem because of the difficulties of anticipating or considering all alternatives and all information.

While this perspective revises the rational action theory, it nevertheless presupposes that people make decisions on the basis of a clear means-ends schema; they know their ends/goals (profit maximization for corporations), know which means will bring out desired ends, and can evaluate alternatives (albeit imperfectly) to select the one they find satisfactory. Thus, Simon's conception of bounded rationality still assumes an objective utility-maximizing function that optimizes the actor's utility within constraints. It is just that subjectively, because of cognitive limitations and imperfect information, the actor cannot know it. A clear implication, as proposed by Simon, is that if the computational capacities of the human mind improved, we could indeed make rational decisions.

Garbage Can Model

While widely influential, Herbert Simon's formulation of bounded rationality does not anticipate that organizational decision-making is more complex than individual decision-making, and that problems may arise where decision makers within organizations have conflicting objectives. In addition, Simon's model does not consider possible "decision inconsistencies and instabilities and the extent to which individuals and organizations do things without apparent reason" (March 1978, 590). This has led a group of scholars building on Simon's work to consider less intentional conceptions of action and launch a different critique of the rational action model. Cohen, March, and Olsen (1972) proposed what they called "a garbage can" model of decision-making. This model suggests that organizations have "garbage cans" into which a variety of problems and solutions are dumped independently of each other by decision makers who generate them. The model implies that problems, solutions, and decision makers, all integral elements of a decision, are not necessarily related to each other. In fact, a decision takes place when problems, solutions, and decision makers align more or less by chance. The alignment depends on the combination of options available at a given time, the combination of problems, the combination of solutions needing problems, and the external demands on the decision makers. Often the alignment of the problems, solutions, and individuals occurs after the opportunity to make a decision has passed, or occurs before the problem has been discovered (Cohen, March, and Olsen, 1972; Cohen and March 1974; March and Olsen 1976).

This model disconnects problems, solutions, and decision makers from each other. Specific decisions do not follow an orderly process from problem to solution but are outcomes of several relatively independent streams of events within the organization. Decisions are not made in a logical or sequential fashion. They are made on an ad hoc basis or when the solutions, problems, and individuals involved in the task happen to align. Actors discover their motives by acting and do not begin action with prior motives in mind. Reflecting upon this perspective after twenty-five years, one of the authors of the garbage can model wrote that it "views organizational life as highly contextual and driven primarily by timing and coincidence" (Olsen 2001, 193). The model itself is one of many possible interpretations of decision-making in an organization but one that tries to account for some features of decision-making that cannot be explained by prevailing perspectives of rational action.

The garbage can model portrays a decision process that seems almost orthogonal to the rational action theory because it focuses on the tendency for people, problems, solutions, and choices to be joined by the relatively arbitrary accidents of their simultaneity rather than by their obvious relevance to the situation. Nevertheless, this model still assumes, as James March, one of its originators states, "contextual rationality" (1978, 594), and thus some simple version of calculated instrumental rationality. Although problems may crystallize only after solutions for them are found, and multiple decision-makers may have conflicting objectives, it is nevertheless supposed that actors' preferences are known, well defined, and well ordered and that they structure choices. But as March (1978) himself notes, when we observe actual behavior, particularly that plagued by uncertainty and ambiguity, this assumption may be unwarranted.

Uncertainty

Uncertainty refers to situations where something is unknown, undetermined, or unsure. According to the instrumentalist perspective, uncertainty in economic processes is not really an issue because it can be estimated by risk probabilities. The world is considered objectively knowable, and any form of uncertainty is a state of mind, ignorance, that decision makers can overcome by assigning mathematical probabilities to it. To take into account uncertainty in decision-making, John von Neumann and Oskar Morgenstern (1944) formulated expected utility theory. The theory predicts utility maximization according to the following logic: the consequences of all possible courses of action, because of uncertainty as to their occurrence, are assigned a probability, that is, an estimation of how likely it is for each (objectively) to occur. Each consequence is also assigned a value (or cost), which arises if this consequence ensues. These values of alternatives and the probabilities of their occurrence are then integrated in a mathematical calculation to derive the course of action, which maximizes one's preferences with the lowest costs.

The assumption that probabilities can be objectively defined was soon questioned. In his formulation of the subjective expected utility theory, Leonard Savage (1954) proposed that people take account of their *subjective* level of confidence in how likely an outcome is to occur, and then make a decision based on subjective expected utility. The evaluation of a course of action in the face of uncertainty then involves the decision maker's preferences, "tastes," for the possible consequences and her beliefs about how likely these consequences are to be realized.

Although it emphasizes subjective as opposed to objective probabilities, this framework nevertheless assumes that people have clear and consistent preferences, that they are able to identify and evaluate all alternative courses of action, and that they are able to judge the likelihood of future events. However, in 1921 Frank Knight had already made a point about the profound uncertainty of the "future course of events," emphasizing that we should clearly distinguish between *measurable* uncertainty (risk) and the *unmeasurable* uncertainty (true uncertainty):

> The practical difference between the two categories, risk and [unmeasurable] uncertainty, is that in the former the distribution of the outcome in a group of instances is known (either through calculation *a priori* or from statistics of past experience), while in the case of [unmeasurable] uncertainty this is not true, the reason being in general that it is impossible to form a group of instances, because the situation dealt with is in a high degree unique. The best example of uncertainty is in connection with the exercise of judgment or the formation of those opinions as to the *future course of events*. (2002, 233; emphasis added)

Or, as John Maynard Keynes later expressed it:

> By "uncertain" knowledge, let me explain, I do not mean merely to distinguish what is known for certain from what is only probable. The game of roulette is not subject, in this sense, to uncertainty [because one can calculate the objective probability of any particular result]. . . . The sense in which I am using the term is that in which the prospect of a European war is uncertain, or the price of copper and the rate of interest twenty years hence. . . . About these matters there is no scientific basis on which to form any calculable probability whatever. *We simply do not know.* (1937, 213–14; emphasis added)

In face of this indeterminacy, the "we simply do not know" condition, intentionally rational actors cannot calculate, even subjectively, probabilities of outcomes. Thus, they cannot maximize utility (Beckert 1996, 2002). To a great extent, people do not know things, or they misjudge them due to limited cognitive capacities. As the work of Amos Tversky and Daniel Kahneman (awarded the 2002 Nobel Prize in economics) shows, people do not have reasonably well defined preferences among different possible outcomes of a decision. They have difficulty assessing their own likes and dislikes or anticipating their future preferences (Kahneman and Snell 1990). Their preferences are not necessarily transitive (Tversky 1969), and they show several biases in their judgments (Kahneman and Tversky 1974). For instance, they show "loss aversion," the "tendency to place greater value on an item when an individual possesses that item than when he or she does not" (Weber and Dawes 2005, 99).[2] Or, as "reflection effect" captures, people are risk averse in the case of gains and risk prone in the case of losses (Higgins 1996, 306). Moreover, people are susceptible to framing effects: "Alternative descriptions of a decision problem often give rise to different preference, contrary to the principle of invariance that underlies the rational theory of choice" (Tversky and Kahneman 1986, S251). If a decision is framed by emphasizing positive outcomes (i.e., rates of survival as opposed to rates of mortality), people will prefer it, even if the objective probability is the same (Kahneman and Tversky 1984). The notion of bounded rationality largely accommodates these decision-making biases and cognitive limitations to rational choice. The growing field of behavioral economics works to test the generality of these limitations and incorporates them in economic models (for a review see Weber and Dawes 2005).

However, cognitive limitations are not the only source of uncertainty. No. Even if actors possessed computer-like calculation capacities without judgment bias, they would often be unable to convert uncertainty into risk because of "situational structure of uncertainty" (Beckert 2002, 40): the ambiguity of meanings of economic processes, unpredictable changes in the environment, and unforeseeable choices made by other actors that influence the decision-making of any particular actor. Hence, it is because socioeconomic worlds are not objectively knowable but socially constructed that uncertainty is a fundamental aspect of life. Part of the situational uncertainty is due to social-structural foundations of economic processes: actors cannot anticipate all probabilities in advance because they do not know how others with whom they are connected will behave, nor what others' beliefs about the future states of the world are, which would all need to be taken into account to form rational expectations (DiMaggio 2002, 85). In addition, because of the importance of macro-institutional and political forces in structuring economic processes, changes in the legal, policy, and political makeup of economic situations have immediate consequences for economic outcomes. If these changes are sudden, they cannot be anticipated in advance. Moreover, ambiguity, that is, uncertainty in meanings, implies the presence of plural, often contradictory logics, practices, and justification regimes that are not eliminated by additional increments of information (March 1994; Bestor 2004). Ambiguity, then, is a result of cultural foundations of economic action, and the resultant multiplicity of potential interpretations of actions, actors, or situations. This also means that a consistent and clear rank-ordering of different principles and preferences is impossible since often these principles are incommensurable (Espeland 1998). Incommensurability between alternatives is also due to the fact that actors simultaneously play different roles in business and other social settings, and this multiplicity of roles provides multiple objectives or preferences that often cannot be reconciled, and the resultant uncertainty cannot be turned into risk.

If socioeconomic worlds in which FDI actors find themselves are not objectively defined but socially constructed, the ambiguity and indeterminacy of the future give rise to situational uncertainty.[3] Hence, complexities related to FDI cannot be fully anticipated and correctly assessed, not even in principle. I presented evidence in chapter 5 of unanticipated actions on the host side of FDI attempts that crucially interfered with the profit-maximizing efforts of investors. (If investors anticipated costly complications caused by the hostile reception of their FDI effort in advance, they would have probably never considered that location.) Furthermore, in the uncertain postsocialist environment, the new institutional rules being put in place almost daily and the frequent political shifts cannot be usefully anticipated by either investors or hosts. Moreover, the transformations after 1989 have increased the ambiguity surrounding economic processes for actors in host countries. Several, often contradictory, institutional orders (socialism, capitalism, nationalism, globalism, European Unionism) have become concurrently available and have provided a multitude of legitimate interpretations of the consequences and value of FDI, and thus several plausible logics of action that postsocialist actors have difficulty evaluating and comparing. Because of all these sources of uncertainty, it is very unlikely that investors and hosts can arrive at an objectively defined optimal solution for their FDI decisions *ex ante,* which rational action presupposes. If so, they cannot maximize or even satisfice (Dequech 2003).

But if understanding FDI as a result of rational profit maximization of investors and hosts makes little sense for environments plagued with situational uncertainty, such as postsocialist Europe, what framework of economic action has more explanatory power? Based on the evidence about the social embeddedness of FDI provided in the previous chapters, I propose that it is most useful to consider that investors and hosts act *practically.*

PRACTICAL ACTION MODEL

The theory of practical action provides microfoundations to neoinstitutional analysis of organizational behavior (see DiMaggio and Powell 1991 for a classic statement). Stimulated by insights from ethnomethodology and cognitive psychology, new institutionalism questioned the usefulness of the monolithic model of rational action of neoclassical economics as

well as Parsonsian value-based rationality rooted in Freudian ego psychology, which provided microfoundations for the old institutional organizational theory (DiMaggio and Powell 1991, 22–27).

Drawing on ethnomethodology, the work of Harold Garfinkel in particular, neoinstitutionalists emphasize the role of routines, conventions, and
practical reason in guiding action. As Garfinkel (1967) observed, actors
in everyday life are practical and largely follow routines. Hence, if the
sphere of economic life and business is just another realm of social life,
theoretical preoccupation with economic actor's rationality as implied by
the rational action model may be unwarranted. In addition, the affective
and evaluative dimensions of action may be intimately bound up with
cognition (DiMaggio and Powell 1991, 22). Moreover, actors may envision a variety of alternatives as plausible strategies (logics) of action since
what is conceived to be rational depends on the intersubjective interpretation of a situation and is not objectively given. Consequently, neoinstitutionalists conceive of a variety of *rationalities* rather than a single rationality in economic action (Dobbin 1993, 1994a, 1994b). The possibility of
multiple rationalities suggests that even in the case of business decision-
making, we should broaden our understanding to include a variety of
possible goals of economic action, not only profit maximization. *Rationality is substantively variable*. Substantively, actors can be rational by
maximizing any goal they define as their subjective utility.

The practical action model also builds on the philosophy of pragmatism
and a view that action is not just *contingent on* the situation; but that the
"situation is *constitutive of* action":

> In order to be able to act, the actor must pass judgment on the nature
> of the situation. Every habit of action and every rule of action contain
> assumptions about the type of situations in which it is appropriate
> to proceed according to the particular habit or rule. In general, our
> perception of situations already incorporates a judgment on the ap-
> propriateness of certain kinds of action. This explains why situations
> are not merely a neutral field of activity for intentions, which were
> conceived outside of that situation, but appear to call forth, to pro-
> voke certain actions already in our perception. (Joas 1996, 160)

Action, then, is not merely teleological, that is, geared toward specific
identified ends, *teloi*, but is creative. Activity itself is a source of ends.
Goals and preferences do not simply derive from the "inside" of actors
but also depend on situations in which these actors find themselves and
the creative solutions they identify in response to novel circumstances
(Whitford 2002, 340). Joas's notion of creative rather than teleological
action uncovers the potential ambiguity in the instrumental relationship
between means and ends, which is the basis of the rational action model.

Rational action (and bounded rationality, for that matter) presupposes that the relationship between means and ends is clearly defined in a rational means-ends schema. This schema presupposes that goals (ends) are known *ex ante*, and that on the basis of these ends, the best strategy of action (or means) is identified, which will allow an actor to best accomplish (maximize) his or her goals. However, in situations plagued with uncertainty, people often cannot know in advance what the consequences of their actions will be, so an optimizing strategy cannot be identified. Moreover, if situations themselves are constitutive of action, then it is possible that the goals and strategies of action (i.e., both ends and means) are modified during the process of action itself. In certain cases, both ends and means emerge out of the situation and are not given prior to it, as assumed by rational action. This suggests that actors engage not merely in procedural rationality, means-end calculations, but in a variety of other procedural types of action, with different logics underlying the means-ends relationship. Just as rationality is substantively variable, action, including economic action, can be *procedurally variable*.

In sum, the practical actor model as outlined above specifies two sources of variation overlooked in the traditional profit-maximization, rational action framework. First, it highlights the possibility of substantive varieties of rationality allowing for goals other than profit maximization. Second, it uncovers procedural variation in the logic of economic action, breaking down the clearly defined means-ends calculations. The next two sections consider each of these sources of variety in turn.

SUBSTANTIVE VARIETIES OF RATIONALITY

While the traditional economic account privileges the understanding that economic actors strive to maximize profits, there may be several other equally likely and legitimate goals of economic action, comprising different substantive varieties of rationality. The claim that economic action is substantively variable rests on the assumption that motives to pursue are not inherent to human nature but that actors are socialized into culturally defined and institutionally legitimized goals, and that they are socialized into culturally available and collectively considered as (in)appropriate means to reach those goals.

In terms of valuable goals, profit maximization is only one option. There are other interests that actors pursue in the economic sphere, interests both economic and noneconomic. Neil Fligstein proposes a framework for the sociology of markets that "replaces profit-maximizing actors with people who are trying to promote the survival of their firm" (2001a, 17) so that the ultimate goal of economic action is not profit-maximization but enhancement of survival. Firms may also explicitly target earnings, shareholder value, or market share. For socialist firms, as described in chapter 2, the goal of economic action in command economies was maximization of surplus (Szelényi, Beckett, and King 1994). Moreover, when states act as economic actors, they can aim at maximization of political power or job protection. In the case of foreign direct investment, decisions could also be informed by value rationality deriving from noneconomic motives. In certain cases of East European émigrés or their children investing in their home countries, economic action may have an ideological basis, such as playing a role in building capitalism after the fall of Communism (Estrin, Hughes, and Todd 1997). These examples make it clear that not all economic activity should be seen as profit-maximizing. Importantly, the substantive rationality thesis also implies that no one goal is more objectively rational than another.

Next to substantive varieties in the goals of action, differences are also prominent in what are considered valued preferences and strategies to achieve economic objectives. Break-even calculations, or SWOT analysis, and a balanced scorecard approach are among the formal analysis models adopted by firms operating in Western capitalism and widely taught in business schools to managers and executives. But to hoard surpluses, socialist firms would find little value in SWOT and much more value in their political connections and personal ties. Moreover, there may be different means that different actors envision as the best way to achieve the same goal. In a macro analysis of the nineteenth-century industrial policy strategies adopted in France, Great Britain, and the United States, Frank Dobbin (1994a) finds that these countries pursued significantly different strategies because of different national conceptions of efficiency. It was these countries' institutions for achieving political order, emphasizing the state, firm, or market, respectively, that influenced their institutions for achieving industrial rationality and economic growth. Likewise, in a perceptive comparison of the Russian and American credit card markets, Alya Guseva and Ákos Róna-Tas (2001) show that banks in different national contexts use different strategies to evaluate the creditworthiness of prospective credit card holders. While Americans rely on a system of computerized calculations of risk utilizing scoring models, Russians rely on trust gleaned from direct and indirect social ties they have to potential cardholders. Like Dobbin, Guseva and Róna-Tas explain these differences in strategies by disparities in the macro-institutions in the two national contexts, which fundamentally structure individual decision-making. But as I have argued, in addition to institutions, other social foundations of economic action, networks, power, and culture also shape the substantive varieties of strategies of action that are available to and considered plausible by economic actors. For instance, as others have widely documented, the adoption of economic and organizational strategies is often based on imitation of others' behavior (DiMaggio and Powell 1983; Tolbert and Zucker 1983; Fligstein 1985; Levitt and March 1988; Davis 1991; Abrahamson and Rosenkopf 1993; Haveman 1993; Marsden and Friedkin 1993; Haunschild 1994; Podolny 1994; Greve 1996; Davis and Greve 1997; Haunschild and Miner 1997; Westphal, Gulati, and Shortell 1997; Avery and Zemsky 1998; Henisz and Delios 2001; Guillén 2002b).

In sum, means and ends of economic action are socially, culturally, and politically defined. Specifically, in terms of FDI transactions, social embeddedness substantively determines:

1. what should be pursued as valued goals (e.g., profits, firm survival, job security, patriotic values),
2. what strategies of action result from these broad objectives (e.g., forming a joint venture with a foreign partner, promoting the company as an investment location, investing in one's home country), and
3. what the means are for evaluating and executing each specific strategy (e.g., imitating other firms in industry, conducting formal cost-and-benefit analysis, using personal affiliate ties).

PROCEDURAL VARIETIES OF ACTION

To be exact, any substantive variety of rationality can be subsumed under the rational action framework, which treats goals and preferences as exogenous. In the formulations of rational action that go beyond allocative efficiency within a market setting, a claim that an act is rational does not refer to its substance (i.e., what is pursued) but to its procedural means-ends logic (i.e., how the action happens). The rational means-ends schema implies internal coherence whereby actors have clear *a priori* defined ends (goals) that determine the selection of means (strategies). Because preferences are stable and known, means are evaluated and ranked in terms of their effectiveness in securing desired goals. Finally, those means that help actors maximize utility are selected and implemented. Certainly, as most of the empirical research on economic decision-making acknowledges, because of cognitive limitations actors can be only bounded-rational, and they create cognitive shortcuts in evaluating the strategies. But even bounded-rational actors maintain the consistent means-ends logic of their decision-making. They have clear goals, and within the constraints of incomplete information and limited cognitive abilities, they rank the possible strategies. They decide on the strategy that is closest to the optimal one (i.e., "good enough" given the limitations) and gets them as close to the utility maximization as possible.

In contrast, the social embeddedness of economic action, the influence of politics, cultural understandings, and social structures on economic activity, often reshuffles the straightforward means-ends calculations and results in alternative economic action principles based on different relationships between means and ends. For instance, political or ideological interests may lead people to strongly identify with certain strategies of action or solutions to problems, so that they may not be able or willing to switch to alternatives even when they are more cost efficient. In such cases, the instrumental rational link between means and ends is reversed because means take precedence over ends. Unlike in the rational means-ends schema, strategies of action here are independent of action goals, which are of secondary importance and often identified only as a consequence of committing to certain means. A position that domestic ownership should be preserved and foreign investment rejected, without regard to whether this is cost efficient, exemplifies such politically and ideologically charged circumstances, where commitment to certain means determines the whole action process.

Moreover, because complex economic actions, such as FDI attempts, are *processes* (i.e., films, not snapshots) that span a significant period of time, we need to acknowledge that the course of interactions and negotiations shapes the final transaction outcome. For instance, shared cultural understandings (or lack thereof), which develop during the course of action between transaction partners, often create emotionally charged circumstances, which can compel actors to change their initial goals or modify their strategies. Likewise, new information that comes to actors via their social networks may induce them to change their preferences when the process of action is already under way. In addition, different types of economic processes in different temporal and spatial contexts have to deal with more or less situational uncertainty, such as changes in legal and political environment or economic crises. Given situational uncertainty, the straightforward means-ends schema will be less likely retained, as actors in their response to novel contingencies may change their preferences, goals, or strategies to reach them. In such circumstances, their strategies will likely be adjusted during the process of action itself. And goals that they reach at the end of the transaction may not be those they wanted at the beginning. All this suggests that social forces not only constitute actors' preferences and goals but also, and crucially, affect their stability; means, or both means and goals, can change during the action process.

In his book, *The Architecture of Markets: An Economic Sociology of Twenty-First-Century Capitalist Societies,* which provides one of the most comprehensive treatments in economic sociology, Neil Fligstein writes

TABLE 6.1
Effects of Uncertain Ends and Preferences on Economic Action

	Preferences stable	Preferences unknown or unstable
Ends determined ex ante	(Bounded) rationality	Muddling through
	Ends set a priori, decision on means based on utility maximization (satisficing)	Means change during the course of action (ends may or may not change as well)
Ends of secondary importance or not determined	Commitment	Improvisation
	Means take precedence over ends	Both means and ends evolve during the action process itself

that "the sociology of markets has accepted the idea that actors are rational (i.e., use means to attain their ends) and that they are trying to produce profits" (2001a, 13). However, based on the above discussion, sociologists and economists would be wise to consider that economic behavior exemplifies multiple action principles. Certainly, one of these principles is rational instrumental action, which is characterized by a means-ends logic: ends are defined *ex ante*, while means are known and selected by optimization, that is, by weighing which strategy will best help achieve the desired goals for the least cost.

However, when uncertainty necessitates reliance on social forces, the rational means-ends logic often breaks down and other types of economic action prevail (summarized in table 6.1). First of all, there are circumstances in which means come before ends. Means are set prior to the action process and goals are of secondary importance. Jim knows he wants to use a particular strategy of action because he is politically or emotionally bound to this strategy, or because he thinks that he *should*, on normative grounds, use this strategy. What goals this strategy will help him achieve is of secondary importance or is not articulated clearly *a priori* because means determine ends, rather than vice versa. Because the focus of action is loyalty or dedication to certain strategies, I call this *commitment-based action*.

The second type of action encompasses circumstances in which ends and means are selected rationally in advance of the transaction but, because of uncertainty and the contingency of situations, means change during the process of action. This may lead to modification in goals as well. Jim starts with a particular goal in mind and with a strategy that seems optimal. However, the indeterminacy of the future and unanticipated changes in the environment and influences of others on his behavior cause

Jim to adjust, to modify his preferences, and to reshuffle his strategies to take into account the new circumstances that come up during the process. Decision-making is incremental; novel circumstances bring new pieces of information that need to be considered in small partial plans. I call this type of action *muddling through situational contingency.*[4]

The third case in which rational means-ends logic does not exist is when ends are unclear, and stability of preferences is also absent. In this case, the action is best characterized by *improvisation*, in which action and cognition occur simultaneously. By immersion in the action process, Jim discovers ends and means as he goes along, on-the-fly. Motivations and actions overlap because situations themselves bring forth the acts (Joas 1996). The guiding principle for such creative action is a *sense* for the situation rather than the full comprehension and conscious command of it (Bourdieu 1980).

Let me illustrate these procedural varieties of economic action—commitment, muddling through, and improvisation—by providing examples of practical experiences of investor firms from the West that pursued FDI opportunities in postsocialist Europe.

Commitment-Based Action

Charles Dole is an American investment banker. His group has recently designed an investment project that brings together several North American and European firms to establish an alternative energy production facility in the Czech Republic. When asked why they chose the Czech Republic as opposed to other investment locations, Charles did not say that they did a cost-benefit analysis of possibilities and decided on the one that will maximize profitability. Rather, he said that the choice of location really has to do with his father. As an official working with the U.S. Trade Commission, Charles's father, James Dole, was assigned to work in then Czechoslovakia, and during this assignment he established multiple contacts in the country that he maintained during Communist times. Charles said that his family had many close ties to people emigrating from Eastern Europe, and that his father helped support and finance people looking to trade in Eastern Europe.

As an investment banker looking for opportunities, Charles used some of his father's contacts to gather more information about a possible location in the Czech Republic. Strongly influenced by his father's legacy, he envisioned that the project would have a social component. The project was structured so that 1 to 2 percent of gross revenue would be donated to the local community. As Charles said, the investors envisioned that part of the funds would be annually distributed to the community for general municipal and medical improvements, and part distributed to implement a vocational and job creation program that they would design together with a local nongovernmental organization.[5]

While we do not have complete information about every step Charles undertook and every thought that guided his decision-making process, we cannot assume that profit maximization played no role. However, it would be also misguided to disregard Charles's own words to the effect that he was primarily guided by his commitment to help a particular community that he felt strongly about, and that he was influenced by his father's legacy. From this vantage, profit maximization seemed to have been secondary. While economic considerations played a role, they were subordinated to social concerns that Charles considered more important.

In chapter 5, we encountered Tom Kovac, whose promotion of investment opportunities in Slovenia was based on his affinity for his grandfather's home country. In chapter 4, I reported the activities of the Polish American Economic Forum, a group of émigrés and Polish-Americans that promoted FDI in Poland to help their home country. We can conclude that certain investment locations are selected on normative grounds and on the conviction that one should do good for that location. Some theorists would explain away these cases as only superficially noninstrumental, assuming that everything is instrumental at a deeper level. From a different theoretical position, it is equally plausible that people do something, not out of pure self-interest, but on the basis of commitment—because they are convinced they *should* do it (Boudon 1998). Economist Amartya Sen (1977) pointed out that commitment to certain objectives cannot be subsumed under the rational action model because action based on commitment is nonegoistic by definition. A decision to invest in a place with which one holds a strong cultural affinity, without regard to whether doing so maximizes one's own welfare, is like that. Such action is better understood as motivated by affect than by cognition. According to Etzioni (1988, 95), "The majority of choices [based on moral commitment] . . . draw largely or exclusively on affective involvements" and operate through shame and guilt rather than reward and punishment (Elster 1989a, 1989b).

Muddling Through Situational Contingency

In the mid-1990s, British Vita, a multinational chemical company, established a wholly owned subsidiary in Poland.[6] This was consistent with the company's strategy of internationalization to lower production costs. Reflecting back on the initial stages of the transaction, managers listed as one of the key reasons for their investment in Eastern Europe the fact that several of Vita's major German customers moved their production to Poland and that the executives from Vita's subsidiary in Germany "helped to bring home to senior management the profitable opportunities opened up by the fall of the Berlin Wall and the opening up of Central Europe" (Estrin, Hughes, and Todd 1997, 167). Hence, the choice to go to Poland was largely determined by managers' business networks.

Vita also had to choose the mode of investment in Poland. The managers explained that the company decided on the acquisition of an existing facility. They wanted to have 100 percent control because they had had bad experiences with joint ventures in Africa and Canada. They did not want to have to negotiate about the way the business was run, which the split control in a joint venture implies. However, when it began the search process, Vita had problems finding a company for outright acquisition. For all the locations considered, the Polish Ministry of Privatization insisted that the Polish side retain significant shares. The company searched for several months, and even considered joint ventures (despite the original resistance to that option because it was *a priori* determined as too costly). Still, Vita could not find any suitable factories. "Vita gradually convinced itself that, despite the recent corporate emphasis on growth by acquisition, this was not the right strategy for it in Poland. However, this did not lead it to drop out of the Polish project, because management felt that it still retained sufficient expertise to attempt a greenfield development" (Estrin, Hughes, and Todd 1997, 171). But looking for a greenfield investment site was not without problems either. The company had to deal with a vast Polish bureaucracy, and to wait eight months for documents covering land registration and ownership to come from Warsaw, much longer than Vita had anticipated. Vita also had problems with local authorities over the electrical supply, which created a major crisis in the investment; Vita threatened to pull out of the deal, which forced the other party to accommodate its wishes. In sum, Vita did not expect all the administrative problems that arose, which substantially delayed its entry into the market, and thus significantly increased the transaction costs of the operation.

How can we characterize Vita's FDI efforts in Poland? As a multinational company, Vita's overall strategy was to look for investment opportunities abroad to lower production costs. Hence, the company had an ultimate goal of cost reduction, and thus profit growth. However, in the case of the investment in Poland, this specific location was not carefully evaluated in advance and not even compared to the profitability of other opportunities. (After all, many of the other East European countries had lower labor costs than Poland, not to mention low labor costs in the Third World). Rather, the decision to go to Poland was made when the opportunity presented itself, largely responding to the practices of the firms in

Vita's network. Basically, Poland was chosen because of network embeddedness: other firms in Vita's network had invested in Poland as well.

Vita also started out with a preference to enter the market via an acquisition, a decision based on previous experience with investments abroad. However, during the process, Vita changed its mode of entry preference because of the political and institutional circumstances of postsocialist Poland. These contingencies were not anticipated in advance, so the company needed to adjust as the attempt proceeded. On the whole, Vita's decision-making process was incremental. While the company had the goal of reducing production costs, strategies to reach this goal emerged in practice, and economic preferences shifted. The decisions carried out in the field were not the strategies initially intended. The institutional and political embeddedness of economic activities in Poland, which Vita could not anticipate because this was its first investment in the region, created situational contingencies to which the firm had to adapt during the process of action. The situation, however, did not fully determine the range of actions. Rather, it presented the firm with different issues that needed attention once stumbled upon. Hence, Vita did not just improvise—converging cognition and action—but did incremental planning, in which cognition is employed before action is taken. Vita was muddling through, adjusting to situational contingencies, and managing the complex situation as it unfolded.

Improvisation

Lycett Industries is a medium-sized company in the steel fabrication industry, based in the United Kingdom.[7] One of its main owners and its managing director is Robert Armitage. In the early 1990s, Armitage thought that the company needed to enter new markets and find lower-cost production sites. He believed that Central and Eastern Europe would be an appropriate place to reach these objectives. Armitage's approach to finding a suitable production site was not very methodical or cost effective. He personally traveled around Poland, then Czechoslovakia, and then Hungary for about two years in search of a site. Once he saw possibilities in the region, he decided that Lycett would not need to acquire all of an existing company, but only buy a share, since this would involve less restructuring. (He did not seem to consider greenfield investment as a possibility.) Armitage finally bought a division of the Hungarian firm Danubius. In retrospect, he argued that Hungary offered a politically stable environment and a good engineering tradition, and that Budapest was centrally located with good communications. It is unclear, however, how many of these reasons were derived in advance of the investment decision. Armitage said at a later point, "If I were to do it again, I would go to

Poland or Slovakia" (quoted in Estrin, Hughes, and Todd 1997, 119). Therefore, it would seem that the justifications provided for the choice of the Hungarian location were *post hoc* rationalizations and that Armitage's decision most likely arose out of circumstances, as a by-product of an unusual search strategy (or, in fact, lack thereof).

As it turned out, Danubius was a division of Ganz shipbuilding group, which was actively searching for a foreign partner for several years. Danubius saw FDI as an opportunity to get capital needed for restructuring and to clarify the relationship with Ganz with regard to ownership of land and buildings. In search of a foreign partner, the management of Danubius distributed pamphlets describing the firm at Hungarian embassies abroad, including the one in London. This is where Armitage learned about Danubius. He established a good relation with a person working at the embassy who arranged a visit to Danubius. (This person ended up on the Lycett Danubius board.) It is likely that Armitage continued to pursue the Hungarian location so seriously because of the rapport he developed along the way with the Hungarian from the embassy. At the same time, being a local, this person was well positioned to facilitate the negotiation process.

On the other side, the managing director of the Danubius part of Ganz Corporation thought that Lycett was a good partner because Lycett's "interest was greater [than that of other investors]" and because he "was impressed with the quality of the sample made" (reported in Estrin, Hughes, and Todd 1997, 119). Other local managers liked Lycett as a potential partner because of the sizable orders it would bring from big customers. None of the managers mentioned the importance of the price that Lycett was willing to pay for Danubius, or the fact that after a careful analysis of all possibilities, cooperation with Lycett had the most advantages and the least disadvantages, proving to be the most optimal for Danubius. In fact, the price was discussed only *after* the top management of Ganz had already agreed to sell Danubius to Lycett. At this point, the negotiations started with two Hungarian state agencies, which between them held a 100 percent share of Ganz. In the end, one of the two agencies, State Holding Company, sold its shares to Lycett, enabling it to acquire a 70 percent stake in Danubius. The other agency, the State Property Agency, "never actually made a decision on the matter of whether to sell, and indeed refused to talk about the price at all because it had not taken a decision in principle about whether or not the firm should be sold" (Estrin, Hughes, and Todd 1997, 120).

Robert Armitage, the key decision-maker, did not seem to have clear goals about the East European investment, except for the fact that he believed that going to Eastern Europe was generally a good idea. (Of course, he reported some reasons for investment after the fact, and since these were rather inconsistent, it is likely they were reconstructed in hindsight.) It is also important to note that Lycett was a relatively small company without FDI experience. Lycett proceeded without clear goals and without knowing what might be the optimal strategy. Investment in postsocialist Hungary was an unprecedented step into the unknown for this U.K.-based company. During the search process (which in this case consisted of traveling around Eastern Europe to look for opportunities), the CEO was discovering the company's goals and the strategies to reach them by responding to circumstances on the fly.

We can say that in his decision-making Robert Armitage improvised. That is, he engaged in a "sequence of relational, informational, and procedural actions and responses created, chosen and carried out . . . during the social interaction" (McGinn and Keros 2002, 445; cf. Moorman and Miner 1998).[8] He worked out the logic in interaction with others, based on his previous understandings and experiences and new ideas that emerged out of situations in which he found himself. In contrast to the muddling through of British Vita, Lycett was less systematic in evaluating the alternatives of action, and his activities were much more characterized by simultaneity of action and cognition with a greater role of chance.[9]

LOGIC OF DECISION-MAKING PRACTICE: ROUTINES, EMOTIONS, CREATIVITY

The evidence from the three cases described above does not align well with the economics textbook definition of business decision-making whereby firms, as independent and unitary rational actors, first identify a goal, then search for pertinent information, then evaluate and rank alternative strategies, and, finally, select the one that maximizes utility. Quite in contrast, investment attempts in postsocialist Europe come across as much more complicated processes because of the various unpredictabilities they involve, the multiple stakeholders they implicate, and the time and negotiation they take to realize. How do Mr. Investor and Mr. Host conduct FDI transactions in such circumstances?

Relying on routines and habits developed from past experiences is one strategy. The more experienced players, such as British Vita, explicitly mentioned their reliance on a repertoire of strategies that they accumulated from their past FDI efforts. And they avoided certain strategies because they were associated with negative experiences. However, firms like Lycett Industries, which were relatively or totally inexperienced with FDI, lacked such a toolkit of practices and, therefore, had to improvise or engage in what often seemed like trial-and-error behavior. This suggests that muddling through situational contingencies will be facilitated by reliance on routines, but in the absence of routines, actors are more likely to improvise.

In either case, it is the action process itself that shapes the economic outcomes, and the final result can rarely be fully anticipated from the beginning. Often, actors adjust in an step-by-step manner, responding to circumstances that present novel challenges. For some, after the initial few decisions are made, path dependency kicks in and is difficult to reverse. After Robert Armitage developed a rapport with a person working at the Hungarian Embassy, who promoted Danubius for him, Lycett pursued only Danubius as the investment location. Once British Vita decided to invest in Poland, it persisted with this decision, even though it encountered a great number of obstacles on the way, which forced a change in the mode-of-entry strategy. Alternatively, focusing on obstacles and constraints, and subsequent inefficiencies, may misrepresent the story. It is also possible that encountering challenges presented Vita with new valuable opportunities that the firm had not previously considered (i.e., greenfield investment) and that adopting different strategies turned out to be more cost effective in the long run. As we saw in the AmeriCo-Slovan case in chapter 5, acquisitions in postsocialist Europe may involve substantial complexities, which may have been costlier for Vita than the delays associated with getting papers for a greenfield investment. As for Armitage, although he later said he would have preferred to invest in Slovakia or Poland, according to EBRD evaluations, in the mid-1990s these two countries were more risky for investment than Hungary. Especially in Slovakia, Mečiar's nationalist government was known to favor domestic ownership, so perhaps meeting that Hungarian Embassy gentleman was actually a very good thing for Armitage's entrepreneurial activities. These thought comparisons serve to make a point: it would be incorrect to assume that uncertainties only bog down economic actors and reduce their efficiency. Although we will never know conclusively, as every FDI effort is unique, we should nevertheless consider the possibility that uncertainties and the subsequent social embeddedness of economic actions present actors with valuable business opportunities that may be a source of greater entrepreneurial profits than the alternatives the actors initially considered (cf. Knight 2002).

Then again, maximization of profits may not be the ultimate concern of investors when commitments and values take precedence. As for Charles Dole, his commitment to investing in the Czech Republic seems a way of honoring his father's legacy. Tom Kovac's lobbying for investments in Slovenia appears motivated by his attachment to his grandfather's homeland. For émigrés from Poland, the involvement in the Polish American Economic Forum that promoted FDI in Poland was a "responsibility to bring help to [their] nation . . . a 'duty' and 'obligation' in order 'to help' Poland '[their] fatherland' " (Erdmans 1998, 173).

Ultimately, the commitment strategy implies that emotions cannot be considered merely peripheral in economic decision-making (cf. Berezin 2005). In particular, the practical actor model presupposes that affect plays an important role in structuring economic action. At a fundamental level, any interest or "motive" for action is grounded in something that "motivates" a person to act, often a basic emotion.[10] More generally, it is the emotions that often help overcome true, unmeasurable, uncertainty. In one of the key sociological statements on the topic, Paul DiMaggio (2002) builds on John Maynard Keynes's (1936) notion of "animal spirits," that is, "emotional feeling states that shape economic behavior above and beyond what a purely cognitive, rational model might lead one to expect" (DiMaggio 2002, 79). According to DiMaggio, when information needed for decision-making is absent, people revert to animal spirits. In the "conditions of Knightian [true] uncertainty, when economic actors with rational intentions have little basis for estimating risk" (80), emotions make a difference.

In an earlier statement, DiMaggio singled out the importance of sympathy for economic transactions in conditions of uncertainty:

[When economic agents] need to go beyond immediate strong ties, power and reputation for probity [become] less useful bases of assessment. . . . Under these conditions, [economic actors] are thrown back on sympathy as an assessment criterion. . . . Sympathy is constructed in part out of categories (like us/not like us) and in part out of ongoing interactions in which participants form strong impressions (confidence, distrust). (DiMaggio 1993, 126–27)

As we have seen from case evidence, building sympathies while searching for a location or negotiating FDI can influence outcomes in a nontrivial manner. Robert Armitage established a rapport with the Hungarian from the embassy, which was crucial for Lycett's investment in Danubius. Even more explicitly, Slovan's rejection of AmeriCo's acquisition attempt showed the importance of sympathy, or in this case, antipathy. Remember that one of Slovan's managers commented that "AmeriCo's attitude was, 'We are going to eat you for breakfast.' " In addition, the media reported on "the American way of doing business," implying lack of care for workers and merciless downsizing, and framed AmeriCo's attempt as "a hostile takeover."[11] These labels and interpretations represented obstacles to developing sympathies between the two transaction partners. In no small way, negative feelings may have fueled the opposition to AmeriCo's investment, which in the end led to the Americans pulling out of the negotiations.

DiMaggio's (1993) comments, quoted above, also suggest that emotions may be crucial because there is a link between sympathy and trust.[12] Trust is instrumental in transactions that involve risks and uncertainties (Macaulay 1963; Zucker 1986; Kollock 1994; Podolny and Page 1998; Kramer 1999). It seems plausible that in transactions where actors used their affiliate ties to make or accept FDI, they relied on their affect as the basis of trust, which led to successful negotiations. Experimental research confirms that, even in cases of simple negotiations, there is a correlation between positive feelings on the part of both parties to an exchange and the likelihood of cooperation (Forgas 1998; McGinn and Keros 2002).

More generally, emotions are important in cases of ambiguity where one needs to make sense of information ready at hand. We hear people say that "gut feelings" (Elster 1996), or intuition, influence their actions, and a volume of research is developing on emotional intelligence as a prerequisite for effective organizational behavior (Bar-On and Parker 2000). Thus, we can modify Hans Joas's (1996) assertion to say that situations are constitutive of action because they call forth not only cognitive schemas already in our perception, which Joas emphasizes, but also emotive states that help us manage ambiguity and uncertainty. Intuition, which economic actors themselves say plays an important part in their decision-making (Agor 1986; Abolafia 1996), may be precisely the state that combines immediate cognition and emotional "gut" reaction in influencing behavior.

Another issue deserves further clarification. The influence of sympathy, and affect more generally, is closely related to the cultural embeddedness of economic processes. Cultural conceptions about the others as more or less likely partners in FDI transactions certainly influence the emotional currents of transactions as they shape the development (or not) of positive evaluations and sympathies between transactors. Even in cases where actors deliberately eschew emotional reactions (since many believe the economic world is characterized by the absence of emotion), a cultural understanding of what is (or is not) appropriate guides repression of emotional reactions, as part of what Arlie Hochschild (1979, 1983) called emotion management.

When we take into account the influence of routines and emotions, coupled with the social embeddedness of economic action, the process of decision-making in FDI attempts can be best characterized as *practical rather than rational action*, in which reasoning is infused with routine, emotional reactions, normative commitments, and "the use of tacit knowledge in an unconscious process" (Abolafia 1996, 26). Indeed, practice is not wholly consciously organized (Bourdieu 1980). It is not random or purely accidental. As a matter of one thing following from another, practice happens. Pierre Bourdieu uses the metaphor of social life as a game to exemplify the scripted and unscripted aspects of practice. First, all games have rules, and they determine what players can and cannot do. Second, games are learned through explicit teaching as well as experientially in practice. Accordingly, most people depend on their social competence, their own experience, or their practical sense of logic rather than an analytical model when they are engaged in social (economic) practices.

Moreover, the notion of practice underscores that action is a *process*. When focusing on economic action as a process, which evolves in time, it becomes even more likely that the means and ends (*teloi*) of economic action (FDI attempts) are not fixed at the beginning of transactions and stable over time. Instead they emerge out of the situation and are shaped by it, so that action is nonteleological (Dewey 1939, 1957; Joas 1993, 1996). This is contrary to the rational action postulates of given and fixed goals, conditions, constraints, and preferences. Thinking of action as nonteleological does not mean that actors are not intentional. They do act to reach some goals. But because of uncertainties, these goals, if defined prior to the action process, are likely transformed during such a process. The end to which actors arrive may not be what they wanted in the beginning. The processual nature of decision-making, and the situational uncertainty that exists in it, often break the stability of preferences and reshuffle tastes—what satisfies the actor at the end of the transaction may not be what would have satisfied him or her at the beginning.

In sum, the actors involved in FDI transactions in postsocialist Europe face cognitive and situational uncertainty. Like anyone else, investors and hosts have cognitive limitations in making rational decisions. They are boundedly rational, and much uncertainty about economic decision-making derives from their lack of knowledge and experience. Hence, in their evaluations, calculations, and estimations, they cannot turn all uncertainties into risk probabilities. Moreover, actors need to deal with situational uncertainty, which is a feature of the social or situational, not psychological or cognitive, environment. Because of situational uncertainty, actors' preferences are unstable. They may have to change strategies during action, and some actors may have unclear goals to begin with. To maneuver the shifting terrain of situational uncertainty, actors rely on their social networks, fall back on cultural conceptions and political alliances, follow routines, and trust emotions. Doing so, they act practically.

In conditions of true, unmeasurable, Knightean uncertainty, actors are unable to retain the clear means-ends logic of decision-making, and would feel incapacitated if they had to precisely calculate the risk and returns of all possible investment alternatives. Should they nevertheless try to design their actions according to a rational means-ends schema ahead of time, they would have to overly simplify and pretend to know *ex ante* things they could only discover during the action process, or *ex post*. Moreover, in this latter case, they would likely give up their investment efforts as soon as circumstances outside their script unexpectedly appeared on the scene. But investors and hosts *do* venture into the unpredictable terrain of cross-border exchanges in transforming postsocialist Europe, and they *do* successfully conclude many FDI attempts. I have argued that this is because investors and hosts opt for practical, more flexible ways to engage in FDI transactions than rational means-ends calculations prescribe: they follow commitments, they muddle through situational contingency, or they improvise. In hindsight some of these strategies may turn out to be suboptimal with respect to material efficiency. FDI business in unsettled times may or may not result in profit maximization. True uncertainty may help open up new strategic opportunities for entrepreneurial profits, but it may also limit efficiency.[13]

Conclusion

If the only thing that is certain is uncertainty, what can economic actors do about it? Von Neumann–Morgenstern expected utility theory or Savage's formulation of subjective expected utility have clear normative implications: if actors make decisions based on rational calculations, they maximize their utility. On the contrary, I tried to show in this chapter that in conditions where cognitive and situational uncertainty abound—and cannot, even in principle, be reduced to (subjective) risk probabilities—trying to strictly follow rational means-ends calculations is, in fact, an impediment. Selecting investment locations based merely on *ex ante* rational calculations of risk and return would most often prevent investors from completing FDI attempts in postsocialist Europe. Trying to reduce the complexity of FDI situations into the rational means-ends framework would incapacitate some, and it would force others to oversimplify, pretending they know things they cannot know in advance and thus sacrifice much-needed flexibility. Fortunately, economic actors are practical and creative. They don't let complexities overwhelm them, and they (usually) don't foolishly pretend to know things they don't. Rather, they rely on social forces: networks, institutions, politics, cultural conceptions, emotions, trust, and routines, which facilitate their economic behavior. These social forces constitute actors' understandings of possibilities available, help them articulate (and adjust when necessary) their preferences, and shape the criteria of strategy evaluation. Doing so, investors and hosts break the rational means-ends logic, but they rely on other principles of practical action: follow commitments, muddle through situational contingencies, or improvise.

It is important to acknowledge that the explanatory power of the practical action model may be pronounced because it is applied to highly uncertain FDI attempts in highly uncertain postsocialist Europe. However, the implications of this analysis for the prevailing understanding of economic processes as rational means-ends calculations should not be dismissed on the grounds of their temporal and spatial uniqueness (i.e., volatile postsocialism) or the peculiar nature of the economic process under scrutiny (i.e., complexities of FDI). Rather, analyses of economic phenomena generally would benefit from conceptualizing and examining the variability in substantive goals as well as the procedural logics of economic action. The task of future research is to apply this approach to other economic processes in other environments and to identify the conditions that sustain certain substantive and procedural varieties of economic action over others.

Chapter 7

EMBEDDED ECONOMIES

THE END of the twentieth century was marked by two momentous processes of social change: the fall of Communism and the rise of globalization. Much has been written and speculated about the complexity and significance of these two transformations. It is surprising, however, that we know little about how they shape each other. How are places undergoing a fundamental social, economic, and political transformation affected by global flows of commodities, capital, and culture?

The point of departure in this book was precisely the intersection of the global and local transformations. I examined the creation and operation of foreign investment markets in Central and Eastern Europe in the first decade after 1989. I analyzed the variation in FDI across postsocialist countries over time and across organizational cases. I argued that studying FDI is part and parcel of analyzing embedded economies: uncovering the social foundations of economic life by identifying and explicating how economic institutions are socially constructed and how economic action, as a relational social process, is enabled and constrained by social structures, power, and culture.

CREATION OF MARKETS: FROM ONE KIND OF EMBEDDEDNESS TO ANOTHER

The transforming postsocialist economies have been referred to in everyday parlance as "emerging markets," which implies that there is something natural and inevitable about how market-based activity in postsocialist Europe has come about. We can trace the scholarly origins of this term to Adam Smith's (1976, 13) remarks on individuals' natural propensity to truck, barter, and exchange. From this perspective, free markets reflect human nature and proliferate spontaneously because they are the most efficient economic organization.

Much scholarship has countered this ahistorical and asocial view of markets (Polanyi 1944; Fligstein 1990, 2001a; Dobbin 1994a; Carruthers 1996; Roy 1997; Swedberg 2005). Among the earliest, Karl Polanyi argued that a self-regulating market is not a natural economic principle, nor is it inevitable. Polanyi traced what he called the great transformation of nineteenth-century England, and the revolutionary attempt to create a new type of economy where market exchange, as opposed to reciprocity or redistribution, became the main form of economic integration. Polanyi pointed to state-led creation of a market-based economy, and the role of industrialists, neoclassical economists, and liberal politicians in setting up the structures that turned land, labor, and capital into "fictitious commodities," and enforced allocation by the market mechanism in all spheres of the economy. Polanyi made a strong case that self-regulating markets do not emerge *ex nihilo*. They are, as other economic arrangements, "embedded and enmeshed in institutions, economic and non-economic" (1957, 248).

In accord with Polanyi, I focused in this book on the social embeddedness of postsocialist economic orders. Whether indeed an end of history (Fukuyama 1989), the fall of Communism nevertheless marked the end of one era and the beginning of a new one for Central and Eastern Europe. Although the ending and the beginning institutional orders, socialism and capitalism, seem utterly different at first sight, I argued that they have much in common. Just as socialism was designed by Communist leaders, capitalism also had to be created by the political will of multiple actors on the postsocialist stage. Just as redistributive arrangements of a command economy were enmeshed and embedded in social forces, so is market exchange. Hence, the key issue of the transformation after the fall of Communist regimes was not an imperative to remove the influence of state, ideology, and politics on economic life. It was not about breaking the redistribution chains and tearing apart the socialist straitjacket so that the natural market spirit, uninhibited by social forces, could emerge spontaneously and unfold inexorably. It could not be so because "market spirit" is fundamentally social. Instead, the central challenge of postsocialist transformations was to institute the kind of social structures, meanings, and power allocations that support a market-based system and facilitate its functioning. The transformation from socialism to capitalism was about a qualitative change in economic organization: a shift in the substantive variety of economic embeddedness, a movement from one kind of embedding to another, a *re*-configuring of structures-power-culture configurations.

Economic change in postsocialism was ultimately a political and cultural project, even if it is rarely recognized as such by economic analysts. It was a matter of decisions by post-Communist elites about which institutional order to understand and choose as the most viable one. The eleven postsocialist countries studied in this book unanimously picked the free-market order. This meant that they had to put in place new social structures, new cultural understandings, and new power allocations, which legitimized the material self-interest of economic actors as a guiding ideational principle, and voluntary exchange between buyers and sellers in the marketplace as a practical economic strategy, in lieu of collective interest and state redistribution. Because nothing about profit maximization is natural, this process could not happen over night and had to involve efforts of a multitude of actors from various spheres. Ultimately, the change has been about institutionalization, a process in which structures and practices of a market-based economy become stable and self-repro-ducing so as to be taken for granted (Meyer and Rowan 1977; Jepperson 1991). As I have shown for FDI, an integral part of this institutionaliza-tion has not only been the setting up of the new *formal* rules of the market game but also socialization of actors into a new, legitimated set of norms, standards, and practices, that is, setting up new *informal* institutions that sustain markets. Because establishment of any institutional order does not happen in a void, the process of market institutionalization in Central and Eastern Europe has really been a *reconfiguration*: transforming that which remains from a previous order into something with a new identity. Therefore, and because of its expansive reach, encompassing all areas of life, such a reconfiguration could only be gradual and differentiated rather than sudden and identical across different national and local settings. Al-though it was largely inspired by neoliberal economic ideas propagated by international institutions and Western advisors (Lipton and Sachs 1990; Sachs 1992; Aslund 1995), and championed by many indigenous East European economists (Bockman and Eyal 2002), the incorporation of neoliberal ideas in practice has varied across countries. The performa-tivity (Callon 1998; MacKenzie and Millo 2003) of the neoliberalism model, that is, the extent to which it has been enacted and implemented, has varied across national contexts, because neoliberal ideas interacted with different preexisting institutions, power structures, and competing discourses.

I focused in my investigation on a particular kind of market behavior, foreign direct investment, which is an integral part of neoliberal reforms of economic liberalization and deregulation (Williamson 1990, 1993; Gore 2000). It is within the context of instituting a market order in post-socialism that FDI has been institutionalized and legitimized. As I showed in chapter 3, FDI flows in Central and Eastern Europe were significantly shaped by the actions of postsocialist states, which created the demand for FDI by instituting rules and regulations of open markets, and legitimating, more or less, FDI transactions as a desirable type of economic behavior in postsocialism. Specifically, after a particular state decided to establish a professional FDI agency, and after it started to sell strategic assets of formerly state-owned monopolies to foreign investors, FDI in that coun-try increased substantially. The state decisions that legitimized FDI prac-tice were not unequivocally linked to an economic necessity to get foreign capital because of dire domestic conditions. In contrast to this explana-tion based on instrumental efficiency, I found that legitimization decisions depended on (*a*) the policy legacy, in particular privatization policy, (*b*) coercive and mimetic pressures from the international environment, in response to the EU and actions of peer states, and (*c*) the prevalence of nationalist protectionist discourse in the newly established states.

While many observers have agued about the importance of state withdrawal from the economy to facilitate restructuring in Central and Eastern Europe, the findings of this analysis show just the opposite. It was the direct and active involvement of the postsocialist states rather than their withdrawal that facilitated marketization and liberalization. In this process of constructing the demand for FDI, states negotiated the various new domestic interests with the previously institutionalized alternatives for action available to political actors, and international pressures. Overall, the instrumental economic considerations turned out to be much less important. In fact, the findings of this book exposed the embedded character of economy: the intricate interactions between domestic and international political interests, discursive meanings and governance structures, and their concurrent influences on state economic policy as well as on actual economic outcomes.

This investigation also demonstrated the utility of a social-constructivist relational view on FDI. If cross-border acquisitions of equity stakes in firms are simply a matter of risk-and-return calculations of profit-minded investors—a unilateral, supply-determined process, as most analysts conceptualize it—then host states' role is either irrelevant or matters only insofar as state policies shape the incentive structures for investors. Profit-minded MNCs would subsume the benefits and costs derived from state policies into risk-and-return calculations and invest in those countries for which the *a priori* calculated return/cost ratio is highest. I have shown that such an investor-centered, *supply*-driven, perspective provides a highly skewed portrayal because it ignores the *demand* side political economy of FDI. Postsocialist states may structure the incentives for investors, but they also—and crucially—help constitute the interests of hosts, and act themselves as market players who are more or less willing to engage in transactions with foreign investors. As such, they construct the demand for FDI in their country. Ultimately, FDI is a product of negotiation between investors *and* hosts. A theory of FDI and its empirical investigation needs to account for active influences from both sides of this relational process.

● ● ●

While the first part of the book focused on the origins of FDI in postsocialism, the second part examined the operation of these newly instituted market-based transactions.

OPERATION OF MARKETS:
STRUCTURES-POWER-CULTURE CONFIGURATIONS

The question of how markets operate has been at the center of political
and sociological analyses of economic processes, but largely assumed by
economists (Barber 1977). Neoclassical economics defined a market as
an abstraction—the interaction between supply and demand to determine
the equilibrium market price. From this view, economic allocations in a
market occur through decentralized, voluntary interactions among independent buyers and sellers, who respond to freely determined market
prices in pursuit of self-interest. Trying to offer a theory that corresponds
better to actual economic transactions, institutional economists modified
this neoclassical view by recognizing that market exchange involves transaction costs. As Nobel laureate Ronald Coase spelled out:

> In order to carry out a market transaction it is necessary to discover
> who it is that one wishes to deal with, to inform people that one
> wishes to deal and on what terms, to conduct negotiations leading
> up to a bargain, to draw up a contract, to undertake the inspection
> needed to make sure that the terms of the contract are being ob-
> served, and so on. (1960, 15)

Within the purview of institutional economics, the key challenge for
rational actors who act to maximize self-interest "with guile" (Williamson 1985, 26) is to find ways to transact that will decrease transaction
costs. In some cases, where uncertainty, asset specificity, and frequency of
exchanges so dictate, it is more cost efficient to organize market transactions by subsuming them within a firm and letting managers coordinate
them than by pursuing them on the market. Market and hierarchy are
two different institutional ways of organizing economic activity, and the
choice between them depends on the amount of transaction costs involved
(Williamson 1975, 1981, 1985).

But even if institutional economists conceptualize a market as an institution, they spend little time elaborating what that entails. Rather, like
their neoclassical colleagues, institutional economists seem to conceive of
a market as a price-setting and resource-allocating "institution," regulating the exchange of commodities, where prices are somehow inherent
properties of objects themselves, and exchanges, writ large, come to be
guided by the famous invisible hand—the almost mystical aggregation of
desires and transactions that comes to embody markets. There is little
recognition in institutional economics that, because of the social nature
of transactions, and interpretive efforts of actors involved, it is often extremely difficult to define and measure transaction costs of exchange (and

thus determine the cost-minimization strategies). Moreover, issues of power are eschewed: little attention is paid to the conflicts of interest among actors and within firms. Transactions are abstracted as autonomous in social context, and because of the focus on actors as self-interested maximizers with guile, there is little consideration of the role of reputation, status, norms, and trust that structure business transactions (Podolny 1994; Granovetter 2002; Nee 2005). If anything, it seems that institutional economists would understand the reliance on social forces a result of economic agents' efforts to lower transaction costs and increase economic efficiency (Williamson 1994).[1]

In contrast, a sociological view of markets is interested precisely in clarifying what is "social" about economic exchanges. By defining markets as *social* institutions, sociologists envision them as repeated patterns of *social interaction* whereby actors orient behavior to each other and attempt to make sense of each other's actions (Weber 1978). Harrison White (1981a, 1981b) was one of the first sociologists whose interest in how markets actually work prompted him to underscore that the basis of markets is the ongoing patterns of social interaction. According to White, markets are "self-reproducing role structures among specific cliques of firms and other actors who evolve roles from observations of each other's behavior" (1981b, 518). This model of markets as cliques of mutually aware actors observing each other and signaling to each other (cf. Spence 1973), gives a sense of how actual market activity comes about and suggests that such activity is firmly grounded in social relations and processes of communication. White's model underscores that market transactions are themselves social relations between people who engage in buying, selling, producing, or consuming.[2] Extending this view, we can conclude that markets, just like family, religion, or education, are a realm of social life, and not something separate from society. It follows that the functioning of markets, as a realm of social life, is influenced by a variety of social forces: networks, institutions, cultural understandings, and politics.

Most obviously, building on White's structural approach, we can see how economic actors exchanging with each other (be they individuals, firms, or countries) are in fact located in a network of social ties. Economic outcomes will be influenced by the structure of the relationships that actors have with each other, that is, whether they are located more or less centrally in networks, whether their ties are weak or strong, and whether they have more or less ties to others who are not connected with each other, that is, their degree of structural autonomy (Granovetter 1974, 1985; Baker 1984, 1990; Burt 1983, 1988, 1992; White 2002).

Yet networks do not function without meaning.[3] Patterns of social relations require attendant frameworks of understandings that enable players to makes sense of their location in the social structure. Thus, to make sense of people's economic behavior, we really need to uncover the cultural understandings that accompany exchanges (Zelizer 1994, 2000).[4] If we take literally the concept of role used by White in his definition of markets, to act people need to know their part: they need to know what expectations in behavior and attitudes are associated with a particular role position. Intersubjectively shared sets of understandings serve as a source of those expectations. Hence, people's economic choices and preferences need to be understood as embedded in culture. The very notion of rational choice, far from inherent to human nature, reflects a cultural account of legitimate action in modern society (Meyer, Boli, and Thomas 1987). What individuals envision as their goals of action, and which strategies they consider plausible for attaining them, are culturally specific. Hence, we should problematize the taken-for-granted notion of economic rationality and consider that what is viewed as rational can take very different forms. This constructivist account is in sharp contrast to the perspective that portrays rationality and efficiency as universal and "naturally" occurring.

Furthermore, the structure of social relations and their subjective meanings for actors are not without consequences for the distribution of power and the political and state dimensions of markets. Along these lines, Neil Fligstein (1990, 1996, 2001a) argues that *markets are politics*: "[Economic] actors engage in political action vis-à-vis one another" (1996b, 657). Institutional preconditions of markets, such as property rights, governance structures, and rules of exchange, define how power is distributed and therefore determine how actors organize to compete or cooperate. The emphasis on the institutional preconditions of exchange also highlights the role of states in markets since it is states that institute laws and policies that guide economic transactions. Indeed, while the traditional economic approach isolates markets from the intervention of states, the embedded economies perspective considers that "state action *always* plays a major role in constituting economies, so that it is not useful to posit states as lying outside of economic activity" (Block 1994, 696). Exemplifying this view, Campbell and Lindberg (1990) argue that the state—even in the United States, where its institutional capacities for intervention are assumed to be weak—is, in fact, always present, shaping the economy through the manipulation of property rights. In other times and places, states assume different roles in the economy (for a review see Block and Evans 2005). Moreover, as economic activity beyond national borders has become more prominent, researchers also highlight the role of international governance structures and international economic arrangements in shaping cross-border exchange and national economic matters (Michie and Smith 1995; Fligstein 2005).

Distancing themselves sharply from the neoclassical conception of a market as an abstraction equilibrating supply and demand via a price-setting mechanism, as well as from the transaction cost orientation of institutional economists, sociologists have attempted to account for network, cultural, political, and state-institutional dimensions of markets. In most cases, however, analysts have privileged the importance of one social force over another. In particular, research on the importance of social relations and networks for the economy is paramount. This largely owes to the legacy of now classic article by Mark Granovetter, in which he asserted that "the behavior and institutions [of economic life] are so constrained by ongoing social relations that to construe them as independent is a grievous misunderstanding" (1985, 481–82). Granovetter's central statement has stimulated an enormous body of research in economic sociology, but its credo status has also contributed to a general impression by most nonspecialists that a sociological perspective on markets is synonymous with the focus on the embeddedness in networks of social relations. As a result, even the concept of embeddedness, which Granovetter borrowed from Polanyi, is often interpreted rather narrowly to mean embeddedness in networks.[5]

However, as the evidence presented here showed, a focus on just one social force, albeit as pervasive as networks of social relations, provides a unidimensional view of economic life. In contrast, I advanced in this book a multidimensional, embedded economies view, which focuses on the structures-power-culture configurations and emphasizes that any economic exchange is influenced *simultaneously* by social structures (i.e., networks and institutions), cultural understandings, and distributions of power. When making their decisions, economic actors rely on their business connections and personal ties. But they also rely on their cultural understandings and affinities. They use their political alliances and vie for power. And they do so in the context of institutional arrangements. The appeal of the multidimensional focus is not only in complicating the sociological portrayal of the economic landscape. The utility of the structures-power-culture focus, as a lens to analyze economic organization and action, is principally in uncovering the socially constructed nature of economy, and then urging the analyst to examine the interrelationships between different social mechanisms to gain a clearer understanding of how and why each individual one matters for economic outcomes.

Uncovering the interrelationships between structures, power, and culture in economic exchanges also questions the dominant assumption that social forces merely regulate economic activity by placing constraints on rational action, and shaping the incentive structures of efficiency-maximizing actors. What the constructivist perspective highlights is that beyond their constraining features, social forces make economic behavior possible because they constitute actors' understandings of economic strategies and goals, enable the evaluation of alternatives that these actors conceive as plausible, empower them to act, and sustain structural conditions in which action takes place.

My analysis of FDI flows and transactions substantiated the utility of disentangling the structures-power-culture configurations of market-based activity. As presented in chapter 4, whether a postsocialist country receives more or less FDI depends not so much on its objective indicators of economic prosperity, stability, and risk, but on political, migration, trade, and cultural relations that it has established with potential investor countries. However, not all kinds of social relations are consequential and not all enhance efficiency. While established business and personal ties forged through trade and migration flows between nations likely decrease costs of FDI transactions, established connections, personal affiliations, and cultural conceptions may also lock actors into a limited number of alternatives. Moreover, the local actors at investment sites may interfere with investors' profit maximization efforts by modifying the investors' original intentions, and sometimes by rejecting investor efforts altogether.

Analyses of FDI transactions at the firm level presented in chapters 5 and 6 provided further evidence that economic action is not always geared to profit maximization, and that it does not always follow a stable and *a priori* known instrumental means-ends logic. Rather, the uncertainty and resultant social embeddedness of economic processes contribute to substantive and procedural variability in FDI transactions. *Substantively*, there are many competing ideas as to what valuable economic goals should be. In particular there are important differences between goals that were emphasized during socialism, like full employment and economic equity, and those goals, such as shareholder value and profits, that guide the actions of capitalist firms. Because of true uncertainty, cognitive and situational, and subsequent structural, political, and cultural embeddedness of economic action, there is also variation in how economic activity is *procedurally* carried out. When uncertainties cannot be subsumed in risk probabilities, straightforward means-ends calculations are replaced by creative practical action strategies emergent during the action process. These include, but are not limited to, actions based on commitment, muddling through situational contingency, and improvisation. Indeed, in conditions of radical uncertainty—precisely what characterized postsocialist Europe the first several years after 1989—strictly following instrumental means-ends calculations represented an impediment for action, not a welfare-enhancing strategy. In face of radical uncertainty, trying to calculate risk probabilities was paralyzing. Rather, to realize FDI attempts, investors and hosts had to be practical and creative and rely on social forces.

Overall, my examination of FDI transactions in uncertain Central and Eastern Europe highlighted the fundamental role of institutions, network, politics, and culture in constituting this form of economic activity, new to the postsocialist environment. Challenging the traditional instrumental account of FDI, which focuses on risk-and-return calculations of efficiency-maximizing investors, I outlined a theory of FDI as a socially constituted relational process whereby practical investors and hosts maneuver the uncertain terrain of cross-border exchanges by drawing resources for their actions from existing social structures, distributions of power, and interpretive frames. These help participants in FDI exchanges deal with uncertainty and identify potential profit-making opportunities, but at the same time they limit the range of alternatives available to them. As such, the resultant exchanges may or may not be efficiency enhancing.

The social-constructivist perspective I advanced in my investigation of FDI in postsocialism has implications for the understanding of economic institutions and action beyond the particular economic process and the particular sociohistorical context examined in this study. My theoretical objective was not to merely dismiss the neoclassical interpretation of markets "emerging" naturally in the presence of rational, independent, self-interested actors. The neoclassical view has a straw-man appeal, but it has been undermined even within the discipline of economics itself. Behavioral and institutional economists all acknowledge social contexts. They see contexts impede the process of rational choice, or as efficiency-enhancing mechanisms employed by strategic actors, the view also shared by rational choice economic sociologists and organizational scholars. But even if they acknowledge the role of social forces in the economy, all of these instrumentalist perspectives conceptualize social forces as a context, which is exogenous to autonomous economic action. In contrast to this instrumentalist "context" account, I provided a constructivist explanation: I showed that "social" is not to be relegated to the context of economic action but is its integral part. It is the stuff economic action is made of, its constituent element. As such, this work advances the kind of economic sociology that not only provides a complimentary perspective to standard instrumentalist economic explanations, by adding a nuanced interpretation of the exogenous social context, but offers a robust alternative analytical framework (cf. Zelizer 2001, 2002a). This framework—a social-constructivist perspective on economic organization and action—challenges the assumptions commonly used to understand economic processes. It conceptualizes the economic and social spheres not as separate but as permeated and embedded. It treats economic worlds not as objectively knowable but as inherently uncertain, whereby much of cognitive and situational uncertainty cannot, even in principle, be turned into calculable risk. Consequently, economic action necessitates reliance on social forces. But actors who maneuver economic landscapes are not passive puppets on the strings of social structures, politics, and culture. These practical actors exercise their agency by pursuing not simply efficiency maximization, but multiple goals, economic and noneconomic. They act practically: they choose from a repertoire of action strategies, which includes not only means-ends profit maximization but also other substantive rationalities and other procedural varieties of creative economic action.

• • •

Finally, this study pursued the sociology of FDI by examining cross-border exchanges of ownership stakes as part and parcel of postsocialist transformations in Central and Eastern Europe. This way, I hoped to contribute to the empirical study of market transition and provide insights about the economic development of this region.

Varieties of Postsocialist Capitalism

Chapter 2 described the varieties of socialist regimes and differences in the paths of extrication. Chapter 3 pointed to the differences in the institutionalization and legitimization of FDI as a desirable economic strategy across postsocialist countries. Considering this diversity, we can hardly expect that postsocialist transformations would evolve toward a singular and universal capitalist system. Indeed, others have proposed that capitalist developments after socialism will result in a distinct variety of economic organization specific to Central and Eastern Europe. This view is consistent with the contemporary examinations of the varieties of capitalism (Hall and Soskice 2001), which begins with the observation that there are different institutional arrangements of capitalist organization and that there is no single or uniform set of economic institutions that is superior in its efficiency. This is because different national contexts offer different endowments to economic actors, and they exhibit different kinds of social regulations, laws, and industrial agreements. In addition, different societies have historically developed different institutionalized patterns of authority, which structure their logic of economic organization. As Nicole Biggart and Mauro Guillén (1999, 740) wrote, "Institutional blueprints guide which actors are constituted as legitimate economic participants, and how they relate to each other as well as to the state." Thus, networked small business firms might be the core pattern of economic organization in Taiwan, *chaebol* based on patrimonial principles in South Korea, and foreign multinationals linked to international technology and marketing channels in Spain (Orrú, Biggart, and Hamilton 1997; Guillén 2001b).

Likewise, researchers have identified specificities of the American, British, German, French, and Japanese national models of economic organization (Dore 1989; Soskice 1991, 1999; Streeck 1992; Albert 1993; Berger and Dore 1996; Crouch and Streeck 1997; Gao 1997, 2001; Hollingsworth and Boyer 1997; Hall and Soskice 2001).

In line with this literature, scholars of transition have proposed that capitalist arrangements in postsocialist Europe constitute a distinctly East European capitalism. One of the most prominent statements in this regard is David Stark's argument about recombinant property and a claim that "recombinant processes are resulting in a new type of mixed economy as a distinctively East European capitalism" (1996, 995). Based on his study of Hungarian firms, Stark proposed that the postsocialist transformation of property rights involved a formation of novel property forms based on inter-enterprise ownership, which "blur the boundaries of public and private, blur the organizational boundaries of firms, and blur the boundaries of the legitimating principles through which [actors] claim stewardship of economic resources" (Stark and Bruszt 1998, 7). These structures of institutional cross-ownership originated, in a path-dependent manner, in the informal reciprocity arrangements established during the socialist period. While Stark's recombinant property thesis has become a widely accepted explanation of postsocialist organizational processes, in a recent article Hanley, King, and Tóth (2002) argued that it "is empirically incorrect" (130). Based on survey data of Hungarian enterprises, these authors claim that *private property*, not recombinant property, has emerged as the predominant category of ownership in Hungary, because of the privatization actions of the Hungarian state and pressures from the international agencies.

Another stream of scholarship proposes that transforming Central and Eastern Europe is characterized by so-called political capitalism, whereby old cadres convert their Communist political privilege into economic advantage. As evidence for this "peculiar linkage of political power and capital" (1991, 128), Jadwiga Staniszkis reports that in 1987 in Poland, there were 80 firms owned by Communist Party officials; by 1990, just a month after Mazowiecki, initiated economic reforms, there were more than 40,000. For Staniszkis this illustrates that the former nomenklatura used its political power to enact privatization laws that enabled it to convert former positions into new forms of post-Communist privilege, and thus private wealth. The result was a creation of political capitalism (cf. Hankiss 1990; King 2001).

In contrast, Gil Eyal, Ivan Szelényi, and Eleanor Townsley (1998), in their study of the new ruling elites in Eastern Europe, found no evidence in favor of the political capitalism thesis. Instead these authors argued that no meaningful class of property owners has been created in postsocialist Central Europe. This was because the institutions of market economy preceded the formation of a propertied class, resulting in a "capitalism without capitalists." Because private property was abolished, there was no propertied capitalist class during socialism, unlike the historical formations of capitalism that Marx and Weber wrote about. Using a survey of political, cultural, and economic elites in Hungary, Poland, and the Czech Republic, these authors also found that "the majority of corporate and industrial managers have acquired no business property at all" (14) and that the only really distinct owners are the state and foreign investors.

Unlike these studies, which examined only one or at most three postsocialist countries over a short period of time, I compared and contrasted the developments in eleven postsocialist states in the first decade after 1989. Casting a wider and longer net, I find that most disagreements in the literature about the character of postsocialist capitalism stem from the narrowness of researchers' cross-national and temporal comparisons, limiting the causal factors that they consider as crucial, and the generalizability of explanations. For instance, Eyal, Szelényi, and Townsley rely on data that cover Hungary, Poland, and the Czech Republic from 1993 to 1996. As my investigation of FDI shows, by 2002 in Bulgaria, Croatia, Romania, and Slovenia, foreign ownership was smaller than in other postsocialist countries, and the state sector was larger. In these countries, managerial and employee ownership as a privatization strategy was more common and the likelihood of the acquisition of property by insiders (i.e., political capitalism) greater than in Hungary and the Czech Republic. Hence, the story of building capitalism without capitalists holds for only a few countries in postsocialist Europe, those where privatization favored outsiders and, consequently, opened doors widely to foreign investors.

Different structural conditions across countries, because of policy legacy and efforts to keep national assets in domestic hands, also contributed to more or less political capitalism and more or less pronounced recombinant property arrangements. Although many observers report that elite members of the old regime have been able to convert their political capital into economic advantage (Staniszkis 1991; Róna-Tas 1994; Szelényi and Kostello 1996; Gerber and Hout 1998; Gerber 2002), a cross-national comparison reveals that those countries that privileged insiders in efforts to avoid foreign investors facilitated this conversion more than others. Structural conditions that provided opportunities for the old cadre elite, and national protectionist efforts that eschewed selling national assets to foreigners, contributed to greater insider privilege, and a greater extent of political capitalism. The situation was different in countries where "political resentment of FDI" (Sinn et al. 1997, 178) was less pronounced and where Communism was fully discredited (if not outlawed). In terms of recombinant property, it seems that those countries that adopted privatization strategies that favored dispersed rather than concentrated owner-ship, less privatization to foreign investors, and a greater role of the state in the economy, such as Croatia, Romania, or Slovenia, will display more prominently the recombinant property patterns that Stark identified, and the blurring of boundaries between private and public.

There is another curious phenomenon in the literature on Central and East European capitalism. Most scholars of market transition point out that the word *transition* implies a common destination, so they prefer the use of *transitions* or *transformations* to suggest multiple paths (Kovacs 1994; Verdery 1996b; Róna-Tas 1997; Smith and Pickles 1998; Burawoy and Verdery 1999; Gal and Kligman 2000; Böröcz 2001). But while the idea of *multiple* paths to capitalism or multiple capitalisms is quite popu-lar, most scholarship still makes claims about *one* variety of capitalism in postsocialist Europe.[6] In contrast, my focus on the postsocialist embed-ded economies elucidated differences across different countries and a strong possibility that a variety of paths of economic development are viable because "effectiveness" and "rationality" have multiple substan-tive instantiations.

There are certainly features that postsocialist European countries have in common. They share a socialist past of a centralized economy with Communist Party rule, which fostered differentiations between the formal and informal spheres of life. After the fall of the Berlin Wall all these countries quickly started on the path to market and democracy. In all of them reforms were implemented rather quickly, in an attempt to squeeze a transformation to markets, which elsewhere took decades, into less than ten years. (The proponents of shock therapy envisioned something even faster). Moreover, the basic institutional outlines of postsocialism were drawn in a specific context of increased economic integration on a global scale, with skyrocketing FDI flows during the 1990s, and rising legitimacy of the neoliberal discourse propounded by international organizations such as the IMF, World Bank, OECD, and EBRD. These pressures created conditions in which the opening up to FDI and the creation of market institutions happened concurrently. As a result, the European postsocial-ist region as a whole is substantially more penetrated by foreign capital than other regions (figure 7.1). For example, in 2003 the average propor-tion of FDI stock in GDP for the eleven countries was 37 percent, almost twice the average for the world or for developed countries.

Within the broadly similar context of transformation, the specific cir-cumstances in each of the Central and East European countries created substantive varieties in their postsocialist economic arrangements. The common contextual forces have been mediated by these countries' histo-ries and by institutions created during state socialism, different privatiza-tion policy legacies, and different discursive and political structures. Based

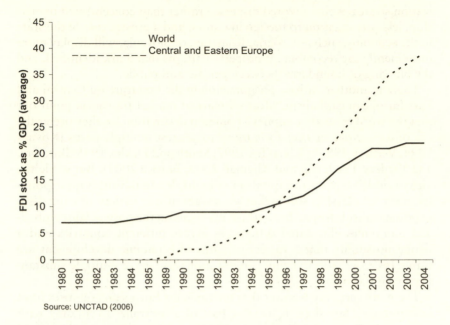

Source: UNCTAD (2006)

Figure 7.1. FDI Stock as a Share in GDP, 1980–2003

on my analysis of FDI, I propose that the configurations of postsocialist embedded economies can be seen as variable along the following, not
necessarily exhaustive or mutually exclusive, dimensions: (1) the role of
postsocialist states, (2) the extent of integration into supranational associations, (3) differences in the prevalence of informality, and (4) the ability
of foreign capital to shape domestic institutional arrangements. Different
configurations of these forces produce different types of social organization of economies *within* Central and Eastern Europe.

Role of States in Postsocialism

While there is little doubt that states in postsocialism have less direct
power over economic production and distribution than they did in a command economy, it would be incorrect to assume that the role of states has
eroded. The implementation of different privatization models (different
in strategy and timing), as one of the key institutional changes after the
collapse of socialism, enabled postsocialist states to exert a significant
influence over the development of their economy. As I showed, the role
of the states has also been crucial for economic liberalization and deregulation, and therefore the amount of FDI that countries have received. Tak-

ing different paths to privatization, liberalization, and deregulation of the economy, postsocialist states have retained different levels of control over productive assets. As table 7.1 shows, in some Central and East European countries the private sector share in GDP is 80 percent, which is comparable to that in the United States (Tanzi 1999). In contrast, some other countries, while decreasing state ownership substantially after the collapse of Communist regimes, have nevertheless maintained larger state sectors. Continued state ownership of productive assets, if it persists, may be one source of variation in economic arrangements across the region.

More generally, this pattern implies that the *nature* of states' role in the economy, that is, the quality of the state-market embeddedness, will vary across the region. Whether states remain owners of productive assets, whether they retain control over some strategic industrial sectors, or whether they focus on the enforcement of property rights and market exchange—all this will also influence the ways in which political interests shape economic matters. In addition, the nature of the state's role in maintaining social equality, and what social protections they offer their citizens, will vary across different countries. Although all of these countries downsized their welfare states after 1989, in 2003 the differences in total government expenditures, or expenditures on health and education, for example, were noticeable; even more so were social outcomes, in particular income inequalities and the estimated share of population living in poverty (table 7.1).

Influence of International Organizations

While states have had an important role to play in postsocialist transition, my inquiry also shows that their role was strongly mediated by pressures from international organizations: EU, IMF, World Bank, EBRD, and a range of credit-rating agencies, which evaluated the "effectiveness" of states in executing reforms, where effective largely meant "in accordance with the neoliberal Washington consensus." For example, the *World Bank Transition Newsletter,* informing the world about the status of one of the most successful transition economies, Slovenia, summarized the country's status in 1996:

> Slovenia has received the highest initial credit rating of any country in transition. . . . Moody's has rated it at A3, while IBCA and Standard & Poor's have given it A ratings. . . . But while the rating agencies praised Slovenia's macroeconomic management, they stressed the need to restrain wage costs, accelerate privatization, and reform the pension and health care systems. (World Bank 1996)

TABLE 7.1
Development Indicators for Central and Eastern Europe

	Bulgaria	Croatia	Czech Republic	Estonia	Hungary	Latvia	Lithuania	Poland	Romania	Slovakia	Slovenia
Gross national income per capita (%PPP)[a]	7,140	10,610	15,600	12,680	13,840	10,210	11,390	11,210	7,140	13,440	19,100
Private sector share in GDP (%)[b]	75	60	80	80	80	70	75	75	65	80	65
Asset share state-owned banks (%)[b]	14	4	4.6	0	10.8	4	0	26.6	43.6	2.9	48.6
Foreign banks among all banks (%)[b]	76	50	70	57	71	63	28.6	76	77	83	27
FDI stock (% GDP)[c]	25	37	50	79	58	32	27	27	23	36	16
Government expenditures (%GDP)[a]	38.4	52.7	44.1	36	46.9	35.4	31.5	44.8	32.3	39.2	48.2
Expenditure on health and education (% GDP)[b]	6.8	11.6	11.3	10.7	11.2	9.1	10	10.3	6.2	7.7	12.5
Informal economy (estimated % GDP)[d]	20–40	11–25[e]	—	30	20–25	40	21–27	16–19	35–50	15	17–30
Unionization rate (%)[g]	30	45	30	15	20	30	15	15	50	40	41.3
Estimated share of population in poverty (%)[b]	6	2	1	7.5	2	4.7	7.8	2	12.9	9	1
Income Inequality (GINI)[a]	35.1	35[e]	24.6	40.2	26.8	37.9	31.8	35.6	35.2	29.9	24.4[f]

[a] 2003. Source: TRANSMONEE.
[b] 2002. Source: EBRD.
[c] 2003. Source: UNCTAD.
[d] 2002. Source: Freedom House.
[e] 1998.
[f] 2001.
[g] Data from Lado 2002 and Petrovic 2002; all figures are estimates except for Slovenia; the figures refer to the years 1999–2001

This evaluation advocates the neoliberal way as the right way in transition, whereby tight monetary policy, restricted fiscal policy, and export-led growth necessitate low social security expenditures and privilege inflation concerns over wage growth. It is noteworthy that this recommendation came though the overall country's economic performance was rated as exemplary.

Tracing how postsocialist states yield to external pressures, my study is congruent with others that propose that integration into global and regional markets has diminished the regulatory autonomy of postsocialist states (Amsden, Kochanowicz, and Taylor 1994). I also show that international pressures have made the formal institutions of these states more and more similar. This is in contrast to research doubting that globalization exerts significant convergence pressures on domestic economies (Fligstein 2001a; Guillén 2001b). To consolidate disparate findings on the convergence hypothesis, I suggest that the extent to which countries yield to international pressures, and thus become more similar in formal policy, depends on (a) the structural position a particular state occupies in the world system, (b) the extent to which neoliberal proponents in a country have domestic political support, and (c) the fragility or newness of domestic institutions. Obviously, developed countries have had centuries to build their institutional arrangements, so it is not surprising that new worldwide ideologies would have a lesser impact, and these countries would continue to maintain distinct paths of development. However, for states in the process of building market-based institutions, global world culture is a source of legitimate models (Meyer et al. 1997), and neoliberal policies are often championed by domestic politicians (Bockman and Eyal 2002).

Addressing the role of international institutions, the EU deserves special mention as the key force structuring postsocialist transformations. All Central and East European states included in this study set out to join the EU after the fall of the Communist regimes. Application for membership involved aligning their emerging institutions with *acquis communautaire*, the EU legislation. This contributed to significant institutional isomorphism across the postsocialist states. However, in many cases the new institutional arrangements were enforced from the outside, as a requirement of EU accession, and sometimes did not reflect the political will of national elites (Bandelj 2004). When this is the case, it is likely that the newly adopted formal rules will be substantially decoupled from actual practice, and that the level of informality will be significant. In general, the dependence of a postsocialist country on international institutions, the extent of its integration into regional associations, and its success in the implementation of externally induced institutions will have an impact on its institutional configurations and economic performance.

Decoupling of Formal and Informal Institutions

While I found clear evidence for the convergence of FDI institutions at the level of national state policy, consistent with the world-society perspective, the empirical evidence is also strong for differentiation between formal institutions and economic activity in practice. Informality looms large in transforming postsocialist economies (cf. Böröcz 2000). Moreover, while we can trace a significant change in the formal institutions adopted by postsocialist states, most notably privatization policies and legal regulation of market-based domestic and international activity, there is greater path dependency in the informal logics of practice from one system to another. As I described in chapter 2, the formal features of the command economy were in practice complemented by informal reciprocity arrangements that helped firms maintain production despite shortages, and helped people compensate for goods and services that the system could not provide. In general, during socialism decoupling of the formal and the informal was part of everyday life. Hence, the key challenge of the postsocialist transformation has not been the reform of formal institutions, but change in the informal logics of practice, arguably a much more difficult task. As Douglass North (1993) stated in his Nobel Prize lecture,

> While the rules may be changed overnight, the informal norms usually change only gradually. Since it is the norms that provide "legitimacy" to a set of rules, revolutionary change is never as revolutionary as its supporters desire and performance will be different than anticipated. And economies that adopt the formal rules of another economy will have very different performance characteristics than the first economy because of different informal norms and enforcement.

Indeed, dismantling the formal institutions of a command economy did not automatically affect the taken-for-granted norms that guided action during socialism. How persistent and durable the effects of old informal arrangements are is in itself an empirical question. We can stipulate that these effects will depend on the interlocking of old logics with the new institutional arrangements, which can either delegitimize or sanction the old ways. We should also remember that institutional rules are accompanied by cultural understandings that are anchored in and reproduced by everyday practices (Swidler 1986). Changing informal rules, then, means changing everyday behavior and the meanings attached to it. It is likely that as long as actors have structural opportunities to use a "socialist logic of action" that is still normatively sanctioned, informality will persist. The extent to which structural opportunities and normative sanctioning differ across postsocialist countries will also have an impact on the size of the informal economy. Table 7.1 shows the variation on this dimension as of 2000.

My findings about the decoupling of formal and informal institutions in relation to FDI also speak to the debate in the globalization literature on convergence or divergence. What we see in postsocialist Europe is, in fact, the simultaneity of convergence and divergence in globalization outcomes, and it is the decoupling that sustains this simultaneity. When we examine a single phenomenon, such as FDI, at different levels of analysis, international, national, and local, we see that coercive and mimetic pressures from international institutions and peer countries encourage similarity in the ideologies concerning economic liberalization and in the formal FDI policies that a country adopts. At the same time, examining the practice of FDI transactions shows creativity of actors and assertion of local interest. Actors particularize the investment process by differentiating between more or less likely partners in FDI transactions. In some cases persistence of protectionist attitudes prevents realization of certain kinds of transactions. This means, as Viviana Zelizer (1999) has said, that uniformity and diversity are two sides of the same coin; while we may get a one-sided impression of convergence when we zero in on a particular segment of economic life, the divergence is revealed when we flip perspectives and move to a different level of analysis.

Foreign Capital Penetration of Domestic Economies

Foreign direct investment was professed as a panacea for hurting postsocialist economies and as a catalyst of market transition. Observers warned that "without massive inflows of foreign capital, successful transition in Central and Eastern Europe is unlikely" (Schmidt 1995, 268). With the analysis presented in this book I established that the process was not as straightforward as described. Different postsocialist countries received varied levels of FDI not only because of differences in economic potential and political risk, but because of greater or lesser efforts to create demand for FDI, that is, to institutionalize commitment to open markets and legitimize FDI practice. Now, what can we say is the role of foreign investment in shaping the variety of capitalisms in Central and Eastern Europe?

As table 7.2 shows, in several countries, notably Estonia, Hungary, and the Czech Republic, foreign investors have penetrated the economy so deeply that they may rightfully be considered a constituency of the new postsocialist elite (Eyal, Szelényi, and Townsley 1998; King and Szelényi 2005). Needless to say, the presence of powerful foreign business actors, on a par with the domestic elite, has serious implications for shaping the development of these economies. As previous research finds, MNCs do

TABLE 7.2
Importance of FDI in National Economies

	1990	1992	2000	2002	2003
Bulgaria	<1	2	18	24	25
Croatia	<1	1	19	31	37
Czech Republic	4	5	39	53	50
Estonia	—	9	51	65	79
Hungary	2	9	49	56	58
Latvia	—	13	29	33	32
Lithuania	—	6	21	26	27
Poland	<1	2	21	25	27
Romania	0	1	18	17	23
Slovakia	<1	3	18	35	36
Slovenia	3	7	15	19	16
Average for CEE	2	5	27	35	37
World	8	8	18	21	22
European Union	11	11	29	35	33
Developed countries	8	8	16	19	21
United States	7	7	12	14	13
Japan	<1	<1	1	2	2
China	5	7	18	17	16

Source: UNCTAD 2006.
Note: FDI stock as a percentage share in GDP.

not shy away from lobbying governments for advantageous changes at the national level (Jensen 2006).

In addition, foreign investors in European postsocialist countries may hold the majority ownership stakes in individual economic sectors. As we can gauge from table 7.1, ownership of one of the most strategic sectors of the postsocialist economies, the banking sector, is mostly in the hands of foreigners, except for Slovenia and Lithuania.[7] In 2001, the EBRD reported that in Bulgaria, 85 percent of the banking sector was foreign owned. In Croatia, "Foreign-controlled banks now account for over 80 percent of banking assets." In Poland, "The majority of assets in the banking sector are controlled by foreign owned banks." In the Romanian banking sector, "About 55 percent is foreign owned." In Slovak Republic, "The largest bank in terms of assets was sold to Erste Bank of Austria," while "the second-largest bank was sold to [an] Italian banking group" (EBRD 2001b, 126–97). These statistics point to the pervasiveness of foreigners in the financial sectors of the postsocialist economies, which may signal an important foreign influence on fiscal issues in these countries.

Still, not all of the Central and East European economies are equally penetrated by foreign investment. The degree of this penetration may be another source of variation in the types of capitalisms consolidating in these countries. Based on my findings, the variation in FDI does not chiefly depend on differences in economic and political characteristics of countries. Postsocialist states play an active and consequential role in structuring FDI inflows by conferring more or less legitimacy on foreign investors as rightful players in the domestic economy. This occurs not only through attractive FDI policies but mostly through active promotion of a country as an FDI destination: the professional support given to potential investors by national FDI agencies as well as the commitment that host states show to FDI as a development strategy by selling major strategic monopolies to foreigners. Postsocialist states' choices regarding FDI legitimization are not driven by the objective economic necessity of budget deficits or external debt but follow institutional legacies and result from an interplay between domestic and international discursive and political structures.

This social embeddedness of economic policy and economic behaviors has led some countries, like Estonia, to privilege the role of FDI in the organization of its postsocialist economy, while it has led others, like Slovenia, to follow a very different strategy. In fact, Estonia and Slovenia are probably most comparable in the set of eleven studied here. Both are very small; both emerged as independent states in 1991 out of large federal and multiethnic states, the Soviet Union and Yugoslavia, respectively; both were instrumental in starting the processes of disintegration of these federations; both were highly developed compared to the federation average; both were among the first to successfully complete EU negotiations. However, as for the role of FDI, Estonia and Slovenia stand at opposite ends of a continuum, with the highest and the lowest levels of relative FDI stock, respectively. By 2003, Estonia accumulated a striking 79 percent of GDP through its FDI stock, but in Slovenia this proportion stood at a meager 16 percent. These differences seem consistent with the more radical and wide-ranging market reform that characterized Estonia's postsocialist transformation, and the more gradual and coordinated restructuring of the Slovenian economy. While this book did not examine the direct consequences of foreign investment for economic development, the tentative evidence about the substantive varieties of market organization consolidating in Estonia and Slovenia offers an important insight for future research. It suggests that FDI may not be as consequential for economic development as international organizations and the neoliberal approach suggest. Based on the findings of my study, an assessment of the effects of FDI for economic, social, and political development would greatly benefit from understanding FDI as an integral part of substantively different embedded economies, allowing for the possibility that the relationship between FDI and different development indicators is varied and not always positive.

CONCLUSION

One hundred million people in Central and Eastern Europe who woke up that morning of November 9, 1989, to witness the destruction of the Berlin Wall could not imagine what the future would bring, what kind of a change lay ahead: how rapid, how fortunate, how devastating, how fundamental. Today, many mornings later, it seems that the changes in Central and Eastern Europe have been all that we could imagine: rapid, fortunate, devastating, and fundamental.

As a social scientist, to find myself in the midst of radical social change was tremendously stimulating because it offered an invaluable opportunity to rethink the taken-for-granted. I used the fertile ground of the shifting postsocialist landscape to ask some basic questions about how markets are created and how they operate. I analyzed how the transformation of the economic order in the first decade after 1989 happened and to what extent rationalist efficiency explanations are useful for understanding the patterns of foreign direct investment that have been pronounced crucial for the successful transformation of postsocialist Europe.

A comparative sociological approach proved fruitful. The evidence gathered from a variety of data sources and with multiple methods of analysis helped uncover the social foundations of economic transformations. It exposed the embeddedness of postsocialist economies. It showed that economic institutions are socially constructed and that economic action, as a relational social process, is enabled and constrained by structures, power and culture, and negotiated by practical actors. I hope that the social-constructivist perspective on the economy and the practical economic actor model outlined in the book provide analytical tools for a sociological analysis of economic change, organization, and action of other kinds, at other times, and in other places. Our understanding of the economy will be richer and better if we integrate into our theories the focus on structures-power-culture configurations, examine the interrelations between these social mechanisms in their influence on economic life, and treat them as constitutive, not merely contextual, forces. Furthermore, we can usefully expand the scope of our economic analyses if we consider the substantive and procedural varieties of practical economic action beyond means-ends profit-maximizing.

The final question worth posing is whether we are observing established forms of market organization in Central and Eastern Europe or whether economic orders and paths to economic development are still shifting. In most countries, reforms are ongoing, and EU accession has presented new member states with new challenges, as have developments at the global level. Almost twenty years into the postsocialist transformations, several of these countries have further embraced FDI and free-market reforms, implementing liberalization provisions with more fervor, it seems, than ever witnessed in the old liberal market economies. Hence, we do not know how thoroughly consolidated postsocialist economic organization is. Much awaits the test of time, providing fertile ground for future research and contentious terrain for policymaking. If anything, the unanticipated changes that occurred with the revolutions of 1989 have made us aware of the liabilities of grand predictions for the future. But while the substantive variety of economic organization is uncertain, I hope this book has shown that our understanding of it will be impaired if we do not pay attention to the specific configurations of social structures, power distributions, and cultural understandings that do not merely impinge on it, but make it possible.

EPILOGUE

In 2006 my father retired. He couldn't wait. Over the past fifteen years, he had run out of the energy needed to keep up with the fast pace of a global business world, the pressures on his firm to be competitive, and the hard decisions of a postsocialist manager's everyday worklife. A possibility that he might be sent to set up a production facility in China was not a welcome challenge but a heavy burden.

No wonder. In the thirty-five years of his professional life, all spent in one firm, my father experienced more than a lifetime of change: he lived one of the most dramatic transformations of the twentieth century. He began as a promising young engineer in self-management socialism, excelling and earning an Honor for Service to the Nation from Marshall Tito. At the peak of his career, he had to let go of most of the practices and values that held his world together and learn capitalism the hard way, as did millions of others after the collapse of Communism. For capitalism was not a state of nature that effortlessly manifested itself when the Red Party relinquished its power. The new institutional pillars of a market-based system have been carried on the shoulders of people who struggled to put them in place and have since been learning to take them for granted. Coming to terms with the global nature of market competition and engaging in foreign direct investment transactions had been part and parcel of these challenges.

As for my father, he is happy now to have passed his duties and responsibilities to the next generations. It will be their beliefs about valuable economic goals, their political choices on how to reach them, and their practical economic action that will create the future embedded economies.

APPENDIX ON METHOD AND DATA SOURCES

How does a lone researcher cover the vast territory of postsocialist Europe? There is an elective affinity between the methodological approach to study social foundations of foreign direct investment in Central and Eastern Europe and an attempt to get at the multidimensionality of economic organization and transformation. Rather than rely on one dataset and a single analytical technique, I adopted a broadly comparative approach based on multiple levels of analysis, using multiple sources of data and multiple methods.

COUNTRY COMPARISONS

Most previous research on postsocialist Europe relies on qualitative case studies of a few countries, which is a fruitful way to inductively develop explanations of postsocialist transformations. For instance, in American sociology Hungary has been the most studied postsocialist country (Stark 1992, 1996; Róna-Tas 1994, 1997; Böröcz 2000), sometimes compared to the Czech Republic, Slovakia, or Poland (Eyal, Szelényi and Townsley 1998; Stark and Bruszt 1998; King 2001). In addition, anthropologists Katherine Verdery (1996b, 2003) and Gerald Creed (1998) studied postsocialist transformations by conducting ethnography of Romanian and Bulgarian villages, respectively.

Building on these mostly qualitative studies, my goal was to determine the patterns of postsocialist transformations across Central and Eastern Europe. Thus, my study includes the following eleven countries: Bulgaria, Croatia, the Czech Republic, Estonia, Hungary, Latvia, Lithuania, Poland, Romania, Slovakia, and Slovenia. Table A.1 presents their basic profiles. These are all the postsocialist countries that had started negotiations for EU membership by 2002 and all can be rightfully considered advanced postsocialist states. It is likely that the patterns of transformation in Russia and the Commonwealth of Independent States (CIS) and southeast Europe have been different (King and Szelényi 2005), so my findings may not be generalizable to the other postsocialist countries. Nevertheless, while recognizing the specificities of these countries (in particular the civil war that southeastern Europe experienced, and the greater endowment with natural resources in Russia and CIS that may attract foreign investors), researchers studying FDI in these countries would benefit from considering the importance of privatization policies, political commitment to market reform, state legitimization of FDI practice, and pressures from international organizations.

The sociological account of FDI in Central and Eastern Europe presents significant methodological challenges. Not only does the embeddedness perspective suggest social-structural (i.e., network and institutional), political and cultural variables as explanatory forces, but to establish the explanatory power of this perspective, we also need to examine its strength relative to the alternative risk-

TABLE A.1
Central and Eastern Europe: Basic Characteristics

	Bulgaria	Croatia	Czech Republic	Estonia	Hungary	Latvia	Lithuania	Poland	Romania	Slovakia	Slovenia
Surface area km^2	111,000	56,540	78,870	45,230	93,030	64,590	65,300	312,700	238,400	49,030	20,270
Population (millions)	7.8	4.4	10.2	1.3	10.1	2.3	3.4	38.2	21.7	5.4	2.0
Life expectancy at birth (years)	72.4	75.4	75.7	71.6	72.6	71.5	71.9	74.5	71.3	74.0	76.6
School enrollment, tertiary (% gross)	41.1	30.8	43.2	65.1	59.6	74.3	73.2	61.0	40.2	36.1	73.7
GNI per capita, Atlas method (current $)	2,760	6,820	9,170	7,080	8,370	5,460	5,840	6,140	2,950	6,480	14,820
Agriculture % GDP	10.8	8.2	3.4	4.3	3.8	4.1	5.9	5.1	14.3	3.6	2.5
Services % GDP	59.3	61.6	58.0	66.9	65.0	73.3	61.3	64.0	50.7	66.7	62.3
Exports % GDP	58.0	47.5	71.2	78.4	65.7	44.1	52.3	37.6	35.9	76.8	60.2
Imports % GDP	68.2	55.7	71.7	86.1	68.8	59.7	59.4	39.6	45.0	79.5	61.4
Internet users per 1,000 people	283.5	293.3	469.8	496.7	267.1	350.2	281.8	265.7	207.5	422.9	475.7

Source: World Bank Development Indicators for 2004.

and-return perspective on FDI. This suggests that the number of explanatory variables is large relative to the number of country cases available to compare. To address this issue I extended the analyses over time (chapter 3) and disaggregated the country FDI flows by investor country of origin (chapter 4).

Combining Macro and Micro Levels of Analysis

To understand the broad processes of social change but also their small-scale instantiations, I combined two levels of analysis in this study: country and firm. Country-level analysis allowed me to establish which supraorganizational factors, revealed at the aggregate level, structure FDI transactions. Analysis of FDI behavior at the firm level allowed me to specify the causal mechanisms underlying country trends and examine activities of actual participants in processes we broadly understand as economic globalization.

Combining two levels of analysis was also intended to bridge the micro-macro gap present in the majority of globalization studies, which find contrasting evidence for one of the key issues: whether increasing international movement of capital, people, and culture make the world more homogenous. For example, research in the world-society tradition finds increasing convergence in institutional arrangements across countries and organizations (McNeely 1995; Meyer et al. 1997). Others report that over the past decades national value differences have persisted (Ingelhardt and Baker 2000) and that in order to cope with globalizing forces, countries and organizations strive to be different and emphasize their unique economic, political, and social advantages (Guillén 2001b). With regard to the presence of multinational corporations, empirical evidence suggests that foreign and local interact to produce hybrid practices (Watson 1997) or Creole cultures (Hannerz 2000).

However, as sociologist Mauro Guillén notes in a review of globalization studies, "Many of the empirical disagreements in the [globalization] literature are primarily due to the various levels of analysis at which different researchers operate" (2001a, 235). In this context, my study of FDI at both national and organizational levels, integrating micro- and macro-analysis, fills an important gap in the research and finds that both uniformity and diversity operate simultaneously.

Analytical Techniques and Data

Empirical analyses presented in this book are problem driven. I followed a multimethod approach whereby the choice of data and analytic techniques depended on the series of specific questions that I wanted to answer in order to tell a bigger story. Since my primary goal was to establish the presence (or lack) of patterns across the region, I based most of my macro-level analyses on quantitative data and statistical techniques. I used pooled cross-sectional time series analysis, including OLS with PCSE, GLS, and fixed effects (FE) specifications of over-time trends, as well as OLS and FE regression of a cross section of FDI flows between country dyads.

Whenever possible, I complemented these quantitative analyses with qualitative evidence gathered from thirty semistructured interviews with state officials responsible for foreign direct investment, as well as FDI researchers in Croatia, the Czech Republic, Hungary, Poland, Slovakia, and Slovenia, conducted between

2001 and 2003. I also gathered information via an email questionnaire to state agencies responsible for FDI in Bulgaria, Estonia, Latvia, Lithuania, and Romania, and by content analysis of official state documents and media accounts available on the Internet.

Analyses of FDI transactions at the firm level rely on twenty-six FDI attempts in Slovenia, the Czech Republic, Hungary, Poland, and Romania. Data come from personal interviews with managers, news articles, company documents, and statistics about cases of realized, unrealized, and modified FDI attempts that happened in the period between 1996 and 2000. For four of the examined cases, matched comparisons could be made because either investor or host was the same across two different transactions, allowing me to control for many intervening variables. One such configuration of FDI attempts included a Slovenian host with an American investor (failed) and then a German investor (realized). Another example included an attempt by an Italian investor in Slovenia (failed), and in Romania (realized).

I supplemented my own field research with ten published cases of FDI in Hungary, the Czech Republic, and Poland in Estrin, Hughes, and Todd (1997). These authors conducted interviews with managers at both investor and host sides about the FDI attempt and subsequent performance of the firm. I analyzed the parts of their data that focused on the decision-making process of investors and hosts during the initial stages of FDI transactions.

For the most detailed case presented in chapter 5, I relied on archival company records, media reports, and seven personal interviews (about 1.5 hour each) with former and current managers of the host and investor firms, conducted between 1999 and 2002. Three of these interviews were conducted with the same person at three different points in time. I used two additional interviews with relevant actors that were published in the media.

CHAPTER 3: DATA STRUCTURE, ANALYSIS, AND SOURCES

Sample

Units of analysis are country/years: 1990–2000 (for Bulgaria, the Czech Republic, Hungary, Poland, Slovenia), 1991–2000 (for Romania, Slovakia), 1992–2000 (for Croatia, Estonia, Latvia, and Lithuania). Time series start at different years because several of these countries did not exist as national units before 1992, and thus data are not available. For models that control for the percentage of labor in agriculture, the following observations could not be included because data were unavailable: Croatia (1992–95), Hungary (1991), Lithuania (1992–96), Slovakia (1991–93).

Analysis

To investigate the phenomena of interest across countries and overtime, we need to pool the individual countries' time series. Pooling creates correlations in the data due to country- and time-specific effects. The specificities of pooled cross-sectional time series analysis necessitate adjustments to the violations of OLS regression. To deal with heteroskedasticity, and contemporaneous and serial error correlation (Frees 2004), which would yield coefficient standard errors smaller than those obtained for independent data, one standard econometric approach used in political science is to estimate OLS with panel corrected standard errors (Beck and Katz 1995; Beck 2001). In sociology, most studies with panel structure use random effect generalized least squares (GLS) or fixed effects (FE) regression models (Halaby 2004). I ran the analyses for all these different model specifications and they show consistent results.

I include a time trend to detrend the data and correct for trend stationarity. Plotting the time series for individual variables shows that all of the time series are trending over time, mostly upwards, as a consequence of social change after 1989, and increasing world FDI flows from 1990 to 2000. Unfortunately, the short time series and small sample that we have is an obstacle to using statistical tests to detect a problem. (For example, the tests recommended by Hadri (2000, 149) are applicable to panel data with large T and moderate N, and in our case some of the time series are as short as $T = 5$.) Hence, I follow Baltagi (2002, 371–72), who suggests introduction of a time trend to correct for trend stationarity. Baltagi (2002) and Beck (1991) also discuss the first-difference model. Such a model is not feasible for this analysis because differencing would eliminate eleven observations from the dataset (which means a significant reduction of the already very scarce degrees of freedom). Moreover, the difference model is not theoretically appropriate. Most of the sociopolitical and institutional variables of interest are levels variables. The theory informs hypotheses about the influence of certain levels, not differences, on the outcome.

The Baltagi-Li Lagrange Multiplier test was applied to check for autocorrelation. To correct for heteroskedasticity in the FE model, HC3 robust standard errors were used, recommended for small samples (Long and Ervin 2000). In addition, all models were tested for outliers and influential cases. The analyses were conducted using the Stata 9.0 statistical package.

The outcome for the analysis of legitimization is the legitimization score for a particular country in a given year. The outcome for the analysis of FDI inflows is the per capita foreign direct investment flow into a particular country in a given year (because of clustering around zero, it is logged to reduce skewness and heterogeneity of error variance). To help establish causal priority, the predictors in both pooled cross-sectional time series analyses are measured at time $t - 1$, and the outcome is measured at time t. Operationalizations and descriptive statistics for analyses reported in table 3.3 are included in table A.2. Operationalizations and descriptive statistics for analyses reported in table 3.4 are included in table A.3.

Models 4–6 in table 3.3 show the robustness of the social embeddedness effects. I take into account a possible objection that legitimization is largely an adaptive response to the volume of FDI. Models 4–6 do not support this objection. Further, Model 5 shows a FE model, a very stringent specification that includes a series of country dummies to control for any country-specific characteristics that may be omitted from the analysis. (Such a model precludes the inclusion of any time-invariant factors, so these had to be omitted from the specification.)

TABLE A.2
Variables Used in the Analysis of the Extent of Legitimization of FDI
Practice by Postsocialist States, 1990–2000

Variable	Description	Mean (SD)	Effect
Dependent Variable			
Legitimization	Ordinal variable indicating the extent of legitimacy granted to FDI transactions through two kinds of host state actions: (A) establishment of FDI agency, (B) first state sale of assets from the banking or telecommunications former monopoly sectors to foreigners (2 = years when both A and B occur; 1 = years in which either A *or* B occurs, 0 = years in which neither occurs)	1.08 (.90)	na
Economic Conditions			
Economic Prosperity	Gross domestic product (US$ per capita, thousands)	3.30 (2.15)	–
Foreign Debt	External debt as percentage of GDP	37.99 (30.18)	+
Government Budget Balance	General government balance as percentage of GDP	−2.95 (2.74)	+
Transnational Pressures			
EU Agreement	Dummy variable indicating whether a country is bound by the EU agreement in a particular year (1 = yes, 0 = no). Due to collinearity, orthogonalized with mimetic isomorphism measure (Draper and Smith 1981).	.64 (.48)	+
IMF Program	Dummy variable indicating whether a country is under IMF loan program in a particular year (1 = yes, 0 = no). Due to collinearity, orthogonalized with GDP/capita (Draper and Smith 1981).	.69 (.46)	+
Mimetic Isomorphism	Average score of the extent of legitimization of FDI practice in other countries, excluding the focal country	1.08 (.62)	+
Political/Cultural Forces			
Political Commitment to Market Reform	Dummy variable indicating whether government in power is committed to market reform (0 = nationalist or Communist government, 1 = otherwise)	.67 (.47)	+

TABLE A.2 (*cont.*)
Variables Used in the Analysis of the Extent of Legitimization of FDI
Practice by Postsocialist States, 1990–2000

Variable	Description	Mean (SD)	Effect
Left Government	Dummy variable indicating whether political party in power is of left orientation (1 = Communist, post-Communist, socialist, 0 = otherwise)	.44 (.50)	–
Newly Established State	Dummy indicating whether the host country is a newly established sovereign state after 1989 (1 = yes, 0 = no)	.51 (.50)	–
Path-dependence			
Insider Preference in Privatization	Openness of privatization methods to insiders (4 = primarily MEBO, 3 = MEBO plus other methods; 2 = vouchers and/or direct sale; 1 = primarily direct sale)	2.38 (1.06)	+
Reform before 1989	Dummy variable indicating whether the country embarked on the reform of their socialist economy before 1989 (1 = yes, 0 = no)	.46 (.50)	–
Controls			
Previous FDI	Inflows of FDI in the previous year ($ per capita). Logged for skewness with a base 10 log transformation. Due to collinearity, orthogonalized with political commitment to market reform measure (Draper and Smith 1981).	105.82 (107.07)	+
Time Trend	Trend where 1990 = 1, 1991 = 2, . . .	5.63 (3.01)	+

Unreported GLS models with AR1 disturbance were also conducted but results remained unchanged.

Model 6 of table 3.3. takes into account possible selection effects into EU agreement and IMF program because assignment of states to these is not random. I conduct a two-stage least-squares (2SLS) regression with robust standard errors, whereby IMF program and EU agreement are first determined by economic growth and the extent to which other states had signed EU agreements, together with all other independent variables that should be included in the model for the consistency of the instrumental variable estimator (Baltagi 2002, 277). In the second stage of the regression reported in Model 6, these selection-adjusted predicted values for IMF and EU are used in place of initial variables to estimate their selection-corrected effects on FDI legitimization efforts. Results show that controlling for selection does not change the results.

2SLS Model 6 of table 3.4 corrects for effects of external pressures and ideological orientation of the government that might work indirectly on FDI flows through

TABLE A.3
Variables Used in the Analysis of FDI Flows to Central and
Eastern Europe, 1990–2000

Variable	Description	Mean (SD)	Effect
Dependent Variable			
Foreign Direct Investment	Inflows of FDI (US$ per capita). Logged for skewness with a base 10 log transformation.	116.08 (107.77)	na
Economic Incentives			
Economic Prosperity	Gross domestic product (US$ per capita, in thousands)	3.30 (2.15)	+
Economic Stabilization	Rate of inflation (%)	98.94 (240.01)	–
Credit Rating	Institutional Investor Country Credit Rating, 100-point scale indicating the expert assessed risk of default on investment for a particular country (0 = highest risk, 100 = lowest risk)	7.11 (13.57)	+
Institutional Foundations			
Privatization	Percentage of private sector contribution to GDP. Due to collinearity, orthogonalized with legitimization variable (Draper and Smith 1981).	52.97 (18.25)	+
Political Commitment to Market Reform	Dummy variable indicating whether government in power is committed to market reform (0 = nationalist or Communist government, 1 = otherwise)	.67 (.47)	+
Legitimization	Ordinal variable indicating the extent of legitimacy granted to FDI transactions through two kinds of host state actions: (A) establishment of FDI agency, (B) first state sale of assets from the banking or telecommunications former monopoly sectors to foreigners (2 = years when A and B occur; 1 = years in which either A *or* B occurs, 0 = years in which neither occurs	1.08 (.90)	+

their effects on the endogenous institutional foundations of FDI. Hence, we should adjust for endogeneity by conducting a two-stage regression analysis: the first stage (unreported) estimated all key variables of interest by regressing them on all the independent variables included in Model 6 as well as a set of country dummies to account for any country-related characteristic on these variables, and to control for panel-correlated errors. The second stage (reported) used those fitted values to estimate effects on FDI flows.

2SLS was conducted using the routine in Stata 9.0 (*ivreg*) with robust standard errors. Wooldridge (2002, 98) recommends that researchers use statistical packages that explicitly incorporate a two-stage least-squares routine because some of the sums of squares produced in the second stage that would be used for hypothe-

TABLE A.3 (*cont.*)
Variables Used in the Analysis of FDI Flows to Central and
Eastern Europe, 1990–2000

Variable	Description	Mean (SD)	Effect
Controls			
Democratization	7-point scale indicating freedom and fairness of elections and popular participation in the political process (7 = highest, 1 = lowest)	6.09 (.96)	+/–
Left Government	Dummy variable indicating whether political party in power is of left orientation (1 = Communist, post-Communist, socialist, 0 = otherwise)	.44 (.50)	–
EU Agreement	Dummy variable indicating whether a country is bound by the EU agreement in a particular year (1 = yes, 0 = no). Due to collinearity, orthogonalized with time trend (Draper and Smith 1981).	.64 (.48)	+
IMF Program	Dummy variable indicating whether a country is under IMF loan program in a particular year (1 = yes, 0 = no).	.69 (.46)	+
Share of Labor in Agriculture	Share of labor employed in agriculture on a scale from 0 to 1. Due to collinearity, orthogonalized with GDP/capita (Draper and Smith 1981).	.18 (.10)	–
Time Trend	Trend where 1990 = 1, 1991 = 2, . . .	5.63 (3.01)	+

sis testing are not appropriate in the two-stage setting (cf. Frees 2004, 207). To my knowledge, no such routine exists for PCSE or GLS models, so I use the *ivreg* routine with robust standard errors. For table 3.3, if I first determine the IMF and EU participation in a probit model (Vreeland 2003; Jensen 2006), and then use these fitted values in a regression on FDI legitimacy, I get the same results.

Data Sources

- Foreign direct investment flows: WIIW 2001, EBRD 2001b
- Legitimization: EBRD 2001b, National Accounts,[1] FDI agency websites, interviews with FDI Agency officials
- GDP per capita: IMF 2001, EBRD 2001b
- GDP growth: IMF 2001, EBRD 2001b
- Country credit rating: Institutional Investor 2003
- Inflation rate: IMF 2001, EBRD 2001b
- Foreign debt: EBRD 2001b
- Government budget balance: EBRD 2001b
- Mimetic isomorphism: Calculated on the basis of the Legitimization variable

- EU Agreement: European Union 2005; http://europa.eu.int/comm /enlargement/pas/europe_agr.htm
- IMF program: Vreeland 2003; http://pantheon.yale.edu/~jrv9 /DATA_PAGE.html
- Private sector share in GDP: EBRD 2001b
- Political commitment to market reform: Freedom House Nations in Transit 2006, http://www.freedomhouse.org; Political Parties in Europe Database, http://www.parties-and-elections.de
- Left government: Freedom House Nations in Transit 2006, http:// www.freedomhouse.org; Political Parties in Europe Database, http:// www.parties-and-elections.de
- Democratization: Freedom House Nations in Transit 2006, http:// www.freedomhouse.org
- Newly established state: National Account
- Insider preference in privatization: EBRD 2001b
- Reform before 1989: National Accounts

CHAPTER 4: DATA STRUCTURE, ANALYSIS, AND SOURCES

Sample

The empirical question in this analysis is what determines how much, if at all, world investor countries invest in postsocialist Europe, and how they choose between individual Central and East European locations. The units of analysis in chapter 4 are dyads between world investor countries and eleven Central and East European countries. To create dyads, I needed to determine the population of world investor countries. I defined world investor countries as those countries that have an established outward FDI position in 1995–97, that is, countries that have MNCs that invested abroad during the time period of the analysis. To identify these investor countries, I selected the world's top twenty investor countries in 1997 (UNCTAD 1998). In order to increase the sample size and capture more potential investors, I added to the top twenty any other country that invested at least $5 million between 1995 and 1997 in at least one of the Central and East European countries. This resulted in additional seven countries. It is important to acknowledge that the twenty-seven investor countries generated in this sampling procedure contributed 94.2 percent of the *total world FDI stock* in 1997 (UNCTAD 1998). This means that I captured well the population of world investor countries. Some of these twenty-seven investor countries do invest in Central and Eastern Europe and others do not. Some invest in all Central and East European countries, and others invest in only one or two. Therefore, there is substantial variation in the sample with respect to the outcome (i.e., FDI flows from investor country i into host country h). Specifically, 35 percent of the sample scores 0 on the outcome variable; min = 0, max = 254, mean = 13, standard deviation = 31.

Because of the specific research question about how investors decide to invest, if at all, in particular Central and East European countries, I needed to include in the analysis only those countries with an established outward FDI position. The fact that I captured the countries that contribute 92.4 percent of outward world FDI makes me confident that I included all significant potential investors. It is true that a few very small investor countries from Latin America, Africa, the Middle East, and South Asia are not included in the analysis. The reason is lack of data on their relations with the eleven host countries on six relational measures of interest. However, should data become available, I believe that the inclusion of these very small investor countries would in fact strengthen my findings about the importance of social relations on investment. Namely, country dyads formed with those investor countries would score a zero on the outcome variable of FDI, and would also score zero on the great majority of the relational measures because Central and Eastern Europe has limited economic, political, and cultural relations with those parts of the world. However, from the risk-and-return perspective, those countries would be expected to score positively on dyads formed with the more economically prosperous and the more politically stable postsocialist countries.

The final sample includes the following host countries: Bulgaria, Croatia, the Czech Republic, Estonia, Hungary, Latvia, Lithuania, Poland, Romania, Slovakia, and Slovenia. Investor countries are Australia, Austria, Belgium, Canada, the Czech Republic, Denmark, Estonia, Finland, France, Germany, Greece, Hong Kong, Italy, Japan, Korea, Latvia, Malaysia, Netherlands, Norway, Poland, Singapore, Spain, Sweden, Switzerland, Turkey, United Kingdom, and United States. According to the $5 million criterion, Ireland and Russia would also qualify as investors but were omitted because data were unavailable. Total outflows from these two countries indicate that they invest abroad relatively little and are not present as investors in the majority of my host countries. If anything, inclusion of Russia, which invests mostly in the Baltic states, would strengthen the impact of relational variables since Russia has cultural ties with the Baltics and has shared business ties with these countries since the time they were part of the USSR. Since four host countries, the Czech Republic, Estonia, Latvia, and Poland also passed my criteria for investor countries, the set of dyads is not a complete 11 x 27= 297, but 293. Data on all the relational characteristics for all host-investor dyads were not available, so 32 observations needed to be dropped. To compare these missing data cases with the rest of the sample, I fitted a dummy variable to the observations with missing data, to see if those observations were significantly different. The results showed that there was no statistically significant difference between those missing data observations and the rest of the sample.

Analysis

The dependent variable in this analysis is the aggregate of 1995–97 FDI inflow in U.S. dollars in the investor-host country dyad, scaled by host country population. I also used an outcome that scales FDI within a dyad by GDP of host country. The results were substantively similar between the two types of operationalizations. I present results for scaling by population because such analysis allows me to establish an independent effect of host country GDP on FDI.

The outcome is measured for the 1995–1997 period because 1995 marks the year of first substantial investment into the region, with FDI flows exceeding 1 percent of total GDP, and 1997 is the most recent year for which all dyadic data are available. Information on predictor variables is from a period before 1995 in

TABLE A.4

Variables Used in the Analysis of FDI Flows in Investor-Host Country Dyads

Variable	Description	Mean (SD)	Effect
Dependent Variable			
Foreign Direct Investment	Cumulative inflows of FDI from investor to host (US$ per capita) 1995–97. Logged for skewness with a base 10 log transformation.	12.67 (30.87)	na
Host Characteristics			
Development	GDP per capita (US$ thousands)	2.49 (1.71)	+
	GDP growth (%)	–3.9 (5.4)	+
	Inflation rate (%)	223.9 (249.6)	–
	Ratio of digital to all phone lines (1996)	262.7 (58.6)	+
	Ratio of highways to all roads (1996)	71.6 (21.4)	+
	Unemployment rate (%)	9.2 (4.1)	+
	Combined first-, second-, and third-level gross school enrollment ratio (%), 1994	69.8 (4.5)	+
	Average monthly wages (US$)	223.6 (164.7)	–
Political Stability	5-point scale indicating stability of government and market oriented policies (1 = lowest, 5 = highest), 1993	3.14 (1.10)	+
FDI Policy	11-point scale measuring openness of host government's FDI policy in 1993 (1 = lowest, 11 = highest)	7.80 (2.40)	+
Propensity to Invest			
Total FDI from Investor	Cumulative FDI outflows from investor (US$ billion) 1995–97 (less investment into host country during that time)	40.03 (61.97)	+
Institutional Arrangements			
Bilateral Investment Treaties	Dummy variable indicating whether countries signed bilateral investment treaty by December 1994	.64 (.48)	+

order to establish causal priority. Since the current political structure of countries in Central and Eastern Europe dates from 1992, predictors are measured for the period 1992–94. I report analyses from two different model specifications: OLS and fixed effects models. The use of dyads as units of this analysis may create correlations in data due to host- or investor-specific effects. Such clustering would yield coefficient standard errors smaller than those obtained for independent data and boost the regression coefficients. To address this concern, the robustness of

TABLE A.4 (*cont.*)
Variables Used in the Analysis of FDI Flows in Investor-Host Country Dyads

Variable	Description	Mean (SD)	Effect
EU Agreement	Three-point scale indicating whether bound by EU agreement by December 1994 (0 = no agreement, 1 = agreement by 1993, 2 = agreement by 1991)	.43 (.77)	+
Political Alliances			
Foreign Aid	Government aid from investor country to host country government (US$ per capita host)	.68 (1.83)	+
Networks			
Migration	Dummy variable indicating registered emigrants from host to investor country	.46 (.50)	+
Export	Exports from investor to host (US$ thousands per capita host)	.03 (.08)	+
Cultural Ties			
Historical-Cultural Ties	Dummy variable indicating a presence of investor country national ethnic minority in host country and vice versa	.11 (.31)	+
Gravity Model Controls			
Geographical Distance	Distance in miles between the capital city of the investor country and the capital city of the host country (in thousands)	2.11 (2.30)	–
Language	Dummy variable indicating whether the official national language in host and investor countries belong to the same linguistic group (e.g., Romance, Germanic, Slavic)	.06 (.24)	+

relational variables is tested in a model that corrects for potential bias by adding fixed effects for each host and investor country. A random effects model for hosts and investors provides a more parsimonious specification. Results from the random effects model were substantively identical to the fixed effects analysis. However, for the purposes of this analysis, the fixed effects model provides the most stringent test to assess the explanatory power of the relational perspective, since it accounts for *any* possible host or investor country characteristic, and thus also controls for any possibly omitted country characteristic variable.

A variety of diagnostics and specification checks were used to study the robustness of the results. Studentized residuals and Cook's distances revealed no influential cases, significant outliers, or severe departures from model assumptions. To assess the sensitivity of the effects (Leamer 1983) to the choice of the GDP/capita predictor as the host country economic indicator, I estimated relational coefficients for all permutations of the following host country variables, measured as annual averages for the 1992–94 period: GDP, GDP/capita, GDP growth, inflation rate, ration of digital to all phone lines, ratio of highways to all roads, unemployment rate, combined first- second- and third-level gross school enrollment ratio, and average monthly wages. The narrow range of coefficients obtained from this large set of alternative models indicated robustness of relational effects to assumptions about host characteristics.

I have also considered the potential issues of endogeneity. Geographical proximity and language similarity, two relational measures proposed by the gravity theory of economics, may be also highly correlated with migration and trade, and language (as a measure of cultural similarity) may be correlated with the indicator of historical-cultural ties. In fact, a correlation matrix of bivariate associations shows that, while statistically significant and in the expected directions, correlations between these variables are relatively modest, so multicollinearity is not an issue. Pearson's correlations are as follows: trade-distance ($-.196$), migration-distance ($-.251$), language-historical/cultural tie ($.273$). Relatively low associations are due to the specificity of the Central and East European region, which was largely closed to Western trade during the socialist period, and the fact that some of the most common migration destinations, such as the United States and Australia, are geographically quite distant.

Data Sources

- Foreign direct investment flows: WIIW 1998, OECD 1998a
- GDP (exchange values): IMF 1998
- GDP per capita: IMF 1998
- GDP growth: IMF 1998
- Inflation rate: IMF 1998
- Unemployment rate: IMF 1998
- Wages: IMF 1998
- Ratio of digital to all phone lines: World Bank 1999
- Ratio of highways to all roads: World Bank 1999
- Combined first-, second-, and third-level gross school enrollment ratio: World Bank 1999
- Political risk indicator: Dunning and Rojec 1993
- FDI policy: Dunning and Rojec 1993 and National Accounts. *Note*: The following five criteria were used in the construction of the FDI policy index of a total 12 points: (*a*) approval/registration of foreign investor required (0 = yes, 1 = no); (*b*) sectors restricted to investment (0 = three or more, 1 = one or two, 2 = none); (*c*) incentives by host government: tax holiday (3 = three or more years, 2 = one to two years, 1 = tax cut, 0 = no tax incentives), exemption from custom tariffs (1 = yes, 0 = no); (*d*) limits on repatriation of profits (0 = yes, 1 = no); (*e*) role of FDI in privatization policy (4 = open early sale to foreigners, 3 = belated open sale to foreigners, 2 = first offer to domestic investors, 1 = required negotiations with privatization agency, 0 = no foreign privatization).
- Total FDI outflows from investor country: OECD 1998a, UNCTAD 1998
- Bilateral investment treaties: UNCTAD 1996b
- EU agreements: EU website, http://europa.eu.int/comm/enlargement/pas /europe_agr.htm
- Foreign aid: OECD 1997

TABLE A.5
Sectoral Composition of FDI and Representative MNCs

Country	Top Three Sectors (in 2000 FDI stock)	Largest Affiliates of Foreign MNCs
Bulgaria[a]	Trade (19%) Food, beverages, and tobacco (17%) Transport, storage, and communications (12%)	Lukoil (Russia), Daewoo (South Korea), Allianz (Germany), Billa (Austria), ING Bank (Netherlands), Danone (France), Nestle (Switzerland), Societe General (France), Interbrew (Belgium), Kraft Foods (U.S.), Vodafone (UK), Raifeissen Bank (Austria)
Croatia	Finance (28%) Chemicals and chemical products (18%) Transport, storage, and communications (17%)	Interbrew (Belgium), Siemens (Germany), Grupo Banca Intesa Milano (Italy), Holcim (Switzerland), ABB (Sweden/Switzerland), Deutsche Telekom (Germany), Raifeissen Bank (Austria), Casa di Risparmio (Italy), Bank Austria Creditanstalt (Austria)
Czech Republic	Trade (15%) Finance (15%) Transport, storage, and communications (11%)	Volkswagen (Germany), Phillip Morris (U.S.), Bank Austria (Austria), Siemens (Germany), Nestle (Switzerland), IBM (U.S.), Galena (U.S.), ABB (Sweden/Switzerland), Coca-Cola (U.S.), Raifeissen Bank (Austria), Citibank (U.S.), Makro Cash and Carry (Germany), Jihomoravska Energetika (Germany), Tesco Stores (UK), IPS AS (Finland), Delvita (Netherlands), KBC Bank (Belgium)
Estonia[b]	Finance (25%) Transport, storage, and communications (22%) Trade (13%)	Eesti Telekom (Finland/Sweden), Neste Eesti AS (Finland), Kreenholmi Valduse (Sweden), Rakvere Lihakombinaat (Finland), Tolaram Grupp (Singapore), E.O.S. AS (U.S.), ABB (Sweden/ Switzerland), Shell (Netherlands/UK), Eesti Uhisbank AS (Sweden), Eesti Toostusliising AS (Finland)

TABLE A.5 (*cont.*)
Sectoral Composition of FDI and Representative MNCs

Country	Top Three Sectors (in 2000 FDI stock)	Largest Affiliates of Foreign MNCs
Hungary	Business activities (16%) Trade (12%) Finance (11%)	Audi (Germany), Philips (Netherlands), IBM (U.S.), Matav (Germany), ABN Amro Bank (Netherlands), Raiffeisen Bank (Austria), Central European International Bank Rt. (Italy), General Electric (U.S.), Unilever (Netherlands), Philip Morris (U.S.), Henkel (Germany), Elektrolux (Sweden), Bank Austria Creditanstalt (Austria), Citibank (U.S.), Allianz (Germany)
Latvia[b]	Trade (22%) Finance (16%) Business activities (16%)	Liepajas metalurgs As (Ireland), Latvija Statoil SIA (Norway), Latvijas Finieris AS (Germany), Lattelekom SIA (Finland), Latvijas Gaze AS (Germany/Russia), Latvijas Mobilais Telefons SIA (Finland/Sweden), Hansabanka AS (Estonia), Kolnische Ruck Riga (Germany), Kellogg (U.S.), Siemens (Germany), Coca-Cola (U.S.), Unilever (Netherlands)
Lithuania	Trade (23%) Telecommunications (17%) Financial intermediation (16%)	Mazeikiu Nafta, AB (U.S.), Lietuva Statoil UAB (Norway), Lietuvos Energija, AB (Sweden), Lietuvos Telekomas, AB (Finland/Sweden), Lietuvos Dujos, AB (Germany), Hansa Lizingas, UAB (Estonia), Vilniaus Bankas Lizingas, AB (Sweden), Kraft Foods (U.S.), Svyturys, AB (Denmark), Coca-Cola (U.S.), Lithuanian Shipping Company (Denmark), Neste (Finland)

• Migration: OECD 1998b and National Accounts. *Note*: There is no one source that collects data on sizes of migration groups in various countries. Contacting immigrant organizations for the eleven host countries revealed that they have only crude estimates on the sizes of immigrant populations of their national origin around the world and that their data are not complete. Moreover, such data would hardly be comparable across countries. Every country issues national reports on emigration,

TABLE A.5 (cont.)
Sectoral Composition of FDI and Representative MNCs

Country	Top Three Sectors (in 2000 FDI stock)	Largest Affiliates of Foreign MNCs
Poland	Finance (20%) Trade (17%) Food, beverages, and tobacco (8%)	Fiat (Italy), Daewoo (South Korea), Volkswagen (Germany), Makro Cash and Carry (Germany), Procter and Gamble (U.S.), General Motors (U.S.), Philips (Netherlands), Renault (France), British American Tobacco (UK), Ford (U.S.), Unilever (Netherlands), Bank Austria Creditanstalt (Austria), Citibank (U.S.), ING Bank (Netherlands), Allianz (Germany)
Romania[c]	Trade Secondary sector Transport, storage, and communication	Automobile Dacia (France), Daewoo (South Korea), Petromidia (Turkey), Metro Cash and Carry (Germany), Interbrands (Cyprus), Mobil Rom SA (France), ABN Amro Bank (Netherlands), Alpha Bank (Greece), Lafarge (France), Coca-Cola (U.S.), Lukoil (Russia), Colgate (U.S.), Unilever (Netherlands), Shell (Netherlands/UK), Banca Turco Romania SA (Turkey)
Slovakia	Transport, storage, and communication (17%) Finance (17%) Trade (12%)	Volkswagen (Germany), Skoda Auto Slovensko (Germany), Slovak International Tabak (Germany), Tesco Stores As (UK), Billa (Austria), Cokoladovny Slovakia (Netherlands), Vagus AS (Czech Republic), Allianz (Germany), Bank Austria Creditanstalt (Austria), Chemion (France), OMV (Austria), Citibank (U.S.), Heineken (Netherlands), Deutsche Telekom (Germany), IBM (U.S.), Nestle (Switzerland)

which list the number of individuals per year who register at a local municipality that they are acquiring a new citizenship. However, not everybody who registers also specifies to which country he or she is emigrating. This means that official reports are likely conservative in terms of numbers and they include only legal emigrants. Using a continuous variable of emigrants from host to investor countries in the 1992–94 period would also obscure the fact that the effect of immigrants might take sev-

TABLE A.5
Sectoral Composition of FDI and Representative MNCs

Country	Top Three Sectors (in 2000 FDI stock)	Largest Affiliates of Foreign MNCs
Slovenia	Finance (26%) Trade (14%) Business activities (13%)	Revoz/Renault (France), Sava Tires/ Goodyear (U.S.), Porsche (Austria), Spar (Austria), Inexa Store (Sweden), Interina (Croatia), Bank Austria (Austria), Societe General (France), Iskratel (Germany), Danfoss (Denmark), Henkel (Austria), Droga (UK), Simobil (Austria), Papirnica Vevce (Austria)

Source: UNCTAD 2006.
[a] Data for 1999.
[b] Data for 2001.
[c] Percentage distributions on sectoral composition of FDI are not available.

eral years to develop. The best measure would therefore be a variable that captures a history of migration trends between a country pair. Since half of the nations included in this analysis did not exist as sovereign political units before 1992, there are no continuous historical data available for the majority of my sample. However, migration studies have documented that people tend to migrate to those destinations with preexistent ethnic communities of their national origin (Zolberg 1989; Portes 1995; Massey et al. 1998). This implies that yearly migration from host to investor country would signal the existence of ethnic communities of host country origin in investor countries. Thus, a decision was made to dichotomize the available data according to whether any emigrants were reported to leave a host country for the investor country during each of the three years (1992–94). Comparison of country pairs scoring 1 on the migration variable and available data on the presence of immigrant communities provided by national immigration organizations revealed a very close fit. Thus I am confident that my migration measure is a good indicator of the presence of migrants of host country origin in an investor country.

- Export: National Accounts
- Historical-cultural ties: Ethnologue, http://www.sil.org/ethnologue/. Note: Presence of a national minority of host country origin in an investor country or vice versa is a proxy for the existence of historical cultural ties between countries. It parallels the indicator or colonial status for non-European countries. It is the best available quantifiable measure that reflects a historical and cultural dimension of the relations between two countries, which warrants its inclusion in the analysis despite its possible shortcomings.

- Geographical distance: Distance calculator, http://www.escapeartist .com/travel/howfar.htm
- Language: Ethnologue, http://www.sil.org/ethnologue/

NATIONAL ACCOUNTS

National Accounts refer to references found in the 1993–2000 issues of the following national statistical yearbooks:

- *Bulgaria: Statistical Yearbook*. National Statistical Institute, Sofia.
- *Statistical Yearbook of the Republic of Croatia*. Central Bureau of Statistics, Zagreb.
- *Statistical Yearbook of the Czech Republic*. Czech Statistical Office, Prague.
- *Statistical Yearbook of Estonia*. Statistical Office of Estonia, Tallinn.
- *Statistical Yearbook of Hungary*. Hungarian Central Statistical Office, Budapest.
- *Statistical Yearbook of Latvia*. Central Statistical Bureau of Latvia, Riga.
- *Statistical Yearbook of Lithuania*. Statistics Lithuania, Vilnius.
- *Statistical Yearbook of the Republic of Poland*. Central Statistical Office, Warsaw.
- *Romanian Statistical Yearbook*. National Institute of Statistics, Bucharest.
- *Statistical Yearbook of the Slovak Republic*. Statistical Office of the Slovak Republic, Bratislava.
- *Republic of Slovenia: Statistical Yearbook*. Statistical Office of the Republic of Slovenia, Ljubljana.

NOTES

CHAPTER 1
SOCIAL FOUNDATIONS OF THE ECONOMY

1. Throughout the book I use Central and Eastern Europe as a geopolitical term to include the following eleven countries: Bulgaria, Croatia, the Czech Republic, Estonia, Hungary, Latvia, Lithuania, Poland, Romania, Slovakia, and Slovenia. This is also the sample of countries included in empirical analyses.

2. The 10 percent cutoff is defined by the international organizations that collect information on FDI, including International Monetary Fund (IMF), Organization for Economic Cooperation and Development (OECD), and United Nations Conference on Trade and Development (UNCTAD), and accepted by most national accounting systems that abide by these international standards.

3. Scholars have claimed that the last two decades of the twentieth century saw rising support on a global scale for economic policies that encourage market deregulation, privatization, and liberalization, often referred to as neoliberal reforms or neoliberalism (Lash and Urry 1987; Albert 1993; Przeworski 1995; Gore 2000; Campbell and Pedersen 2001). Neoliberals welcome such economic changes because they believe a market released from government intervention will select the most efficient policies.

4. References to socialism and capitalism used here are ideal-typical. As I discuss in further detail, (a) the actual experienced socialism varied across countries (chapter 2), and (b) the capitalist economic organization consolidating in postsocialist countries shows within-regional variation (chapter 7).

5. Karl Polanyi (1957, 148) used the term *embeddedness* to indicate that actually existing market economies are not analytically autonomous but "embedded and enmeshed in institutions, economic and noneconomic. The inclusion of the noneconomic is vital. For religion or government may be as important for the structure and functioning of the economy as monetary institutions or the availability of tools and machines that lighten the toil of labor." This notion of economic embeddedness has been used in later work to examine the variety of social organization of capitalist systems (e.g., Hollingsworth and Boyer 1997; cf. Barber 1995; Block 2003). Since the publication of Mark Granovetter's influential article "Economic Action and Social Structure: The Problem of Embeddedness" (1985), the term *embeddedness* has been often (narrowly) associated with the influence of social networks on economic activity. Close to Polanyi's original statement, I adopt a "thicker," "substantivist," notion of embeddedness, which covers the influence of all social forces on the economy, not only networks.

6. In their delineation of forces that structure economic life, Zukin and DiMaggio (1990) also include cognition. Since I am primarily interested in social forces, I subsume the category of social cognition under culture, assuming that shared cultural understandings manifest themselves for each individual as cognitive sche-

mata, mental models, or typifications that help individuals to perceive, interpret, and act upon the phenomena around them (Berger and Luckmann 1967; DiMaggio and Powell 1991; DiMaggio 1997).

7. Ann Swidler (1986) has distinguished between settled and unsettled lives (periods) to differentiate between times perturbed by social change and those characterized by stability.

8. The claim that social forces constitute economic behavior does not imply an oversocialized conception of action (critiqued by Wrong 1961; Granovetter 1985) because it maintains a strong focus of human agency. Social forces structure how economic actors engage in transactions because they provide resources that actors use to compose strategies of action rather than because they provide ultimate values that unilaterally determine individuals' behavior, like puppets on a string (cf. Swidler 1986).

9. Representative research in this subfield includes Granovetter 1974, 1985; White 1981a, 1981b, 2002; Baker 1984, 1990; Burt 1992; Podolny 1993; Portes and Sensenbrenner 1993; Powell, Koput, and Smith-Doerr 1996; Uzzi 1996, 1997, 1999; DiMaggio and Louch 1998; Gulati and Gargiulo 1999, Fernández, Castilla, and Moore 2000; Yakubovich 2005; for review see Smith-Doerr and Powell 2005. The network approach adopted in this research is often equated with the embeddedness perspective. But the focus on just networks leads to a thin version of embeddedness in which economic processes seem to operate autonomously in the context of networks and social ties. The social constructivist view I am adopting here leads to a thick conception of embeddedness in which social interaction is treated as constitutive of economic activity.

10. In fact, economist Michael Piore characterized economic sociology as "an enormous hodge-podge of ideas and insights, existing at all sorts of different levels of abstraction, possibly just incommensurate, without a basic theory or structure to sort them out, or order them" (1996, 742).

11. A notable exception here is the work of Neil Fligstein (1996, 2001a) who integrates several social forces in his analyses of economic life, arguing for a political-cultural approach to markets and for paying attention to the role of states in building market institutions.

12. For example, a substantive varieties approach can be applied to the investigation of political structures in the economy. Since modernity, states have been key political structures constituting economic systems (Block 1994), although the kind of influence that states have varies across context. As Evans (1995) distinguished, predatory and developmental states exert different influences under different circumstances. In developed liberal capitalism, the state's role is relegated to manipulation of property rights (Campbell and Lindberg 1990). In socialist economies, state control of economic activity is all-encompassing (Szelényi, Beckett, and King 1994). In postsocialism, states may act as market agents selling property in the process of privatization.

13. Several existing empirical analyses in economic sociology are in line with the examination of substantive varieties of embeddedness proposed here. A perspective on capitalism that proposes that capitalism comes in various institutional configurations can be seen as an inquiry into substantive varieties of capitalist economic organization (Katzenstein 1985; Campbell, Hollingsworth, and Lind-

berg 1991; Streeck 1991, 1992; Crouch and Streeck 1997; Hollingsworth and Boyer 1997; Guillén 2001b; Hall and Soskice 2001). Because of different institutionalized patterns of authority (social structures) and organizational logics (cultural understandings), networked small business firms may be the core of economic organization in Taiwan, *chaebol* based on patrimonial principles in South Korea, and foreign multinationals linked to international technology and marketing channels in Spain (Biggart and Guillén 1999; Guillén 2001b). Furthermore, Zelizer's (1994, 2000, 2002b, 2004, 2005) analysis of multiple markets and multiple monies is congruent with the view that there are substantive varieties of embeddedness. Differentiated social relationships (e.g., friendship, sexual intimacy, employment relations) give rise to differentiated interpretations of the appropriateness of certain kinds of monetary transactions to that particular relationship over alternatives (e.g., gifts over entitlements or compensation). Likewise, substantively different media of transfer (e.g., cash, gifts, alimony) are used to maintain the distinctions between varieties of social relations.

14. See Stark (1992) on use of the term *transformation* instead of *transition* and a suggestion that the transformation in Eastern Europe is from plan to clan, rather than from plan to market.

15. In fact, some have proposed that the current sociological perspective on economy lacks a clear model of action (Beckert 1996; Fligstein 2001a). Some economic sociologists, primarily from a network perspective, accept the view that economic actors are rational profit-maximizing agents and that social relations in which they are located are efficiency enhancing (e.g., Granovetter 1985; Uzzi 1996, 1997, 1999; Gulati and Gargiulo 1999). Other scholars are more skeptical about the usefulness of the rational action model and the preeminence of efficiency in guiding economic outcomes (Meyer and Rowan 1977; Fligstein 1990, 1996, 2001a, 2002; Roy 1997).

16. This thinking aligns well with the "garbage can" model of decision-making, which suggests that organizations have "garbage cans" into which a variety of problems and solutions are dumped independently of each other by decision makers who generate them. A decision takes place when problems, solutions, and decision makers align more or less by chance. Often the alignment of the problems, solutions, and individuals occurs after the opportunity to make a decision has passed or occurs before the problem has been discovered (Cohen, March, and Olsen 1972; Cohen and March 1974; March and Olsen 1976).

17. The term *muddling through* was introduced by Lindblom (1959) to describe incremental political decision-making in public administration. I use the term not to wholeheartedly transpose Lindblom's concept but to suggest that in economic decision-making incrementalism is likely as well. Even if actors have clear goals in the beginning, situational contingency will destabilize their preferences so they will need to adjust their objectives during the course of action itself; i.e. they will muddle through the action process. In the end, their goals and preferences will be quite different from those articulated in the beginning.

18. The dependency school actually does not characterize MNCs' impacts as unilaterally negative for development of countries in the periphery. Cardoso and Faletto (1979) argue that the interaction of local social classes and multinational enterprises can explain growth in peripheral economies. According to Evans

(1979) the state can mediate the negative role of foreign capital if it effectively takes part in a "triple alliance" together with the local bourgeoisie and MNCs. Gereffi (1978, 1983) emphasizes that supportive state policies are key. Without those, MNCs are more likely to contribute to national development than local corporations, but with the right policies, local corporations can contribute more.

19. While much research in the world-systems and dependency literature reports the deleterious effects of foreign capital penetration on economic growth and income equality in host nations, earlier studies have also been critiqued for faulty interpretations. Firebaugh (1992) demonstrated that negative growth effects found for foreign investment stock were an artifact of introducing both foreign direct investment (FDI) flow (the yearly inflow) and FDI stock (the cumulated inflow) in the same equation, which resulted in spurious "denominator effects." Firebaugh showed that the correct interpretation for the findings from these studies is that the foreign investment rate (the ratio of flow/stock) benefits developing countries, but that it doesn't benefit them as much as domestic investment. Some recent studies, taking into account Firebaugh's critique, find negative effects of long-term FDI on economic growth and income inequality (Dixon and Boswell 1996; Kentor 1998; Alderson and Nielsen 1999). In contrast, De Soysa and O'Neal (1999) offer a reanalysis of Firebaugh's (1992, 1996) and Dixon and Boswell's (1996) studies, and largely replicate Firebaugh's findings. In addition, we should note that some studies conclude that foreign direct investment has no effect on economic growth (Hein 1992; Dutt 1997).

Chapter 2
From Socialism to Postsocialism

1. Although *socialism* and *communism* are often used interchangeably to describe the system put in place in countries ruled by the Communist parties, the two terms are not synonymous. In theory, socialism is a transitional phase between the exploitative capitalist system of private ownership of the means of production, and the classless society of communism. Actually existing regimes with Communist parties in power never achieved this high stage of communist development. For this reason I refer to the Central and East European societies between World War II and 1989 as socialist.

2. The Communist Party attained power in the Soviet Union in 1917 (Kornai 1992, 6). In 1987, the World Development Report characterized the following countries as socialist: Soviet Union, Mongolia, Albania, Yugoslavia, Bulgaria, Czechoslovakia, Hungary, Poland, Romania, North Korea, China, East Germany, Vietnam, Cuba, Congo, Somalia, South Yemen, Benin, Ethiopia, Angola, Cambodia, Laos, Mozambique, Afghanistan, Nicaragua, and Zimbabwe (reported in Kornai 1992).

3. In reality, not 100 percent of all the productive forces were nationalized when the Communist regimes were installed. For example, a notable exception was the agriculture sector in Poland, which was not taken into state hands.

4. To call those who were in charge in socialist enterprises managers is a bit misleading. Their role was quite different from that of managers in capitalist firms.

In fact, as Michal Čakrt, Czech professor of organizational behavior wrote, "The communist regime hated and feared *management*. . . . During those times, anything Western, especially American, was viewed with suspicion and management was considered a word of capitalism" (1993, 63). Managing was not deemed necessary and was equated with manipulation. The key function of those in charge was to control and supervise the execution of the plan. Indeed, management was a function rather than a profession. Hence, officials did not consider any need for management training. Professional and expert knowledge sufficed.

5. Economists who championed the economic theory of socialism, in particular Oskar Lange (1938), argued that socialist economic planning would achieve efficiency and rational pricing (see also Schumpeter 1976). Bockman and Eyal (2002) summarize Lange's logic: "First, the central planning authority drafts clear and binding rules, which include the instruction for managers to approximate in their pricing the marginal cost of production. These rules are published, so all economic actors are familiar with them. At the second stage, production and competition begin on the basis of these rules and prices. The third stage is iterative, as the central planning authority continuously adjusts the rules and prices in accordance with the feedback it gets from the managers. Eventually, efficiency and equilibrium are reached" (319).

6. "Greater Serbia" would consist of Serbia proper, the semiautonomous republics of Vojvodina and largely ethnically Albanian Kosovo, the Serb-populated parts of Croatia, large sections of Bosnia and Herzegovina, and possibly Macedonia.

7. This may not be surprising. Since the late 1980s, a neoliberal development practice summarized in the so-called Washington consensus has been espoused by the World Bank and the International Monetary Fund (Gore 2000). The principles of mass privatization align well with the principles of stabilization, liberalization, privatization, and deregulation that form a core of the Washington consensus.

8. Mass privatization was also adopted in Russia and most of the former Soviet republics. It is also important to note that by the late 1990s, some economists posed their doubts about the efficacy of rapid reform (Nellis 1999; Stiglitz 2000). Reviewing empirical privatization studies, Megginson and Netter (2001, 338) arrive at the following conclusion: "One thing we can say is that . . . the evidence demonstrating the benefits of privatization is weakest for countries in Eastern Europe, where privatization was implemented rapidly. This may suggest that privatization should have proceeded along a more gradual path." That said, empirical studies largely find that private ownership is associated with better firm-level performance in terms of revenue growth and efficient restructuring than is continued state ownership (Claessens, Djankov, and Pohl 1997; Frydman et al. 1999, 2000). Megginson and Netter (2001) also conclude that privatization positively affects economic performance of firms.

9. As Mencinger (2004, 77) reports Slovenia considered two alternative strategies of privatization. One advocated by the majority of Slovenian academic economists was "decentralized, gradual and commercial privatization, which the government would only monitor; the other [codified in a Jeffrey Sachs–Peterle-Umek act] advocated massive and speedy privatization administered by the government and relying on the free distribution of enterprise shares [via vouchers]." After long negotiations in the parliament, the Ownership Transformation Act was passed in

November 1992, which "combined the decentralization, gradualism, and diversity of privatization methods of the first approach with the free distribution of vouchers called for under the second" (Mencinger 2004, 77).

CHAPTER 3
INSTITUTIONALIZATION OF FDI IN POSTSOCIALISM

1. Janez is a common Slovenian name. Johann and Giovanni are its German and Italian equivalents, respectively.

2. This argument builds on a famous article by Paul David (1985) "Clio and the Economics of QWERTY," where David tries to explain the standardization of the peculiar organization of letters on a keyboard even when it was less efficient than the abandoned alternative would have been.

3. The positive statistically significant coefficient for mimetic isomorphism variable captures the fact that the higher the average legitimization score for all countries but the focal country in a particular year, the higher the legitimacy efforts in the focal country in the subsequent year.

4. In a related argument about the role of nationalism in postsocialism, some analysts emphasize that those states that were under Soviet dominance had to rebuild their national sovereignty after 1989. So we might expect that this hindered FDI legitimization. However, I could not test this hypothesis because there is too little variation on this variable in my sample, since all but two countries were under direct Soviet dominance.

5. Because economic indicators for the sample of eleven Central and East European countries are strongly related to each other, additional analyses were conducted, which checked separately the importance of country risk rating, GDP growth, wages, unemployment, trade, budget deficit, foreign debt, level of education, infrastructure support, and corruption, to make sure that the weakness of economic factors was not related to the choice of economic indicators. None of these other alternative measures of economic risk and return showed a statistically significantly relationship to FDI flows.

6. Because country credit rating incorporates the information on economic prosperity and economic stability, it would be incorrect to include it in a model that combines it with the other two economic indicators.

7. Among these controls, only democratization seems to have a significant effect on FDI, but its coefficient is negative, signaling that higher levels of democratic consolidation actually hinder FDI flows to a particular country. This puts in perspective previous research on the role of democracy. The explanation pointing to the positive effects of democracy on FDI, most recently elaborated by Nathan Jensen (2006), does not distinguish between the possibly contradictory effects that various aspects of democratization have on the activities of MNCs. While it is likely the case that democratization, as Jensen argues, decreases political risks because it insures protection of property rights and lower risks of expropriation of assets (cf. North and Weingast 1989; Olson 1993, 2000; Bates 2001), Quan Li and Adam Resnick (2003) also point out that democracy-related emergence and empowerment of various political and social interests has a potentially

negative effect on FDI. My analysis of the role of FDI takes into account the government's commitment to market reform, which includes protection of private property rights as part and parcel of building markets. Hence, the net effect that the variable democratization captures is related to the strength of political participation of various interest groups. The greater democratization score indicates the strengthening of pluralism and empowerment of social interests to organize and participate in political competition. As such, democratization is an impediment because it implies the greater likelihood that domestic groups will assert their own interests against those of foreign MNCs. In particular, in the case of postsocialist Europe, these interests may be resonant with patriotic and protectionist sentiments. This explanation also points to the importance of a relational perspective on FDI, considering both investors and host actions. A level of democracy in a potential host country is not only a part of the risk-and-return calculus of foreign investors, who fear expropriation, but it also actively structures the demand for foreign investment on the side of the hosts.

8. See Zelizer (2000, 2005) for an elaboration and critique of the "separate spheres" argument as it pertains to visions of the relationship between intimacy and economy.

CHAPTER 4
CROSS-COUNTRY PATTERNS IN FDI FLOWS

1. Others have critiqued network research for being inattentive to culture (Zelizer 1988; Emirbayer and Goodwin 1994; Spillman 1999) or politics and institutions (Barber 1995; Fligstein 2001a, 2002).

2. Personal interview, May 3, 2002, Ljubljana, Slovenia.

3. Personal interview, July 20, 1999, Zagreb, Croatia.

4. Personal interview, October 30, 2001, Moščenička Draga, Croatia.

5. *Delo* (Ljubljana, Slovenia), June 10, 1997.

6. Later, based on a study among students in twenty-three countries, using a questionnaire designed by Chinese scholars, Hofstede added a fifth dimension to denote differences between societies that value long-term orientations such as perseverance and thrift and those that value short-term orientations such as saving face (Hofstede 2006).

7. Hofstede's survey did not cover most of the postsocialist countries, as there were no IBM subsidiaries established there.

8. I elaborate on this notion of cultural matching in the next chapter, where I explicate the cultural embeddedness at the level of FDI firm-to-firm transactions.

9. For further elaboration of this methodological issue, see the appendix.

10. Other studies on the effects of relational variables have used dyads as units of analysis (Galaskiewicz and Wasserman 1989; Lincoln, Gerlach, and Takahashi 1992).

11. Following the constructivist perspective, I conceptualize national cultures as *historically* developed cultural repertoires. To emphasize this distinction from the essentialist uses of culture, I refer to the cultural ties variable as *historical-cultural ties*.

12. See Chakrabarti's (2001, 96) explanation of this convention.

13. Because Poland and the Czech Republic are also included among the investor countries, and they invest very little in other Slavic countries, except for the Czech Republic in Slovakia, the direction of the language similarity coefficient with dyadic FDI flows is in fact negative, but since this relationship is not statistically significant, we should not try to interpret the negative sign as meaningful.

14. Personal interview, January 10, 1999, Ljubljana, Slovenia.

CHAPTER 5
EMBEDDEDNESS OF ORGANZIATIONAL FDI ATTEMPTS

1. Private investment funds burgeoned when privatization in Slovenia started, when groups of individuals created these funds by persuading citizens to invest their ownership certificates in their funds instead of directly into firms.

2. *Delo* (Ljubljana, Slovenia) June 10, 1997.

3. *Mag* (Ljubljana, Slovenia), June 1997.

4. Based on the findings in chapter 3, we could say that the professed attitude of the Slovenian officials may have been pro-market and pro-FDI, but since Slovenia was the state that legitimized FDI practice last among Central and East European states, there was not much will to show actual commitment to FDI in practice.

5. *Gorenjski Glas* (Kranj, Slovenia), June 10, 1997.

6. *Mag* (Ljubljana, Slovenia), June 1997.

7. *Delo* (Ljubljana, Slovenia) June 10, 1997.

8. This case is based on information gathered from seven semistructured face-to-face interviews (average length 1.5 hours) with Slovan and AmeriCo managers, two published interviews with actors involved in the transaction, media reports, and companies' documents.

9. Personal interview, Venice, Italy, June 23, 2001.

10. This study has not specifically addressed the issue of translation during the negotiation processes, primarily because the use of translators in the cases I examined was not very common. Nevertheless, based on the little evidence gathered, I can speculate about two contradicting ways in which the role of translators in cross-country business transactions is crucial. First, translators may aid in the transaction when they help to establish common ground between the two parties, i.e., they serve as mediators. Alternatively, the presence of translators is an obvious sign that the two parties do not speak the same language, creating friction in the communication process and consequent difficulties for the transaction.

11. Research is divided on whether mimicking the behavior of other firms is a rational efficiency-enhancing strategy. The legitimacy of a particular behavior is enhanced if more firms engage in it or if firms with more prestige (usually bigger in size and success) do so. These actions may or may not make the organization more profitable or enable it to better achieve its goals. For example, conglomerate acquisitions were very popular for U.S. firms in the 1960s, despite their negative financial outcomes for the firms that engaged in them (Davis, Diekmann, and Tinsley 1994). Alternatively, others propose that frequency of use may serve as a

signal that a particular practice is really superior because it enhances efficiency. Following the practices of more successful firms may be a valid indicator that these practices are indeed more cost efficient. Abrahamson and Rosenkopf (1993) point to the rational nature of the imitation process, where looking for market signals from peers leads to efficiency. Researchers have also differentiated between more or less experienced firms and their reliance on social cues. Haunschild and Miner (1997) found that an inexperienced firm relies more on social cues to make decisions, while a more experienced firm places greater reliance on technical decision-making as opposed to social clues. This would suggest that firms new to FDI transactions would rely on their networks more heavily than more experienced multinationals. The fact that AmeriCo's managers strongly emphasized the importance of networks goes against this claim. Reliance on social networks may have less to do with the experience of a firm than with the environmental uncertainty in which they operate. In such conditions, imitation may seem like a practical strategy; sometimes it is the best the actors have available, although it provides no guarantees of efficiency.

12. But even if we accept that economic action can be guided by different motives, and that there are multiple equally successful ways of achieving the same goals, we leave unaffected the assumption of self-interest as the natural principle of action. But should self-interest really be taken for granted? Albert Hirschman (1977) in *The Passions and the Interests* traces the acceptance, and even glorification, of selfishness and greed in modern society and thus shows that even self-interest, as one of the "natural" human characteristics, is historically variable. Hirschman argues that economic and political philosophers transformed the passion of greed into a virtue that facilitated the modernization project.

13. Personal interview, Prague, Czech Republic, June 21, 2002

14. Personal interview, Ljubljana, Slovenia, February 1, 2002.

15. Personal interview, Venice, Italy, June 23, 2001

16. Personal interview, Ljubljana, Slovenia, February 1, 2002.

17. *Delo* (Ljubljana, Slovenia), October 12, 2002, 10.

18. *Delo* (Ljubljana, Slovenia), November 9, 2001, 1. The Rapal contract was signed between Italy and Yugoslavia in 1920; one-third of Slovenian territory, the Primorska region, was given to the Italians. The contract was reconsidered in 1947 with a peace treaty between states allied and associated with Italy, although a considerable Slovene minority remained on the Italian territory.

19. *Delo* (Ljubljana, Slovenia), November 15, 2001, 13.

20. With a policy set by the National Assembly, any privatization and foreign investment related to the banking sector in Slovenia has to get an approval from the National Bank of Slovenia.

21. This case also illustrates how cultural conceptions can interfere with issues of power and control. It is precisely because of Slovenian attitudes toward Italians that a majority share and thus control over a bank became a pressing issue.

22. *Delo* (Ljubljana, Slovenia), January 11, 2002.

23. Personal interview, Ljubljana, Slovenia, April 25, 2002.

24. Based on the information provided by the owner of the land sold to the Dutch investor (December 23, 2000).

25. Zukin and DiMaggio (1990) proposed that there are many substantive aspects to embeddedness (cognitive, structural/network, political, and cultural), which is also integral with Karl Polanyi's (1944, 1957) use of the concept. Nevertheless, Granovetter (1985) reformulated "embeddedness" to mean the influence of networks on economic action, which is how many economic sociologists think of it today, substantially narrowing the scope of their analyses to only one social force—networks. My explicit statement that embeddedness should be treated as structures-power-culture configuration recovers the significance of different social influences on economic life.

26. Even when ties are lacking, we can trace network effects because being an isolate denotes a particular structural position in a network and thus shapes economic action.

27. One the most prominent economic sociologists, Richard Swedberg (2003, 2005), has recently called for economic sociology that pays attention to the role of interests in economic processes. In fact, linking the cultural, political, and structural aspects of economic action helps us see how interests are articulated and how they are pursued in transactions.

CHAPTER 6
UNCERTAINTY AND THE PRACTICE OF FDI TRANSACTIONS

1. Phrases in quotes are from a personal interview with a representative of a foreign chamber of commerce in Prague, the Czech Republic, June 26, 2002.

2. As evidence of "loss aversion" in financial markets, O'Dean (1998) shows that people sell stocks that have risen in value too early and hold on to stocks that have declined in value for too long. Traditional economic theory would predict that decisions to buy or sell stocks would have nothing to do with whether stock has increased or decreased in value since acquired because decisions will be based solely on the future expected value of the stock (Weber and Dawes 2005, 100).

3. Certainly, beside "social" sources of uncertainty, there are also unpredictable natural or technological disasters. Interestingly, sociological research on risks shows that risk judgments in such situations depend on social contexts (Beck 1992; Vaughn 1997; Tierney 1999).

4. Charles Lindblom (1959) used the term *muddling through* to describe the decision-making of the U.S. executive bureaucracy, which, as boundedly rational actors, uses "successive limited comparison" (81) in formulating policy. My use is not meant to adopt Lindblom's thinking about administrative and policy decision-making wholesale. I primarily use it to focus on the incremental nature of complex decision-making where, because of situational uncertainty, decision-steps need to be rethought and reevaluated in light of novel information or contingencies along the way.

5. Information based on two phone conversations and email correspondence with the author, between March and June 2004.

6. The information is based on case evidence collected by Estrin, Hughes, and Todd (1997, 163–78) in their study of multinationals in Central and Eastern Europe. For each case, Estrin and colleagues interviewed several managers in both

investor and host companies. They asked general questions about the FDI transactions, and they were not primarily interested in the process of decision-making. They didn't directly ask respondents to recall how exactly the decisions of where to invest were made, so there is less chance that respondents substantially reconstructed the processes that happened in the past. The fact that organizational decision-makers tend to *post hoc* rationalize the events that happened when their attention is brought to the process is an obvious methodological disadvantage involved in interviewing. As research in psychology shows, postoutcome estimates by subjects of their preoutcome judgments are closer to the outcomes than their preoutcome judgments were, the I-knew-it-all-along effect. When actors look back, they rationalize their action, so it seems as if they employed teleological rationality to achieve it. When looking back, actors cannot help but include information acquired during the process in the information out of which a decision is made, resulting in a hindsight bias in economic expectations (Hölzl, Kirchler, and Rodler 2002).

7. The information is based on case evidence collected by Estrin, Hughes, and Todd (1997, 114–29). See note 6 for a description.

8. McGinn and Keros (2002, 469) also proposed an understanding of economic transactions as social improvisations, i.e., as "attempts at mutual sense-making within an economic context." They argued that such a characterization better reflected their empirical data on simple economic negotiations between pairs of students than a characterization that "transactions are individually strategic attempts at profit maximization" (469).

9. Klaus Meyer and Ane Skak (2002) report about the importance of serendipity in entry into Eastern Europe.

10. According to Albert Hirschman (1977), moneymaking became the "calm *passion*" as in the late Renaissance interests emerged as the term for conducting a more balanced public and private life, curtailing passions.

11. *Delo* (Ljubljana, Slovenia), June 10, 1997.

12. As Berezin (2005, 111) states, it is important to analytically separate emotions from trust (but see Pixley 2002, 2004).

13. How do we know whether any particular FDI effort is profitable or not? This is extremely difficult to determine. Supposedly, investors and hosts could *ex post* calculate all the transaction costs and compare those to targeted earnings. They would also have to determine the time span in which they want to evaluate the transaction, whether short term or long term. Unfortunately, such data on FDI in Central and Eastern Europe are not available. We can mention that in their review of privatization literature, Megginson and Netter (2001) conclude that in Central and Eastern Europe "foreign ownership, where allowed, is associated with greater post privatization performance improvement [in terms of profitability] than is purely domestic ownership" (360). Whether this says something about profitability for investor corporations is a different question. We have to remember that none of the surveys of existing FDI firms in the region includes firms that pulled out or did not successfully realize their investment effort. And if firms pulled out, most likely they did so out of economic concerns.

CHAPTER 7
EMBEDDED ECONOMIES

1. The institutional economists acknowledge the institutional bases of markets, but generally do not problematize their efficiency. But see North (1990, 2005), who points out that markets do not always promote efficiency.

2. White actually focuses almost exclusively on production, not exchange or consumption (see also White 2002).

3. Critics of the networks perspective on markets point to the inadequacy of the "anti-categorical imperative" (Emirbayer and Goodwin 1994, 1414), i.e., undermining the importance of the qualities of individual categories (actors), and the content of social relationships that connect them (Zelizer 1988, Krippner 2001, Fligstein 2002).

4. In a theoretical statement on the role of culture in economy, Zelizer (2002a) claims that economic sociology has had an "uneasy" relationship to culture, and that culturalist analyses have been primarily applied to "nonstandard" economic topics (such as household or care labor). This slant leads many to assume that some economic phenomena are "more cultural" than others, and that perhaps the more "standard" economic processes have little or no place for culture. I challenged this position and investigated how a "standard" economic phenomenon, foreign direct investment, is constrained and enabled by cultural understandings of plausible economic partners, desirable economic goals, and available strategies to reach them.

5. Polanyi used the notion of embeddedness to underscore that the economy is an integral part of society (Barber 1995; Swedberg 1997). In Granovetter's appropriation, Polanyi's focus on institutions was reduced to one single aspect of social life, i.e., social relationships, specifically network ties between economic actors (Krippner 2001).

6. In a recent overview of post-Communist systems, Lawrence King and Ivan Szelényi (2005) differentiate between varieties of post-Communist capitalism: capitalism from without, capitalism from above, capitalism from below. In their classification, most countries examined in my study fall into the "capitalism from without" category, where the dominant class formation comprises multinationals, and FDI presents the main dynamic of accumulation. My findings show that we should recognize that even *within* this category, differences across countries are substantial.

7. The ownership structures are shown for 2000 and are certainly not fixed. In fact, in all the countries that showed weaker foreign penetration, talks are going on about selling more state-owned banks to the highest bidder, and often this means to foreign investors. For the case of Slovenia, see Bandelj (2006).

APPENDIX ON METHOD AND DATA SOURCES

1. For the meaning of this source, see the subheading "National Accounts" at the end of the appendix.

REFERENCES

Abolafia, Mitchel. 1996. *Making Markets: Opportunism and Restraint on Wall Street*. Cambridge: Harvard University Press.

————. 1998. "Markets as Cultures: An Ethnographic Approach." Pp. 69–85 in *The Laws of the Markets*, ed. Michel Callon. Oxford: Blackwell.

Abrahamson, Eric, and Lori Rosenkopf. 1993. "Institutional and Competitive Bandwagons: Using Mathematical Modeling as a Tool to Explore Innovation Diffusion." *Academy of Management Review* 18:487–517.

Agarwal, Jamuna P. 1980. "Determinants of Foreign Direct Investment: A Survey." *Weltwirtschaftliches Archiv* 116:739–73.

Agarwal, Sanjeev. 1994. "Socio-cultural Distance and the Choice of Joint Ventures: A Contingency Perspective." *Journal of International Marketing* 2 (2): 63–80.

Agor, Weston H. 1986. *The Logic of Intuitive Decision Making*. New York: Quorum Books.

Aharoni, Yair. 1966. *The Foreign Investment Decision Process*. Cambridge: Harvard Graduate School of Business.

Albert, Michel. 1993. *Capitalism vs. Capitalism*. Trans. Paul Haviland. New York: Four Walls Eight Windows.

Alderson, Arthur, and François Nielsen. 1999. "Inequality, Development and Dependence: A Reconsideration." *American Sociological Review* 64:606–31.

Aldrich, Howard. 2005. "Entrepreneurship." Pp. 451–77 in *The Handbook of Economic Sociology*, ed. Neil J. Smelser and Richard Swedberg. 2nd ed. Princeton, N.J.: Princeton University Press; New York: Russell Sage Foundation.

Aldrich, Howard, and Roger Waldinger. 1990. "Ethnicity and Entrepreneurship." *Annual Review of Sociology* 16:111–35.

Alesina, Alberto, and David Dollar. 1998. "Who Gives Foreign Aid to Whom and Why?" NBER Working Paper No. 6612.

Allen, Michael P., and John L. Campbell. 1994. "State Revenue Extraction from Different Income Groups: Variations in Tax Progressivity in the United States, 1916 to 1986." *American Sociological Review* 59 (2): 169–86.

Allison, Graham T. 1971. *Essence of Decision: Explaining the Cuban Missile Crisis*. Boston: Little, Brown.

Alter, Rolf, and Frederic Wehrle. 1993. "Foreign Direct Investment in CEE: An Assessment of the Current Situation." *Intereconomics* 28 (3): 1–5.

Amable, Bruno. 2000. "Institutional Complementarity and Diversity of Social Systems of Innovation and Production." *Review of International Political Economy* 7:645–87.

Amsden, Alice, Jacek Kochanowicz, and Lance Taylor. 1994. *The Market Meets Its Match*. Cambridge: Harvard University Press.

Anderson, Erin, and Hubert Gatignon. 1986. "Modes of Foreign Entry: A Transaction Cost Analysis and Propositions." *Journal of International Business Studies* 17 (3): 1–26.

Antal-Mokos, Zoltan. 1998. *Privatization, Politics and Economic Performance in Hungary.* Cambridge: Cambridge University Press.

Ash, Timothy Garton. 1984. *Polish Revolution: Solidarity.* New York: Scribner.

Aslund, Anders. 1992. *Post-communist Economic Revolutions: How Big a Bang?* Washington, D.C.: Center for Strategic and International Studies.

———. 1994. "Lessons of the First Four Years of Systemic Change in Eastern Europe." *Journal of Comparative Economics* 19:22–38.

———. 1995. *How Russia Became a Market Economy.* Washington, D.C.: Brookings Institution Press.

Avery, Christopher, and Peter Zemsky. 1998. "Multidimensional Uncertainty and Herd Behavior in Financial Markets." *American Economic Review* 88:724–48.

Babb, Sarah. 2001. *Managing Mexico: Economists from Nationalism to Neoliberalism.* Princeton, N.J.: Princeton University Press.

Baker, Wayne. 1984. "The Social Structure of a National Securities Market." *American Journal of Sociology* 89:775–811.

———. 1990. "Market Networks and Corporate Behavior." *American Journal of Sociology* 96:589–625.

Balasubramanyam, V. N., M. Salisu, and David Sapsford. 1999. "Foreign Direct Investment as an Engine of Growth." *Journal of International Trade and Economic Development* 8 (1): 27–40.

Baltagi, Badi H. 2002. *Econometrics.* 3rd ed. Springer-Verlag.

Bandelj, Nina. 2002. "Embedded Economies: Social Relations as Determinants of Foreign Direct Investment in Central and Eastern Europe." *Social Forces* 81 (2): 411–44.

———. 2003. "Particularizing the Global: Reception of Foreign Direct Investment in Slovenia." *Current Sociology* 51 (3–4): 377–94.

———. 2004. "Negotiating Global, Regional, and National Forces: Foreign Investment in Slovenia." *East European Politics and Societies* 18 (3): 455–80.

———. 2006. "Cultural Understandings of Economic Globalization: Discourse on Foreign Direct Investment in Slovenia." MPIfG Discussion Paper 06/1. Max Planck Institute for the Study of Societies.

Bar-On, Reuven, and James D.A. Parker. 2000. *The Handbook of Emotional Intelligence: Theory, Development, Assessment, and Application at Home, School and in the Workplace.* San Francisco: Jossey-Bass.

Barber, Bernard. 1977. "Absolutization of the Market." Pp. 15–31 in *Markets and Morals,* ed. Gerald Dworkin, Gordon Bermant, and Peter G. Brown. Washington, D.C.: Hemisphere Publishing.

———. 1995. "All Economies are Embedded: The Career of a Concept and Beyond." *Social Research* 62 (2): 388–413.

Barro, Robert J., and Xavier Sala-i-Martin. 1995. *Economic Growth.* Cambridge: MIT Press.

Bartlett, David. 1997. *The Political Economy of Dual Transformations: Market Reform and Democratization in Hungary.* Ann Arbor: University of Michigan Press.

Basi, R. S. 1963. *Determinants of United States Private Direct Investment in Foreign Countries.* Kent, Ohio: Kent State University Press.

Bates, Robert. 2001. *Prosperity and Violence: The Political Economy of Development*. New York: Norton.

Bauer, Tamas. 1983. "The Hungarian Alternative to Soviet-Type Planning." *Journal of Comparative Economics* 11 (3): 304–16.

Beck, Nathaniel. 1991. "Comparing Dynamic Specifications." *Political Analysis* 3:51–87.

———. 2001. "Time-Series–Cross-Section Data: What Have We Learned in the Last Few Years?" *Annual Review of Political Science* 4:271–93.

Beck, Nathaniel, and Jonathan Katz. 1995. "What to Do (and Not to Do) with Time-Series Cross-Section Data." *American Political Science Review* 89:634–47.

Beck, Ulrich. 1992. *Risk Society: Towards a New Modernity*. London: Sage.

Beck, Ulrich, Anthony Giddens, and Scott Lash. 1994. *Reflexive Modernization*. Stanford, Calif.: Stanford University Press.

Becker, Gary. 1957. *The Economics of Discrimination*. Chicago: University of Chicago Press.

Beckert, Jens. 1996. "Uncertainty and the Embeddedness of Economic Action." *Theory and Society* 25:803–40.

———. 2002. *Beyond the Market: The Social Foundations of Economic Efficiency*. Princeton, N.J.: Princeton University Press.

———. 2004. *Unverdientes Vermögen. Soziologie des Erbrechts*. Frankfurt am Main: Campus Verlag.

Beer, Linda, and Terry Boswell. 2002. "The Resilience of Dependency Effects in Explaining Income Inequality in the Global Economy: A Cross-National Analysis, 1975–1995." *Journal of World-Systems Research* 8 (1): 30–59.

Bendix, Reinhard. 1956. *Work and Authority in Industry: Ideologies of Management in the Course of Industrialization*. Berkeley and Los Angeles: University of California Press.

Benito, Gabriel, and Geir Gripsrud. 1992. "The Expansion of Foreign Direct Investments: Discrete Rational Location Choices or a Cultural Learning Process?" *Journal of International Business Studies* 23:461–76.

Bennett, Peter D., and Robert T. Green. 1972. "Political Instability as a Determinant of Direct Foreign Investment." *Journal of Marketing Research* 9:182–86.

Berezin, Mabel. 2005. "Emotions and the Economy." Pp. 109–29 in *Handbook of Economic Sociology*, ed. Neil J. Smelser and Richard Swedberg. 2nd ed. Princeton, N.J.: Princeton University Press; New York: Russell Sage Foundation.

Berger, Peter, and Thomas Luckmann. 1967. *The Social Construction of Reality: A Treatise in the Sociology of Knowledge*. Garden City, N.Y.: Anchor.

Berger, Suzanne. 2000. Globalization and Politics. *Annual Review of Political Science* 3:43–62.

Berger, Suzanne, and Ronald Dore. 1996. *National Diversity and Global Capitalism*. Ithaca, N.Y.: Cornell University Press.

Bergstrand, Jeffrey H. 1985. "The Gravity Equation in International Trade: Some Microeconomic Foundations and Empirical Evidence." *Review of Economics and Statistics* 67 (3): 474–81.

———. 1989. "The Generalized Gravity Equation, Monopolistic Competition, and the Factor-Proportions Theory in International Trade." *Review of Economics and Statistics* 71 (1): 143–53.

Bestor, Theodore C. 2004. *Tsukiji: The Fish Market at the Center of the World*. Berkeley and Los Angeles: University of California Press.

Bevan, Alan, and Saul Estrin. 2004. "The Determinants of Foreign Direct Investment into European Transition Economies." *Journal of Comparative Economics* 32:775–87.

Bhagwati, Jagdish N. 2003. *Free Trade Today*. Princeton, N.J.: Princeton University Press.

Bhagwati, Jagdish N., Elias Dinopoulos and Kar-Yiu Wong. 1992. "Quid Pro Quo Foreign Investment." *American Economic Review* 82:186–90.

Biggart, Nicole. 1989. *Charismatic Capitalism: Direct Selling Organizations in America*. Chicago: University of Chicago Press.

———. 1991. "Explaining East Asian Economic Organization: Toward a Weberian Institutional Perspective." *Theory and Society* 20:199–232.

Biggart, Nicole, and Mauro Guillén. 1999. "Developing Difference: Social Organization and the Rise of the Auto Industries of South Korea, Taiwan, Spain, and Argentina." *American Sociological Review* 64 (5): 722–47.

Billington, Nicholas. 1999. "The Location of Foreign Direct Investment: An Empirical Analysis." *Applied Economics* 31:65–76.

Blanchard, Olivier, Rudiger Dornbusch, Paul Krugman, Richard Layard, and Lawrence Summers. 1991. *Reform in Eastern Europe*. Cambridge: Cambridge University Press.

Blanchard, Oliver, Kenneth A. Froot, and Jeffrey D. Sachs. 1994. *The Transition in Eastern Europe*. Chicago: University of Chicago Press.

Block, Fred. 1994. "The Roles of the State in the Economy." Pp. 691–710 in *Handbook of Economic Sociology*, ed. Neil J. Smelser and Richard Swedberg. Princeton, N.J.: Princeton University Press.

———. 2003. "Karl Polanyi and the Writing of *The Great Transformation*." *Theory and Society* 32:275–306.

Block, Fred, and Peter Evans. 2005. "State and Economy." Pp. 505–26 in *The Handbook of Economic Sociology*, ed. Neil J. Smelser and Richard Swedberg. 2nd ed. Princeton, N.J.: Princeton University Press; New York: Russell Sage Foundation.

Blomstrom, Magnus, and Ari Kokko. 1997. "How Foreign Investment Affects Host Countries." World Bank Policy Research Working Paper 1745.

Blonigen, Bruce, and Robert Feenstra. 1996. "Protectionist Threats and Foreign Direct Investment." NBER Working Paper No. 5475.

Bockman, Johanna, and Gil Eyal. 2002. "Eastern Europe as a Laboratory for Economic Knowledge: The Transnational Roots of Neoliberalism." *American Journal of Sociology* 108:310–52.

Bollen, Kenneth A. 1979. "Political Democracy and the Timing of Development." *American Sociological Review* 44:572–87.

Boltanski, Luc. 1990. "Visions of American management in Postwar France." Pp. 343–72 in *Structures of Capital: Social Organization of the Economy*, ed. Sharon Zukin and Paul DiMaggio. Cambridge: University of Cambridge Press.

Bornschier, Volker, and Thanh-Huyen Ballmer-Cao. 1979. "Income Inequality: A Cross National Study of the Relationships Between MNC-Penetration, Dimensions of the Power Structure and Income Distribution." *American Sociological Review* 44:438–506.

Bornschier Volker, and Christopher Chase-Dunn. 1985. *Transnational Corporations and Underdevelopment*. New York: Praeger.

Böröcz, József. 2000. "Informality Rules." *East European Politics and Societies* 14 (2): 348–80.

———. 2001. "Change Rules." *American Journal of Sociology* 106:1152–68.

Boudon, Raymond. 1998. "Limitations of Rational Choice Theory." *American Journal of Sociology* 104:817–28.

Bourdieu, Pierre. 1980. *The Logic of Practice*. Stanford, Calif.: Stanford University Press.

———. 2005. "Principles of an Economic Anthropology." Pp. 75–89 in *The Handbook of Economic Sociology*, ed. Neil J. Smelser and Richard Swedberg. 2nd ed. Princeton, N.J.: Princeton University Press; New York: Russell Sage Foundation.

Boycko, Maxim, Andrei Shleifer, and Robert Vishny. 1995. *Privatizing Russia*. Cambridge: MIT Press.

———. 1996. "A Theory of Privatisation." *Economic Journal* 106:309–19.

Brady, David, Jason Beckfield, and Martin Seeleib-Kaiser. 2005. "Economic Globalization and the Welfare State in Affluent Democracies, 1975–2001." *American Sociological Review* 70:921–48.

Brainard, Lacl. 1997. "An Empirical Assessment of the Proximity-Concentration Trade-off Between Multinational Sales and Trade." *American Economic Review* 87:520–44.

Brewer, Thomas. 1993. "Government Policies, Market Imperfections, and Foreign Direct Investment." *Journal of International Business Studies* 24:67–80.

Brubaker, Rogers. 1996. *Nationalism Reframed: Nationhood and the National Question in the New Europe*. New York: Cambridge University Press.

Brune, Nancy, Geoffrey Garrett, and Bruce Kogut. 2004. "The International Monetary Fund and the Global Spread of Privatization." *IMF Staff Papers* 51 (2).

Bruszt, László. 1992. "Transformative Politics: Social Costs and Social Peace in East Central Europe." *Eastern European Politics and Societies* 6 (1): 55–76.

Buch, Claudia, Robert Kokta, and Daniel Piazolo. 2003. "Does the East Get What Would Otherwise Flow to the South? FDI Diversion in Europe." *Journal of Comparative Economics* 31:94–109.

Buckley, Peter J., and Mark C. Casson. 1976. *The Future of the Multinational Enterprise*. London: Homes and Meier.

Bunce, Valerie. 1999. *Subversive Institutions: The Design and Destruction of Socialism and the State*. Cambridge: Cambridge University Press.

Burawoy, Michael, and Katherine Verdery. 1999. *Uncertain Transition: Ethnographies of Change in the Postsocialist World*. Lanham, Md.: Rowman and Littlefield.

Burt, Ronald. 1983. *Corporate Profits and Cooptation*. New York: Academic Press.

———. 1988. "The Stability of American Markets." *American Journal of Sociology* 94:356–95.

Burt, Ronald. 1992. *Structural Holes: The Social Structure of Competition*. Cambridge: Harvard University Press.

———. 2004. "Structural Holes and Good Ideas." *American Journal of Sociology* 110:349–99.

Čakrt, Michal. 1993. "Management Education in Eastern Europe: Toward Mutual Understanding." *Academy of Management Executive* 7 (4): 63–69.

Calavita, Kitty. 1992. *Inside the State: The Bracero Program, Immigration and the I.N.S.* New York: Routledge.

Calhoun, Craig. 1993. "Nationalism and Ethnicity." *Annual Review of Sociology* 19:211–39.

Callon, Michel. 1998. *The Laws of the Market*. Oxford: Blackwell.

Campbell, John C. 1980. "Tito: The Achievement and the Legacy." *Foreign Affairs* 58:1045–59.

Campbell, John L. 1996. "An Institutional Analysis of Fiscal Reform in Post-Communist Europe." *Theory and Society* 251:45–84.

———. 1998. "Institutional Analysis and the Role of Ideas in Political Economy." *Theory and Society* 27:377–409.

———. 2004. *Institutional Change and Globalization*. Princeton, N.J.: Princeton University Press.

Campbell, John L., and Leon Lindberg. 1990. "Property Rights and the Organization of Economic Activity by the State." *American Sociological Review* 55: 634–47.

Campbell, John L., and Ove K. Pedersen, eds. 1996. *Legacies of Change: Transformations of Postcommunist European Economies*. New York: Aldine de Gruyter.

———. 2001. *The Rise of Neoliberalism and Institutional Analysis*. Princeton, N.J.: Princeton University Press.

Campbell, John L., Rogers Hollingsworth, and Leon Lindberg. 1991. *Governance of the American Economy*. New York: Cambridge University Press.

Caratan, Branko. 1997. "The New States and Nationalism in Eastern Europe." *International Politics* 34:285–302.

Cardoso, Fernando Henrique, and Enzo Faletto. 1979. *Dependency and Development in Latin America*. Trans. Marjory Mattingly Urquidi. Berkeley and Los Angeles: University of California Press.

Carruthers, Bruce G. 1996. *City of Capital: Politics and Markets in the English Financial Revolution*. Princeton, N.J.: Princeton University Press.

Carruthers, Bruce G., Sarah L. Babb, and Terence C. Halliday. 2001. "Institutionalizing Markets, or the Market for Institutions? Central Banks, Bankruptcy Law, and the Globalization of Financial Markets." Pp. 94–126 in *The Rise of Neoliberalism and the Institutional Analysis*, ed. John Campbell and Ove Pedersen. Princeton, N.J.: Princeton University Press.

Caves, Richard E. 1996. *Multinational Enterprise and Economic Analysis*. Cambridge: Cambridge University Press.

Cerulo, Karen. 1997. "Identity Construction: New Issues, New Directions." *Annual Review of Sociology* 23:385–409.

Chakrabarti, Avik. 2001. "The Determinants of Foreign Direct Investments: Sensitivity Analyses of Cross-Country Regressions." *Kyklos* 54 (1): 89–114.

Chase-Dunn, Christopher. 1975. "The Effects of International Economic Dependence on Development and Inequality: A Cross-National Study." *American Sociological Review* 40:720–38.

Chase-Dunn, Christopher, and Peter Grimes. 1995. "World-Systems Analysis." *Annual Review of Sociology* 21:387–417.

Chase-Dunn, Christopher, Yukio Kawano, and Benjamin D. Brewer. 2000. "Trade Globalization since 1795: Waves of Integration in the World-System." *American Sociological Review* 65:77–95.

Chibber, Vivek. 2002. "Bureaucratic Rationality and the Developmental State." *American Journal of Sociology* 107:951–89.

Choi, Sang Rim, Daekeun Park, and Adrian E. Tschoegl.1996. "Banks and the World's Major Banking Centers, 1990." *Weltwirtschaftliches Archiv* 132 (4): 774–93.

Claessens, Stijnm, Simeon Djankov, and Gerhard Pohl. 1997. "Ownership and Corporate Governance: Evidence from the Czech Republic." World Bank Policy Research Paper 1737.

Coase, Ronald. 1960. "The Problem of Social Cost." *Journal of Law and Economics* 3:1–44.

Cohen, Michael D., and James G. March. 1974. *Leadership and Ambiguity: The American College President.* New York: McGraw-Hill.

Cohen, Michael D., James G. March, and Johan Olsen. 1972. "A Garbage Can Theory of Organizational Choice." *Administrative Science Quarterly* 17:1–25.

Collins, Randall. 1981. "On Microfoundations of Macrosociology." *American Journal of Sociology* 86:984–1014.

Comisso, Ellen. 1991. "Property Rights, Liberalism, and the Transition from 'Actually Existing' Socialism." *East European Politics and Societies* 5 (1): 162–88.

———. 1995. "Legacies of the Past or New Institutions: The Struggle over Restitution in Hungary." *Comparative Political Studies* 28 (2): 200–238.

Condrescu, Andrei. 1992. *The Hole in the Flag: A Romanian Exile's Story of Return and Revolution.* New York: Avon.

Cox, Robert W. 1996. "A Perspective on Globalization." Pp. 21–30 in *Globalization: Critical Reflections*, ed. James H. Mittelman. Boulder, Colo.: Lynne Rienner.

Creed, Gerald. 1998. *Domesticating Revolution: From Socialist Reform to Ambivalent Transition in a Bulgarian Village.* University Park: Pennsylvania State University Press.

Crouch, Colin, and Wolfgang Streeck. 1997. *Political Economy of Modern Capitalism: Mapping Convergence and Diversity.* London: Sage.

Cyert, Richard, and James G. March. 1963. *Behavioral Theory of the Firm.* New York: Prentice Hall.

CzechInvest. 2005. "Annual Report 2004." Retrieved March 25, 2005, http://www.czechinvest.org/web/pwci.nsf/dwnl/B35DEBE63465BD52C1256EEB00326DC7/$File/annual%20report%202004.pdf.

Dallago, Bruno, Gianmaria Ajani, and Bruno Grancelli. 1992. *Privatization and Entrepreneurship in Post-socialist Countries: Economy, Law, and Society.* New York: St. Martin's Press.

David, Paul. 1985. "Clio and Economics of QWERTY." *American Economic Review* 75:332–37.

Davidson, William H. 1980. "The Location of Foreign Direct Investment Activity: Country Characteristics and Experience Effects." *Journal of International Business Studies* 12:9–22.

Davis, Gerald F. 1991. "Agents without Principles? The Spread of the Poison Pill through the Intercorporate Network." *Administrative Science Quarterly* 36:583–613.

Davis, Gerald F., Kristina A. Diekmann, and Catherine H. Tinsley. 1994. "The Decline and Fall of the Conglomerate Firm in the 1980s: The Deinstitutionalization of an Organizational Form." *American Sociological Review* 59:547–70.

Davis, Gerald F., and Henrich R. Greve. 1997. "Corporate Elite Networks and Governance Changes in the 1980s." *American Journal of Sociology* 103:1–37.

Delios, Andrew, and Witold J. Henisz. 2000. "Japanese Firms' Investment Strategies in Emerging Economies." *Academy of Management Journal* 43 (3): 305–23.

della Porta, Donatella, Hanspeter Kriesi, and Dieter Rucht. 1999. *Social Movements in a Globalizing World.* London: Palgrave.

DeMartino, George. 1998. "Foreign Direct Investment." In *Foreign Policy in Focus*, ed. Martha Honey and Tom Barry. Retrieved April 24, 2005, http://www.fpif.org/briefs/vol3/v3n14fdi.html.

de Mortanges, Charles P., and Wilem B. Caris. 1994. "Investment in Eastern Europe: The Case of the Netherlands." Pp. 249–66 in *The Economics of Change in East and Central Europe*, ed. Peter J. Buckley and Pervez N. Ghauri. London: Academic Press.

de Nevers, Renee. 2003. *Comrades No More: The Seeds of Change in Eastern Europe.* Cambridge: MIT Press.

Dequech, David. 2003. "Uncertainty and Economic Sociology: A Preliminary Discussion." *American Journal of Economics and Sociology* 62 (3): 509–32.

De Soysa, Indra, and John R. O'Neal. 1999. "Boon or Bane? Reassessing the Effects of Foreign Capital on Economic Growth." *American Sociological Review* 64 (5): 766–82.

Dewey, John. 1939. *Theory of Valuation.* Chicago: University of Chicago Press.

———. 1957. *Human Nature and Conduct.* New York: Modern Library.

Dicken, Peter. 2003. *Global Shift: Reshaping the Global Economic Map in the 21st Century.* 4th ed. New York: Guilford.

DiMaggio, Paul. 1993. "Nadel's Paradox Revisited: Relational and Cultural Aspects of Organizational Structures." Pp. 118–42 in *Networks and Organization*, ed. Nitin Nohria and Robert Eccles. Boston: Harvard Business School Press.

———. 1994. "Culture and Economy." Pp. 27–57 in *The Handbook of Economic Sociology*, ed. Neil J. Smelser and Richard Swedberg. Princeton, N.J.: Princeton University Press; New York: Russell Sage Foundation.

———. 1997. "Culture and Cognition." *Annual Review of Sociology* 23: 263–88.

———. 2002. "Endogenizing 'Animal Spirits': Toward a Sociology of Collective Response to Uncertainty and Risk." Pp. 79–100 in *The New Economic Sociology: Developments in an Emerging Field*, ed. Mauro F. Guillén, Randall Collins, Paula England, and Marshall Meyer. New York: Russell Sage Foundation.

DiMaggio, Paul, and Hugh Louch. 1998. "Socially Embedded Consumer Transactions: For What Kinds of Purchases Do People Most Often Use Networks?" *American Sociological Review* 63:619–37.

DiMaggio, Paul, and Walter Powell. 1983. "The Iron Cage Revisited: Institutional Isomorphism and Collective Rationality in Organizational Fields." *American Sociological Review* 48:147–60.

———. 1991. "Introduction." Pp. 1–40 in *The New Institutionalism in Organizational Analysis*, ed. Walter Powell and Paul DiMaggio. Chicago: University of Chicago Press.

Dixon, William, and Terry Boswell. 1996. "Dependency, Disarticulation, and Denominator Effects: Another Look at Foreign Capital Penetration." *American Journal of Sociology* 102:543–62.

Dobbin, Frank. 1993. "The Social Construction of the Great Depression: Industrial Policy During the 1930s in the United States, Britain, and France." *Theory and Society* 22:1–56.

———. 1994a. *Forging Industrial Policy*. Cambridge: Cambridge University Press.

———. 1994b. "Cultural Models of Organization: The Social Construction of Rational Organizing Principles." Pp. 117–42 in the *Sociology of Culture*, ed. Diana Crane. Cambridge, Mass.: Blackwell.

Dobosiewicz, Zbigniew. 1992. *Foreign Investment in Eastern Europe*. London: Routledge.

Dore, Ronald. 1989. *British Factory, Japanese Factory: The Origins of National Diversity in Industrial Relations*. Berkeley and Los Angeles: University of California Press.

Dow, Sheila. 1985. *Macroeconomic Thought: A Methodological Approach*. London: Basil Blackwell.

Draper, Norman R., and Harry Smith. 1981. *Applied Regression Analysis*. New York: John Wiley and Sons.

Drori, Gili S., John W. Meyer, Francisco O. Ramirez, and Evan Schofer. 2003. *Science in the Modern World Polity: Institutionalization and Globalization*. Stanford, Calif.: Stanford University Press.

Dunning, John H. 1958. *American Investment in British Manufacturing Industry*. London: Allen and Unwin.

———. 1979. "Explaining Changing Patterns of International Production: In Defence of the Eclectic Theory." *Oxford Bulletin of Economics and Statistics* 41:269–95.

———. 1980. "Towards an Eclectic Theory of International Production: Some Empirical Tests." *Journal of International Business Studies* 11 (2): 9–31.

———. 1981. *International Production and the Multinational Enterprise*. London: Allen and Unwin.

Dunning, John H. 1995. "Reappraising the Eclectic Paradigm in the Age of Alliance Capitalism." *Journal of International Business Studies* 26 (3): 461–91.

Dunning, John H., and Matija Rojec. 1993. *Foreign Privatization in Central and Eastern Europe.* Ljubljana: CEEPN Technical Paper Series No. 2.

Dutt, Amitava K. 1997. "The Pattern of Direct Foreign Investment and Economic Growth." *World Development* 25:1925–36.

Earle, John S., Roman Frydman, and Andrzej Rapaczynski. 1993. *Privatization in the Transition to a Market Economy: Studies of Preconditions and Policies in Eastern Europe.* New York: St. Martin's Press.

European Bank for Restructuring and Development (EBRD). 2001a. *Investment Profile.* London: EBRD. Retrieved April 15, 2003, http://www.ebrd.com/about/index.htm.

———. 2001b. *Transition Report 2001.* London: EBRD.

———. 2003. *Transition Report 2003.* London: EBRD.

The Economist. 2006. "French Economic Nationalism: Colbert was Here." March 25, p. 65.

Edelman, Lauren N. 1992. "Legal Ambiguity and Symbolic Structures: Organizational Mediation of Civil Rights Law." *American Journal of Sociology* 97:1531–1976.

Eisenstadt, Shmuel N. 1964. "Social Change, Differentiation and Evolution." *American Sociological Review* 29 (3): 375–86.

Ekiert, Grzegorz. 1996. *The State against Society: Political Crises and their Aftermath in East Central Europe.* Princeton, N.J.: Princeton University Press.

Ekiert, Grzegorz, and Stephen Hanson. 2003. *Capitalism and Democracy in Central and Eastern Europe: Assessing the Legacy of Communist Rule.* New York: Cambridge University Press.

Eliasoph, Nina, and Paul Lichterman. 2003. "Culture in Interaction." *American Journal of Sociology* 108:735–94.

El Kahal, Sonia. 1994. *Introduction to International Business.* New York: McGraw-Hill.

Ellingsen, Tore, and Karl Wärneryd. 1999. "Foreign Direct Investment and the Political Economy of Protection." *International Economic Review* 40 (2): 357–79.

Elster, Jon. 1989a. *The Cement of Society: A Study of Social Order.* Cambridge: Cambridge University Press.

———. 1989b. *Nuts and Bolts for the Social Sciences.* Cambridge: Cambridge University Press.

———. 1996. "Rationality and the Emotions." *Economic Journal* 106 (438): 1386–97.

Emirbayer, Mustafa, and Jeff Goodwin. 1994. "Network Analysis, Culture, and the Problem of Agency." *American Journal of Sociology* 99:1411–54.

Erdmans, Mary Patrice. 1998. *Opposing Poles: Immigrants and Ethnics in Polish Chicago, 1976–1990.* University Park: Pennsylvania State University Press.

Espeland, Wendy Nelson. 1998. *The Struggle for Water: Politics, Rationality, and Identity in the American Southwest.* Chicago: University of Chicago Press.

Estrin, Saul, Kristy Hughes, and Sarah Todd. 1997. *Foreign Direct Investment in CEE: Multinationals in Transition*. London: Royal Institute of International Affairs.

Etzioni, Amitai. 1988. *The Moral Dimension: Toward a New Economics*. New York: Free Press.

European Union. 2005. "Europa: The EU On-line." Retrieved June 5, 2005, http://europa.eu.int/.

———. 2006. "Phare." Retrieved March 20, 2006, http://ec.europa.eu/comm/enlargement/pas/phare/.

Evans, Peter. 1979. *Dependent Development: The Alliance of Multinational, State and Local Capital in Brazil*. Princeton, N.J.: Princeton University Press.

———. 1995. *Embedded Autonomy: States and Industrial Transformation*. Princeton, N.J.: Princeton University Press.

———. 1997. "The Eclipse of the State?" *World Politics* 50:62–87.

Evans, Peter, and James Rauch. 1999. "Bureaucracy and Growth: A Cross-National Analysis of the Effects of 'Weberian' State Structures on Economic Growth." *American Sociological Review* 64:748–65.

Evans, Peter, Dietrich Rueschemeyer, and Theda Skocpol. 1985. *Bringing the State Back In*. New York: Cambridge University Press.

Evans, Peter, and Michael Timberlake. 1980. "Dependence, Inequality, and the Growth of the Tertiary: A Comparative Analysis of Less Developed Countries." *American Sociological Review* 45:531–52.

Eyal, Gil, Ivan Szelényi, and Eleanor Townsley. 1998. *Making Capitalism Without Capitalists*. New York: Verso.

Featherstone, Mike, and Scott Lash, eds. 1999. *Spaces of Culture: City, Nation, World*. Thousand Oaks, Calif.: Sage

Feenstra, Robert, James Markusen, and Andrew Rose. 2001. "Using the Gravity Equation to Differentiate among Alternative Theories of Trade." *Canadian Journal of Economics* 34 (2): 430–47.

Fernández, Roberto M., Emilio J. Castilla, and Paul Moore. 2000. "Social Capital at Work: Networks and Employment at a Phone Center." *American Journal of Sociology* 105:1288–1356.

Firebaugh, Glenn. 1992. "Growth Effects of Foreign and Domestic Investment." *American Journal of Sociology* 98:105–30.

———. 1996. "Does Foreign Capital Harm Poor Nations? New Estimates Based on Dixon and Boswell's Measure of Capital Penetration." *American Journal of Sociology* 102:563–75.

Fischer, Stanley, and Allan Gelb. 1991. "The Process of Socialist Economic Transformation." *Journal of Economic Perspectives* 4:91–106.

Fiss, Peer C., and Paul M. Hirsch. 2005. "The Discourse of Globalization: Framing and Sensemaking of an Emerging Concept." *American Sociological Review* 70:29–52.

Fligstein, Neil. 1985. "The Spread of the Multidivisional Form." *American Sociological Review* 50:377–91.

———. 1990. *The Transformation of Corporate Control*. Cambridge: Harvard University Press.

Fligstein, Neil. 1996. "Markets as Politics: A Political-Cultural Approach to Market Institutions." *American Sociological Review* 61 (4): 656–73.

———. 2001a. *The Architecture of Markets: An Economic Sociology of Twenty-First-Century Capitalist Societies*. Princeton, N.J.: Princeton University Press.

———. 2001b. "Social Skill and the Theory of Fields." *Sociological Theory* 19:105–25.

———. 2002. "Agreements, Disagreements, and Opportunities in the 'New Sociology of Markets.'" Pp. 61–78 in *The New Economic Sociology: Developments in an Emerging Field*, ed. Mauro Guillén, Randall Collins, Paula England, and Marshall Meyer. New York: Russell Sage Foundation.

———. 2005. "The Political and Economic Sociology of International Economic Arrangements." Pp. 183–204 in *The Handbook of Economic Sociology*, ed. Neil J. Smelser and Richard Swedberg. 2nd ed. Princeton, N.J.: Princeton University Press; New York: Russell Sage Foundation.

Fligstein, Neil, and Peter Brantley. 1992. "Bank Control, Owner Control, or Organizational Dynamics: Who Controls the Large Modern Corporation?" *American Journal of Sociology* 98:280–309.

Fligstein, Neil, and Iona Mara-Drita. 1996. "How to Make a Market: Reflections on the Attempt to Create a Single Market in the EU." *American Journal of Sociology* 102:1–33.

Fligstein, Neil, and Alec Stone Sweet. 2002. "Constructing Polities and Markets: An Institutionalist Account of European Integration." *American Journal of Sociology* 107:1206–43.

Foreign Investment Advisory Service (FIAS). 2000. *Slovenia—Administrative Barriers to Investment*. Washington, D.C.: FIAS.

Forgas, Joseph. 1998. "On Feeling Good and Getting Your Way: Mood Effects on Negotiating Strategies and Outcomes." *Journal of Personality and Social Psychology* 74:565–77.

Frank, Andre Gunder. 1967. *Capitalism and Development in Latin America*. New York: Monthly Review Press.

Frank, David John, Ann Hironaka, and Evan Schofer. 2000. "The Nation-State and the Natural Environment over the Twentieth Century." *American Sociological Review* 65:96–116.

Freedom House. 2006. "Nations in Transit." Retrieved June 2, 2006, http://www.freedomhouse.org.

Frees, Edward. 2004. *Longitudinal and Panel Data: Analysis and Applications in the Social Sciences*. Cambridge: Cambridge University Press.

Frydman, Roman, Cheryl W. Gray, Marek Hessel, and Andrzej Rapaczynski. 1999. "When Does Privatization Work? The Impact of Private Ownership on Corporate Performance in Transition Economies." *Quarterly Journal of Economics* 114 (4): 1153–91.

———. 2000. "The Limits of Discipline: Ownership and Hard Budget Constraints in the Transition Economies." C. V. Starr Center for Applied Economies Working Paper. New York University.

Frydman, Roman, Kenneth Murphy, and Andrzej Rapaczynski. 1996. "Capitalism with a Comrade's Face." *Transition* 2 (2): 5–11.

Frydman, Roman, and Andrzej Rapaczynski. 1994. *Privatization in Eastern Europe: Is the State Withering Away?* Budapest: Central European University Press.

Fukuyama, Francis. 1989. "The End of History?" *National Interest* 16 (Summer): 3–18.

Gal, Susan. 1991. "Bartók's Funeral: Representations of Europe in Hungarian Political Rhetoric." *American Ethnologist* 18 (3): 440–58.

Gal, Susan, and Gail Kligman. 2000. *The Politics of Gender After Socialism: A Comparative-Historical Essay.* Princeton, N.J.: Princeton University Press.

Galaskiewicz, Joseph, and Stanley Wasserman. 1989. "Mimetic Processes within an Interorganizational Field: An Empirical Test." *Administrative Science Quarterly* 34:454–79.

Galaskiewicz, Joseph, Stanley Wasserman, Barbara Rauschenbach, Wolfgang Bielefeld, and Patti Mullaney. 1985. "The Influence of Corporate Power, Social Status, and Market Position on Corporate Interlocks in a Regional Market." *Social Forces* 64:403–31.

Galtung, Johan. 1971. "A Structural Theory of Imperialism." *Journal of Peace Research* 2:81–117.

Gao, Bai. 1997. *Economic Ideology and Japanese Industrial Policy: Developmentalism from 1931 to 1965.* New York: Cambridge University Press.

———. 2001. *Japan's Economic Dilemma: The Institutional Origins of Prosperity and Stagnation.* New York: Cambridge University Press.

Garfinkel, Harold. 1967. *Studies in Ethnomethodology.* Englewood Cliffs, N.J.: Prentice- Hall.

Gastanga, Victor, Jeffrey B. Nugent, and Bistra Pashamova. 1998. "Host Country Reforms and FDI Flows: How Much Difference Do They Make?" *World Development* 26: 1299–1314.

General Agreement on Tariffs and Trade (GATT). 1992. *Trade Policy Review: Poland.* Vol. 1. Geneva: GATT.

Gerber, Theodore P. 2002. "Structural Change and Post-socialist Stratification: Labor Market Transitions in Contemporary Russia." *American Sociological Review* 67:629–59.

Gerber, Theodore P., and Michael Hout. 1998. "More Shock than Therapy: Market Transition, Employment, and Income in Russia, 1991–1995." *American Journal of Sociology* 104:1–50.

Gereffi, Gary. 1978. "Drug Firms and Dependency in Mexico: The Case of the Steroid Hormone Industry." *International Organization* 32 (1): 237–86.

———. 1983. *The Pharmaceutical Industry and Dependency in the Third World.* Princeton, N.J.: Princeton University Press.

———. 2005. "The Global Economy: Organization, Governance, and Development." Pp. 160–82 in *The Handbook of Economic Sociology,* ed. Neil J. Smelser and Richard Swedberg. 2nd ed. Princeton, N.J.: Princeton University Press; New York: Russell Sage Foundation.

Giddens, Anthony. 1984. *The Constitution of Society: Outline of the Theory of Structuration.* Berkeley and Los Angeles: University of California Press.

———. 1991. *Modernity and Self-Identity.* Cambridge, Mass.: Polity Press.

Gilpin, Robert. 1987. *The Political Economy of International Relations*. Princeton, N.J.: Princeton University Press.

Gore, Charles. 2000. "The Rise and Fall of the Washington Consensus as a Paradigm for Developing Countries." *World Development* 28 (5): 789–804.

Grabbe, Heather. 2003. "Europeanization Goes East: Power and Uncertainty in the EU Accession Process." Pp. 303–25 in *The Politics of Europeanization*, ed. Kevin Featherstone and Claudio Radaelli. Oxford: Oxford University Press.

Grabbe, Heather, and Kristy Hughes. 1998. *Enlarging the EU Eastwards*. London: Pinter.

Grabher, Gernot, and David Stark. 1997. "Organizing Diversity: Evolutionary Theory, Network Analysis and Postsocialism." *Regional Studies* 31 (5): 533–44.

Granacki, Victoria. 2004. *Chicago's Polish Downtown*. Charleston, S.C.: Arcadia.

Granovetter, Mark. 1974. *Getting a Job: A Study of Contacts and Careers*. Cambridge: Harvard University Press.

———. 1985. "Economic Action and Social Structure: The Problem of Embeddedness." *American Journal of Sociology* 91:481–510.

———. 2002. "A Theoretical Agenda for Economic Sociology." Pp. 35–60 in *The New Economic Sociology: Developments in an Emerging Field*, ed. Mauro Guillén, Randall Collins, Paula England, and Marshall Meyer. New York: Russell Sage Foundation.

Greve, Heinrich. 1996. "Patterns of Competition: The Diffusion of a Market Position in Radio Broadcasting." *Administrative Science Quarterly* 41:29–60.

Grubaugh, Stephen. 1987. "Determinants of Direct Foreign Investment." *Review of Economics and Statistics* 69:149–52.

Grzymala-Busse, Anna M. 2002. *Redeeming the Communist Past: The Regeneration of Communist Parties in East Central Europe*. Cambridge: Cambridge University Press.

Guidry, John A., Michael D. Kennedy, and Mayer N. Zald, eds. 2001. *Globalizations and Social Movements: Culture, Power, and the Transnational Public Sphere*. Ann Arbor: University of Michigan Press.

Guillén, Mauro. 1994. *Models of Management: Work, Authority and Organization in a Comparative Perspective*. Chicago: University of Chicago Press.

———. 2001a. "Is Globalization Civilizing, Destructive or Feeble? A Critique of Five Key Debates in Social Science Literature." *Annual Review of Sociology* 27:235–60.

———. 2001b. *The Limits of Convergence*. Princeton, N.J.: Princeton University Press.

———. 2002a. "Organized Labor's Images of Multinational Enterprise: Divergent Foreign Investment Ideologies in Argentina, South Korea, and Spain." *Industrial and Labor Relations Review* 53 (3): 419–42.

———. 2002b. "Structural Inertia, Imitation and Foreign Expansion: South Korean Firms and Business Groups in China, 1987–95." *Academy of Management Journal* 45 (3): 509–25.

Gulati, Ranjay. 1995. "Social Structure and Alliance Formation Patterns: A Longitudinal Analysis." *Administrative Science Quarterly* 40:619–52.

Gulati, Ranjay, and Martin Gargiulo. 1999. "Where do Interorganizational Networks Come From?" *American Journal of Sociology* 104:1439–93.

Gulati, Ranjay, and James Westphal. 1999. "Cooperative or Controlling? The Effects of CEO-Board Relations and the Content of Interlocks on the Formation of Joint Ventures." *Administrative Science Quarterly* 44:473–506.

Guseva, Alya, and Ákos Róna-Tas. 2001. "Uncertainty, Risk and Trust: Russian and American Credit Card Markets Compared." *American Sociological Review* 66 (5): 623–46.

Hadri, Kaddour. 2000. "Testing for Stationarity in Heterogeneous Panel Data." *Econometrics Journal* 3:148–61.

Haggard, Stephan, and Robert Kaufman. 1995. *The Political Economy of Democratic Transitions*. Princeton, N.J.: Princeton University Press.

Hall, Peter, and David Soskice. 2001. *Varieties of Capitalism: The Institutional Foundations of Comparative Advantage*. Oxford: Oxford University Press.

Hamilton, Gary G., and Nicole Woosley Biggart. 1988. "Market, Culture, and Authority: A Comparative Analysis of Management and Organization in the Far East." *American Journal of Sociology* 94 (Supplement): S52–S94.

Hankiss, Elemer. 1990. *East European Alternatives*. Oxford: Clarendon Press.

Hanley, Eric, Lawrence King, and János Istvan Tóth. 2002. "The State, International Agencies, and Property Transformation in Postcommunist Hungary." *American Journal of Sociology* 108:129–61.

Hannerz, Ulf. 2000. "Scenarios for Peripheral Cultures." Pp. 331–34 in *The Globalization Reader*, ed. Frank Lechner and John Boli. New York: Blackwell.

Hanousek, Jan, and Eugene Kroch. 1998. "The Two Waves of Voucher Privatization in the Czech Republic: A Model of Learning in Sequential Bidding." *Applied Economics* 30 (1): 133–43.

Haque, Nadeem, and Mohsin S. Khan. 1998. "Do IMF-Supported Programs Work? A Survey of the Cross-Country Empirical Evidence." *IMF Working Paper* WP/98/169.

Hare, Paul, and Tamas Révész. 1992. "Hungary's Transition to the Market: The Case against a 'Big-Bang.'" *Economic Policy* 7 (14): 227–64.

Harsanyi, Nicolae, and Michael D. Kennedy. 1994. "Between Utopia and Dystopia: The Labilities of Nationalism in Eastern Europe." Pp. 149–79 in *Envisioning Eastern Europe*, ed. Michael D. Kennedy. Ann Arbor: University of Michigan Press.

Harvey, David. 1989. *The Condition of Postmodernity*. Oxford: Blackwell.

Haunschild, Pamela. 1994. "How Much Is That Company Worth? Interorganizational Relationships, Uncertainty and Acquisition Premiums." *Administrative Science Quarterly* 39:391–411.

Haunschild, Pamela, and Ann Miner. 1997. "Modes of Interorganizational Imitation: The Effects of Outcome Salience and Uncertainty." *Administrative Science Quarterly* 42:472–500.

Hausner, Jerzy, Bob Jessop, and Klaus Nielsen. 1995. *Strategic Choice and Path-Dependency in Post-Socialism: Institutional Dynamics in the Transformation Process*. Aldershot: Edward Elgar.

Haveman, Heather A. 1993. "Follow the Leader: Mimetic Isomorphism and Entry into New Markets." *Administrative Science Quarterly* 38:593–627.

Hein, Simeon. 1992. "Trade Strategy and the Dependency Hypothesis: A Comparison of Policy, Foreign Investment, and Economic Growth in Latin America and East Asia." *Economic Development and Cultural Change* 40 (3): 495–521.

Hejazi, Walid, and Edward Safarian. 1999. "Trade, Foreign Direct Investment, and R&D Spillovers." *Journal of International Business Studies* 30:491–511.

Helpman, Elhanan. 1984. "A Simple Theory of International Trade with Multinational Corporations." *Journal of Political Economy* 92 (3): 451–71.

Henisz, Witold. 2000. "The Institutional Environment for Multinational Investment." *Journal of Law, Economics and Organization* 16:334–64.

———. 2002. "The Institutional Environment for Infrastructure Investment." *Industrial and Corporate Change* 11:355–89.

Henisz, Witold J., and Andrew Delios. 2001. "Uncertainty, Imitation, and Plant Location: Japanese Multinational Corporations, 1990–1996." *Administrative Science Quarterly* 46:443–75.

Henisz, Witold J., Bennet A. Zelner, and Mauro Guillén. 2005. "World-Wide Diffusion of Market-Oriented Infrastructure Reform, 1977–1999." *American Sociological Review* 70:871–97.

Hennart, Jean-François. 1982. *A Theory of Multinational Enterprise.* Ann Arbor: University of Michigan Press.

Hickson, David J. 1987. "Decision-Making at the Top of Organizations." *Annual Review of Sociology* 13:165–92.

Higgins, Tory. 1996. *Social Psychology: Handbook of Basic Principles.* London: Guilford Press.

Hill, Charles, Peter Hwang, and Chan W. Kim. 1990. "An Eclectic Theory of the Choice of International Entry Mode." *Strategic Management Journal* 11: 117–28.

Hirschman, Albert. 1977. *The Passions and the Interests.* Princeton, N.J.: Princeton University Press.

Hirst, Paul Q., and Grahame Thompson. 1999. *Globalization in Question: The International Economy and the Possibilities of Governance.* 2nd ed. Malden, Mass.: Blackwell.

Hochschild, Arlie Russell. 1979. "Emotion Work, Feeling Rules, and Social Structure." *American Journal of Sociology* 85:551–75.

———. 1983. *The Managed Heart: Commercialization of Human Feeling.* Berkeley and Los Angeles: University of California Press.

Hofstede, Geert. 2001. *Culture's Consequences: Comparing Values, Behaviors, Institutions and Organizations across Nations.* 2nd ed. Thousand Oaks, Calif.: Sage.

———. 2006. "A Summary of My Ideas about National Culture Differences." Retrieved March 23, 2006, http://feweb.uvt.nl/center/hofstede/page3.htm.

Hollingsworth, J. Rogers. 2003. "On Institutional Embeddedness." Pp. 87–107 in *Advancing Socio-Economics: An Institutional Perspective,* ed. J. Rogers Hollingsworth, Karl. H. Müller, and Ellen Jane Hollingsworth. Lanham, Md.: Rowman and Littlefield.

Hollingsworth, J. Rogers, and Robert Boyer. 1997. *Contemporary Capitalism: The Embeddedness of Institutions.* Cambridge: Cambridge University Press.

Hollingsworth, J. Rogers, Philippe Schmitter, and Wolfgang Streeck. 1994. *Governing Capitalist Economies.* New York: Oxford University Press.

Hölzl, Erik, Erich Kirchler, and Christa Rodler. 2002. "Hindsight Bias in Economic Expectations: I Knew All Along What I Want to Hear." *Journal of Applied Psychology* 87 (3): 437–43.

Horvat, Branko. 1976. *The Yugoslav Economic System: The First Labor-Managed Economy in the Making.* White Plains, N.Y.: International Arts and Sciences Press.

Huber, Evelyne, and John D. Stephens. 2001. *Development and Crisis of the Welfare State.* Chicago: University of Chicago Press.

Huntington, Samuel. 1984. "Will More Countries Become Democratic?" *Political Science Quarterly* 99:193–218.

Hymer, Stephen. 1976. *The International Operations of National Firms: A Study of Direct Foreign Investment.* Cambridge: MIT Press.

Ingham, Geoffrey. 1996. "The 'New Economic Sociology.' " *Work, Employment and Society* 10:549–64.

Inglehart, Ronald, and Wayne Baker. 2000. "Modernization, Cultural Change, and the Persistence of Traditional Values." *American Sociological Review* 65 (1): 19–51. 2000.

Ingram, Paul, and Peter Roberts. 2000. "Friendships among Competitors in the Sydney Hotel Industry." *American Journal of Sociology* 106:387–423.

Institutional Investor. 2003. "Country Credit Rankings." Retrieved April 5, 2003, http://institutionalinvestor.com.

International Monetary Fund (IMF). 1997. *World Economic Outlook.* Washington, D.C.: IMF.

———. 1998. *International Financial Statistics Yearbook.* Washington, D.C.: IMF.

———. 1999. *Balance of Payments Statistics Yearbook.* Washington, D.C.: IMF.

———. 2001. *International Financial Statistics Yearbook.* Washington, D.C.: IMF.

———. 2005a. "Articles of Agreement of the International Monetary Fund: Article VII—General Obligations of Members." Retrieved June 18, 2005, http://www.imf.org/external/pubs/ft/aa/aa08.htm.

———. 2005b. "IMF—International Monetary Fund Homepage." Retrieved June 5, 2005, http://www.imf.org/.

———. 2006. "The Process of IMF Lending." Retrieved March 20, 2006, http://www.imf.org/external/np/exr/facts/howlend.htm.

InvestBulgaria Agency. 2005. "About InvestBulgaria Agency." Retrieved May 6, 2005, http://investbg.government.bg/.

Jackman, Robert. 1973. "On the Relations of Economic Development to Democratic Performance." *American Journal of Political Science* 17:611–21.

Javorcik, Beata Smarzynska. 2004. "Does Foreign Direct Investment Increase the Productivity of Domestic Firms? In Search of Spillovers through Backward Linkages." *American Economic Review* 94:605–27.

Jenkins, Craig, and Zeynep Benderlioglu. 2005. "Mass Protest and the Democratic Transitions in Eastern Europe, 1984–1994." Unpublished manuscript, Department of Sociology, Ohio State University.

Jensen, Nathan. 2006. *Nation-States and the Multinational Corporation: A Political Economy of Foreign Direct Investment*. Princeton, N.J.: Princeton University Press.

Jepperson, Ronald. 1991. "Institutions, Institutional Effects and Institutionalism." Pp. 143–63 in *The New Institutionalism in Organizational Analysis*, ed. Walter Powell and Paul DiMaggio. Chicago: University of Chicago Press.

Jessop, Bob. 2002. "Liberalism, Neoliberalism, and Urban Governance: A State Theoretical Perspective." Pp. 105–25 in *Spaces of Neoliberalism*, ed. N. Brenner and N. Theodore. Malden, Mass.: Blackwell.

Joas, Hans. 1993. *Pragmatism and Social Theory*. Chicago: University of Chicago Press.

———. 1996. *The Creativity of Action*. Cambridge: Polity Press.

Jun, Kwang W., and Harinder Singh. 1996. "The Determinants of Foreign Direct Investment in Developing Countries." *Transnational Corporations* 5 (2): 67–105.

Kahneman, Daniel, and Jackie Snell. 1990. "Predicting Utility." Pp. 295–310 in *Insights in Decision Making*, ed. Robin Hogarth. Chicago: University of Chicago Press.

Kahneman, Daniel, and Amos Tversky. 1974. "Judgment under Uncertainty: Heuristics and Biases." *Science* 185:1124–31.

———. 1984. "Choices, Values, and Frames." *American Psychologist* 39:341–50.

Karatnycky, Adrian, Alexander Motyl, and Charles Graybow, eds. 1999. *Nations in Transit, 1998: Civil Society, Democracy and Markets in East Central Europe and Newly Independent States*. New Brunswick, N.J.: Transaction Publishers.

Katzenstein, Peter. 1985. *Small States in World Markets*. Ithaca, N.Y.: Cornell University Press.

———. 1996. *Cultural Norms and National Security: Police and Military in Postwar Japan*. Ithaca, N.Y.: Cornell University Press.

Kaufman, Daniel, and Paul Siegelbaum. 1997. "Privatization and Corruption in Transition Economies." *Journal of International Affairs* 50:419–58.

Keck, Margaret E., and Kathryn Sikkink. 1998. *Activists beyond Borders: Advocacy Networks in International Politics*. Ithaca, N.Y.: Cornell University Press.

Kennedy, Michael D. 2002. *Cultural Formations of Postcommunism: Emancipation, Transition, Nation and War*. Minneapolis: University of Minnesota Press.

Kennedy, Paul. 1993. *Preparing for the Twenty-First Century*. New York: Random House.

Kentor, Jeffrey. 1998. "The Long-Term Effects of Foreign Investment Dependence on Economic Growth 1940–1990." *American Journal of Sociology* 103:1024–46.

Kerr, Robert M. 1982. "The Role of Operational Research in Organizational Decision Making." *European Journal of Operational Research* 14:270–78.

Keynes, John Maynard. 1936. *The General Theory of Unemployment, Interest, and Money*. London: McMillan.

———. 1937. "The General Theory of Unemployment." *Quarterly Journal of Economics* 51:209–23.

King, Lawrence. 2001. *The Basic Features of Postcommunist Capitalism in Eastern Europe: Firms in Hungary, the Czech Republic and Slovakia.* Westport, CT: Praeger.

King, Lawrence, and Patrick Hamm. 2006. "The Governance Grenade: Mass Privatization, State Capacity and Economic Development in Postcommunist and Reforming Communist Societies." Paper presented at the American Sociological Association Meetings, Montreal, Canada.

King, Lawrence, and Ivan Szelényi. 2005. "Post-communist Economic Systems." Pp. 205–32 in *The Handbook of Economic Sociology,* ed. Neil J. Smelser and Richard Swedberg. 2nd ed. Princeton, N.J.: Princeton University Press; New York: Russell Sage Foundation.

King, Lawrence, and Balazs Varadi. 2002. "Beyond Manichean Economics: Foreign Direct Investment and Growth in the Transition from Socialism to Capitalism." *Communist and Post-Communist Studies* 35:1–21.

Kindleberger, Charles P. 1970. *The International Corporation.* Cambridge: MIT.

Knickerbocker, Frederick. 1973. *Oligopolistic Reaction and Multinational Enterprise.* Cambridge: Harvard University Press.

Knight, Frank. 2002. *Risk, Uncertainty and Profit.* Washington, D.C.: Beard Books.

Kobrin, Stephen J. 1982. *Managing Political Risk Assessment: A Strategic Response to Environmental Change.* Berkeley and Los Angeles: University of California Press.

———. 1984. "Expropriation as an Attempt to Control Foreign Firms in LDCs: Trends from 1960–1979." *International Studies Quarterly* 28 (3): 329–48.

Kogut, Bruce. 1988. "Joint Ventures: Theoretical and Empirical Perspectives." *Strategic Management Journal* 9:319–32.

———. 1996. "Direct Investment, Experimentation, and Corporate Governance in Transition Economies." Pp. 293–332 in *Corporate Governance in Central Europe and Russia: Banks, Funds and Foreign Investors,* ed. Roman Frydman, Cheryl Gray, and Andrzej Rapaczynski. Budapest: Central European University Press.

Kogut, Bruce, and Sea-Jin Chang. 1991. "Technological Capabilities and Japanese Foreign Direct Investment in the United States." *Review of Economics and Statistics* 73:401–13.

Kogut, Bruce, and J. Muir Macpherson. 2003. "The Decision to Privatize as an Economic Policy Idea: Epistemic Communities, Palace Wars and Diffusion." Unpublished manuscript, Wharton Business School, University of Pennsylvania.

Kogut, Bruce, and Harbir Singh. 1988. "The Effect of National Culture on the Choice of Entry Mode." *Journal of International Business Studies* 19 (3): 411–32.

Kogut, Bruce, and Udo Zander. 1993. "Knowledge of the Firm and the Evolutionary Theory of the Multinational Corporation." *Journal of International Business Studies* 24:625–45.

———. 2000. "Did Socialism Fail to Innovate? A Natural Experiment of the Two Zeiss Companies." *American Sociological Review* 65 (2): 169–90.

Kollock, Peter. 1994. "The Emergence of Exchange Structures: An Experimental Study of Uncertainty, Commitment and Trust." *American Journal of Sociology* 100:313–45.

Kornai, János. 1959. *Overcentralization in Economic Administration*. Oxford: Oxford University Press.

———. 1980. *Economics of Shortage*. Amsterdam: North-Holland.

———. 1986. "The Soft Budget Constraints." *Kyklos* 39 (1): 3–30.

———. 1992. *Socialist System: Political Economy of Communism*. Princeton, N.J.: Princeton University Press; Oxford: Oxford University Press.

Koslowski, Rey. 1992. "Market Institutions: East European Reform, and Economic Theory." *Journal of Economic Issues* 26:673–705.

Kovacs, János Matyas. 1994. "Introduction: Official and Alternative Legacies." Pp. xi–xxiii in *Transition to Capitalism? The Communist Legacy in Eastern Europe*, ed. János Matyas Kovacs. New Brunswick, N.J.: Transaction Publishers.

Kramer, Roderick. 1999. "Trust and Distrust in Organizations: Emerging Perspectives, Enduring Questions." *Annual Review of Psychology* 50:569–98.

Krippner, Greta. 2001. The Elusive Market: Embeddedness and the Paradigm of Economic Sociology." *Theory and Society* 30:775–810.

Križnik, Božena. 2002. "Ob istih pogojih prednost Janezu." *Delo*, January 10, 2002. Retrieved March 28, 2005, http://www.delo.si/index.php?sv_path=43,50&id=7cb91833dce168c4785707c9297ec62d04&source=Delo.

Kurtz, Marcus, and Andrew Barnes. 2002. "The Political Foundations of Post-Communist Regimes: Marketization, Agrarian Legacies, or International Influences." *Comparative Political Studies* 35 (5): 524–53.

Lado, Maria. 2002. "Industrial Relations in the Candidate Countries." *European Industrial Relations Observatory On-line*. Retrieved April 5, 2003, http://www.eiro.eurofound.ie/2002/07/study/TN0207102Fa.html.

Lamont, Michèle. 1992. *Money, Morals and Manners: The Culture of the French and American Upper-Middle Class*. Chicago: University of Chicago Press.

Lamont, Michèle, and Laurent Thevenot. 2001. *Rethinking Comparative Cultural Sociology: Repertoires of Evaluation in France and the United States*. Cambridge: Cambridge University Press.

Lang, James, and Daniel Lockhart. 1990. "Increased Environmental Uncertainty and Changes in Board Linkage Patterns." *Academy of Management Journal* 33:106–28.

Lange, Oskar. 1938. "On the Economic Theory of Socialism." Pp. 55–143 in *On the Economic Theory of Socialism*, ed. Benjamin E. Lippincott. Minneapolis: University of Minnesota Press.

Langley, Ann. 1989. "In Search of Rationality: The Purposes Behind the Use of Formal Analysis in Organizations." *Administrative Science Quarterly* 34:598–631.

Lankes, Hans-Peter, and Anthony J. Venables. 1996. "Foreign Direct Investment in Economic Transition: The Changing Pattern of Investments." *Economics of Transition* 4:331–47.

Lash, Scott, and John Urry. 1987. *The End of Organized Capitalism*. Madison: University of Wisconsin Press.

Leamer, Edward E. 1983. "Let's Take the Con out of Econometrics." *American Economic Review* 23:31–43.

Lechner, Frank, and John Boli. 2000. "General Introduction." Pp. 1–3 in *The Globalization Reader*, ed. Frank Lechner and John Boli. New York: Blackwell.

Levitt, Barbara, and James March. 1988. "Organizational Learning." *Annual Review of Sociology* 14:319–40.

Li, Quan, and Adam Resnick. 2003. "Reversal of Fortunes: Democratic Institutions and Foreign Direct Investment Inflows to Developing Countries." *International Organization* 57:175–211.

Lie, John. 1997. "Sociology of Markets." *Annual Review of Sociology* 23:341–60.

Lincoln, James, Michael Gerlach, and Peggy Takahashi. 1992. "Keiretsu Networks in the Japanese Economy: A Dyad Analysis of Intercorporate Ties." *American Sociological Review* 57:561–91.

Lincoln, James, M. Hanada, and J. Olson. 1981. "Cultural Orientations and Individual Reactions to Organizations: A Study of Employees of Japanese Owned Firms." *Administrative Science Quarterly* 25:93–115.

Lindblom, Charles. 1959. "The Science of 'Muddling Through.' " *Public Administration Review* 19:79–88.

Linneman, Hans. 1961. *An Economic Study of International Trade Flows*. Amsterdam: North Holland.

Linz, Juan, and Alfred Stepan. 1997. *Problems of Democratic Transition and Consolidation*. Baltimore: Johns Hopkins University Press.

Lipset, Seymour Martin. 1959. "Some Social Requisites of Democracy: Economic Development and Political Legitimacy." *American Political Science Review* 53:69–105.

Lipset, Seymour Martin, and György Bence. 1994. "Anticipations of the Failure of Communism." *Theory and Society* 23:169–210.

Lipton, David, and Jeffrey Sachs.1990. "Privatization in Eastern Europe: The Case of Poland." *Brookings Papers on Economic Activity* 2:293–341.

Lomnitz, Larissa. 1988. "Informal Exchange Networks in Informal Systems: A Theoretical Model." *American Anthropologist* 90:42–56.

London, Bruce, and Robert J. S. Ross. 1995. "The Political Sociology of Foreign Direct Investment." *International Journal of Comparative Sociology* 36 (3–4): 198–218.

Long, Scott J., and Laurie H. Ervin. 2000. "Using Heteroscedasticity Consistent Standard Errors in the Linear Regression Model." *American Statistician* 54 (3): 217–24.

Lopata, Helena. 1994. *Polish Americans*. New Brunswick, N.J.: Transaction Publishers.

Lyles, Marjorie A., and Howard Thomas. 1988. "Strategic Problem Formulation: Biases and Assumptions Embedded in Alternative Decision-making Models." *Journal of Management Studies* 25 (2): 131–45.

Macaulay, Stewart. 1963. "Non-contractual Relations in Business: A Preliminary Study." *American Sociological Review* 28:55–69.

MacKenzie, Donald, and Yuval Millo. 2003. "Constructing a Market, Performing Theory: The Historical Sociology of a Financial Derivatives Exchange." *American Journal of Sociology* 109:107–45.

March, James. 1978. "Bounded Rationality, Ambiguity, and the Engineering of Choice." *Bell Journal of Economics* 9:587–607.

———. 1994. *A Primer on Decision Making: How Decisions Happen*. New York: Free Press.

March, James, and Johan Olsen. 1976. *Ambiguity and Choice in Organizations*. Oslo: Universitetsforlaget.

Markusen, James R. 1984. "Multinationals, Multi-Plant Economies, and the Gains from Trade." *Journal of International Economics* 16 (3–4): 205–26.

Markusen, James R., and Anthony J. Venables. 1999. "Foreign Direct Investment as a Catalyst for Industrial Development." *European Economic Review* 43 (2): 335–56.

Markusen, John. 1995. "The Boundaries of Multinational Enterprises and the Theory of International Trade." *Journal of Economic Perspectives* 9 (2): 169–89.

Marsden, Peter, and Noah Friedkin 1993. "Network Studies of Social Influence." *Sociological Methods and Research* 22:125–49.

Marx, Karl. 1974. *The German Ideology*. New York: International Publishers.

Marx, Karl, and Friedrich Engels. 1978. "The Communist Manifesto." Pp. 469–500 in *The Marx-Engels Reader*, ed. Robert C. Tucker. 2nd ed. New York: Norton.

Mason, David, and James Kluegel. 1995. "Introduction: Public Opinion and Political Change in the Postcommunist States." Pp. 1–25 in *Social Justice and Political Change: Public Opinion in Capitalist and Post-Communist States*, ed. David Mason, James Kluegel, and Bernd Wegener. Hawthorne, N.Y.: Aldine de Gruyter.

Massey, Douglas, Joaquin Arango, Graeme Hugo, Ali Kouaoci, Adela Pellegrino, and J. Edward Taylor. 1998. *Worlds in Motion: Understanding International Migration at the End of the Millennium*. Oxford: Oxford University Press.

McDermott, Gerald. 2002. *Embedded Politics: Industrial Networks and Institutional. Change in Post-Communism*. Ann Arbor: University of Michigan Press.

McFaul, Michael. 2002. "The Fourth Wave of Democracy and Dictatorship: Noncooperative Transitions in the Postcommunist World." *World Politics* 54 (2): 212–44.

McGinn, Kathleen L., and Angela T. Keros. 2002. "Improvisation and the Logic of Exchange in Socially Embedded Transactions." *Administrative Science Quarterly* 47:442–73.

McMichael, Phillip. 1996. *Development and Social Change: A Global Perspective*. Thousand Oaks, Calif.: Pine Forge Press.

McNeely, Connie. 1995. *Constructing the Nation-State: International Organizations and Prescriptive Action*. London: Greenwood Press.

McSweeney, Dean, and Clive Tempest. 1993. "The Political Science of Democratic Transition in Eastern Europe." *Political Studies* 41:408–19.

Mead, Richard. 1994. *International Management: Cross Cultural Dimensions*. Cambridge: Blackwell Business.

Megginson, William, and Jeffry Netter. 2001. "From State to Market: A Survey of Empirical Studies on Privatization." *Journal of Economic Literature* 39 (2): 321–89.

Mencinger, Jože. 2004. "Transition to a National and a Market Economy: A Gradualist Approach." Pp. 67–82 in *Slovenia: From Yugoslavia to the EU*, ed. Mojmir Mrak, Matija Rojec, and Carlos Silva-Jáuregui. Washington, D.C.: World Bank.

Meyer, Allan D. 1984. "Mingling Decision Making Metaphors." *Academy of Management Review* 9 (1): 6–17.

Meyer, John, John Boli, and George M. Thomas. 1987. "Ontology and Rationalization in the Western Cultural Account." Pp. 12–38 in *Institutional Structure: Constituting State, Society, and the Individual*, ed. George M. Thomas, John W. Meyer, Francisco O. Ramirez, and John Boli. Newbury Park, Calif.: Sage.

Meyer, John, John Boli, George M. Thomas, and Francisco Ramirez. 1997. "World Society and the Nation-State." *American Journal of Sociology* 103:144–81.

Meyer, John, and Brian Rowan. 1977. "Institutionalized Organizations: Formal Structure as Myth and Ceremony." *American Journal of Sociology* 83:340–63.

Meyer, Klaus. 1995. "Foreign Direct Investment in the Early Years of Economic Transition: A Survey." *Economics of Transition* 2:301–20.

———. 1998. *Direct Investment in Economies in Transition*. Northhampton, Mass.: Edward Elgar.

———. 2002. "Management Challenges in Privatisation Acquisitions in Transition Economies." *Journal of World Business* 37:266–76.

Meyer, Klaus, and Ane Skak. 2002. "Networks, Serendipity and SME Entry into Eastern Europe." *European Management Journal* 20 (2): 179–88.

Michie, Jonathan, and John Grieve Smith. 1995. *Managing the Global Economy*. Oxford: Oxford University Press.

Mills, C. Wright. 1956. *The Power Elite*. Oxford: Oxford University Press.

Mintz, Beth, and Michael Schwartz. 1985. *The Power Structure of American Business*. Chicago: University of Chicago Press.

Mishra, Ramesh. 1999. *Globalization and the Welfare State*. Northhampton, Mass.: Edward Elgar.

Mizruchi, Mark, and Lisa Fein. 1999. "The Social Construction of Organizational Knowledge: A Study of the Uses of Coercive, Mimetic, and Normative Isomorphism." *Administrative Science Quarterly* 44:653–83.

Mizruchi, Mark, and Linda Stearns. 1988. "A Longitudinal Study of the Formation of Interlocking Directorates." *Administrative Science Quarterly* 33: 194–210.

Molnár, Virág. 2005. "Cultural Politics and Modernist Architecture." *American Sociological Review* 70 (1): 111–35.

Monks, Robert, and Nell Minow. 2004. *Corporate Governance*. Malden, Mass. Blackwell.

Moorman, Christine, and Anne S. Miner. 1998. "Organizational Improvisation and Organizational Memory." *Academy of Management Review* 23 (4): 698–723.

Mosley, Layna. 2003. *Global Capital and National Governments*. Cambridge: Cambridge University Press.

MTI Econews. 1994. February 28. MTI Hungarian News Agency.

Murrell, Peter. 1992. "Conservative Political Philosophy and the Strategy of Economic Transition." *East European Politics and Societies* 6 (1): 3–16.

———. 1993. "Evolutionary and Radical Approaches to Economic Reform." Pp. 215–31 in *Stabilization and Privatization in Poland: An Economic Evaluation of the Shock Therapy Program*, ed. Kazimierz Z. Poznanski. Boston: Kluwer.

Natlačen, Tomaž. 2002. "Predsedniške volitve 2002." *Nedelo* November 3. Retrieved March 28, 2005, http://www.delo.si/index.php?sv_path=43,50&id=a895dd2040e446f24dcac4dfcc278ba504&source=Nedelo.

Nee, Victor. 2005. "The New Institutionalisms in Economics and Sociology." Pp. 49–74 in *The Handbook of Economic Sociology*, ed. Neil J. Smelser and Richard Swedberg. 2nd ed. Princeton, N.J.: Princeton University Press; New York: Russell Sage Foundation.

Nee, Victor, and Paul Ingram. 1998. "Embeddedness and Beyond: Institutions, Exchange, and Social Structure." Pp. 19–45 in *The New Institutionalism in Sociology*, ed. Mary Brinton and Victor Nee. New York: Russell Sage Foundation.

Nellis, John. 1999. *Time to Rethink Privatization in Transition Economies*. Washington, D.C.: World Bank.

Niklasson, Tomas. 1994. "The Soviet Union and Eastern Europe, 1988–9: Interactions between Domestic Change and Foreign Policy." Pp. 191–219 in *Democratization in Eastern Europe: Domestic and International Perspectives*, ed. Geoffrey Pridham and Tatu Vanhanen. London: Routledge.

North, Douglass. 1990. *Institutions, Institutional Change, and Economic Performance*. New York: Cambridge University Press.

———. 1993. "Economic Performance through Time." Nobel Memorial Prize Lecture. Stockholm: Nobel Foundation. Retrieved March 15, 2003, http://www.nobel.se/economics/laureates/1993/north-lecture.html.

———. 2005. *Understanding the Process of Economic Change*. Princeton, N.J.: Princeton University Press.

North, Douglass, and Barry Weingast. 1989. "Constitutions and Credible Commitments: the Evolution of the Institutions of Public Choice in 17th Century England." *Journal of Economic History* 49:803–32.

Obstfeld, David. 2005. "Social Networks, the Tertius Iungens Orientation, and Involvement in Innovation." *Administrative Science Quarterly* 50:100–130.

O'Dean, Terry. 1998. "Are Investors Reluctant to Realize Their Losses?" *Journal of Finance* 53:1775–98.

O'Donnell, Guillermo, Philippe Schmitter, and Laurence Whitehead. 1986. *Transitions from Authoritarian Rule: Tentative Conclusions about Uncertain Democracies*. Baltimore: Johns Hopkins University Press.

Offe, Klaus. 1991. "Capitalism by Democratic Design? Democratic Theory Facing the Triple Transition in East Central Europe." *Social Research* 58 (4): 865–92.

Olsen, Johan. 2001. "Garbage Cans, New Institutionalism and the Study of Politics." *American Political Science Review* 95 (1): 191–98.

Olson, Mancur. 1993. Dictatorship, Democracy, and Development." *American Political Science Review* 87 (3): 567–76.

———. 2000. *Power and Prosperity: Outgrowing Communist and Capitalist Dictatorships*. New York: Basic Books.

Oneal, John R. 1994. "The Affinity of Foreign Investors for Authoritarian Regimes." *Political Research Quarterly* 47 (3): 565–88.

Orenstein, Mitchell. 1998. "A Genealogy of Communist Successor Parties in East-Central Europe and the Determinants of Their Success." *East European Politics and Societies* 12:472–99.

Organization for Economic Co-operation and Development (OECD). 1997. *Geographical Distribution of Financial Flows to Aid Recipients 1992–1996*. OECD.

———. 1998a. *International Direct Investment Statistics Yearbook*. Paris: OECD.

———. 1998b. *Trends in International Migration*. Paris: OECD.

———. 1998c. "Survey of OECD Work on International Investment." Working paper. Paris: OECD

Ó Riain, Sean 2000. "States and Markets in an Era of Globalization." *Annual Review of Sociology* 26:187–213.

Orrú, Marco, Nicole Biggart, and Gary Hamilton. 1997. *The Economic Organization of East Asian Capitalism*. Thousand Oaks, Calif.: Sage.

O'Toole, L. J. 1997. "Networking Requirements, Institutional Capacity, and Implementation Gaps in Transitional Regimes: The Case of Acidification Policy in Hungary." *Journal of European Public Policy* 4 (1): 1–17.

Oxley, Joanne E. 1997. "Appropriability Hazards and Governance in Strategic Alliances: A Transaction Cost Approach." *Journal of Law, Economics and Organization* 13:387–409.

Panitch, Leo. 1996. "Rethinking the Role of the State." Pp. 83–113 in *Globalization: Critical Reflections*, ed. James H. Mittelman. Boulder, Colo.: Lynne Rienner.

Perrow, Charles. 1990. "Economic Theories of Organization." Pp. 121–52 in *Structures of Capital: The Social Organization of the Economy*, ed. Sharon Zukin and Paul DiMaggio. Cambridge: Cambridge University Press.

———. 2002. *Organizing America: Wealth, Power, and the Origins of Corporate Capitalism*. Princeton, N.J.: Princeton University Press.

Petrovic, Jasna. 2002. "Countering the New Masters: Central and East European Workers Struggle to Hold their Ground in Hard Economic Times." *Multinational Monitor* 23 (5). Retrieved April 5, 2003, http://multinationalmonitor.org/mm2002/02may/may02interviewpetrovic.html.

Pfeffer, Jeffrey, and Gerald Salancik. 1974. "Organizational Decision Making as a Political Process: The Case of a University Budget." *Administrative Science Quarterly* 19:135–51.

———. 1978. *The External Control of Organizations: A Resource Dependence Perspective*. New York: Harper and Row.

Piore, Michael J. 1996. "Review of the Handbook of Economic Sociology." *Journal of Economic Literature* 34:741–54.

Piroska, Dora. 2002. "Varieties of Debt Management in CEECs: An Institutional Investigation of International Financial Transactions." Paper presented at EPIC Third Workshop, Florence, Italy.

Pixley, Joycelyn. 2002. "Emotions and Economics." Pp. 69–89 in *Emotions and Sociology*, ed. Jack Barbalet. Oxford: Basil Blackwell.

———. 2004. *Emotions in Finance*. Cambridge: Cambridge University Press.

Podolny, Joel. 1993. "A Status-Based Model of Market Competition." *American Journal of Sociology* 98:829–72.

———. 1994. "Market Uncertainty and the Social Character of Economic Exchange." *Administrative Science Quarterly* 39:458–83.

Podolny, Joel, and Karen Page. 1998. "Network Forms of Organization." *Annual Review of Sociology* 24:57–76.

Polanyi, Karl. 1944. *The Great Transformation: The Economic and Social Origins of Our Time*. Boston: Beacon Press.

———. 1957. "The Economy as Instituted Process." Pp. 243–70 in *Trade and Market in the Early Empires*, ed. K. Polanyi, C. Arensberg, and H. Pearson. New York: Free Press.

Polish Information and Foreign Investment Agency. 2005. "About Polish Information and Foreign Investment Agency." Retrieved May 6, 2005, http://www.paiz.gov.pl/index/?id=65b9eea6e1cc6bb9f0cd2a47751a186f.

Portes, Alejandro. 1995. *The Economic Sociology of Immigration: Essays on Networks, Ethnicity, and Entrepreneurship*. New York: Russell Sage Foundation.

Portes, Alejandro, William J. Haller, and Luis Eduardo Guarnizo. 2002. "Transnational Entrepreneurs: An Alternative Form of Immigrant Adaptation." *American Sociological Review* 67:278–98.

Portes, Alejandro, and Julia Sensenbrenner. 1993. "Embeddedness and Immigration: Notes on the Social Determinants of Economic Action." *American Journal of Sociology* 98:1320–50.

Posner, Richard. 1986. *Economic Analysis of Law*. 3rd ed. Boston: Little, Brown.

Powell, Walter, and Paul DiMaggio. 1991. *The New Institutionalism in Organizational Analysis*. Chicago: University of Chicago Press.

Powell, Walter, Kenneth Koput, and Laurel Smith-Doerr. 1996. "Interorganizational Collaboration and the Locus of Innovation: Networks of Learning in Biotechnology." *Administrative Science Quarterly* 41:116–45.

Powell, Walter, Kenneth Koput, Laurel Smith-Doerr, and Jason Owen-Smith. 1999. "Network Position and Firm Performance: Organizational Returns to Collaboration in the Biotechnology Industry." *Research in the Sociology of Organizations* 16:129–59.

Powell, Walter, Kenneth Koput, Douglas White, and Jason Owen-Smith. 2005. "Network Dynamics and Field Evolution: The Growth of Interorganizational Collaboration in the Life Sciences." *American Journal of Sociology* 110:1132–1205.

Poznanski, Kazimierz Z. 1993. "An Interpretation of Communist Decay: The Role of Evolutionary Mechanisms." *Communist and Post-Communist Studies* 26 (1): 3–24.

Prauser, Steffen, and Arfon, Rees. 2004. "The Expulsion of the 'German' Communities from Eastern Europe at the End of the Second World War." EUI Working Paper HEC No. 2004/1. European University Institute, Florence.

Premik. 2005. "Slovene-Italian Relations 1880–1956." Retrieved June 6, 2005, http://www.kozina.com/premik/poreng_enastran.htm.

Przeworski, Adam. 1991. *Democracy and the Market*. Cambridge: Cambridge University Press.

———. 1995. *Sustainable Democracy*. New York: Cambridge University Press.

Przeworski, Adam, Michael E. Alvarez, Jose Antonio Cheibub, and Fernando Limongi. 2000. *Democracy and Development. Political Institutions and Well-Being in the World, 1950–1990*. Cambridge: Cambridge University Press.

Przeworski, Adam, and Fernando Limongi. 1997. "Modernization: Theories and Facts." *World Politics* 49:155–83.

Ranney, David. 1998. "Investment Liberalization Agenda." In *Foreign Policy in Focus*, ed. Martha Honey and Tom Barry, vol. 3, no. 21. Retrieved April 24, 2005, http://www.fpif.org/briefs/vol3/v3n21trad.html.

Rivoli, Pietra, and Eugene Salori. 1996. "Foreign Direct Investment under Uncertainty." *Journal of International Business Studies* 27:335–57.

Robertson, Roland 1992. *Globalization: Social Theory and Global Culture*. London: Sage.

Robinson, Ian. 1995. "The NAFTA Labour Accord in Canada: Experience, Prospects, and Alternatives." *Connecticut Journal of International Law* 10 (2): 475–531.

Rodrik, Dani, Scott Bradford, and Robert Lawrence. 1997. "Has Globalization Gone Too Far?" Institute for International Economics.

Rojec, Matija, et al. 2001. *Slovenia: FDI Review*. Ljubljana: Faculty of Social Sciences.

Romania Factbook. 2005. "Foreign Investment." Retrieved June 5, 2005, http://www.factbook.net/forinvcountry.php?sort=value&dash=DESC.

Róna-Tas, Ákos. 1994. "The First Shall Be Last? Entrepreneurship and Communist Cadres in the Transition from Socialism." *American Journal of Sociology* 100:40–69.

———. 1997. *The Great Surprise of the Small Transformation: The Demise of Communism and the Rise of the Private Sector in Hungary*. Ann Arbor: University of Michigan Press.

———. 1998. "Social Capital and Path Dependence: Sociology of the Post-communist Economic Transformation." *East European Politics and Societies* 12 (1): 107–31.

Roy, William G. 1997. *Socializing Capital: The Rise of the Large Industrial Corporation in America*. Princeton, N.J.: Princeton University Press.

Rugman, Alan. 1981. *Inside the Multinationals: The Economics of Internal Markets*. New York: Columbia University Press.

Sachs, Jeffrey. 1989. "My Plan for Poland." *International Economics* 3:24–29.

———. 1992. "Privatization in Russia: Some Lessons from Eastern Europe." *American Economic Review* 82:43–48.

———. 1994. *Poland's Jump to the Market Economy*. Cambridge: MIT Press.

———. 1998. "The IMF and the Asian Flu." *American Prospect* 9 (37). Retrieved May 5, 2005, http://www.prospect.org/print/V9/37/sachs-j.html.

Sachs, Jeffrey, and David Lipton. 1990. "Poland's Economic Reform." *Foreign Affairs* 69:47–66.

Safarian, Edward. 1966. *Foreign Ownership of Canadian Industry*. Toronto: McGraw-Hill.

Sakamoto, Yoshikazu. 1994. "A Perspective on the Changing World Order: a Conceptual Prelude." Pp. 15–54 in *Global Transformation*, ed. Yoshikazu Sakamoto. Tokyo: United Nations University Press.

Sassen, Saskia. 1991. *The Global City*. Princeton, N.J.: Princeton University Press.

———. 1996. *Losing Control? Sovereignty in an Age of Globalization*. New York: Columbia University Press.

Savage, Leonard. 1954. *The Foundations of Statistics*. New York: Wiley.

Schimmelfennig, Frank, and Ulrich Sedelmeier. 2005. *The Europeanization of Central and Eastern Europe*. Ithaca, N.Y.: Cornell University Press.

Schmidt, Klaus-Dieter. 1995. "Foreign Direct Investment in Eastern Europe: State-of-the-art and Prospects." Pp. 268–89 in *Transforming Economies and European Integration*, ed. Rumen Dobrinsky and Michael Landesmann. Aldershot, U.K.: Edward Elgar.

Schneiberg, Marc. 2005. "Combining New Institutionalisms: Explaining Institutional Change in American Property Insurance." *Sociological Forum* 20 (1): 93–137.

Schneper, William, and Mauro Guillén. 2004. "Stakeholder Rights and Corporate Governance: A Cross-National Study of Hostile Takeovers." *Administrative Science Quarterly* 49:263–95.

Schumpeter, Joseph. 1976. *Capitalism, Socialism and Democracy*. New York: Harper and Row.

Schutz, Alfred. 1962. *Collected Papers*. Vol. 1. The Hague: Nijhoff.

Schwartzman, Kathleen. 1998. "Globalization and Democracy." *Annual Review of Sociology* 24:159–81.

Seleny, Anna. 1991. "Hidden Enterprise and Property Rights Reform in Socialist Hungary." *Law and Policy* 13 (2): 149–69.

Seljak, Iztok. 2002. "Zakaj daje ta oblast prednost tujemu kapitalu." *Sobotna Priloga* March 2. Retrieved March 28, 2005, http://www.delo.si/index.php?sv_path=43,50&id=34ad7a71ec407034c0e21c7f92f5208304&source=Sobotna+priloga.

Sen, Amartya. 1977. "Rational Fools: A Critique of the Behavioral Foundations of Economic Theory." *Philosophy and Public Affairs* 6:317–44.

Sewell, William. 1992. "A Theory of Structure: Duality, Agency, and Transformation." *American Journal of Sociology* 98:1–29.

Shenkar, Oded. 2001. "Cultural Distance Revisited: Towards a More Rigorous Conceptualization and Measurement of Cultural Differences." *Journal of International Business Studies* 32 (3): 519–35.

Shleifer, Andrei, and Robert Vishny. 1994. "Privatization in Russia: First Steps." Pp. 137–64 in *The Transition in Eastern Europe*, vol. 2: *Restructuring*, ed. Oliver Blanchard, Kenneth Froot, and Jeffrey Sachs. Chicago: University of Chicago Press.

Silver, Beverly J. 2003. *Forces of Labor: Workers' Movements and Globalization since 1870*. Cambridge: Cambridge University Press.

Simon, Herbert. 1957. *Administrative Behavior*. New York: Macmillan.

Simoneti, Marko, Matija Rojec, and Aleksandra Gregorič. 2004. "Privatization, Restructuring, and Corporate Governance of the Enterprise Sector." Pp. 224–

43 in *Slovenia: From Yugoslavia to the EU*, ed. Mojmir Mrak, Matija Rojec, and Carlos Silva-Jáuregui. Washington, D.C.: World Bank.

Sinn, Hans-Werner, Alfons J. Weichenrieder, Bruno S. Frey, and Ailsa A. Röell. 1997. "Foreign Direct Investment, Political Resentment and the Privatization Process in Eastern Europe." *Economic Policy* 12 (24): 177–210.

Sklair, Leslie. 1991. *Sociology of the Global System*. New York: Harvester Wheatsheaf.

Smelser, Neil, and Richard Swedberg, eds. 2005. *The Handbook of Economic Sociology*. 2nd ed. Princeton, N.J.: Princeton University Press; New York: Russell Sage Foundation.

Smith, Adam. 1976. *An Inquiry into the Nature and Causes of the Wealth of Nations*. Oxford: Oxford University Press.

Smith, Adrian, and John Pickles. 1998. *Theorizing Transition*. London: Routledge.

Smith, Charles. 1990. *Auctions: The Social Construction of Values*. Berkeley and Los Angeles: University of California Press.

Smith-Doerr, Laurel, and Walter Powell. 2005. "Networks and Economic Life." Pp. 379–402 in *The Handbook of Economic Sociology*, edited by Neil Smelser and Richard Swedberg. Princeton, NJ: Princeton University Press.

Solow, Robert M. 1956. "A Contribution to the Theory of Economic Growth." *Quarterly Journal of Economics* 70:65–94.

Soskice, David. 1991. "The Institutional Infrastructure for International Competitiveness: A Comparative Analysis of the UK and Germany." Pp. 45–66 in *The Economics of the New Europe*, ed. A. B. Atkinson and R. Brunetta. London: Macmillan.

———. 1999. "Divergent Production Regimes: Coordinated and Uncoordinated Market Economies in the 1980s and 1990s." Pp. 101–34 in *Continuity and Changes in Contemporary Capitalism*, ed. H. Kitschelt, P. Lange, G. Marks, and J. D. Stephens. Cambridge: Cambridge University Press.

Spence, Michael. 1973. "Job Market Signaling." *Quarterly Journal of Economics* 87:355–74.

Spicer, Andrew, Gerald McDermott, and Bruce Kogut. 2000. "Entrepreneurship and Privatization in Central Europe: The Tenuous Balance Between Destruction and Creation." *Academy of Management Review* 25 (3): 630–49.

Spillman, Lyn. 1999. "Enriching Exchange: Cultural Dimensions of Markets." *American Journal of Economics and Sociology* 58 (4): 1047–73.

Stack, Steven 1980. "The Political Economy of Income Inequality: A Comparative Analysis." *Canadian Journal of Political Science* 13:273–86.

Staniszkis, Jadwiga. 1991. *The Dynamics of Breakthrough*. Berkeley and Los Angeles: University of California Press.

Stark, David. 1992. "Path Dependence and Privatization Strategies in East Central Europe." *East European Societies and Politics* 6 (1): 17–54.

———. 1996. "Recombinant Property in East European Capitalism." *American Journal of Sociology* 101:993–1027.

Stark, David, and László Bruszt. 1998. *Postsocialist Pathways: Transforming Politics and Property in East Central Europe*. Cambridge: Cambridge University Press.

Steinmo, Sven, Kathleen Thelen, and Frank Longstreth. 1992. *Structuring Politics: Historical Institutionalism in Comparative Analysis.* New York: Cambridge University Press.

Stiglitz, Joseph. 2000. "Whither Reform? Ten Years of Transition." Pp. 27–56 in *Annual World Bank Conference on Economic Development,* ed. Boris Pleskovič and Joseph Stiglitz. Washington, D.C.: World Bank.

Stopford, John, and Luis Wells. 1972. *Managing the Multinational Enterprise.* New York: Basic Books.

Strang, David, and John Meyer. 1993. "Institutional Conditions for Diffusion." *Theory and Society* 22:487–511.

Strange, Susan. 1996. *The Retreat of the State: The Diffusion of Power in the World Economy.* New York: Cambridge University Press.

Streeck, Wolfgang. 1991. "On the Institutional Conditions of Diversified Quality Production." Pp. 21–61 in *Beyond Keynesianism: The Socio-Economics of Production and Employment,* ed. Egon Matzner and Wolfgang Streeck. London: Edward Elgar.

———. 1992. *Social Institutions and Economic Performance.* Beverly Hills, Calif.: Sage.

Streeck, Wolfgang, and Kathleen Thelen. 2005. *Beyond Continuity: Institutional Change in Advanced Political Economies.* Oxford: Oxford University Press.

Suchman, Mark C. 1995. "Managing Legitimacy: Strategic and Institutional Approaches." *Academy of Management Review* 20 (3): 571–610.

Summary, Rebecca. 1989. "A Political-Economic Model of U.S. Bilateral Trade." *Review of Economics and Statistics* 71 (1): 179–82.

Sun, Haishun. 1999. "Entry Modes of Multinational Corporations into China's Market: A Socioeconomic Analysis." *International Journal of Social Economics* 26 (5): 642–60.

Sutton, John R., Frank Dobbin, John W. Meyer, and Richard Scott. 1994. "The Legalization of the Workplace." *American Journal of Sociology* 99:944–71.

Swan, Trevor W. 1956. "Economic Growth and Capital Accumulation." *Economic Record* 32:334–61.

Swedberg, Richard. 1994. "Markets as Social Structures." Pp. 255–82 in *The Handbook of Economic Sociology,* ed. Neil J. Smelser and Richard Swedberg. New York: Russell Sage Foundation.

———. 1997. "New Economic Sociology: What Has Been Accomplished, What Is Ahead?" *Acta Sociologica* 40:161–82.

———. 2003. *The Principles of Economic Sociology.* Princeton, N.J.: Princeton University Press.

———. 2005. "Markets in Society." Pp. 233–53 in *The Handbook of Economic Sociology,* ed. Neil J. Smelser and Richard Swedberg. 2nd ed. Princeton, N.J.: Princeton University Press; New York: Russell Sage Foundation.

Swedberg, Richard, and Mark Granovetter. 1992. *The Sociology of Economic Life.* Boulder, Colo.: Westview Press.

Swidler, Ann. 1986. "Culture in Action: Symbols and Strategies." *American Sociological Review* 51:273–86.

Szelényi, Ivan, Katherine Beckett, and Lawrence P. King. 1994. "The Socialist Economic System." Pp. 234–51 in *The Handbook of Economic Sociology*, ed. Neil J. Smelser and Richard Swedberg. New York: Russell Sage Foundation.

Szelényi, Ivan, and Eric Kostello. 1996. "The Market Transition Debate: Toward a Synthesis?" *American Journal of Sociology* 101:1082–96.

Szelényi, Ivan, and Balazs Szelényi. 1994. "Why Socialism Failed: Toward a Theory of System Breakdown—Causes of Disintegration of East European State Socialism." *Theory and Society* 23:211–31.

Tanzi, Vito. 1999. "Transition and the Changing Role of Government." *Finance and Development* 36 (2): 20–23.

Teece, David J. 1985. "Multinational Enterprise, Internal Governance and Industrial Organization." *American Economic Review* 75:233–38.

Thelen, Kathleen. 1999. "Historical Institutionalism in Comparative Politics." *Annual Review of Political Science* 2:369–404.

Tierney, Kathleen. 1999. "Toward a Critical Sociology of Risk." *Sociological Forum* 14:215–42.

Tilly, Charles. 1992. *Coercion, Capital, and European States, A.D. 990–1992.* Cambridge: Basil Blackwell.

Tolbert, Pamela and Lynne Zucker. 1983. "Institutional Sources of Change in the Formal Structure of Organizations: The Diffusion of Civil Service Reform, 1880–1935." *Administrative Science Quarterly* 28:22–39.

Trade and Investment Promotion Office. 1998. *Raziskava podjetij s tujim in mešanim kapitalom* (Research on companies with foreign and mixed capital). Ljubljana: Trade and Investment Promotion Office. Mimeo.

Tversky, Amos. 1969. "Intransitivity of Preferences." *Psychological Review* 76:31–48.

Tversky, Amos, and Daniel Kahneman. 1986. "Rational Choice and the Framing of Decisions." *Journal of Business* 59 (4): S251–S278.

Ungar, Sanford. 1998. *Fresh Blood: The New American Immigrants*. Urbana: University of Illinois Press.

United Nations Conference on Trade and Development (UNCTAD). 1996a. *International Investment Instruments: A Compendium*. Vols. 1–3. Washington, D.C.: UNCTAD.

———. 1996b. *World Investment Report.* Washington, D.C.: UNCTAD.

———. 1998. *World Investment Report.* Washington, D.C.: UNCTAD.

———. 2001. *World Investment Report.* Washington, D.C.: UNCTAD.

———. 2002. *World Investment Report.* Washington, D.C.: UNCTAD.

———. 2006. "World Investment Report: Search by Country/Economy." Retrieved March 20, 2005, http://www.unctad.org/Templates/Page .asp?intItemID=3198&lang=1.

U.S. Library of Congress. 2006. "Poland—United States." Retrieved March 20, 2006, http://www.country-data.com/cgi-bin/query/r-10772.html.

Uzzi, Brian. 1996. "The Sources and Consequences of Embeddedness for the Economic Performance of Organizations: The Network Effect." *American Sociological Review* 61:674–98.

Uzzi, Brian. 1997. "Social Structure and Competition in Interfirm Networks: The Paradox of Embeddedness." *Administrative Science Quarterly* 42:35–67.

———. 1999. "Embeddedness in the Making of Financial Capital: How Social Relations and Networks Benefit Firms Seeking Financing." *American Sociological Review* 64:481–505.

Van Rossem, Ronald. 1996. "The World System Paradigm as General Theory of Development: A Cross-National Test." *American Sociological Review* 61:508–27.

Vaughn, Diane. 1997. *The Challenger Launch Decision: Risky Technology, Culture, and Deviance at NASA.* Chicago: University of Chicago Press.

Velthuis, Olav. 2005. *Talking Prices: Symbolic Meanings of Prices on the Market for Contemporary Art.* Princeton, N.J.: Princeton University Press.

Verdery, Katherine. 1991. *National Ideology under Socialism: Identity and Cultural Politics in Ceauşescu's Romania.* Berkeley and Los Angeles: University of California Press.

———. 1996a. "Nationalism, Postsocialism, and Space in Eastern Europe." *Social Research* 63 (1): 77–95.

———. 1996b. *What Was Socialism and What Comes Next?* Princeton, N.J.: Princeton University Press.

———. 1998. "Transnationalism, Nationalism, Citizenship, and Property: Eastern Europe since 1989." *American Ethnologist* 25 (2): 291–306.

———. 2003. *The Vanishing Hectare: Property and Value in Postsocialist Transylvania.* Ithaca, N.Y.: Cornell University Press.

Vernon, Raymond. 1971. *Sovereignty at Bay: The Multinational Spread of U.S. Enterprises.* New York: Basic Books.

———. 1983. "Organizational and Institutional Responses to International Risk." Pp. 191–216 in *Managing International Risk*, ed. Richard J. Herring. New York: Cambridge University Press.

———. 1999. "The Harvard Multinational Enterprise Project in Historical Perspective." *Transnational Corporations* 8 (2): 35–49.

Vickers, John Stuart. 1985. "Pre-emptive Patenting, Joint Ventures and the Persistence of Oligopoly." *International Journal of Industrial Organization* 3:261–73.

von Neumann, John, and Oskar Morgenstern. 1944. *Theory of Games and Economic Behavior.* Princeton, N.J.: Princeton University Press.

Vreeland, James. 2003. *The IMF and Economic Development.* Cambridge: Cambridge University Press.

Walder, Andrew. 1994. "The Decline of Communist Power: Elements of a Theory of Institutional Change." *Theory and Society* 23:297–323.

———. 1995. "Local Governments as Industrial Firms: An Organizational Analysis of China's Transitional Economy." *American Journal of Sociology* 101:263–301.

Wallerstein, Immanuel. 1974. *The Modern World System.* New York: Academic Press.

Waters, Malcolm. 1995. *Globalization.* New York: Routledge.

Watson, Ian. 1994. *The Baltics & Russia Through the Back Door.* 2d ed. Edmonds, Wash.: Rick Steves' Europe Through the Back Door.

Watson, James. 1997. "Transnationalism, Localization, and Fast Foods in East Asia." Pp. 1–38 in *Golden Arches East: McDonald's in East Asia*, ed. James Watson. Stanford, Calif.: Stanford University Press.

Weber, Max. 1978. *Economy and Society*. Berkeley and Los Angeles: University of California Press.

Weber, Roberto, and Robyn Dawes. 2005. "Behavioral Economics." Pp. 90–108 in *The Handbook of Economic Sociology*, ed. Neil J. Smelser and Richard Swedberg. 2nd ed. Princeton, N.J.: Princeton University Press; New York: Russell Sage Foundation.

Wei, Shang-Jin. 2000. "How Taxing is Corruption on International Investors?" *Review of Economics and Statistics* 82 (1): 1–11.

Weintraub, Roy. 2005. "Neoclassical Economics." *Concise Encyclopedia of Economics*. Retrieved June 20, 2005, http://www.econlib.org/library/Enc/NeoclassicalEconomics.html.

Wejnert, Barbara. 2005. "Diffusion, Development, and Democracy, 1800–1999." *American Sociological Review* 70:53–81.

Welfens, Paul J. J. 1993. "The Growth of the Private Sector: Privatization and Foreign Direct Investment in Eastern Europe." Pp. 119–66 in *Overcoming the Transformation Crisis*, ed. Horst Siebert. Tübingen, Germany: J. C. B. Mohr.

Welsh, Helga A. 1994. "Political Transition Processes in Central and Eastern Europe," *Comparative Politics* 26 (4): 379–94.

Westphal, James, Ranjay Gulati, and Stephen Shortell. 1997. "Customization or Conformity? An Institutional and Network Perspective on the Content and Consequences of TQM Adoption." *Administrative Science Quarterly* 42:366–94.

Wheeler, David, and Ashoka Mody. 1992. "International Investment Location Decisions: The Case of US Firms." *Journal of International Economics* 33:57–76.

White, Harrison C. 1981a. "Production Markets as Induced Role Structures." Pp. 1–59 in *Sociological Methodology*, ed. Samuel Leinhardt. San Francisco: Jossey-Bass.

———. 1981b. "Where Do Markets Come From?" *American Journal of Sociology* 87:517–47.

———. 2002. *Markets from Networks: Socioeconomic Models of Production*. Princeton, N.J.: Princeton University Press.

Whitford, Josh. 2002. "Pragmatism and the Untenable Dualism of Means and Ends: Why Rational Choice Theory does not Deserve Paradigmatic Privilege." *Theory and Society* 31:325–63.

Whitley, Richard. 1992a. *Business Systems in East Asia: Firms, Markets and Societies*. London: Sage.

———. 1992b. *European Business Systems: Firms and Markets in their National Contexts*. London: Sage.

Wiener Institut für Internationale Wirtschaftsvergleiche (WIIW). 1998. *Foreign Direct Investment in Central and East European Countries and the Former Soviet Union*. WIIW-WIFO Database.

———. 2001. *Foreign Direct Investment in Central and East European Countries and the Former Soviet Union*. WIIW-WIFO Database.

Williamson, John. 1990. *Latin American Adjustment: How Much Has Happened?* Washington, D.C.: Institute for International Economics.

Williamson, John. 1993. "Democracy and the Washington Consensus." *World Development* 21:1329–36.

Williamson, Oliver. 1975. *Markets and Hierarchies: Analysis and Antitrust Implications.* New York: Free Press.

———. 1981. "The Economics of Organization: The Governance of Contractual Relations." *American Journal of Sociology* 87:548–77.

———. 1985. *The Economic Institutions of Capitalism.* New York: Free Press.

———. 1994. "Transaction Cost Economics and Organization Theory." Pp. 77–107 in *The Handbook of Economic Sociology,* ed. Neil J. Smelser and Richard Swedberg. Princeton, N.J.: Princeton University Press; New York: Russell Sage Foundation.

Wolff, Stefan. 2000. *German Minorities in Europe: Ethnic Identity and Cultural Belonging.* New York: Berghahn Books.

Wooldridge, Jeffrey. 2002. *Econometric Analysis of Cross Section and Panel Data.* Cambridge: MIT Press.

World Bank. 1996. *World Bank Transition Newsletter.* May–June. Retrieved March 20, 2007, http://web.worldbank.org/WBSITE/EXTERNAL/NEWSLETTERS/EXTTRANSITION/EXTDECBEYTRANEWLET/0,,contentMDK:20691268~menuPK:1544646~pagePK:64168445~piPK:64168309~theSitePK:1542353,00.html.

———. 1999. *World Development Report.* Washington, D.C.: World Bank.

World Trade Organization. 1998. *Trade Policy Review: Hungary.* Geneva: World Trade Organization.

Wrong, Denis. 1961. "The Oversocialized Conception of Man in Sociology." *American Sociological Review* 26:183–93.

Yakubovich, Valery. 2005. "Weak Ties, Information, and Influence: How Workers Find Jobs in a Local Russian Labor Market." *American Sociological Review* 70:408–21.

Yergin, Daniel, and Joseph Stanislaw. 1998. *The Commanding Heights: The Battle between Government and the Marketplace That Is Remaking the Modern World.* New York: Simon and Schuster.

Zeitlin, Maurice. 1974. "Corporate Ownership and Control: The Large Corporation and the Capitalist Class." *American Journal of Sociology* 79:1073–1119.

Zelizer, Viviana. 1979. *Morals and Markets: The Development of Life Insurance in the United States.* New York: Columbia University Press.

———. 1987. *Pricing the Priceless Child: The Changing Social Value of Children.* New York: Basic Books.

———. 1988. "Beyond the Polemics on the Market: Establishing a Theoretical and Empirical Agenda." *Sociological Forum* 3:614–34.

———. 1994. *The Social Meaning of Money.* New York: Basic.

———. 1999. "Multiple Markets: Multiple Cultures." Pp. 193–212 in *Diversity and Its Discontents,* ed. Neil J. Smelser and Jeffrey C. Alexander. Princeton, N.J.: Princeton University Press.

———. 2000. "The Purchase of Intimacy." *Law and Social Inquiry* 25:817–48.

———. 2001. "Economic Sociology." Pp. 4128–31 in *International Encyclopedia of the Social and Behavioral Sciences,* ed. Neil J. Smelser and Paul B. Baltes. Amsterdam: Elsevier.

———. 2002a. "Enter Culture." Pp. 101–28 in *The New Economic Sociology: Developments in an Emerging Field*, ed. Mauro Guillén, Randall Collins, Paula England, and Marshall Meyer. New York: Russell Sage Foundation.

———. 2002b. "Intimate Transactions." Pp. 274–302 in *The New Economic Sociology: Developments in an Emerging Field*, ed. Mauro Guillén, Randall Collins, Paula England and Marshall Meyer. New York: Russell Sage Foundation.

———. 2004. "Circuits of Commerce." Pp. 122–44 in *Self, Social Structure, and Beliefs: Explorations in the Sociological Thought of Neil Smelser*, ed. Jeffrey Alexander, Gary T. Marx, Christine Williams. Berkeley and Los Angeles: University of California Press.

———. 2005. *The Purchase of Intimacy*. Princeton, N.J.: Princeton University Press.

Zolberg, Aristide. 1989. "The Next Waves: Migration Theory for a Changing World." *International Migration Review* 23:403–30.

Zubrzycki, Geneviève. 2001. " 'We, the Polish Nation': Ethnic and Civic Visions of Nationhood in Post-communist Constitutional Debates." *Theory and Society* 30:629–68.

Zucker, Lynne G. 1986. "Production of Trust: Institutional Sources of Economic Structure, 1840–1920." *Research on Organizational Behavior* 8:53–111.

Zukin, Sharon, and Paul DiMaggio. 1990. "Introduction." Pp. 1–36 in *Structures of Capital: The Social Organization of the Economy*, ed. Sharon Zukin and Paul DiMaggio. New York: Cambridge University Press.

INDEX